The Berkshire Hills & Pioneer Valley of Western Massachusetts

The Berkshire Hills & Pioneer Valley of Western Massachusetts

Christina Tree & William Davis

Principal photography by Kim Grant

The Countryman Press ✳ Woodstock, Vermont

DEDICATION

To our family: Liam, Topher, Tim, Yuko, and Aki

We welcome your comments and suggestions. Please contact Explorer's Guide Editor, The Countryman Press, P.O. Box 748, Woodstock, VT 05091, or e-mail countrymanpress@wwnorton.com.

Copyright © 2004 by Christina Tree and William Davis

First Edition

ISSN: 1547-2205
ISBN: 0-88150-590-0

Cover and interior design by Bodenweber Design
Composition by PerfecType, Nashville, TN
Cover photograph of the Bridge of Flowers in Shelburne Falls, MA, courtesy of Shelburne Falls Area Business Association, www.shelburnefalls.com

Maps by Mapping Specialists Ltd., Madison, WI, © The Countryman Press

Published by The Countryman Press,
P.O. Box 748, Woodstock, Vermont 05091

Distributed by W. W. Norton & Company, Inc.,
500 Fifth Avenue, New York, NY 10110

Printed in the United States of America

10 9 8 7 6 5 4 3 2 1

EXPLORE WITH US!

Welcome to the Berkshire Hills and Pioneer Valley of Western Massachusetts. In writing this guide, we have been increasingly selective in making recommendations based on years of conscientious research and personal experience. What makes us unique is that we describe the state by locally defined regions, giving you Western Massachusetts' communities, not simply its most popular destinations. With this guide you'll feel confident to venture beyond the tourist towns, along roads less traveled, to places of special hospitality and charm.

WHAT'S WHERE

In the beginning of the book you'll find an alphabetical listing of special highlights, with important information and advice on everything from antiques to weather reports.

LODGING

Prices: Please don't hold us or the respective innkeepers responsible for the rates listed as of press time in 2004. Some changes are inevitable. Massachusetts has a statewide 5.7 percent lodging and meals tax. Communities also have the option of levying an additional local tax of up to 4 percent and most resort towns opt for the full amount.

Smoking: Statewide ban in restaurants, bars, and night clubs, takes effect July 5, 2004.

RESTAURANTS

Note the distinction between Dining Out and Eating Out. By their nature, restaurants listed in the Eating Out group are generally inexpensive.

KEY TO SYMBOLS

- ⚑ The special value symbol appears next to lodging and restaurants that combine high quality and moderate prices.
- ✒ The kids-alert symbol appears next to lodging, restaurants, activities, and shops of special appeal to youngsters.
- ♿ The wheelchair symbol appears next to lodging, restaurants, and attractions that are partially or fully handicapped-accessible.
- 🐾 The dog paw symbol appears next to lodgings that accept pets (usually with a reservation and deposit) as of press time.
- ∞ The wedding rings symbol appears beside inns that frequently serve as venues for weddings and civil unions.

We would appreciate your comments and corrections about places you visit or know well in the state. Please use the card enclosed in this book, or e-mail Chris: ctree@traveltree.net.

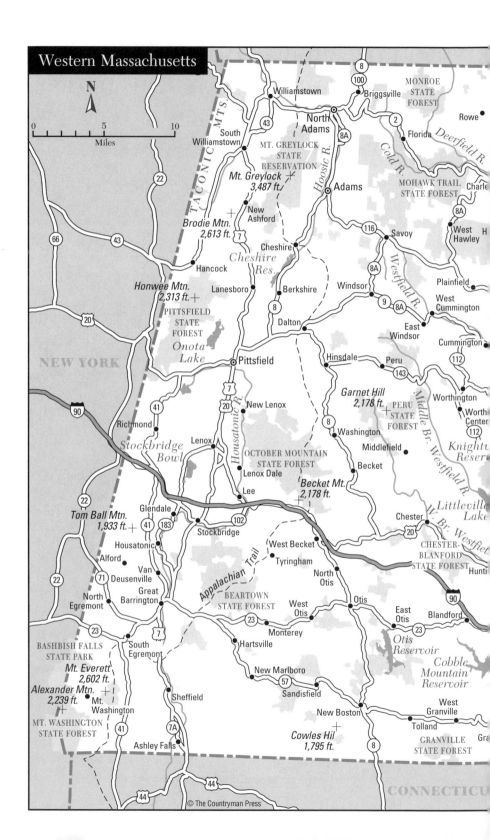

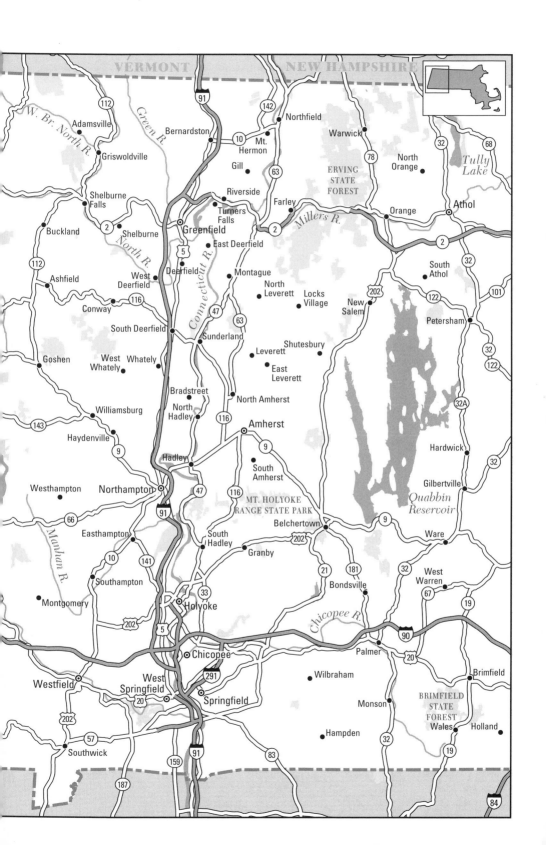

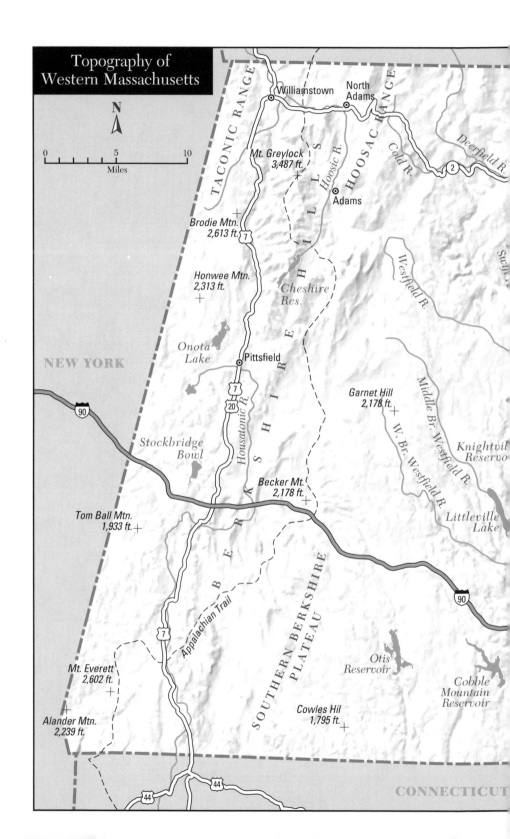

Topography of
Western Massachusetts

N

0   5   10
Miles

TACONIC RANGE

Williamstown   North Adams

HOOSAC RANGE

Cold R.

Deerfield R.

2

Mt. Greylock
3,487 ft.

Hoosic R.

Adams

Brodie Mtn.
2,613 ft.

7

Honwee Mtn.
2,313 ft.

Cheshire
Res.

Westfield R.

NEW YORK

Onota
Lake

Pittsfield

7

20

Housatonic R.

Garnet Hill
2,178 ft.

Middle Br. Westfield R.

Knightvil
Reservo

W. Br. Westfield R.

90

Stockbridge
Bowl

Littleville
Lake

Becker Mt.
2,178 ft.

Tom Ball Mtn.
1,933 ft.

B
E
R
K
S
H
I
R
E

Appalachian Trail

SOUTHERN BERKSHIRE PLATEAU

90

Otis
Reservoir

Cobble
Mountain
Reservoir

7

Mt. Everett
2,602 ft.

Alander Mtn.
2,239 ft.

Cowles Hil
1,795 ft.

44

44

CONNECTICUT

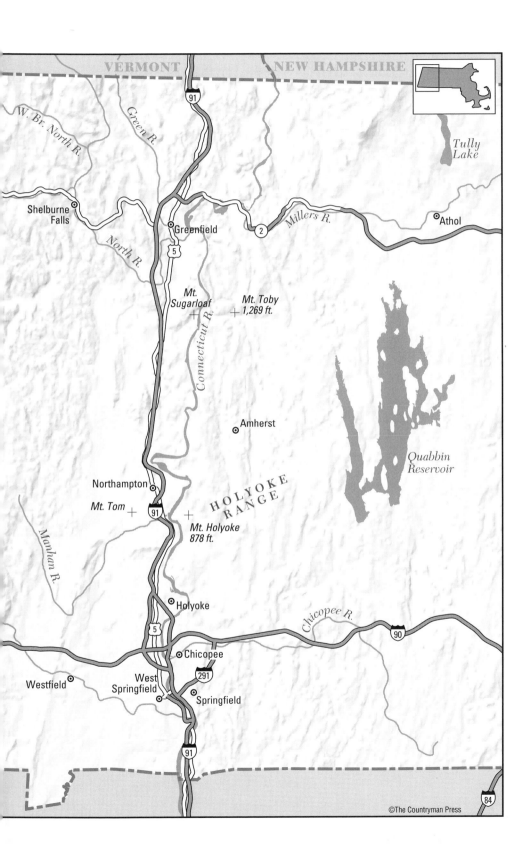

VERMONT   NEW HAMPSHIRE

W. Br. North R.

Green R.

Tully
Lake

Shelburne
Falls

Greenfield

Millers R.

Athol

North R.

Mt.
Sugarloaf

Mt. Toby
+1,269 ft.

Connecticut R.

Amherst

Quabbin
Reservoir

Northampton

Mt. Tom +

HOLYOKE
RANGE

Mt. Holyoke
878 ft.

Manhan R.

Holyoke

Chicopee R.

West
Springfield

Chicopee

Westfield

Springfield

©The Countryman Press

CONTENTS

INTRODUCTION

Too often when we begin to enthuse about Western Massachusetts, we watch eyes glaze over, but when we mention "the Berkshires" people listen up. We talk about the "Pioneer Valley" and even Berkshire residents are puzzled. We go on about the "Berkshire Hilltowns" and they are really confused. By bundling these three neighboring, variously known, and very different—but all culturally rich and scenic—areas into one book, we hope to suggest what an altogether amazing region Western Massachusetts is.

We make the case that "Culture in the Country"—a slogan coined for Berkshire County—applies to all Western Massachusetts. Berkshire County is indeed the setting for internationally famous summer music, theater, and dance festivals, and the Pioneer Valley is home to a dozen colleges, an equal number of outstanding museums, and numerous concerts and performances, adding up to far more year-round "culture" within a small radius than can be found in many major cities.

The semantics of what's where in Western Massachusetts is, admittedly, confusing and unrelated to topography. Berkshire County posts WELCOME TO THE BERKSHIRES signs at its borders, while in fact the Berkshire Hills roll eastward, in places almost to the Connecticut River valley—which of course needs a name other than "Connecticut," because this is Massachusetts. Suggestions have included Asparagus Valley, Happy Valley, King Philip's Realm, and Knowledge Corridor, but "Pioneer Valley" is what's stuck since the 1940s. It refers to the 17th-century arrival of English colonists a century before they settled the flanking hills.

Politically the Pioneer Valley encompasses three counties—Franklin, Hampshire, and Hampden—that extend far into those hills. Physically the east–west Holyoke Range divides the valley itself into the Springfield area to the south and the more rural Upper Valley to the north, and the Upper Valley in turn divides into the Five-College Area (with Amherst and Northampton as its dual hubs) and the Deerfield/Greenfield area in the narrowest, northernmost end of the valley. Technically part of the Pioneer Valley, the Berkshire Hilltowns are salted through the roll of the Berkshire Hills between Berkshire County and the Connecticut River valley. They are the state's highest and most remote towns, with the kind of white-clapboard villages, orchards, sugarbushes, and farmscapes generally associated with Vermont.

Our definition of Western Massachusetts stops east of the Quabbin Reservoir and measures, based on the way the roads run, little more than 50 miles from east to west and less than 70 miles north to south. Divided as this small area is, however, by hills and mind-sets, it seems larger.

In 1910 Jacob's Ladder (the hilly stretch of Route 20 east of Becket) was graded so that motor cars could access south Berkshire County from the east. In 1914 the more dramatic Mohawk Trail (Route 2 between Greenfield and North Adams), including a dramatic stretch over the higher Hoosac Range, was engineered and promoted as the country's first scenic auto route. Today both roads have been backroaded by the Massachusetts Turnpike (I-90), as the river roads have been by north–south I-91 along the Connecticut. It's all about scenic roads, once you are here.

Lodging includes the state's most elegant and expensive inns, resorts, and spas, and its most reasonably priced and rural B&Bs. Dining runs the same gamut—from exquisite gourmet to farm snack bars at which everything is home grown as well as baked. With the exception of its most famous towns and attractions, little in this entire region is obvious. Few signs point the way to waterfalls and mountain summits, to bike trails, or even to world-class museums.

More so than other parts of New England, Western Massachusetts resembles European landscapes in the sense that the centuries have stamped it, leaving few

CHESTERFIELD BARN

Kim Grant

corners untouched in a variety of ways, yet preserving things both natural and human-made that deserve to be preserved. It's a landscape that generously rewards those who explore it.

When the predecessor of this book, *Massachusetts: An Explorer's Guide*, was initially published, it was the first complete 20th-century guide to the state. This book has, however, been researched once more from scratch. We have visited and otherwise checked out almost every place to stay we list and driven thousands of miles, much of it over unpaved roads. To our amazement this book is actually almost as large as the original guide to the entire state, which included Boston and Cape Cod. Read on and you will see why.

Chris would like to thank, first and foremost, Ann Hamilton and her assistant Nancy Stone of Franklin County and both Art Schwenger and Jeff Potter of Shelburne Falls for their unfailing support. In the Berkshires Nick Noyes and Ann Claffie of the Berkshire Visitors Bureau, Rod Bunt of North Adams, and Joy Doane and Claudia Leibert of Great Barrington were particularly helpful. Heartfelt thanks also go to Harry Dodson of Ashfield, Arnold Westwood of West Cummington, Carolyn Taylor of Blandford, Susan Grader of Buckland, Julia and Ed Berman of Whatley, Ann Zieminski and John Koull of Amherst, Suzanne Beck of Northampton, and Sandy Ward of Holyoke. Thanks too to Clint Richmond for his help with the Mohawk Trail.

Bill would like to thank Cherie McBride in the Pioneer Valley; Marianne Gambaro and Meghan Hamel in Springfield; Tom and Suky Werman, Elizabeth Aspenlieder, and Pamela Kueber in Lenox; Christina Alsop, Marty Gottron, and John Felton in Stockbridge. To many more who helped us along the way, as well, and to The Countryman Press staff, who permitted us to stretch our deadline and to illustrate this book with the many images and entirely new maps that make all the difference. Thanks too to our speedy and competent copy editor Laura Jorstad for keeping us precise and grammatical. We appreciate your comments and welcome your suggestions for the next edition of this guide. Feel free to contact as directly: ctree@traveltree.net or bill@davistravels.com.

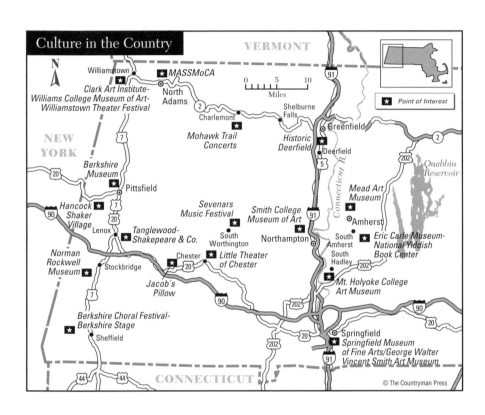

Culture in the Country

N

VERMONT

Williamstown
★ MASSMoCA
Clark Art Institute-
Williams College Museum of Art-
Williamstown Theater Festival

North
Adams

0   5   10
Miles

91

Point of Interest ★

NEW
YORK

Charlemont
★
Mohawk Trail
Concerts

Shelburne
Falls

Greenfield

Historic
Deerfield ★

Deerfield

2

202

Quabbin
Reservoir

Berkshire
Museum
★ Pittsfield

Hancock ★
Shaker
Village
Lenox

Sevenars
Music Festival
★
South
Worthington

Smith College
Museum of Art
★

Northampton

Mead Art
Museum
★
Amherst

South
Amherst

Eric Carle Museum-
National Yiddish
Book Center ★

Tanglewood-
Shakepeare & Co.

Chester
★
★ 20

Little Theater
of Chester

South
Hadley

202

Norman
Rockwell
Museum ★
Stockbridge

Jacob's
Pillow

90

202

Mt. Holyoke College
Art Museum ★

90

20

Berkshire Choral Festival-
Berkshire Stage
★
Sheffield

202

20

Springfield
Springfield Museum ★
of Fine Arts/George Walter
Vincent Smith Art Museum

91

44   44

CONNECTICUT

© The Countryman Press

WHAT'S WHERE IN WESTERN MASSACHUSETTS

AGRICULTURAL FAIRS The Berkshire Agricultural Society, incorporated February 15, 1811, was this country's first such society, and Elkanah Watson, its founder, is recognized as "the father of American fairs." The first was held in Pittsfield in 1814. By 1818 the state's agricultural societies included Northampton, which still holds its annual Three County Fair on Labor Day weekend. The Franklin County Fair at the Greenfield Fairgrounds is usually the following weekend. It's also worth checking out the colorful old-fashioned fairs in small towns that feature pulling contests (by oxen, draft horses, and trucks), plenty of livestock, and live music. The Littleville Fair in Chester and the Middlefield Fair are early in August, and the Cummington and Blandford Fairs are in late August.

Kim Grant

The **Eastern States Exposition** (www.thebige.com), held mid- to late September in West Springfield, is in a class by itself, a six-state event with thousands of animals competing for prizes along with a midway, concession stands, big-name entertainment, and the Avenue of States. Up-to-date lists of fairs are available from the **Massachusetts Agricultural Fairs Association** (781-834-6629; www.mafa.org) and from the **Massachusetts Department of Food and Agriculture** (617-626-1720; www.massgrown.org).

AIRPORTS Contact the **Massachusetts Aeronautics Commission** (617-973-8881; www.massaeronautics.org) in Boston for a database about the state's airports, big and small. **Bradley International Airport** (1-888-624-1533; www.bradleyairport) in Windsor Locks, Connecticut, is the region's major airport, served by most major airlines with connecting flights to just about anywhere you want to go. With its new, centralized terminal and easy highway access (I-91, exit 40), it's one of New England's more visitor-friendly gateways. **Albany International Airport** (518-242-2200) is also handy to much of Berkshire County.

AMTRAK Amtrak (1-800-USA-RAIL; www.amtrak.com). On its way from New York to Burlington (Vermont), the **Vermonter** stops in Springfield and Amherst. Springfield is also a stop on some Boston-bound trails, and the **Lakeshore Limited** stops in Pittsfield en route to Chicago. There is frequent service from New York to Albany. *Note:* Canny Berkshire residents take reasonably priced Metro-North (www.mta.info) from Grand Central Station to Wassaic Station, New York; on July through Labor Day weekends a connecting bus drops passengers in Great Barrington.

AMUSEMENT PARK While all the state's other amusement parks (all founded in the late 19th century by trolley companies as an inducement to ride the cars out to the end of the line) have bitten the dust, Riverside Park in Agawam is now **Six Flags New England** (www.sixflags.com), the region's largest theme and water park, home to "Superman Ride of Steel."

ANIMALS Forest Park in Springfield (www.forestparkzoo.com) and the much smaller **Christenson Zoo** (native deer, peacocks, peasants and raccoons) in Northampton's Look Memorial Park are the area's only formal zoos. There are many menageries, however, such as those found at **McCray Farm** in South Hadley and at the **Long View Tower** in Greenfield on the Mohawk Trail. The most exotic collection of animals in Western Massachusetts is probably at **Tregellys Fiber Farm** (www.tregellysfibers.com) in Hawley, where animals number around 200 and include unusual heritage breeds such as Galloway cattle, yaks, camels, Icelandic sheep, Navajo Churro sheep, llamas, and Bactrian (two-humped) camels from Mongolia, not to mention peacocks and an assortment of birds. At **Flayvors of Cook Farm** in Hadley you can see the cows that supply your ice cream, and at **Keldaby** in Colrain visitors are welcome to mingle with the angora goats. **Ioka Valley Farm** in Hancock features a barnyard with pigs, sheep, goats, calves, and rabbits. Check out our farm listings in each chapter for many more friendly animals to visit.

ANTIQUARIAN BOOKSELLERS For a descriptive listing of local dealers, check out the web site of the **Massachusetts and Rhode Island Antiquarian Booksellers** (MARIAB; www.mariab.org) or pick up their booklet guide at one of the shops. Western Massachusetts is studded with antiquarian bookstores; you'll find them listed in each chapter. Many, like the **Bookmill** in Montague (www.montaguebookmill.com) and **Meetinghouse Books** in South Deerfield (www.meetinghouse-books.com), are destinations in their own right.

ANTIQUES Berkshire County represents a major antiques center; the **Berkshire County Antiques Dealers Association** (www.berkshireantiquesandart.com) publishes a pamphlet listing most of the shops, which we describe individually in each chapter under *Selective Shopping.* Sheffield alone has two dozen galleries, while the **Buggy**

Whip Factory (www.buggywhipan-
tiques.com) in nearby Southfield (70
dealers) is a popular destination. In
the Pioneer Valley, Northampton has
its share of antiques shops, and auctions are frequent in the Deerfield/
Greenfield area.

APPALACHIAN TRAIL The AT runs
87.7 miles through the Berkshires,
beginning near Sages Ravine in
Mount Everett State Forest in the
town of Mount Washington in the
very southwestern corner of
Massachusetts. It leads up over
Mount Race and Mount Everett, then
turns east through Sheffield and continues on up by Benedict Pond in
Beartown State Forest; heads through
Tyringham and on up through
October Mountain State Forest; proceeds through Dalton and Cheshire,
and on up along the eastern flank of
Mount Greylock to the summit. Then
it's down to Route 2 in North Adams
and on up through Clarksburg State
Forest to the Vermont state line.
Access points, with and without parking, are far more frequent here than
along the AT in northern New
England, and many stretches are
spectacularly beautiful.

Kim Grant

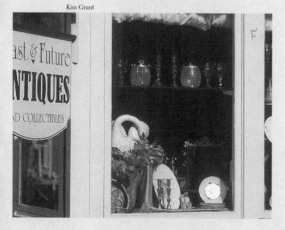

APPLES Contact the **Massachusetts
Department of Food and
Agriculture** (617-626-1720;
www.massgrown.org) for the *Pick-
Your-Own* guide. The Berkshire
Hilltowns represent one of the state's
prime orchard areas. For apple wine
lovers, **West County Winery** (413-
424-348; www.westcountycider.com)
in Colrain (just 3 miles off Route 2) is
worth a special trip. While its hard
ciders are widely distributed, it's
difficult to find all six of the hard
ciders produced here from local fruit.
Anything you want to know about
apples can be found through the **New
England Apple Association** (www.
apples-ne.com), headquartered in
Hatfield.

AREA CODE 413 applies to all of
Western Massachusetts.

ART MUSEUMS Within Western
Massachusetts, an area little more
than 50 miles wide and less than 70
miles long, are found several major
art museums and as many smaller
museums with world-class art pieces
in their collections. The most famous
is the **Sterling and Francine Clark
Art Institute** (www.clarkart.edu) in
Williamstown, drawing art lovers from
throughout the world to see its
French impressionists and 19th-cen-
tury American artists. Just around the
corner is the **Williams College
Museum of Art** (www.wcma.org),
with its wealth of works by Maurice
Prendergast and other choice
American pieces donated by alumni.
These museums in turn are complemented by **MASS MoCA
(Massachusetts Museum of
Contemporary Art;** www.massmo-
ca.org), which opened in 1999 and is
billed as one of the world's largest

contemporary art centers.

Continue west along the Mohawk Trail and down to Deerfield, site of **Historic Deerfield** (www.historic-deerfield.org) with its many portraits and decorative art pieces, then zip down I-91 to Northampton, where the recently expanded **Smith College Museum of Art** (www.smith/edu/artmuseum) showcases a superb collection of primarily 19th- and early-20th-century art as well as major contemporary exhibits. Drive east 9 miles to Amherst to see the **Mead Art Museum** (www.amherst.edu/mead) with its well-rounded permanent collection, much of it again contributed by alumni. In another corner of Amherst the newly opened **Eric Carle Museum of Picture Book Art** (www.picturebookart.org) shows work by the world's top children's book illustrators, recognizing this as an art form in its own right. In the neighboring **National Yiddish Book Center** (www.yiddishbookcenter.org) there are also frequently art exhibits worth stopping for.

A short drive south on the scenic Notch Road (Route 116) over the Holyoke Range to South Hadley takes you to the **Mount Holyoke College Art Museum** (www.mtholyoke.edu/go/artmuseum), one of the country's oldest collegiate art collections, ranging from ancient Asian and Egyptian works through 19th-century landscapes and contemporary pieces. Another short ride to I-91 and into Springfield brings you to the **Quadrangle** (www.quadrangle.org) of museums. This includes the **Museum of Fine Arts**—18th-century portraits and 20th-century works, complemented by decorative arts—and the **George Walter Vincent Smith Art Museum,** with an out-

Kim Grant

standing collection of Japanese armor and cloisonné.

Hop on the Mass Pike (1-90) and in less than an hour you are back in Berkshire County at the **Norman Rockwell Museum** (www.nrm.org) in West Stockbridge, exhibiting not only works by its eminent namesake illustrator but also changing exhibits by other noted illustrators. Finally, north on Route 7 in Pittsfield are the **Berkshire Museum** (www.berkshire-museum.org), a fine regional museum with a respectable collection of American paintings, and nearby **Hancock Shaker Village** (www.hancockshakervillage.org), which displays distinctive Shaker spirit paintings as well as furnishings.

Obviously no one should try to complete this marathon circuit in a day, but it could easily make up a 2- to 5-day tour given the scenery, shopping, lodging and dining along the way. Art lovers will also find quality galleries along the way (listed in each chapter under *Selective Shopping*).

BALLOONING Both **Pioneer Valley Balloons** (www.northampton-airport.com) in Northampton and **Worthington Hot Air Ballooning** (413-238-5514) in Worthington offer hot-air balloon flights year-round, weather permitting.

BASKETBALL The Naismith Memorial Basketball Hall of Fame (www.hoophall.com) in Springfield celebrates Dr. James Naismith's invention of basketball at a local YMCA college in 1891. The present $45 million Hall of Fame museum is Springfield's pride, its most visible landmark (it's shaped like a giant basketball and illuminated in different colors at night), and its biggest tourist attraction. A combination history museum, shrine, computer game arcade, and gymnasium—there's nothing else quite like it.

BED & BREAKFASTS A B&B used to be just a private home in which guests paid to stay and to breakfast. The definition has broadened in recent years to include farms and fairly elaborate and formal lodging places that resemble inns but do not serve dinner. Happily, B&Bs are now widely scattered throughout the state and remain reasonably priced, especially in less touristed areas. Many are run by longtime residents who are knowledgeable about the surrounding area and delighted to orient their guests. Our lodging focus here is on B&Bs. In the process of updating this book, we visited every B&B we could find. **We do not charge for listings in this book and include only those that we would like to stay in ourselves**.

BICYCLING We have noted rentals and outstanding bike routes in most sections. The 10-mile **Norwottuck Rail Trail** between Northampton and Amherst is a popular bike path, and it's possible to come from New York City to Amherst on Amtrak's Vermonter and pedal off to a B&B in either town. A new trail, the 11-mile **Ashuwillticook Rail Trail** (www.berkshirebikepath.org), connects Adams and Cheshire paralleling Route 8 but hugging the shores of Berkshire Pond and Cheshire Reservoir. An even newer 4-mile **Canalside Rail Trail** running south from the Discovery Center in Turners Falls is set for completion in 2004.

A glossy *Massachusetts Bicycle Guide* pamphlet available from the

Kim Grant

Massachusetts Office of Travel and Tourism (1-800-227-MASS; www.massvacation.com) lists state forests with bicycle facilities. Cyclists should secure a copy of the *Rubel Western Massachusetts Bicycle and Road Map* (www.bikemaps. com). At this writing a "Berkshire Bike Touring" map—a free version of the county's section of the Rubel map—is available from the Berkshire Visitors Bureau (www.berkshires.org). *Bike Rides in the Berkshire Hills* by Lewis C. Cuyler (Berkshire House Publishers) and *Bicycling the Pioneer Valley . . . and Beyond* by Marion Gorham (New England Carto-graphics) are also recommended.

Serious mountain bikers should check out River Road south from Chesterfield Gorge to the Knightville Dam (see "Hidden Hills"). Many state forests offer trails beloved by moun-tain bikers. Check out the Department of Conservation and Recreation web site: www.massparks. org. Also see www.massbike.org.

BIRDING The **Massachusetts Audubon Society** (781-259-9500; www.massaudubon.org), founded in 1896 to discourage the use of wild bird plumage as hat decorations, also pioneered the idea of wildlife sanctu-aries. Mass Audubon maintains two staffed sanctuaries in the Pioneer Valley—**Arcadia Nature Center** (413-584-3009) on the Oxbow of the Connecticut River in Easthampton/ Northampton, and **Laughing Brook Education Center** (413-655-8034) in Hampden. In Berkshire County the major wildlife sanctuaries are **Pleasant Valley** (413-637-0320) and **Canoe Meadows,** both in Lenox. In addition, numerous smaller sanctuar-ies are scattered through this area

and described within individual chapters.

Hawk-watchers, we should add, converge on the Connecticut Valley in September, watching these birds ride the thermal highs; favorite lookout spots are Mount Tom and Mount Holyoke. The most famous birds in Western Massachusetts are, however, probably the nesting eagles in Barton Cove. TV cameras are trained on the nest and can be viewed at the Discovery Center in Turners Falls. *Birding Western Massachusetts* (New England Cartographics) by Robert Tougias describes more than two dozen birding sites.

BOAT EXCURSIONS Seasonal cruises of the Connecticut in the Five-College Area are offered aboard the *Spirit of South Hadley* (413-315-6342) and in the Greenfield area on the *Quinnetukut II* (1-800-859-2960), based at Northfield Mountain.

Kim Grant

BOAT LAUNCHES Sites are detailed in brochures on salt- and freshwater fishing available from the **Massachusetts Division of Fisheries and Wildlife** (617-626-1590; www.masswildlife.org), 251 Causeway Street, Suite 400, Boston 02114-2104.

BUTTERFLIES **Magic Wings** (www.MagicWings.net) in South Deerfield is a flowery, lush, year-round oasis filled with thousands of butterflies.

BUS SERVICE **Bonanza Bus** (1-800-556-3815; www.bonanza.com) runs from New York City to Sheffield, South Egremont, Great Barrington, Lee, Lenox, and Pittsfield, with connections to Williamstown. **Peter Pan Bus–Trailways** (1-800-343-9999; www.peterpanbus.com) connects Boston with Springfield, Holyoke, Northampton, Amherst, Lee, Lenox, and Pittsfield. From Albany, Bonanza and **Greyhound** (www.greyhound.com) both offer service to Pittsfield.

CAMPING The **Department of Conservation and Recreation** details information about camping in state forests in a *Camping* brochure as well as listing sites in its *Massachusetts Forests and Parks Recreational Activities* brochure and in and on its web site: **www.massparks.org.** Campsites can be reserved through **www.Reserve-America.com** (1-877-422-6762). Site occupancy is limited to four people or one family, and to 14 days. Rates vary with the park or site; many parks also offer log cabins.

Check out the **Beartown State Forest** in Monterey (413-528-0904); **DAR State Forest** in Goshen (413-268-7098); **Mohawk Trail State Park** in Charlemont (413-339-5504); **Mount Greylock State Reservation** in Lanesborough (413-499-4262; www.massparks.org); **October Mountain State Park** in Lee (413-243-1778); **Pittsfield State Forest** (413-442-8992); **Savoy Mountain State Park** in Savoy (413-664-9567); **Tolland State Forest** in East Otis (413-269-6002); and **Windsor State Forest** (413-684-0948). A *Massachusetts Campground Directory* to commercial campgrounds is available from the **Massachusetts Association of Campground Owners** (781-544-3475; www.camp-mass.com).

CANALS The country's first canal is said to have been built in South Hadley in 1794 (scant trace remains). The **Farmington Canal,** which ran from Northampton through Westfield and Southwick on its way to New Haven, is still visible in parts. In Holyoke power canals have become important parts of a Heritage State Park; in **Turners Falls,** near the new Discover Center, both power and transportation canals are still visible.

CANOEING AND KAYAKING The canoe is making a comeback, and kayaks demanding less skill are now even more popular, increasing interest in paddling Western Massachusetts ponds, lakes, and rivers. Rentals have proliferated, and we detail them in specific chapters.

CHEESE Not only is **Monterey Chèvre** (413-528-2138) delicious, but buying it at the source—Rawson Brook Farm in Monterey—also makes a great excuse to visit with the goats that contribute their milk to its cause. Never mind that **Granville Cheese** (www.granvillestore.com) is made now in upstate New York; it's aged, as it has been since 1851, in the Granville Country Store, one of a number described in the "Hidden Hills" chapter.

CHILDREN, ESPECIALLY FOR Many Western Massachusetts attractions appeal to children age 3 to 93, but those we note under *Families, Especially for* and with the ✍ sign highlight things of special interest to families with young children, as well as child-friendly lodging and restaurants. Such destination attractions include **Eric Carle Museum of Picture Book Art** (www.picture-bookart.org) in Amherst and **Six Flags New England** (www.sixflags.com), the region's largest theme and water park. In Old Deerfield the **Old Indian House** (www.old-deerfield.org) houses activities geared to young visitors, and Holyoke offers a fine **Children's Museum** and adjacent **merry-go-round** in the Holyoke Heritage State Park. In Springfield there's the **Forest Park Zoo** (see *Animals*); the **Quadrangle,** with its **Dr. Seuss figures** (the father of the real Dr. Seuss ran the Forest Park Zoo); and the

Kim Grant

Science Museum (www.quadrangle.com), with its many child-geared exhibits and dinosaurs. We also describe where to find real dinosaur prints in the Pioneer Valley and the "Dino Dig" that's among the many interactive exhibits at the **Berkshire Museum** (www.berkshire-museum.org) in Pittsfield. The nearby **Hancock Shaker Village** (www.hancockshakervillage.org) includes a great hands-on Discovery Room—and visitors under 18 are free.

CHRISTMAS TREES The **Massachusetts Christmas Tree Association** (1-800-521-3550; www.ChristmasTrees.org), P.O. Box 375, Greenfield 01302, supplies a list of farms at which you can cut your own.

COVERED BRIDGES Covered bridges are found in Charlemont, Colrain, Conway, Greenfield, and Sheffield.

CRAFTS The country's largest concentration of craftspeople is reportedly in the Five-College Area and the hills just to the west. **Northampton's Main Street** showcases much of their work, as do several shops in **Shelburne Falls.** The region's outstanding crafts fairs are the **Paradise City Arts Festivals** held in June and on Columbus Day weekend at the Three-County Fairground in Northampton, and the **Deerfield Crafts Fairs** showcasing traditional crafts in June and September at Memorial Hall in Old Deerfield. We list outstanding crafts galleries and studios in each chapter under *Selective Shopping.*

EVENTS This region generates several very different kinds of events. (1) There are the seasonal happenings:

sugaring sit-down breakfasts in the Upper Pioneer Valley and Berkshire Hilltowns in March, the white-water races on the Westfield in April, and crop festivals and PYO as they ripen (see *Farms, Farmer's Markets, and Farm Stands*). August is the season for small-town agricultural fairs, and September for the big ones. Then come fabulous fall foliage festivals, followed by November and early-December crafts fairs combined with holiday lighting festivals. (2) Cultural happenings staged for the general public (as opposed to the rich Five-College Area academic-year events and theater, music, and lecture offerings—which are almost all open to the public) begin in mid-June and end in August. The Tanglewood Music Festival in Lenox is the most famous of these, but there are many more, along with theater and dance, all staged primarily in south Berkshire County but also found throughout the region. (3) Town celebrations. Many of these are annual events but some of the best are frequently just one-time celebrations. For instance: In 2004 Montague (all five villages) celebrates its 250th anniversary, and Old Deerfield celebrates the 300th anniversary of its famous Indian raid. A percentage of all events are found at www.massvacation.com (1-800-227-6277), and we try to list all the best under *Special Events* at the end of each chapter.

FACTORY OUTLETS The **Prime Outlets** at Lee (www.primeoutlets. com) are an attractive grouping of five dozen fairly upscale "outlets" just off the Mass Pike, exit 2. Several old-fashioned outlets are found off the beaten path. In Adams **Interior Alternatives** is an outlet for Waverly

Kim Grant

fabrics and wallpaper, while the **Old Stone Mill** offers bargain-priced wallpapers with some matching fabrics. In North Adams **Berkshire Sportswear** in the Windsor Mill is also the real thing (cash only). Within chapters we describe outlets under *Selective Shopping*.

FALL FOLIAGE AND FOLIAGE FESTIVALS The most colorful small-town fall festivals in the state (ranking right up there with the most colorful in all of New England) are the **Conway Festival of the Hills,** the first weekend in October, and the **Fall Foliage Festival** in Ashfield on Columbus Day weekend (see "West County"). The Northern Berkshire Fall Foliage Festival in North Adams, the first weekend in October, is a huge old event, and on Columbus Day weekend you can join residents of Adams who turn out in force to hike "their" side of the mountain.

Western Massachusetts is unquestionably as beautiful a region to explore in fall as any in New England, given its wealth of maple trees and back roads, many of them dirt. Be advised that color comes first to the higher reaches of Mount Greylock and spreads through the Berkshire Hills the first weeks of October, filling both the Berkshire and Pioneer Valleys a week or two later and lingering on there through October. We decry the lodging practice of charging "foliage rates" throughout October. When it's over, it's really over.

FARMS, FARMER'S MARKETS, AND FARM STANDS "Agritourism" is big in Massachusetts. Several farms offer B&B and cottage rentals on their property. Many more farms have pick-your-own (apples, strawberries, and blueberries, for example), depending on the season; still others invite you in to see their animals, and one (Flayvors of Cook Farm) in Hadley makes fabulous ice cream from the cows grazing beside the shop. Farms in South Hadley, Hancock, and Hawley feature large collections of animals (see *Animals*).

A visit to a farm invariably gets you off the main drag and into beautiful countryside you might otherwise not find. The **Massachusetts Department of Food and Agriculture** (1-877-MASS-GROWN) maintains an extensive web site (www.massgrown.org) detailing information about farms that allow you to pick your own vegetables and fruit. Request or download the *Down on the Farm Directory* of farms that welcome visitors with farm stands, PYO, B&B, or in other ways. The **Community Involved in Sustaining Agriculture** (413-559-5404 or 1-877-623-6633; www.buylocalfood.com) publishes an annual

guide to farmers in Franklin, Hampshire, and Hampden Counties who sell directly to the public; their web site promotes current events and local "fruit loop" tours. **Berkshire Grown** (www.berkshiregrown.org) publishes an annual map/guide and performs a similar service for farmers in Berkshire County.

Look for asparagus in May in the Pioneer Valley (also known as "Asparagus Valley"); for strawberries throughout the area in June; for blueberries, raspberries, and sweet corn after July 4 and—through August—peaches, too. September is apple season, October is all about pumpkins, and in December it's time to cut Christmas trees. Also see *Maple Sugaring*.

Kim Grant

Kim Grant

FISHING Freshwater fishing options range from mountain streams in the Berkshires and Hilltowns to the wide Connecticut. For a listing of stocked fishing sites, best bets, and areas with handicapped access, call the **Massachusetts Division of Fisheries and Wildlife** (1-800-ASK-FISH or 275-3474; www.mass.gov/masswildlife). Also check *Fishing* under each of the chapters in this guide.

GOLF We have listed golf courses under *To Do* in each chapter.

GUIDANCE At the beginning of each chapter we list the regional and local sources of information for that area. The web site www.masscountryroads.com is a helpful travel site devoted to the northern tier of Western Massachusetts towns. The **Massachusetts Office of Travel and Tourism** (MOTT; 617-973-8500,

1-800-227-6277, or 1-800-447-6277) publishes the free *Massachusetts Getaway Guide*. MOTT's web site is www.massvacation.com.

HERITAGE STATE PARKS Conceived and executed by the state as a way of revitalizing old industrial areas, each "park" revolves around a visitors center in which multivisual exhibits dramatize what makes the community special. Though they have served as prototypes for similar parks throughout the country, the Heritage State Parks within the scope of this book have all suffered severe financial cutbacks under recent administrations. The **Holyoke** and **Western Gateway** (in North Adams) parks are, however, still operating as envisioned.

HIGHWAYS I-91 parallels the Connecticut River in its north–south passage through Western Massachusetts, and I-90—the Massachusetts Turnpike—is a quick way across the southern tier of the state (see *Massachusetts Turnpike*). Much of the area described in this book is, however, blessedly far from any major highway—unless you want to count Route 2, which is four lanes, even six lanes in places, from Boston all the way to Wendell in the Pioneer Valley. From Boston, if you are heading west to the Amherst/Northampton area as well to most of the Berkshire Hilltowns and northern Berkshire County, Route 2 is actually quicker as well as more scenic and cheaper than the Mass Pike. For more on the westernmost stretch of Route 2, see *Mohawk Trail*.

HIKING AND WALKING The **Department of Conservation and Recreation** (DCR, formerly DEM) maintains hundreds of miles of hiking trails in the 47 state parks and forests in Western Massachusetts. The **Appalachian Trail** winds 87.7 miles through Berkshire County (see above). The **Taconic Crest Trail** offers many spectacular views along its 35-mile route, also in the Berkshires, including sections in New York and Vermont. Another dramatic, but not easy, hike follows the ridge-line of the east–west Holyoke Range (accessible from the state-run Notch Visitors Center in Granby). Elsewhere in the Five-College Area, the Amherst Conservation Commission maintains some 45 miles of walking and hiking trails. Within this book several walks are suggested in each chapter (see *Hiking* and *Green Space*). The bible for hiking throughout the state is the Appalachian Mountain Club's *Massachusetts Trail Guide*.

HISTORY Within this book a fair amount of Massachusetts history is told through descriptions of many places that still commemorate or dramatize it.

The Connecticut River valley was farmed by Native Americans for thousands of years before the first "Pioneers" arrived, but today only place-names recall their tribes: **Woronoco** (Westfield), **Agawam** (Springfield/West Springfield), **Norwottuck** (Hadley and Northampton), **Pocumtuck** (Deerfield area) and **Squakheag** (Northfield area). It's difficult to estimate how many people lived in this area before a smallpox epidemic, contracted through contact with English and Dutch traders, decimated these tribes in 1633. William Pynchon of Roxbury took advantage of this situation to establish a settlement at present-day **Springfield** in 1636, buying

the land for for 18 fathom of wampum, 18 coats, 18 hatchets, 18 hoes, and 18 knives. Settlers and Indians tentatively coexisted for several decades, but in 1675 the 24-year-old Wampanoag Indian chief Metacomet, better remembered as King Philip, attempted to unite all tribes east of the Hudson River to rise up against the colonists, who already outnumbered them. The uprising began in Plymouth Colony, but King Philip and more than 1,000 Wampanoags escaped to the Connecticut River valley, killing 60 settlers at Deerfield. An obelisk in **South Deerfield** marks the site of this "Bloody Brook Massacre," and the nearby summit of **Mount Sugarloaf,** now a state reservation accessible by road and offering a spectacular view down the valley, is still known as "King Philip's Seat." Philip himself, however, barely escaped capture in a devastating ambush at **Turners Falls** (named for the English captain who directed it) and was slain soon after on the coast.

Local Indian tribes, understandably angry at being pushed off their land, began forming alliances with the French in Canada, then locked in a struggle with Britain for the control of the continent. A series of conflicts known as the French and Indian Wars

Kim Grant

(1689–1763) devastated settlements over much of Western Massachusetts despite the efforts of the citizen soldiers of the colonial militia. During one campaign the song "Yankee Doodle" was written in Charlemont by a British army doctor to poke fun at the typical unmilitary-looking militiaman, whose idea of dressing up was to "stick a feather in his cap." Ignoring the doctor's sarcasm, Americans enthusiastically adopted the song, which became one of the marching tunes of the Revolution. **Charlemont** annually commemorates its composition with a festival called **Yankee Doodle Days** in July.

The most destructive and dramatic of all the French and Indian attacks occurred at **Old Deerfield** in February 1704. A large force of French soldiers and Indian allies from several tribes swarmed over the stockade just before dawn, catching the sleeping village completely by surprise. In the ensuing battle 50 of the town's 291 inhabitants were killed and 112 were captured and carried away to Montreal, while many of its houses were burned. Most of the captives were eventually ransomed and returned home, but some children, adopted by Indian or French families, remained in Canada. Serious settlement in the hills of the Connecticut River valley commenced only after the end of the French and Indian Wars.

Deerfield was rebuilt and, although it was attacked twice more in the next 40 years, was never again captured. The stories (not just the settlers' side) of the 1704 attack are well told at **Memorial Hall Museum** and **Indian House Memorial** in Deerfield, which among other things display a door covered with gashes made by Indian tomahawks during the raid.

Native Americans in the southwestern corner of Massachusetts had been trading amicably with Dutch settlers along the Hudson for several decades before the English arrived in the 1730s. Families from the Connecticut River valley settled **Sheffield,** and a young missionary, John Sergeant, was dispatched to **Stockbridge** from Yale College to propagate the Gospel to the Mohegans. The town's unusually wide street dates from its use as the site on which these friendly Indians built their wigwams, and Sergeant's **Mission House** survives, portraying how well a white family could survive in these backwoods in the early 18th century, but little about the Indians remains. Despite their service to Washington during the American Revolution, the Stockbridge Indians were forced west by the end of the 18th century, carrying their heavy, leather-bound Bible with them.

Berkshire residents played a significant role in the Revolution. In 1773 Sheffield townspeople gathered in the **Colonel Ashley House** to draft the Sheffield Declaration, a petition against British tyranny, observing that "Americans are entitled to all the liberties, privileges and immunities of natural born British subjects." The following August a Berkshire Congress dedicated to taking practical action in defense of such rights met at Stockbridge, and when the British ministerial judges attempted to convene at the courthouse in Great Barrington, they found their way barred by angry locals. Tombstones of those who lost their lives in the Revolutionary War can be found throughout the area.

Boston merchants actually profited from filling war needs, but residents of rural towns in the west of the state found themselves hard hit in the years immediately following the war, especially when payment was required in hard currency, which farmers usually lacked. A farmer who could not pay was stripped of his lands and sent to prison. In 1786, at the height of this rural depression, farmers held a 3-day convention in Hatfield and decided to attack the county courthouse in Northampton. Led by Daniel Shays, a debt-ridden war hero from Pelham, they next attacked the Springfield Arsenal and failed miserably. A few forgotten plaques tell the remaining story. A marker beside the **Pelham Town Hall** (just off Route 202, the **Daniel Shays Highway**) commemorates the spot where the rebels camped for more than 2 winter weeks in their stand "against unjust laws." Another monument along the **Sheffield–South Egremont Road** records the finale of the uprising: HERE 100 REBELS WERE ROUTED AFTER PLUNDERING STOCKBRIDGE AND GREAT BARRINGTON. Shays himself escaped to Vermont, and a recorded 700 families from Western Massachusetts followed him.

The first decades of the 19th century were also the era of the quintessential New England village with its steepled church and grouping of handsome houses around a common, a picture for which Greenfield architect Asher Benjamin is largely responsible. Aware of rural carpenters' need for a do-it-yourself guide, Benjamin in 1796 wrote *The Country Builder's Assistant*, then six more books that went through 44 editions and resulted in the **Greenfield Public Library, Memorial Hall** in Old Deerfield, and

hundreds of handsome homes and churches in the area and throughout the region.

The Civil War fueled the state's industrial growth. At the **Springfield Armory National Historic Site** you learn that it also turned that city into a boomtown, the "Arsenal of the Union," which produced about half the rifled muskets used by northern troops. The story of the region's first major planned mill city built from scratch in the 1840s is told in the **Holyoke Heritage State Park,** while that of the state's last industrial-era boom city—North Adams—spawned by the 25-year construction of the then world's longest railroad tunnel is dramatized in the **Western**

Kim Grant

Gateway Heritage State Park.
Such manufacturing cities continued
to prosper, thanks to immigrant labor,
until the 1920s when the textile and
other industries began moving out of
the state. Innovative uses have been
found for many old mill buildings,
notably the **Massachusetts Museum
of Contemporary Art** (MASS
MoCA) in North Adams, which occupies most of a sprawling industrial
complex originally built as a textile
plant.

What's generally forgotten is the
flip side to this "industrial revolution."
In the agricultural era farmers rarely
left their land, but city dwellers who
punched clocks also took vacations.
Moneyed visitors from throughout the
country flocked to summer hotels; to
upward of 100 summer estates such
as **Naumkeag** and **Blantyre,
Cranwell, Wheatleigh, Seven
Hills,** and **Eastover** in Lenox; and to
more modest country houses like the
William Cullen Bryant Homestead
in Cummington. Many blue-collar
workers and their families traveled
the ubiquitous trolley lines to amusement parks, all now vanished except
for Riverside in Agawam (currently
Six Flags New England). Less affluent
folks also traveled the trolleys and rail
lines to farms catering to guests
throughout Western Massachusetts.

In 1910 **Jacob's Ladder,** a stretch
of Route 20 over the hills into south
Berkshire County, was constructed to
accommodate autos; in 1914 the
Mohawk Trail (Route 2 west over
higher and more dramatic Hoosac
Mountain, then down into North
Adams) was created specifically as one
of the country's first scenic auto touring routes. The **Hotel Northampton**
opened as a "motoring destination" in
1927 featuring a mini museum village

of Americana, and at the same time
Storrowtown, a larger gathering of
rural historic buildings, was assembled at the **Eastern States
Exposition.** In ensuing decades, as
train service atrophied and car travel
increased, virtually all the old summer
hotels disappeared, replaced by
motels.

In the last few decades of the 20th
century the settlement pattern of the
19th century was actually reversed,
with people moving back to the country as urban refugees found ways to
support themselves in rural places.
Educational centers such as
Northampton and Amherst became
lively destinations in their own right,
creating the need for lodging in surrounding hills.

Currently many of the state's true
beauty spots are far more easily accessible than they were for most of the
20th century, thanks in large part to
the the state's enterprising
**Department of Conservation and
Recreation** (www.massparks.org) and
to private land preservation groups
like the **Trustees of Reservations**
(www.thetrustees.org), the
Massachusetts Audubon Society
(see *Birding*), and many local conservation trusts. Lodging has also once
more proliferated throughout the
area. More so than other parts of New
England, Western Massachusetts now
resembles European landscapes in
the sense that the centuries have
stamped it, leaving few corners
untouched in a variety of ways, yet
preserving things both natural and
human-made that deserve to be
preserved.

HORSEBACK RIDING Over the past
decade a number of Massachusetts
livery stables have closed or limited

Kim Grant

themselves to lessons and clinics. In Lenox trail rides are offered at **Undermountain Farm** (413-637-3365) and **Berkshire Horseback Adventure** (413-623-5606); in Becket at **Sunny Banks Ranch** (413-623-5606); and in Williamstown at **DeMayo's Bonnie Lea Farm** (413-458-3149). Trail rides are also available to guests at **High Pocket Farm** (www.highpocket.com) in Colrain.

HUNTING The source for information about licenses, rules, and wildlife management areas is the **Massachusetts Division of Fisheries and Wildlife** (617-626-1590; www.gov/masswildlife), 251 Causeway Street, Suite 400, Boston 02114. Request the current *Abstracts* and a list of the division's wildlife management areas.

LITERARY LANDMARKS In Amherst poet **Emily Dickinson** (1830–1886) was born, lived virtually her entire life, and wrote most of her finest verse in an imposing mansion at 280 Main Street. Her second-floor bedroom has been restored to look much as it did when she was in residence. She is buried in **West Cemetery** on Triangle Street.

The **Jones Library** at 43 Amity Street has a collection of 8,000 items relating to Dickinson, including original handwritten poems. Seven panels in the research wing depict her life in Amherst. The library also has a collection devoted to poet **Robert Frost,** who lived in Amherst from 1931 to 1938 and later taught at Amherst College. For more information on both Dickinson and Frost, see "Upper Pioneer Valley."

Poet and editor **William Cullen Bryant** was born in Cummington in 1794. At the height of his fame, when he was editor and co-owner of the *New York Post*, he transformed the original humble family homestead off Route 112 into a graceful mansion, now owned by the Trustees of Reservations. Filled with memorabilia of Bryant and his era, the **Bryant Homestead** also has an expansive view of a beautiful countryside (see "Hidden Hills").

The Mount, novelist **Edith Wharton**'s home on Plunkett Street in Lenox, is a turn-of-the-20th-century copy of a 17th-century English mansion, but it incorporates a lot of her own ideas of gracious living (she was a wealthy New York socialite). It was here that she wrote *Ethan Frome*, which is set in the Berkshires. **Edith Wharton Restoration, Inc.,** manages the property and conducts tours (see "South Berkshire").

In 1850 **Herman Melville** bought **Arrowhead,** an 18th-century Pittsfield farmhouse, where he wrote his masterpiece *Moby-Dick*. The house at 789 Holmes Road has a fine view of Mount Greylock, the mass of which may have inspired his vision of a great whale. The house is now headquarters for the Berkshire Historical

Society. (See "Central and North Berkshire.") The **Berkshire Athenaeum** on the Pittsfield common has a Melville Room with every book he ever wrote, and most of those written about him. Artifacts displayed include the desk at which he wrote *Billy Budd*.

MAPLE SUGARING Native Americans reportedly taught this industry to early settlers in Tyringham (southern Berkshire County) in the early 18th century. Sugaring is thriving today, primarily in the Hilltowns, an area with more sugarhouses than the rest of the state put together. During sugaring season in March, visitors are welcome to watch producers "boil off" the sap, reducing it to the sweet liquid that is traditionally sampled on ice or snow. The *Massachusetts Maple Producers Directory*, listing dozens of sugarhouses that welcome visitors when they are boiling in March and that cater to customers year-round, is available from the **Massachusetts Maple Producers Association** (413-628-3912; www.massmaple.org), Watson–Spruce Corner Road, Ashfield 01330.

MAPS Most of the Massachusetts this book explores has been backroaded by the limited-access highways—the Massachusetts Turnpike, Route 2, I-91, and I-3—and the free state road map available at this writing is of limited use. In this edition we have made a special effort to provide detailed maps to the areas that merit them, striving for accuracy both in the way back roads run and in the extensive amount of open space accessible to visitors (within each chapter, we detail it under *Green Space*). We recommend, however, that you secure copies of the detailed **Rubel Bicycle and Road Maps** to eastern and Western Massachusetts (see *Bicycling*). We also recommend the Jimapco Western Massachussetts Road Map. Franklin County and the "Hidden Hills" also publish free detailed maps, available from the *Guidance* sources listed in those chapters.

MASSACHUSETTS TURNPIKE It's impossible to explore much of Massachusetts without encountering the "Mass Pike" (I-90). Completed in 1965, this superhighway cuts as straight as an arrow 135 miles across the state from Boston to the New York State line, with just 25 exits, 14 of them east of I-495. It was the first road in Massachusetts on which you could officially drive 65 miles per hour (between Auburn and Ludlow and again between Westfield and the New York line). Eleven service centers (most with fast-food restaurants) are scattered along the route, and four of these include information desks. They are located near the intersection with I-84 in Charlton (eastbound, 508-248-4581; westbound, 508-248-3853); in Lee (413-243-4929); and in Natick (508-650-3698).

MOHAWK TRAIL Traditionally this is the ancient trail blazed through the hilly northwestern corner of the state by Native Americans on their way between the Connecticut River and the Hudson River valleys. However, no one pretends that it's the exact route (check out the Mahican-Mohawk Trail in "Along the Mohawk Trail"). What's certain is the fact that on October 22, 1914, the 38-mile stretch of Route 2 between

Greenfield and Williamstown was officially opened as New England's first "Scenic Road." At the time only a small percentage of roads in the region were paved, and this particularly hilly section was specifically designed to lure "tourists," touring in their first cars. In its namesake chapter we describe the 1920s and 1930s viewing towers and trading posts, which are strategically spaced to permit those old autos to take on water after a steep climb. Thanks to white-water rafting and the dramatic renaissance of Shelburne Falls, visitors and residents alike are rediscovering this genuinely scenic road. The Mohawk Trail Highway has, incidentally, grown over the years and now extends a full 63 miles, beginning in Millers Falls. Web site: www.mowhawktrail.com.

MOUNTAINS Mount Greylock is the state's highest, and you can get to the top (3,491 feet) by car. You can also drive up **Mount Sugarloaf, Mount Tom,** and **Mount Holyoke.** All these offer hiking trails, as does **Mount Toby.** Note that you can stay on top of Mount Greylock; see the sidebar in "Central and North Berkshire."

MUSEUM VILLAGES Unlike most museum villages, both **Hancock Shaker Village,** a restored Shaker community in central Berkshire County, and **Historic Deerfield,** a street lined with more than a dozen 18th- and 19th-century homes in the Upper Pioneer Valley, are composed of buildings still in their original locations. Both therefore evoke an unusual sense of place as well as illustrating their respective stories. Both are also serious research centers. In East Springfield the much smaller **Storrowton** represents one of the

Kim Grant

country's earliest re-created villages; **Greenfield Village,** just west of Greenfield on Route 2, is one man's collection, housed in a building he constructed himself.

MUSIC The best known is the **Tanglewood Music Festival** (www.bso.org) during July and August in Lenox. Other prestigious summer series of note include the **Aston Magna Festival** (www.aston-magna.org) in Great Barrington, the **Berkshire Choral Festival** (www.choralfest.org) in Sheffield, the **Sevenars** concerts in South Worthington, and the **Mohawk Trail Concerts** (www.mohawktrailconcerts.org) in Charlemont.

PETS, TRAVELING WITH The dog-paw symbol 🐾 indicates lodgings that accept pets. Most require prior notice and a reservation; many also require an additional fee.

PUBLIC RADIO Albany-based **WAMC-FM** (90.3) enjoys a wide reception throughout western Massachusetts thanks to a transmitter atop Mount Greylock. There's also Great Barrington–based **WAMQ-FM** (105.1) and Amherst–based **WFCR-FM** (88.5).

RAIL EXCURSIONS The **Berkshire Scenic Railway** (413-637-2210; www.berkshirescenicrailroad.org) offers seasonal 20-mile round trips between Lenox and Stockbridge. Also check out the **Railroad Depot Museum** in Chester (see *Hidden Hills*).

ROOM TAX In contrast to most states, which impose one state tax throughout, Massachusetts has given local communities the option of adding an extra 4 percent—theoretically for local promotion—to the basic 5.7 percent room tax. Although resort towns tend to add the extra 4 percent, there is no hard-and-fast rule. It's worth asking. It's also worth noting that B&Bs with only two or three rooms are exempt from the room tax.

SKIING, CROSS-COUNTRY Trails are

noted throughout the book under *Cross-Country Skiing* and *Green Space*. The state's most dependable snow conditions are found in the Berkshire Hilltown snowbelt, which runs north–south through **Stump Sprouts** (a lodge and touring center; www.stumpsprouts.com) in East Hawley; the **Windsor Notch Reservation** (www.thetrustees.org) in Windsor; **Hickory Hill Ski Touring Center** in Worthington; and both **Bucksteep Manor** (www.bucksteep-manor.com) and **Canterbury Farm** (www.canterbury-farms.com) in Washington.

SKIING, DOWNHILL Within this book we have described each area. In Central and North Berkshire **Jiminy Peak** (www.jiminypeak.com) has expanded substantially in recent years and now owns Brodie, which offers only snow tubing and cross-country; **Bousquet** (www.bousquets.com), founded in 1932, continues to offer beginner, intermediate, and night skiing. In South Berkshire **Catamount** (www.catamountski.com) and **Butternut** (www.butternutbasin.com) both offer vertical drops of 1,000 feet and a variety of trails, while **Otis Ridge** (www.otisridge.com) is a family-geared area limiting lift tickets to 800 per day. Up in West County **Berkshire East** (www.berkshire-east.com) bills itself as southern New England's largest ski area with 45 trails and five lifts, including a new quad for the 2004 season.

SHAKERS The Shakers are the oldest and most successful of America's many 19th-century communal religions, and interest in Shaker furniture and clothing, drawings, and entire, architecturally distinctive Shaker vil-

Kim Grant

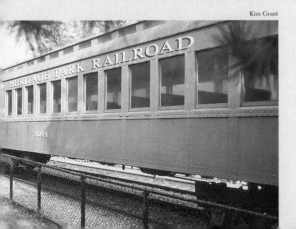

lages runs wide and deep. So does fascination with the people who created these "visible prayers." The Shakers once numbered 6,000 celibate brethren and sisters scattered in 20 self-contained villages from Maine to Ohio. Today only eight villages survive in good enough shape to tell their story—and the Hancock Shaker Village in Central Berkshire is one of the best.

In the 1770s Ann Lee was the leader of England's small sect of the United Society of Believers in Christ's Second Appearing, known for their expressive style of worship as "Shaking Quakers." With her husband, brother, and six followers, Mother Ann settled in Watervliet, near Albany, New York, in 1776. These were years of religious revival as well as political revolution. Whole communities of New Light Baptists—those in New Lebanon, New York (just over the boarder from Hancock), and Hancock—embraced Mother Ann's dictates of celibacy, shared property, pacifism, equality of the sexes, and a firm belief that life could be perfected in this world.

This last philosophy bred not only fine workmanship but also an astounding array of inventions: the flat broom, circular saw, clothespin, seed packet, and no-iron fabric, to name a few.

The Shaker Vatican, so to speak, was Mount Lebanon Shaker Village, straddling the Massachusetts–New York border just west of Hancock. Mount Lebanon elders and eldresses codified rules for all aspects of Shaker life. With 600 residents by the mid–19th century, this was the largest as well as most important Shaker community. On the Sabbath, brethren gathered to pray, sing, and dance in the theater-sized meetinghouse that

had been ingeniously designed in 1824 without interior supports, and it was not unusual for more than 1,000 "World's People" (non-Shakers) to come for this "Sunday Show."

"They filed off in a double circle, one going one way, one the other—two or three abreast—laboring around this large hall with knees bent, hands paddling like fins and voices chanting weird airs," recorded Fanny Appleton Longfellow.

Today Mount Lebanon's surviving Shaker buildings are almost all part of the Darrow School, also the venue for summer Concerts at Tannery Pond and the prime showcase for all things Shaker in Hancock Shaker Village, just east of New Lebanon in Hancock, Massachusetts. Another former Shaker village can be found in Tyringham, and yet another vanished community existed deep in Savoy State Forest.

Hancock Shaker Village

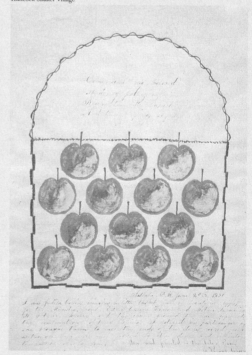

SNOWMOBILING **The Snow-mobiling Association of Massachusetts** (413-369-8092; www.sledmass.com), P.O. Box 55, Heath 01346. SAM coordinates local clubs and offers guidance to some 500 miles of trails throughout the state.

SPAS Lenox is the spa capital of New England. Admittedly, there are relatively few spas in New England, and only two of the three major facilities in Lenox—**Canyon Ranch** (www.canyonranch.com) and **Cranwell** (www.cranwell.com)—are technically spas. The third, the **Kripalu Center for Yoga and Health** (www.kripalu.org), is, however, also a mainstream mecca for thousands seeking physical and mental renewal. The staff requirements at all these centers have drawn a large number of both New Age and traditional fitness practitioners to the area; several have opened small day spas catering to patrons of the many local inns, a situation worth noting, especially in winter and spring, when inn prices drop well below Tanglewood-season rates.

STATE FORESTS AND PARKS Would you believe that Massachusetts has the eighth largest state park system in the country? The **Department of Conservation and Recreation** (DCR, formerly DEM) is responsible for more than a quarter million acres of public forests and parks. It's the largest single landholder in the state. The system began in 1898 with the gift of 8,000 acres around Mount Greylock. Initially its mandate was to purchase logged-over, virtually abandoned land for $5 per acre, and during the Great Depression the Civilian Conservation Corps (CCC) greatly expanded the facilities (building roads, trails, lakes, and other recreation areas).

This book describes 47 forests and parks in their respective chapters under *Green Space,* suggesting opportunities for camping, boating, swimming, skiing downhill (Butternut) and cross-country—not to mention hiking. *The Massachusetts Forest and Park Map/Guide* is an indispensable key to this vast system, available along with the Massachusetts Outdoor Recreation Map (including state wildlife management areas) and the pamphlet guides *Universal Acccess* (detailing handicapped-accessible facilities) and *Massachusetts Historic State Parks,* from the DCR (for the Berkshires, 413-442-8928; for the Pioneer Valley, 413-545-5993; www.massparks.org).

THEATER The **Williamstown Theatre Festival** (www.WTFestival.org), late June through August, is the premier summer theater festival of the Northeast. **Shakespeare & Company** (www.shakespeare.org) in Lenox, performing May through October, is in a class of its own, and the **Berkshire Theatre Festival** (www.berkshiretheatre.org) in Stockbridge is still thriving after 75 years of summer productions. **Barrington Stage Company** (www.barringtonstageco.org), based at Consolati Performing Arts Center in Berkshire, offers both main-stage summer musicals and black-box presentations. The **Miniature Theatre of Chester** (www.miniaturetheatre.org) offers superb small productions. **Pioneer Valley Summer Theatre** (www.summertheatre.net) at the Williston Northampton School offers performances June through mid-

August in Easthampton; **New Century Theatre** (www.smith.edu/theatre/nct) has developed a reputation for quality performances, staged late June through mid-August on the Smith College campus in Northampton and at the **Arena Civic Theatre** in Greenfield. The **New World Theater** (www.newworldtheater.org) at UMass addresses minority themes during the academic year and on weekends in June and July. **City Stage** in Springfield stages professional theater September through May, as does **Shea Community Theater** in Turners Falls.

TRACKING With or without snow-shoes, tracking is proving to be a new way into the woods year-round for many people. The idea is to track animals for purposes other than hunting. The tracking guru in Massachusetts is the naturalist and photographer Paul Rezendes (978-249-8810), who offers workshops and guided tours in the Quabbin area. Massachusetts Audubon Sanctuaries (see *Birding*) throughout the state also now offer tracking programs.

TRUSTEES OF RESERVATIONS The nation's oldest private statewide conservation and preservation organization, the **Trustees** (413-298-3239; www.thetrustees.org), as this non-profit is simply known, was founded in 1891 by Charles Eliot, who proposed to preserve parcels of land "which possess uncommon beauty and more than usual refreshing power . . . just as the Public Library holds books and the Art Museum pictures—for the use and enjoyment of the public." So it happens that the Trustees now own and manage hilltops, waterfalls, islands, barrier beach-es, bogs, historic houses, and designed landscapes among other things, 20 in Western Massachusetts alone. Within this book we describe properties as they appear within chapters. Note that holdings include the outstanding Guest House at Field Farm in Williamstown. Also note the beautifully maintained historic houses in Stockbridge, Ashley Falls, and Cummington.

WATERFALLS Someone should make a poster of Massachusetts waterfalls—not only because there are so many, but also because most are so little known and varied. We have visited and described them all. Check out Ashfield, Becket, Blandford, Cheshire, Chesterfield, Dalton, Middlefield, Mount Washington, New Marlboro, North Adams, Sheffield, Shelburne Falls, Williamsburg, and Worthington.

WEATHER The web site www.mass-countryroads is a good bet for 5-day weather forecasts for Western Massachusetts.

WHEELCHAIR ACCESS The wheel-chair symbol & indicates lodging and dining places that are handicapped accessible. Also note the pamphlet detailing the universal-access program in state forests and parks (see above).

WHITE-WATER RAFTING Since 1989, when New England Electric began releasing water on a regular basis from its Fife Brook Dam, white-water rafting has become a well-established pastime on the Deerfield River. **Zoar Outdoor** (www.zoaroutdoor.com) in Charlemont pioneered the sport in this area and offers lodging and a variety of programs. Maine-based **Crab**

Apple (www.crabapplewhitewater.com) now has its own attractive base on the river down the road—stiff competition—as does **Moxie** (www.wild-rivers.com), also headquartered in Maine.

WINERIES West County Winery (www.westcountycider.com) in Colrain has been producing widely marketed and respected apple wines since 1984 and welcomes visitors June through December. **Chester Hill Winery** (www.blueberrywine.com) in Chester makes three kinds of blueberry wine, as well as a white wine with grapes from New York, and welcomes visitors in its tasting room June through December.

The Berkshire Hills

BERKSHIRE COUNTY

ALONG THE MOHAWK TRAIL

THE BERKSHIRE HILLTOWNS

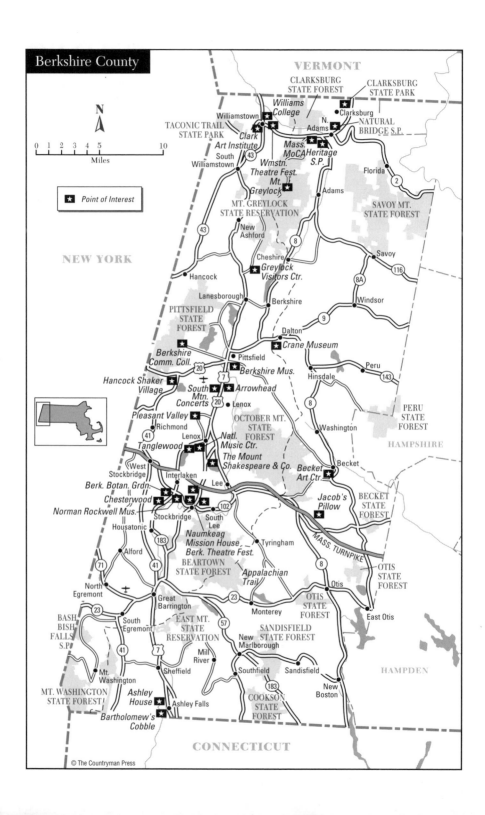

Berkshire County

VERMONT

CLARKSBURG
STATE FOREST

CLARKSBURG
STATE PARK

N

0 1 2 3 4 5 10
Miles

★ Point of Interest

Clarksburg

Williamstown ★ Williams
College

TACONIC TRAIL
STATE PARK

Clark
Art Institute

N.
Adams

NATURAL
BRIDGE S.P.

South
Williamstown

43

Mass.
MoCA Heritage
S.P.

Wmstn.
Theatre Fest.

Florida

2

Mt.
Greylock

Adams

MT. GREYLOCK
STATE RESERVATION

SAVOY MT.
STATE FOREST

NEW YORK

New
Ashford

43

8

Cheshire

Savoy

116

Greylock
Visitors Ctr.

Hancock

8A

Windsor

Lanesborough

Berkshire

PITTSFIELD
STATE
FOREST

9

Dalton

Peru

Berkshire
Comm. Coll.

Crane Museum

Pittsfield

143

20

Berkshire Mus.

7

Hancock Shaker
Village

South
Mtn.
Concerts

Arrowhead

Hinsdale

PERU
STATE
FOREST

20

Lenox

8

Pleasant Valley

41

Richmond

OCTOBER MT.
STATE
FOREST

Washington

HAMPSHIRE

Tanglewood

Lenox

Natl.
Music Ctr.

West
Stockbridge

The Mount
Shakespeare & Co.

Becket

Interlaken

Becket
Art Ctr.

Berk. Botan. Grdn.

Lee

Chesterwood

102

Jacob's
Pillow

BECKET
STATE
FOREST

Norman Rockwell Mus.

Stockbridge

South
Lee

Housatonic

183

Naumkeag
Mission House
Berk. Theatre Fest.

Tyringham

MASS. TURNPIKE

Alford

BEARTOWN
STATE FOREST

Appalachian
Trail

North
Egremont

71

41

8

OTIS
STATE
FOREST

Great
Barrington

23

Otis

BASH
BISH
FALLS
S.P.

23

South
Egremont

EAST MT.
STATE
RESERVATION

57

Monterey

OTIS
STATE
FOREST

East Otis

41

7

Mill
River

SANDISFIELD
STATE FOREST

New
Marlborough

HAMPDEN

Mt.
Washington

Sheffield

Southfield

Sandisfield

MT. WASHINGTON
STATE FOREST

Ashley
House

Ashley Falls

COOKSON
STATE
FOREST

New
Boston

183

Bartholomew's
Cobble

CONNECTICUT

© The Countryman Press

BERKSHIRE COUNTY

SOUTH BERKSHIRE
CENTRAL AND NORTH BERKSHIRE

Berkshire has the best name recognition of any Massachusetts county. Ask residents where they come from and the answer is invariably "the Berkshires," not "Massachusetts."

"The Berkshires" is actually a fairly recent name created to promote Berkshire County. Never mind that the Berkshire Hills themselves roll east through the Hilltowns almost to the Connecticut River.

This westernmost strip of Massachusetts has, however, always been a place apart. Its first settlers were easygoing Dutchmen rather than the dour Puritans, and while parts of Berkshire County are equidistant from both Boston and New York City, visitors and ideas tend to flow from the south rather than the east.

Berkshire County is a distinctive roll of hill and valley that extends the full 56-mile length of the state. Its highest mountains, including Mount Greylock (3,491 feet) in North Berkshire and Mount Everett (2,264 feet) in South Berkshire, are actually strays from New York's Taconic Range; the county is walled from New York State on the west by the Taconics and from the rest of "the Bay State" by hills high enough for 18th-century settlers to have called them "the Berkshire Barrier."

History, topography, and politics aside, what sets the Berkshires apart from anywhere else in the United States, let alone Massachusetts, is the quantity and quality of the music, art, dance, and theater staged here during July and August. Summer festivals are scattered through a wide swath of largely forested countryside: from MASS MoCA, one of the world's largest contemporary arts centers, housed in a vast redbrick mill complex up in North Adams, to the prestigious Jacob's Pillow Dance Festival, in a corner of "South County."

Admittedly, it's the manicured old resort towns of Lenox and Stockbridge that visitors have come to equate with summer culture. Writers and artists were the first Berkshire summer residents; wealthier rusticators began arriving with the trains from New York and Boston. Between 1880 and 1920 some 75 grandiose summer mansions were built around Lenox and Stockbridge. Then came the stock market crash and depression years, but neither Boston nor New York society forgot their former summer playground. In the 1930s the Boston Symphony

Orchestra selected an estate in Lenox as its summer home, and the cultural and summer social tide began to turn once more. It was interrupted, however, by World War II, and after came the years in which illustrator Norman Rockwell vividly recorded sleepy small-town America, based on what he saw within bicycling distance of his Stockbridge studio.

Unexpectedly, the Cold War boosted Berkshire County as a cultural destination. Fearing a nuclear attack on Manhattan, Singer Sewing Machine heirs Sterling and Francine Clark chose to display their legendary art collection in the ivied college town of Williamstown, building a marble museum to house it. The 1955 opening of the Clark Art Institute drew art lovers from around the world—and the steady stream continues.

Even more unexpectedly, the Vietnam War brought the Berkshires a different artistic fame. Folksinger Arlo Guthrie wrote "Alice's Restaurant," an 18-minute-long saga recounting Guthrie's arrest for illegally dumping litter and how it kept him out of the draft. The song became the anti-battle cry of a generation, and the 1969 movie version brought it all visually home: the same small-town scenes and people that Norman Rockwell had depicted, and once more evoking the feel—this time a different feel—of small towns across the country.

In the 21st century Berkshire County is once more enjoying a Gilded Era, and this time it's shared by a far larger group than that of 100 years ago. Once more there's no question that Stockbridge and Lenox are not just any small towns. Visitors from everywhere rock on the porch of the Red Lion Inn (which was almost torn down to make way for a gas station at the early 1960s tourism ebb), and while the Curtis in Lenox is no longer a hotel, the town now offers dozens of princely mansions in which to sleep, and half a dozen in which you can dine at princely prices. In all, the Berkshires now can accommodate 4,000 visitors on any given night, offer them 60 cultural attractions, and feed them in 200 restaurants.

Admittedly many of the cultural attractions are highly seasonal, but few lodging places or restaurants now close for the winter. Lodging rates, on the other hand, vary wildly with the season and even with the day of the week. On weekends during "Tanglewood season" (July and August), you can pay Manhattan prices for a modest room and frequently must stay a minimum of 3 days. Weekdays, even in August, may cost less. Rates remain high through October, but justifiably. Foliage colors linger here, weeks after they have faded from northern New England. Winter offers skiing at some of the country's oldest family-geared ski areas and reduced prices for all those elegant rooms with fireplaces; it's also a good time to take advantage of lower rates at both the day and full-service spas that now cluster in South Berkshire.

We have divided Berkshire County in two: "South Berkshire" (also known as South County) includes Lenox and Stockbridge as well as Great Barrington and the surrounding rural villages. The central Berkshire communities of Pittsfield, Hancock, and Dalton we have combined with the Williamstown and North Adams in "North Berkshire."

Year-round the countryside remains far more than a backdrop. Since the 1840s, both picnicking and hiking along bench-spotted paths and up gentle mountains have been considered the thing to do in summer, and now snowmobiles as well as snowshoes and cross-country skis access many trails in the county's more than 125,000 acres of public preserves.

GUIDANCE

Countywide information sources

Berkshire Visitors Bureau (413-743-4500 or 1-866-444-1815; www.berk-shires.org) offers a countywide reservation service. Request *The Berkshires Vacation Guide,* a thick annual listing of attractions, lodgings, and dining.

Massachusetts Department of Conservation and Recreation (DCR) publishes a handy map/guide to state forests and parks and maintains a visitor-friendly regional office on Route 7 south of Pittsfield (413-442-8928; www.massparks.org), open 9–5 weekdays, serving the entire area.

SOUTH BERKSHIRE

The southwest corner of Massachusetts has its own distinctive beauty and pace. The Housatonic River is slower and the roads are more heavily wooded, winding through classic old villages, by swimming holes, and past hiking paths that lead to waterfalls.

In July and August, however, this serene landscape is the backdrop for the liveliest music, theater, and dance presentations in the Northeast, arguably in the entire country. It's a phenomenon that's been more than a century in the making.

Writers Nathaniel Hawthorne, Herman Melville, and Oliver Wendell Holmes Sr. were among the first Berkshire summer residents. Their lyrical descriptions of its inspirational scenery helped attract wealthy rusticators, who built great summer mansions (coyly called "cottages") and terraced cornfields into formal gardens, especially in and around Lenox and Stockbridge. The stock market crash of 1929, the depression, and the federal income tax thinned the ranks of the Berkshires' wealthy elite. The mansions remained, however, and were frequently taken over by private schools, religious orders, or cultural institutions.

NEAR NEW MARLBORO

Kim Grant

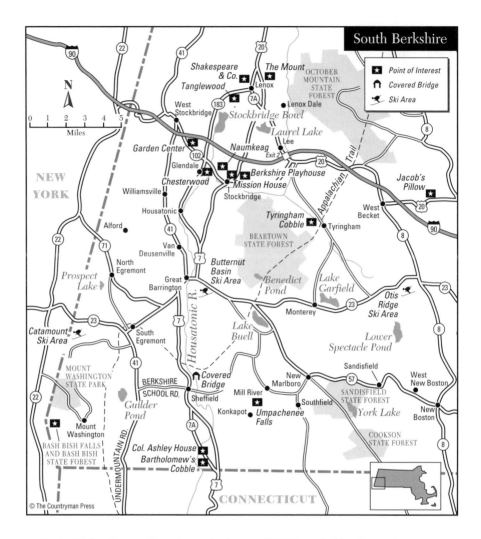

In 1937 the Boston Symphony Orchestra (BSO) made Tanglewood, an estate donated by an orchestra patron, its summer home. Dancers, musicians, actors, and writers began flocking to the Lenox area, lured by the presence of the Berkshire Playhouse (now the Berkshire Theatre Festival), Jacob's Pillow Dance Festival, and the BSO—all presenting summer programs at former private estates.

The audience for these, and the many more live performances that currently form the South Berkshire summer arts scene, is composed primarily of New Yorkers. Great Barrington is said to be equidistant from both New York and Boston—2 hours, 15 minutes (traffic permitting) from both—but New York accents predominate here. This isn't a bad thing. New Yorkers are a famously discerning audience for music, theater, and the arts and bring a discerning palate to restaurants. They not only support the arts and patronize the places to eat, to shop, and to stay, but also tend to be the people operating most visitor-geared ventures.

In and around Lenox and Stockbridge, many mansions are now inns and bed & breakfasts, and three former Lenox estates are now destination resorts in their own right: Canyon Ranch is New England's premier spa, Cranwell is both a golfing resort and a spa, while Kripalu is the region's largest yoga-based retreat center. The other resort villages are South Egremont (blink and you're through), with its clutch of restaurants and antiques shops, and Sheffield, the Berkshires' oldest town and now aptly synonymous with antiques dealers.

The towns that have changed most visibly in south and central Berkshire County in recent years are the formerly workaday Lee and Great Barrington. In Lee paper is still made and lime, even a little marble, still, and both Johansson's Five & Dime and Joe's Diner are Main Street staples, but the Victorian buildings and the vintage-1855 Morgan House have been restored, placed on the National Register, and offer a variety of dining. Capitalizing on its status as the county's prime gateway—the gate being a Massachusetts Turnpike tollbooth—Prime Outlets, a large designer outlet mall, sits on a hillside just off the Pike exit, and there are gracious B&Bs scattered along the town's wooded upland roads.

Great Barrington, the largest town in south Berkshire County, has changed even more dramatically. It has always been a place to buy a wrench, catch a bus, and see a dentist or a movie. Recently it's also become a place to shop for linen clothing and country furnishings, for artist materials and vintage posters, to find a rental kayak or a guide for fly-fishing. The tiny visitors center has opened a Half Tix window, selling same-day, half-price tickets for musicals and plays at the Barrington Stage Company, dance at Jacob's Pillow, and music in numerous South Berkshire venues.

South from Great Barrington, the Housatonic spirals lazily through a broad valley hemmed in by rolling hills to the west and walled by the abrupt range that includes Mount Everett on the west. Sheffield's village of Ashley Falls, almost on the Connecticut line, is the site of the Colonel Ashley House in which the Sheffield Declaration, a 1773 statement of grievances against Bristish rule, was drafted. This exceptional home is owned by the Trustees of Reservations, the venerable Massachusetts organization that also maintains several of the area's outstanding historic houses and preserves.

South Berkshire harbors thousands of acres of state park and forest, acquired when land was cheap, after 75 percent of its trees were chopped down to feed either the area's lime kilns or its paper mills. In the 1890s vast estates were also acquired by private owners, and segments of these are also now preserved by the state and by the Trustees. Public lands offer camping, swimming, and fishing as well as hiking and cross-country skiing. The Appalachian Trail cuts across the Housatonic Valley, offering numerous access points, from the heights of Mount Race to Benedict Pond in Beartown State Forest.

East of the Housatanic Valley gentle hills are webbed with back roads, many still dirt, climbing through old farms and still some estates dating from land speculation before railway routes were determined. A railway never materialized, and the east–west Massachusetts Turnpike followed Route 20 through Becket to Lee, backroading Otis, Tyringham, and Monterey and even further backroading the 18th-century towns of Sandisfield and New Marlborough.

AREA CODE 413.

GUIDANCE The **Berkshire Visitors Bureau.** See the "Berkshire County" introduction.

Lenox Chamber of Commerce (413-637-3646 or 1-800-25-LENOX; www.lenoxchamber.org), Curtis Building, 5 Walker Street, Lenox 01240-0646. A walk-in, volunteer-staffed information center providing free lodging referral, which during Tanglewood season includes many private homes, along with guidance about shopping, dining, and attractions.

Stockbridge Information Booth. A kiosk-style booth on Main Street is open daily in summer months (but just noon–2 on Sunday). The **Stockbridge Chamber of Commerce** (413-298-5200; www.stockbridgechamber.org) is good for help by phone weekdays 8:30–2:30. Lodging hot line: 1-866-626-5327.

The Stockbridge Lodging Association publishes its own brochure (write Box 224, Stockbridge 01262) and operates a lodging hot line: 413-298-5327.

The Lee Chamber of Commerce (413-243-0852; www.leechamber.org), 3 Park Place, is right on the park with plenty of adjoining parking in the middle of town. Open daily 10–6 in-season, 10–5 off-season.

Southern Berkshire Chamber of Commerce (413-528-1510; www.southern-berkshires.com), 362 Main Street at the southern edge of Great Barrington (Route 23/Route 7), across from the long gray wall of "Searles Castle." Open year-round Tuesday through Saturday 10–4:30, until 6 July, August, and October. The lodging hot line is 413-528-4006 or 1-800-269-4825.

GETTING THERE *By air:* See **Albany Airport** and **Bradley International Airport** in Windsor Locks, Connecticut, under *Airports* in "What's Where."

By bus: From Boston, **Peter Pan–Trailways** (1-800-343-9999) serves Lee and Lenox via Springfield. From Manhattan, **Bonanza** (1-800-556-3815) runs up Route 7, stopping on the green in Sheffield, South Egremont, Great Barrington (Bill's Pharmacy: 413-528-1590), Stockbridge (Main Street), Lee (McClelland Drugs: 413-243-0135), and Lenox (Lenox News & Variety: 413-637-2815).

By train: From New York City, Metro-North (212-532-4900 or 1-800-METRO-INFO; www.mta.info). On July through Labor Day weekends Friday-evening trains from Grand Central to Wassaic Station, New York, connect with buses to Great Barrington. The return service is offered Monday morning, and the price is surprisingly reasonable.

By car: From Boston, the obvious route is the Massachusetts Turnpike to exit 2 at Lee (2 hours on the button). For a more scenic approach take exit 3 in Westfield and either drive the 45 miles via Route 20 to Route 23 west to **Otis** and **Monterey,** or (in good weather) follow Routes 10/202 south to Route 57 west (see *Scenic Drives*).

From New York City, the obvious approach is the Major Deegan Expressway or the Henry Hudson Parkway to the Saw Mill River Parkway, then to the Taconic Parkway; take the South Berkshire exit, Hillsdale/Claverack, Route 23.

GETTING AROUND A car is the way to go, but if you are a car-free urban dweller you still have options: You can get to several key towns by bus from Boston or, easier still, from Manhattan (see *Getting There*), then hire a taxi or rent a car (check chamber listings in Lee and Great Barrington) to get around. Local rental car agencies deliver cars to the bus stops or local inns. Given the many scenic but confusing roads that web this area in particular, we recommend securing a *Berkshire Bike Touring* map, free from the sources listed under *Guidance*.

The **Berkshire Regional Transit Authority** (413-499-2782 or 1-800-292-2782) links Great Barrington, Lee, Lenox, and Stockbridge with Pittsfield; hours are geared to commuters rather than to visitors.

PARKING It's free in Lenox, Stockbridge, and Great Barrington, but there's a 2-hour limit, strictly enforced. In Great Barrington the big downtown lot is at the end of Railroad Street; there's a smaller lot at the end of Castle Street.

MEDICAL EMERGENCY Dial **911.**

❋ Towns and Villages

Egremont (population: 1,150). There is no village of Egremont; instead there's North Egremont and South Egremont, divided by Baldwin Hill. **South Egremont** is the livelier village, one of the few in the Berkshires to retain its original, rambling old inn, and the Old Mill houses one of the most prestigious restaurants in the Berkshires. The village is also known for antiques shops. Note the fan window in the **Congregational Church** and the town hall in the southern village. Don't miss **Baldwin Hill,** with its surviving farms and sense of serenity. **North Egremont** consists of a general store, an inn, and lakeside campground.

Great Barrington (population: 7,288). The shopping hub of southern Berkshire County, Great Barrington has become known in recent years for the quality and quantity of its restaurants, and also of its downtown shopping. Railroad Street, not too long ago one of the dingier corners of town, is now restaurant row, home to some of the county's leading places to eat, while the Triplex Theater with its first-run films, Café Helsinki with its live music, and the newly restored Mahaiwe Theater on Castle Street complement the dining and shopping. Intriguing shops and restaurants have recently also spread up and down Main Street, complementing long-established grocery and hardware shops. Still a place to get your shoes or your camera fixed, it's also now the place to find the right wedding present or an inflatable kayak. During the August-through-September "season" a surprising variety of music, theater, and other live performances also contribute to Great Barrington's claim to be the liveliest downtown in all Berkshire County.

While it has had its ups and downs, Great Barrington has always been visitor-friendly. Around the turn of the 20th century there were three large and fashionable inns in town, including the Berkshire Inn, operating from

THE OLD INN ON THE GREEN, NEW MARLBOROUGH GEDNEY FARM

Kim Grant

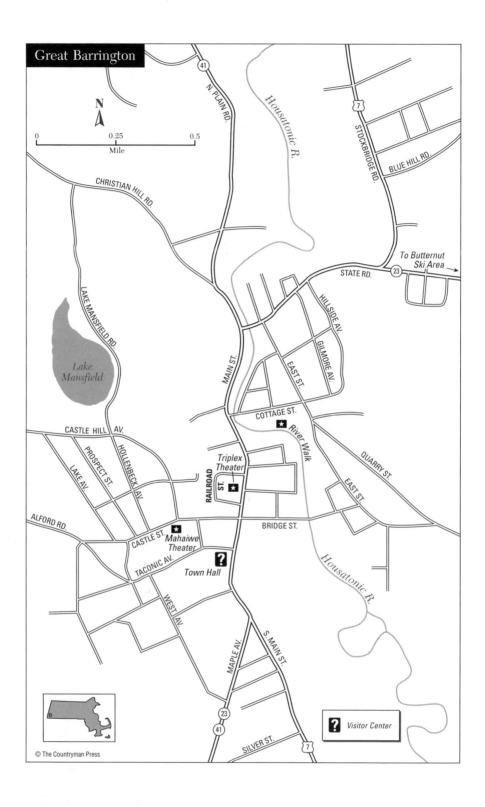

1868 until 1963, which more than filled the site that's now occupied by the chamber of commerce booth, Bill's Pharmacy, and the Days Inn. Across Main Street loom the walls and turrets of Searles Castle, designed by Stanford White and built of local blue dolomite stone between 1882 and 1886 for the widow of a founder of the Central Pacific Railroad. Main Street's three stone churches also evoke this opulent era.

Worth noting: The ancient-looking (and barely readable) stone marker in front of town hall with the inscription:

NEAR THIS SPOT STOOD THE FIRST COURT HOUSE OF BERKSHIRE COUNTY HERE AUGUST 16, 1774 OCCURRED THE FIRST OPEN RESISTANCE TO BRITISH RULE IN AMERICA.

Worth finding: River Walk, still evolving but offering benches and views of the Housatonic in several segments as it flows behind Main Street. At the entrance beside Brooks Drugs, a brief history credits William Edward Burghardt DuBois with inspiring the project, pleading with townspeople to "Rescue the Housatonic . . . restore its ancient beauty." Sociologist and civil rights activist W. E. B. DuBois (1868–1966) was born in Great Barrington by what he called this "golden river," explaining that it was "golden because of the woolen and paper waste that soiled it." The woolen and paper mills were, however, several miles upstream in Housatonic, a village that still has a working paper mill as well as a number of artists working in former mill buildings.

Two more famous men are closely associated with Great Barrington: William Cullen Bryant, while born in Cummington, began married life and practiced law ("forced to drudge for the dregs of men, / And scrawl strange words with the barbarous pen") in Great Barrington. Many of his most famous poems, including "Monument Mountain" and "Green River," were inspired by local landmarks. It was on Monument Mountain, just north of town on Route 7, that Nathaniel Hawthorne and Herman Melville met, at an 1850 picnic.

RIVER WALK, GREAT BARRINGTON

Kim Grant

North and south of Great Barrington, Route 7 is lined with restaurants and smallish malls, not easily dismissed because of the many independent shops and restaurants studding both commercial strips.

Lenox (population: c. 6,000) evolved in stages. Its 1787 status as county seat gave it graceful Federal buildings like the courthouse; the recently renovated library with its luxurious reading rooms, gallery, and outdoor reading park; the Academy; and the Church on the Hill. In the 1860s county government shifted to Pittsfield and summer visitors began buying up large holdings. By the turn of the century more than 90 elaborate summer "cottages" were scattered along every ridge in the area. Lenox's glory years as the inland Newport were brief, ended by the Great Depression and the federal income tax. The resort might have vanished entirely had it not been for the Boston Symphony Orchestra's Berkshire Music Festival. Concert halls were not yet air-conditioned, and symphony music typically ceased during summer. The orchestra selected Lenox as its summer home because Tanglewood (a forested estate named by Nathaniel Hawthorne, who wrote *Tanglewood Tales* there) was given to it by a patron. More than 50 grand "Berkshire Cottages" still cluster in and around Lenox. The Mount, former residence of novelist Edith Wharton (whose best-known work, *Ethan Frome,* is set in the Berkshires), was recently restored and is open to the public. Shakespeare & Company performs the works of the Bard along with contemporary plays in a complex of buildings on a 63-acre former estate that includes Spring Lawn, an opulent turn-of-the-20th-century mansion. Bellefontaine, another baronial cottage, is now a spa (Canyon Ranch), several are inns, and the site of one of the grandest (Andrew Carnegie's mansion unfortunately burned) is now the Kripalu Center for Yoga and Health.

Stockbridge (population: 2,300) was founded in 1734 to contain and educate the local Mohicans. Just four white families were permitted to settle, theoretically to "afford civilizing examples to the Indians." But predictably, the whites multiplied and the Native Americans dwindled. After distinguishing themselves as the only tribe to serve in the Revolution and the first to be given U.S. citizenship, the Stockbridge tribe was shipped west, eventually to Wisconsin, where a few hundred descendants still live. Stockbridge boasts that the Laurel Hill Association was the country's first village-improvement society. Residents will tell you that the same number of notables have been summering in town for the past century; only the faces change periodically. The rambling, wooden Red Lion Inn, a short walk from the restored Mission House, forms the heart of the village. Naumkeag, the quintessential Gilded Age mansion, is just a short way up the hill, and the Berkshire Theatre Festival is on the northern fringe of town. The village green is actually west of the Route 102–Route 7 junction, and many visitors miss it entirely. Here stand the imposing brick Congregational Church (1824), the pillared Old Town Hall (1839), and the Field Chime Tower, which marks the site of the original Native American mission. The Indian Burial Ground is nearby—the large mound topped by a stone obelisk and overlooking the golf course. The Village Cemetery, across from the green, contains the remains of John Sergeant, Native American chief John Konkapot, 19th-century tycoons like Joseph Choate, and town aristocrats like

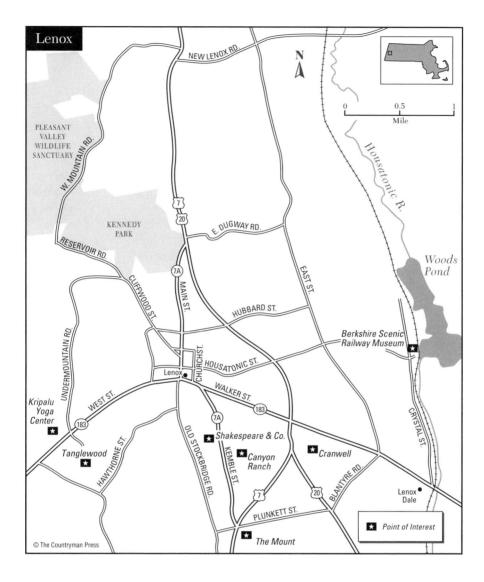

Lenox

PLEASANT VALLEY WILDLIFE SANCTUARY

W. MOUNTAIN RD.

RESERVOIR RD.

KENNEDY PARK

NEW LENOX RD.

E. DUGWAY RD.

N

0   0.5   1
Mile

Housatonic R.

Woods Pond

CLIFFWOOD ST.

UNDERMOUNTAIN RD.

7A

MAIN ST.

CHURCH ST.

HOUSATONIC ST.

HUBBARD ST.

EAST ST.

Berkshire Scenic Railway Museum

Lenox

WALKER ST.

WEST ST.

Kripalu Yoga Center

183

Tanglewood

HAWTHORNE ST.

OLD STOCKBRIDGE RD.

7A

KEMBLE ST.

183

Shakespeare & Co.

Canyon Ranch

Cranwell

BLANTYRE RD.

CRYSTAL ST.

7

20

Lenox Dale

PLUNKETT ST.

The Mount

★ Point of Interest

© The Countryman Press

the Fields and Sedgwicks, the latter buried in a large, circular family plot known as "the Sedgwick pie."

Monterey (population: 918). Much of this town has been absorbed into **Beartown State Forest,** and it is largely a second-home community. Lake Garfield is ringed with summer homes, and its beach is private. The **General Store** is, however, hospitable, with a deli and snacks at tables in the rear. Head north from the village center and turn onto Art School Road to find the **Bidwell House,** an exceptionally well-furnished 18th-century home with walking trails through its extensive grounds. This was once a dairy center producing more cheese than any other location in the county, and **Monterey Chèvre** from Rawson Brook Farm is still the county's best cheese.

Mount Washington (population: 135). Mount Washington looms like a solitary green island above the valleys in three states. The town is the southwesternmost, the highest, and one of the smallest in Massachusetts. Best known as the home of **Bash Bish Falls,** the state's most photographed cascade, it is also the site of one of the highest peaks (2,600-foot-high Mount Everett) and the highest lake (Guilder Pond) in Massachusetts. The community is also arguably the oldest in Berkshire County (settled by the Dutch in the 1690s). The town is webbed with hiking trails—including one of the more dramatic, open ridgeline sections of the **Appalachian Trail.** Given that you can drive almost to the top of Mount Everett and that you can park at several other trailheads that access high-elevation trails—and paths to several waterfalls (the cascades of Race Brook and Bear Rock as well as Bash Bish)—you would assume this place was one of the better-known, more popular spots to hike. Not so. Mount Washington seems to be a well-kept hikers' secret. Population is less than 200 and triples in summer. The center of the village is marked by the small **Union Church** (ecumenical, open summers only) and tiny town hall. Note the old cemetery on West Street and Blueberry Hill Farm.

New Marlborough (population: 918). A beautiful roll of hills pocked by shallow valleys carved by the Konkapot River and its offshoots. The town is webbed with roads connecting its villages: Mill River, Southfield, Hartsville, New Marlborough Center, and Clayton. At the center stand the Old Inn on the Green and a domed white-clapboard meetinghouse, the venue for late-summer-through-fall music, films, etc., sponsored by More and More: 413-229-3126.

Sheffield (population: 2,967). This town was the first in the Berkshires to be chartered (1733). Its wide main street (Route 7) is lined with stately old homes, and the town boasts the greatest number of antiques dealers of any town in the Berkshires. North of the green, the 1770s brick **Dan Raymond House,** maintained by the Sheffield Historical Society (413-229-2694), is open Memorial Day through October (Thursday through Saturday 11–4 and by appointment).

COVERED BRIDGE IN SHEFFIELD

Kim Grant

It reflects the lifestyle of this prosperous merchant, his wife, and their nine children and is part of a seven-building complex that includes a regional research center (Monday and Friday 1:30–4 and by appointment), a vintage-1820 law office, a carriage house with a tool exhibit, and an oddly shaped building once used to grow vegetables for nearby hotels, now an education center. There's also an 1830s smokehouse and a stone store housing changing exhibitions and a museum store. The 1760 **Old Parish Church** is a beauty, one of the oldest churches in Berkshire County and the site of a seasonal Friday-afternoon farmer's market (4–7) as well as of the annual 3-day **Sheffield Antiques Fair,** always the third weekend in August. Several miles south on Route 7 is Ashley Falls, well worth allotting several hours in which to tour the **Colonel Ashley House** (1735), the oldest in the Berkshires, and to walk along the glassy Housatonic in **Bartholomew's Cobble.** Note the covered bridge, built originally in 1827, just off Route 7 at the northern end of the village.

Tyringham (population: 375). Hemmed in on three sides by mountains, this village was the site of a major Shaker community from the 1790s until the 1870s (a group of privately owned Shaker buildings still stands on Jerusalem Road near Shaker Pond). The village then began attracting prominent summer residents, including Samuel Clemens. A number of 19th-century writers eulogized Tyringham. See **Tyringham Cobble,** the **McLennan Reservation,** and **Ashintully.**

Sandisfield (population: 809). Between 1840 and 1870 this was a booming industrial town with six taverns and churches and a population said to surpass Pittsfield's. It's difficult to believe. Land sales boomed when a railroad was proposed to run through town, but it never happened; the last surviving industrial vestige is the **Buggy Whip Factory,** which operated from 1792 until 1973 and is now an antiques center housing more than 80 dealers. A museum corner also dramatizes the history of the tanning industry in town. The most visible village in Sandisfield is New Boston, at the junction of Routes 8 and 57. The **New Boston Inn** is said to date from 1737 and is unquestionably one of the state's oldest inns, still offering food and lodging, retaining even its old ballroom as second-floor common space.

Kim Grant

✳ To See

THE ARTS In no other rural corner of the country are so many quality music, dance, and theater productions found so near each other. In July and August you can choose from a rich menu of live performances, many at prices far below what they would be in New York or Boston.

Note: For Jacob's Pillow, Great Barrington Stage, and several concert series, half-price tickets are frequently available after 2 PM the day of the performance through Half Tix, a service based at Southern Berkshire Chamber of Commerce (see *Guidance*).

MUSIC Tanglewood Music Festival (413-637-5165; off-season, 617-266-1492; box office, 617-266-1200 or

1-888-266-1200; www.bso.org), Tanglewood, entrance on West Street (Route 183) west of Lenox village. The Boston Symphony Orchestra's summer concert series, which opens July 4 and runs through August, has been held since the 1930s in a fan-shaped, open-sided hall understatedly referred to as "the Shed." The Koussevitzky Music Shed actually seats 5,000 people and has splendid acoustics. More than 14,000 patrons regularly converge on Tanglewood on weekends, but a concert is rarely sold out, and then it's usually for an appearance by a pop music superstar such as James Taylor. There is always room on the 500-acre grounds, though parking lots can fill up and postconcert traffic jams are legendary (which is why inns and B&Bs within walking distance of the main gate can charge premium rates). Many concertgoers actually prefer sitting on the lawn and come several hours early, dressed in high resort style (or any old way at all), bearing elaborate picnic hampers that have been known to include white linen tablecloths and candelabra. (*Note:* It does rain and bugs do bite on the lawn, so come prepared.) The lawn at Tanglewood is one of New England's great people-watching places. Many concerts are now also staged in the 1,200-seat Seiji Ozawa Hall, which also has an adjoining lawn that can accommodate several hundred. Symphonic concerts (Friday and Saturday evenings and Sunday afternoons) aside, the Tanglewood calendar is filled, beginning in mid-June, with chamber music and other special concerts; there's also an annual Festival of Contemporary Music and a Labor Day weekend Jazz Festival, plus almost daily concerts by young musicians of the Tanglewood Music Center (TMC) Orchestra. The Boston Pops performs each summer, and there are Friday Prelude Concerts and Saturday-morning open rehearsals. Prices for seats in the Shed are $17–85 depending on the place and event, while lawn seats run $15–20; Ozawa Hall,

TANGLEWOOD MUSIC FESTIVAL

Walter Scott

$27–65. Open rehearsals in the Shed are $16, and dress rehearsals in the theater are $15–20. TMC tickets are $10–25. Request a detailed schedule and order form. Children 12 and under are free on the lawn.

Aston Magna Festival (413-528-3595 or 1-800-875-7156; www.astonmagna.org), St. James Church, Main Street, Great Barrington. Five Saturdays in July and August. The counry's oldest annual summer festival devoted to baroque, classical, and early romantic music, very professionally played on period instruments.

Berkshire Choral Festival (413-229-8526; www.choralfest.org), 245 Undermountain Road (Route 41) in the concert shed of the campus of the nearby Berkshire School, stages a 5-week summer series of concerts combining hundreds of voices with music by the Springfield Symphony. Come early for a picnic and a preconcert talk.

Stockbridge Chamber Concerts (413-442-7711 or 1-888-528-7728), Searles Castle, Great Barrington. A series of midweek chamber music concerts in July and August; tours of Searles Castle, now the John Dewey Academy, are offered before the tour.

DANCE **Jacob's Pillow Dance Festival** (413-243-0745; www.jacobspillow.org), George Carter Road, Becket (off Route 20, 8 miles east of Lee). America's oldest dance festival and still its most prestigious, Jacob's Pillow presents a 10-week summer program of classic and experimental dance. Located on a onetime hilltop farm, the Pillow was founded in the 1930s by the famed dancer Ted Shawn as both a school for dancers and a performance center. As well as scheduled productions, informal impromptu performances are going on all the time. There is a pleasant café. Tickets for performances in the Ted Shawn Theater, the first in the country built exclusively for dance, are $20–55. Inquire about performances in the Doris Duke Studio Theater and about free performances inside and out.

JACOB'S PILLOW DANCE FESTIVAL

THEATER **Shakespeare & Company** (box office, 413-637-3353; off-season, 413-637-1197; www.shakespeare.org), 70 Kemble Street, Lenox. Productions late May through October; tickets run $8–45, depending on seating, theater, and performance. Students, seniors, and groups get a 10 percent discount. Some free performances. In existence for more than 25 years, this exciting theater company, long based at the Edith Wharton mansion, the Mount, now has its own expansive home: a 63-acre property that incorporates three estates including Spring Lawn, a splendid Gilded Age mansion almost as grand as the Mount. The grounds are open to the public for strolling and picnicking. Although Shakespeare is the main dramatic fare, the company also does other classic plays, such as works of Chekhov, as well as plays by contemporary authors, and short "salon" pieces based on stories by Edith Wharton and others, the latter usually presented at Spring Lawn. Major productions are staged at Founders Theatre, which can seat nearly 500 people. One of the company's long-term projects is a re-creation of The Rose—a three-tiered, thatch-roofed Elizabethan-era London theater. Until the money is raised to begin construction, the group makes do with "The Rose Footprint." This is a simple outdoor theater covered with a tent in midsummer (often used for productions featuring student actors) that is on the site and has the same dimensions as the planned Elizabethan replica.

Berkshire Theatre Festival (413-298-5576; www.berkshiretheatre.org), 6 East Main Street (Route 102), Stockbridge. Since 1928 the July-through-August festival has been staged in a building designed by Stanford White in 1887 as the Stockbridge Casino. The building was restored and moved to its present site in the 1920s by Mabel Choate, mistress of Naumkeag. Katharine Hepburn, Ethel Barrymore, James Cagney, and Dustin Hoffman all performed here early in their careers. The festival program is varied and usually includes one or two premieres each season. Children's theater is staged Wednesday through Saturday at 11 AM at the Berkshire Museum in Pittsfield in July and the festival's 100-seat Unicorn Theatre in August. Tickets are $29–55.

Barrington Stage Company (413-528-8888 or 413-528-8806; www.barringtonstageco.org), Consolati Performing Arts Center at the regional high school, Berkshire School Road, Sheffield. This relatively new but enthusiastically reviewed and received theater group, directed by Julianne Boyd, offers musicals on the main stage and smaller plays on Stage II throughout the summer and fall. The main stage is at the Berkshire School, but venues vary. Free for those age 13 and under, discounts for students and seniors, and frequently discounted tickets through Half Tix.

Mahaiwe Performing Arts Center (413-644-9040; www.mahaiwe.org), 14 Castle Street, Great Barrington. This ornate and intimate (700-seat) vaudeville house was built in 1905 and is presently undergoing thorough restoration. To date all the infrastructure has been updated and much of the ornate detailing has been restored, but the ambitious plans for total restoration are still in progress. In the meantime, it serves as the venue for frequent live presentations—from full operas to nationally known folk musicians—as well as for a film and lecture series.

Also see the **Williamstown Theatre Festival** in "North Berkshire."

ART MUSEUM The Norman Rockwell Museum (413-298-4100; www.nrm.org), Route 183 south of its junction with Route 102, 3 miles west of Stockbridge. Norman Rockwell (1894–1978), America's most beloved illustrator, spent his last 50 years in Stockbridge and often used it as a backdrop and local residents as models. The museum displays some 200 of his works, including the

HOME FOR CHRISTMAS AT THE NORMAL ROCKWELL MUSEUM. PRINTED BY PERMISSION OF THE NORMAN ROCKWELL FAMILY AGENCY, © 1967 THE NORMAN ROCKWELL FAMILY ENTITIES.

famous World War II poster series *The Four Freedoms,* along with many original paintings done for covers of the *Saturday Evening Post* magazine, at the time a national institution. Even if you didn't grow up with the *Post,* Rockwell's iconic yesteryear images of small-town American life retain their charm and are a delight to look at. Also on view are powerful paintings, quite different from the folksy *Post* covers, that he did for *Collier's* magazine to illustrate articles on 1960s civil rights incidents. Although Rockwell is the focus, the museum always also has major special exhibits on other illustrators and aspects of contemporary illustration. The handsome museum building, which includes a large gift shop, is on a 36-acre former estate with tranquil views from benches (and picnic facilities) overlooking the Housatonic River. Open daily 10–5 in summer; November through April, weekdays 10–4, weekends 10–5. Rockwell's studio, located on the museum grounds, is open May through October. Closed Thanksgiving, Christmas, and New Year's Day. $12 adults, $7 students, under 18 free.

Also see the **Clark Art Institute, MASS MoCA,** the **Williams College Art Museum,** the **Berkshire Museum,** and **Hancock Shaker Village** in "Central and North Berkshire."

HISTORIC HOMES Chesterwood (413-298-3579; www.chesterwood.org), Route 183, south of its junction with Route 102 in the Glendale section of Stockbridge. Open May through October, daily 10–5. $10 adults, $9 seniors and students, $5 age 6–18, family rate $25. This 160-acre estate served as the summer home for 33 years to Daniel Chester French (1850–1931), whose *Minute Man* statue in Concord established his eminence as a sculptor at age 25. By 1895, when he discovered Stockbridge, he was internationally respected and able to maintain this elaborate summer home and studio, which commands, as he put it, the "best dry view" he'd ever seen. The National Trust offers guided tours of the residence, of a newly renovated barn gallery with special exhibits, and of the studio, now exhibit space for plaster casts of many of the sculptor's works, including the statue that now sits in Washington's Lincoln Memorial. Visitors are welcome to stroll the grounds, which include a wooded path—the Hemlock Glade—overlooking Monument Mountain. Frequent events are staged throughout the summer, notably an antique auto show in May and an outdoor sculpture show July through October, also a November sale (at the newly expanded gift store) and a Christmas tour. Inquire about "Fridays at Home": tea served Fridays June through October in the studio. The year is 1920 and Margaret, the sculptor's daughter, is serving. Meadowlark, a studio-hideaway squirreled away across the road and thoroughly private, is available for rent year-round (see Red Lion Inn under *Lodging*).

Mission House (413-298-3239), Main Street, Stockbridge. Open Memorial Day weekend through Columbus Day, daily 10–5. Adults $5, children $3. John Sergeant, idealistic young missionary to the Stockbridge tribe of the Mohican nation, built this house for his bride in 1739. He built it not on Route 102 where it now stands (known as the Plain at the time, this site held Native American wigwams), but up on the hill where the town's few white families lived, among them the Williamses. Sergeant's wife was Abigail Williams, a lady of pretensions, and the house is elaborately built for its time and place. It was salvaged and moved to this site in 1929 and is maintained by the Trustees of Reservations. An outbuilding houses an exhibit on the Stockbridge Indians. The beautiful "colonial revival" garden, a mix of flowers and herbs, is the work of the noted landscape architect Fletcher Steele, who also designed the famous formal gardens at Naumkeag.

Naumkeag (413-298-3239), Prospect Hill Road, Stockbridge. Open daily late May through Labor Day, then weekends and holidays through Columbus Day; 10–4:15. $10 adults for house and garden, $8 for garden only; $3 age 6–12. The Trustees of Reservations maintain this fantasy gabled and shingled 26-room "cottage." It was designed by McKim, Mead & White in 1885 for one of the leading lawyers of the day, Joseph Hodges Choate, who endeared himself to his wealthy colleagues by securing the reversal of an income tax law that Congress had passed in 1894. It's the most evocative of the region's Gilded Age mansions because it retains many of its original furnishings and because the tours are so good. The view from the terrace is one of the finest in the Berkshires. The gardens, designed by leading landscaper Fletcher Steele, are as exceptional as the house and filled with imaginative touches and surprising elements, such as the famous curving blue steps set for contrast in a grove of white birches. The gardens are also the scene of a concert series in July and August.

NAUMKEAG, STOCKBRIDGE

Christina Tree

Frelinghuysen Morris House & Studio (413-637-0166; www.frelinghuysen.org), 92 Hawthorne Street, Lenox. Open July 4 weekend through Labor Day, Thursday through Sunday 10–4; June, September, and October, Thursday through Sunday 10–4. $8 adults, $3 children. An architecturally interesting 1940s house (a starkly white Bauhaus-style building with art

THE MOUNT

(413-637-1899 or 1-888-637-1902; www.edith-wharton.org), 2 Plunkett Street (junction of Route 7 and Route 7A), Lenox. Open daily 9–5 Memorial Day weekend through October; $16 adults, $8 students, free under 12. Novelist Edith Wharton's Georgian-style home, built in 1902, is an English mansion designed by Christopher Wren but incorporates many of the ideas articulated in her book *The Decoration of Houses*. Wharton had a hand in designing the formal gardens as well as the building and also chose its furnishings. The resulting mansion is special

PORTRAIT OF EDITH WHARTON, 1902

Beinecke Library/Yale University

indeed and once more looks as it did in Wharton's day: Nearly $9 million was spent to restore the 42-room house and magnificent formal gardens for their centennial in 2002. Also meticulously restored was Wharton's sumptuous bedroom suite—it has French marble fireplaces, oil-painted floral wall panels, gilded mirrors, and the best views of the gardens, where she did much of her writing. Tours conveying a sense of Wharton's life and work are offered by Edith Wharton Restoration, Inc. Inquire about the Women of Achievement lecture series, presented on Mondays in July and August at 4 PM ($18 at the door, $16 in advance for lecture and reception).

THE MOUNT

deco decor) on 46 acres bordering Tanglewood. The furnishings are original (cutting-edge modern for the era) and the walls hung with paintings by the owners and their contemporaries, including Picasso, Braque, Léger, and Gris.

Ventfort Hall (413-637-3206; www.gildedage.org), 104 Walker Street, Lenox. Open Memorial Day through October, daily 10–3 (the last tour is at 2 PM). In winter admission is by appointment. An imposing Elizabethan-style mansion in the center of Lenox built in 1894 for Sarah Morgan, sister of financier J. P. Morgan, Ventfort Hall is now "The Museum of the Gilded Age." The building is used for lectures and theatrical performances and has some exhibits, but only a couple of downstairs rooms have been restored and furnished in period style. Much more needs to be done before it can fully embody the opulent era it represents. Admission with guided tour $8 adults, $4 children 5–17.

The Bidwell House (413-528-6888; www.bidwellhousemuseum.org), Art School Road, Monterey. Open Memorial Day through mid-October, Tuesday through Sunday 11–4; $6 adults, $5 seniors and students, $2 under age 18. A genuine center-chimney colonial house, built circa 1750 as a parsonage by the Reverend Adonijah Bidwell, but what's special about this place is the way it's furnished. In the 1960s it was purchased by Jack Hargis and David Brush, New York interior designers who not only painstakingly restored the home but also expertly furnished it with their collections of earthenware and china, including redware, slipware, and delft, some fine early samplers, antique quilts, pewter, domestic hand tools, and lighting devices. It's a must for anyone interested in 18th-century decorative arts. The house is set in period gardens, and footpaths lead through 196 acres of fields and woods. Inquire about lectures, workshops, and other special events.

Colonel John Ashley House (413-298-3239), Cooper Hill Road in Ashley Falls, well marked from Route 7, south of Sheffield Village. Open June through Labor Day, Wednesday through Sunday 1–5, also weekends and holidays from Memorial Day weekend until Columbus Day. $5 adults, $3 children. The oldest in Berkshire County (1735), this house was the site of the 1773 drafting of the Sheffield Declaration denouncing the British Parliament. The home is beautifully paneled, restored, and furnished. You learn about Mum Bet, purportedly the first slave to sue for, and win, her freedom under due process of law. Along with nearby Bartholomew's Cobble, also maintained by the Trustees of Reservations, this is one of the most interesting corners of south Berkshire County.

SCENIC DRIVES Southwick to New Marlborough. Take exit 3 off the Massachusetts Turnpike at Westfield and head down Routes 10/202 south. Traffic may be initially sticky in Westfield, but the rewards are great as soon as you turn onto Route 57 in Southwick. Note the several family restaurants, good way stops. **Granville,** 5 miles west, is a classic beauty with a general store that's worth a stop to pick up the Granville Cellar Aged Cheddar that's been aged and sold on this spot since the 1850s (open most days until 6:30). It only gets prettier after that, passing though **West Granville** with its early-18th-century meetinghouse and **Tolland** with its state forest (with lakeside campsites on Otis Reservoir).

Note the New Boston Inn that's been standing at the junction of Routes 57 and 8 since 1737 and still boasts good food and lodging. Just over the New Marlborugh line, note the turnoff for **York Lake** (swimming and fishing). Farther along in **New Marlborough,** the Old Inn on the Green, vintage 1760, also offers hospitality. From here roads radiate to most corners of South Berkshire.

Great Barrington to Lee is one of our favorite routes. Follow Route 23 east to Route 57, wandering through the historic village of New Marlborough, and turn north at the Old Inn on the Green onto the (dirt) New Marlborough–Monterey Road. It climbs up into high meadows then dips down through woods. Bear left at the fork and you soon see a sign for Rawson Brook Farm; stop to visit the goats and pick up some exceptional goat cheese. At Route 23 turn left into the center of Monterey and head north on the Tyringham Road (also called Main Road). A left turn will take you to the **Bidwell House;** otherwise continue into the breathtaking Tyringham Valley. Stop at **Tyringham Cobble,** parking by the cow pasture just above the village, and walk to the top of the cobble (a limestone hill); the trail also winds through forest and meadow. The road brings you into Lee, near Route 102 and exit 2 on the Mass Pike.

Egremont/Sheffield Road: For both history and beauty, it's difficult to beat the road from South Egremont to Sheffield. This country road runs south from the South Egremont Inn, and woods soon give way to fields with views of the hills to the west. This is the "Sheffield Plain." At the corner of Kiln Road look for the suitably ancient-looking marble monument commemorating the last battle of **Shays Rebellion** in 1787. Follow the road on down to Route 7 and look on your left for the **Covered Bridge,** originally built in 1837 and reconstructed in 1998.

✳ To Do

BICYCLING *Berkshire Bike Touring,* a version of the *Rubel Western Massachusetts Bicycle and Road Map* (see *Bicycling* under *What's Where*), is currently available from local info booths and centers. *Best Rides in the Berkshire Hills* by Lewis C. Cuyler is also worth picking up. Bicycles can be rented from **Berkshire Bike & Blade** (413-528-5555), Barrington Plaza (south on Route 7), Great Barrington; or the **Arcadian Shop** (413-637-3010), 91 Pittsfield Road, Lenox, open daily (also cross-country skis, snowshoes, backpacking equipment, and clothing).

BIRDING **Pleasant Valley Wildlife Sanctuary** (413-637-0320; www.massaudubon.org), 472 West Mountain Road, Lenox. This Massachusetts Audubon sanctuary includes an evolving education center and year-round programs. Its 730 acres include part of Lenox Mountain, Yokum Brook, beaver ponds, a hemlock gorge, and 7 miles of trails used for cross-country skiing in winter. It harbors hooded mergansers, great blue herons, and belted kingfishers as well as beavers, snapping turtles, and many other animals. Inquire about guided canoe trips on the Housatonic, mid-May through early October.

Thousand Acre Swamp, off Norfolk Road, south of Southfield, left on Hotchkiss. A birder's delight.

BOATING The placid **Housatonic** is ideal for lazy rides down the river, especially between Great Barrington and Bartholomew's Cobble. Trips are detailed in the *AMC River Guide: Massachusetts, Connecticut, Rhode Island.* **Expeditions, Butternut's Outdoor Store** (413-528-7737), 276 Main Street, Great Barrington, rents kayaks. By far the largest lake in the area is Otis Reservoir in the **Tolland State Forest** (413-269-6002); rowboats can be rented at **Camp Overflow** (413-269-3036) and both rowboats and canoes from **J&D Marina** (413-269-4839), both in Otis.

Also see **Pleasant Valley Wildlife Sanctuary,** above.

CAMPING The obvious way to beat the high cost of lodging during the Tanglewood season is to take advantage of one of the four state park campgrounds in this area. The best bet for finding a site is in **Tolland State Forest** (93 campsites, 26 lakeside). The other options are **October Mountain State Forest** (50 sites) and **Beartown State Forest** (12 year-round sites). For reservations, phone 1-877-422-6762. The Department of Environmental Management (DEM) maintains an excellent web site—www.state.mass.gov/dem—as well as a friendly visitors information center on Route 7 south of downtown Pittsfield (413-442-8928). Each of the state forests is described in more detail under *Green Space.* Also see "Central and North Berkshire" and "Berkshire Hilltowns" for more state-maintained camping.

For commercial campgrounds, check out the free guide published by the **Massachusetts Association of Campground Owners** (781-544-3475; www.camp-mass.com).

CAR RACING **Lime Rock Park** (203-435-0896; www.limerock.com), 497 Lime Rock Road, Lakeville, Connecticut. Open April through October, Saturday and holidays. Sports car superstars who race here include Paul Newman. Free parking and free on-site camping; admission under age 12 is free.

FISHING Licenses for fishing (currently $11.50 for those age 15–17; otherwise $12.50 for a resident and $23.50 for a nonresident for 3 days) are required for everyone 15 or over. They are available at local sporting stores and by contacting the Division of Fisheries and Wildlife (413-447-9789), 400 Hubbard Avenue, Pittsfield. Log onto www.state.ma.us/dfwele or www.masswildlife.org.

South Berkshire's many trout-stocked waters include Center Pond and Yokum Pond in Becket, Prospect Lake in Egremont, Goose Pond and Laurel Lake in Lee, Benedict Pond in Monterey, Thousand Acre Swamp in New Marlborough, Benton Pond and East Otis Reservoir in Otis, and Stockbridge Bowl in Stockbridge.

For equipment and guide service, visit **River Run** (413-528-9600; www.berkshirefishing.com). Michael Flach features Orvis equipment in his sporting goods store at 271 Main Street, Great Barrington. He also offers guided fly-fishing trips on the Housatonic in Massachusetts and Connecticut, on the Farmington in Connecticut, and on ponds and rivers throughout southwestern Massachusetts.

Housatonic River Outfitters (413-528-8811; www.dryflies.com), 684 South Street in Great Barrington, an offshoot of the long-established store (860-672-1010) at 24 Kent Road in Cornwall, also offers guided fishing on the Housatonic and Farmington.

FOR FAMILIES ✍ **Rainbow's End Miniature Golf** (413-528-1220), 18 holes at the **Cove Lanes,** 109 Stockbridge Road, Great Barrington (Route 7). If the kids are along, this indoor mini golf is a great for evenings or rainy days.

✍ **Berkshire Theatre Festival** offers children's theater written by local children.

✍ **The Norman Rockwell Museum** is free to children under age 18.

✍ **Pleasant Valley Wildlife Center** (413-637-0320; www.massaudubon.org) in Lenox and **Berkshire Botanical Garden** (413-298-3926; www.berkshirebotanical.org) in Stockbridge offer special programs for children.

✍ Both the **Stockbridge Library** (413-298-5501) and **Lenox Library** (413-637-0197) have extensive children's collections; inquire about story hours.

Also see *Farms.*

GOLF Cranwell Golf Course (413-637-1364; www.cranwell.com), 18-hole championship par 70 course. Golf Digest School, Lee Road in Lenox; driving range, pro shop, full-service spa. Sloane's Tavern serves lunch. Also see *Lodging.*

Egremont Country Club (413-528-4222), Route 23, South Egremont. 18 scenic holes, driving range, pro shop, private lessons, moderate greens fees.

Greenock Country Club (413-243-3323), West Park Street, Lee, has nine holes; moderate greens fees.

HIKING More than 100,000 acres of Berkshire County (75 percent) is wooded, and 86 miles of the **Appalachian Trail** traverse the county. The number and variety of walking and hiking trails, many dating back to the 19th century, are amazing. They are described in several books, notably *Hikes & Walks in the Berkshire Hills* by Lauren R. Stevens, *A Guide to Natural Places in the Berkshire Hills* by René Laubach, and *Wildflowers of the Berkshire & Taconic Hills* by Joseph G. Strauch Jr., all published by Berkshire House, based in South Lee. The *Appalachian Mountain Club Guide to Massachusetts* is also extremely helpful, published by AMC Books. Also see the trails described in this chapter's *Green Space.*

HORSEBACK RIDING Undermountain Farm (413-637-3365), Undermountain Road, Lenox. Year-round lessons, trail rides. $45 an hour for

SIGN ON THE APPALACHIAN TRAIL

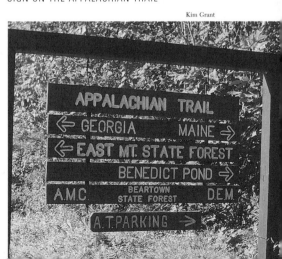

Kim Grant

trail rides; no children under 12. When it comes to setting, views, and total experience, innkeepers tell us that this is by far the best local trail ride.

Berkshire Horseback Adventure (413-637-9090), 293 Main Street, Lenox. Scenic trail rides. $50 an hour, $130 half day, $200 overnight.

Sunny Banks Ranch (413-623-5606), Route 8, Becket. Rodeos every Saturday, lessons, trail rides, western saddle.

LLAMA HIKES **Berkshire Mountain Llama Hikes** (413-243-2224; www.bcn. net/llamahike), 322 Landers Road, Lee. Hourly and sunset scenic hikes with llamas. Accommodations available.

PICNICKING **Bowker Woods,** Route 183 between Stockbridge and Chesterwood; drive in at the sign. There's a pine grove by a small pond, good for picnics. Picnicking is also allowed on the grounds of Shakespeare & Company on Kemble Street in Lenox.

∞ ♪ **Berkshire Botanical Garden** (413-298-3926; www.berkshirebotanical.org), Stockbridge, junction of Routes 102 and 183. Gardens and gift shop open May through October, 10–5. Greenhouses open year-round. The 15 acres include a pond, woodland trail, and children's garden. There are shrubs, trees, perennial borders, greenhouses, herbs, a gift shop, and periodic lectures and workshops. There are also a number of annual special events, including a sculpture show mid-June through October and a flower show in August. Picnickers welcome. Weddings encouraged. Admission—$7 adults, $5 seniors and students—is charged mid-May to mid-October.

RAILWAY EXCURSION **Berkshire Scenic Railway Museum** (413-637-2210; www.berkshirescenicrailroad.org), 10 Willow Creek Road, Lenox. Thanks to a state grant, this long-absent excursion is back in business, making a 20-mile round trip between Lenox and Stockbridge. Vintage coaches and a veteran diesel locomotive are used, and a uniformed conductor narrates the scenic trip along the banks of the Housatonic River. Excursions begin from the old Lenox depot, which houses a gift shop and a museum that includes model train displays and an exhibit on the role of railroads in the Berkshires' Gilded Age boom years. $12 adults, $10 seniors, $8 children under 14.

SWIMMING For a fee, you can swim at **Prospect Lake Park** (413-528-4158), a private campground in North Egremont with a sandy swim beach; at the **Egremont Country Club** (413-528-4222), South Egremont; and at **Card Lake** in West Stockbridge. Inquire locally about swimming in the **Stockbridge Bowl** and **Laurel Lake.** Another favorite local spot is the swimming hole in the **Green River** on Route 23 about a mile west of Great Barrington between Route 71 and Alford Road, and on Route 23 south of Great Barrington (look for the lineup of cars).

Under *Green Space,* check 40-acre **York Lake,** off Route 57 in Sandisfield State Forest; **Otis Reservoir** in Tolland State Forest; **Benedict Pond** in Beartown State Forest; and **Umpachene Falls** in New Marlborough.

TENNIS **Tennis Village School,** West Stockbridge, two hard-surface courts. **Sheffield Racquet Club** (413-229-7968), four clay courts, clubhouse. **Greenock Country Club** (413-243-3323), Lee, two courts. **Egremont Country Club** (413-528-4222), South Egremont, four courts.

✳ Winter Sports

ALPINE SKIING ✍ **Butternut** (413-528-2000; www.butternutbasin.com), Great Barrington; west on Route 23. Still owned by the same family that founded it in 1963. Butternut is known for its grooming and for the beauty of its design by founder Channing Murdock—both on and off the slopes. Mountaineers for 4- through 12-year-olds; also snowboarding programs. *Vertical drop:* 1,000 feet. *Terrain:* 22 trails, 110 skiable acres; longest run: 1.5 miles. *Lifts:* One quad, one triple, four double chairs, and two new beginner lifts. *Snowmaking:* 100 percent of area. *Rates:* Adults $45 weekends, $32 weekdays; juniors and seniors $34 weekends, $22 weekdays; half-day and other discounts. On every nonholiday, Monday and Tuesday lifts are $15. Inquire about tubing.

✍ **Catamount** (413-528-1262; www.catamountski.com), South Egremont, Route 23. Straddling the New York–Massachusetts line, overlooking the rolling farm country of the Hudson Valley, Catamount has been in business 65 years as a family area. The base lodge is pleasant. Mountain Cats for age 4–12; also Tiny Tot lessons for age 4–6. *Vertical drop:* 1,000 feet. *Terrain:* 20 slopes and trails including 1-mile-long (intermediate) "Sidewinder." *Lifts:* Seven lifts, snowboard megaplex with 400-foot half-pipe. *Snowmaking:* 95 percent of area. *Rates:* Adults $45 weekends, $30 weekdays; juniors and seniors $42 weekends, $30/27 weekdays; night skiing Wednesday through Saturday.

✍ **Otis Ridge** (413-269-4444; www.otisridge.com), Route 23 in Otis. A long-established family ski area that operates a ski camp (age 8–15) near the top of its trails. *Vertical drop:* 400 feet. *Terrain:* 10 slopes and trails. *Lifts:* One double chair, five tows. *Snowmaking:* 80 percent of area. *Facilities:* Lodging and food at the slope-side Grouse House (413-269-4446). *Rates:* Adults $25 weekends and $15 weekdays; seniors $10, $5 during the week.

Also see **Jiminy Peak** in "Central and North Berkshire."

CROSS-COUNTRY SKIING **Bucksteep Manor** (413-623-5535 or 1-800-645-2825; www.bucksteepmanor.com), Washington Mountain Road, Washington. With an 1,800-foot elevation and 25 km of trails on 400 acres, this area is usually snow-covered in winter. Trails are groomed and tracked, and there are rentals and guided tours into neighboring 16,000-acre October Mountain State Forest; also lodging and dining on the premises.

Butternut Basin (413-528-2000; snow conditions, 1-800-438-SNOW), Great Barrington. Adjacent to the alpine area are 8 km of trails connecting with Beartown State Forest cross-country skiing.

Canterbury Farm (413-623-0100; www.canterbury-farms.com), 1986 Fred Snow Road, Becket. Generally open December through March, 9–5. Offers 12 miles of tracked wide trails to a lake and around a beaver pond, with an average elevation of 1,700 feet, rental equipment, lessons, fireplaced room with drinks, hot soup, chili, snacks, or space for your own picnic. Snowshoes, ski rentals, lessons.

Cranwell (413-637-1364; 1-800-272-6935; www.cranwell.com), Lee Road, Lenox, offers snowmaking along groomed golf course trails, equipment rentals, and instruction. Full-service spa. Also see *Lodging*.

Also see *Green Space*. Some of the best cross-country skiing is to be found in public preserves. Because of its elevation, the **Mount Washington State Forest** is a standout, as is **Bartholomew's Cobble** in Ashley Falls and **Beartown State Forest** in Monterey. **Kennedy Park** in Lenox also offers easy access to an extensive trail system; rental equipment is available next door at the Arcadian Shop.

SNOWMOBILING Several state forests and parks in this region permit snowmobiling; see *Green Space* below. For guided tours, contact Wild n'wet Sport Rentals in Lenox (413-445-5211; caseycare@peoplepc.com).

✳ Green Space

STATE PARKS AND FORESTS *Note:* The Massachusetts Department of Conservation and Recreation (DCR) publishes a handy map and guide and maintains a visitor-friendly regional office on Route 7 south of Pittsfield (413-442-8928; www.massparks.org).

Beartown State Forest (413-528-0904), Blue Hill Road, Monterey; 10,555 acres. This is high tableland stretching northwest from Monterey, the upper end dropping down to the Housatonic River in South Lee. Accessible from Route 102 in South Lee, and in Monterey from both Blue Hill Road off Route 23 and the Tyringham Road. In summer the big attraction is 35-acre **Benedict Pond,** an artificially formed pond good for swimming (there are sanitary but no changing facilities), picnicking, and boating (no motors). The Appalachian Trail skirts the pond, and a trail circles it. There are also a dozen campsites (open year-round; reservations are needed in summer, but from October through April it's first come, first served) plus lean-tos along the Appalachian Trail. Inquire about the trail to the summit of Mount Wilcox; a 1.5-mile trail circles the pond there.

Four DCR properties cluster in the extreme southwestern corner of the state. The best known of these is **Bash Bish Falls State Park,** a dramatic falls that rushes down a 1,000-foot-deep gorge, finally plunging some 80 feet around two sides of a mammoth boulder and dropping into a perfect pool that's labeled NO SWIMMING. Needless to say this sign is frequently ignored (rangers are on duty weekends only) and, sad to say, divers occasionally die here. Don't swim, but do explore this special place. Access is via Route 23, Route 41, and Mount Washington Road in South Egremont; take Mount Washington Road to East Street, then Cross Road back up West Street to Falls Road to the parking lot. Signage here, at this writing, is dreadful. The rugged quarter-mile trail meanders steeply down through pines to the falls. Don't lose heart at the point the blue blazes disappear (after you cross the stream); they pick up below. Locals who want to bring folding chairs and picnics usually continue down the road instead to the "lower parking lot" in New York's **Taconic State Park.** It's a longer, but level walk in to the bottom of the falls. From this lot you can also access the steep but short trail to the upper rim of the falls—which continues (via the South Taconic Trail) to Alander Mountain in **Mount Washington State Forest** (413-582-0330), East Street, Mount Washington (see directions above from South Egremont to East Street). Forest Headquarters are on East Street, south of the Cross Road turnoff for Bash Bish Falls. Inquire about primitive, walk-in (half a mile) camping sites with pit toilets, springwater, and fireplaces, and about access to the Appalachian Trail. The AT is also accessible from Jug End Road in the **Jug End Reservation,** an extension of the Mount Everett State Reservation that's accessible both from Route 41 and from the Mount Washington Road in South Egremont. The **Mount Everett State Reservation,** accessible from East Street (north of Cross Street) in the town of Mount Washington, seems sadly neglected. At this writing the road to the top of Mount Everett, the 2,602-foot-high mountain (second highest in Massachusetts) that commands an overview of Berkshire County to the north, is closed with, we are told, no plans for its reopening. Dogwood blooms in spring, mountain laurel in June and early July, and there are wild blueberries in late July and early August. **Guilder Pond,** a little more than half a mile up the road, is filled with pink water lilies during late July and much of August; the Appalachian Trail leads north and south of the pond along the ridgeline. Within the reservation a popular trail climbs up to the AT via **Race Brook Falls** from Route 41 in Sheffield. South of Mount Race, the AT skirts beautiful Plantain Pond. Also see Mount Washington under *Villages.*

BASH BISH FALLS

Christina Tree

October Mountain State Forest (413-243-1178), a total of 15,710 acres accessible from Route 20 in both Lenox and Lee. Camping (Memorial Day through Columbus Day) is the big draw here, but there are just 46 sites (flush toilets, showers, picnic tables, dumping station). **Schermerhorn Gorge** is a popular hike and has many miles of trails also used for winter skiing and snowmobiling. Much of this area was once impounded by Harry Payne Whitney as a game preserve (it included buffalo, moose, and Angora goats as well as smaller animals). **Halfway Pond** is a good fishing spot.

Otis State Forest (413-269-6002), off Route 23 on Nash Road in West Otis. Boating (no motors) is permitted on **Upper Spectacle Pond;** cross-country skiing and snowmobiling on the unplowed roads, which include the original road that Henry Knox labored over with cannons in the winter of 1775–76.

Tolland State Forest (413-269-6002), off Route 23 in Otis, offers 92 campsites, Memorial Day through Columbus Day (most for tents; flush toilets, showers, picnic tables, fireplaces). Campsites are on a peninsula jutting out into **Otis Reservoir.** There is a picnic area with a sandy swim beach and a boat launch; also fishing and boating in the reservoir. This is a spot to hike and cross-country ski.

Sandisfield State Forest (in winter, 413-528-0904; in summer, 413-229-8212). The state forest holdings are scattered around Sandisfield; the most popular section is just over the New Marlborough line (Route 57) on **York Lake,** a 40-acre dammed area near the headquarters of Sandy Brook. Here you can swim, boat (no motors), and picnic (there are tables, grills, and fireplaces). The forest harbors five more lakes, all stocked with trout and accessible to nonmotorized boats. Winter trails for skiing and snowmobiling. Hunting is permitted in-season.

TRUSTEES OF RESERVATIONS Contact 413-298-3239 or www.thetrustees.org.

🐾 **Bartholomew's Cobble** (413-229-8600), marked from Route 7A in Ashley Falls, south of Sheffield. Open year-round but closed Sunday and Monday, December through March. The visitors center with exhibits, restrooms, and a naturalist on duty is open 9–4:30. Admission for non–Trustees members is $4 per adult, $1 per child. This 329-acre tract takes its name from the high limestone knolls or cobbles of marble and quartzite that border the glass-smooth Housatonic River. We recommend the pine-carpeted Ledges Trail, a (theoretically) 45-minute loop with many seductive side trails down to the river or up into the rocky heights. The Cobble is noted for the diversity of its fern species and woodland wildflowers. A booklet guide is available from the naturalist. There are exhibits and restrooms in the visitors center. Leashed dogs welcome. Inquire about special kayaking and nature programs. Note that the Colonel Ashley House (see *Historic Homes*) is just up the road.

Monument Mountain on Route 7 north of Great Barrington. This peak is one of the most distinctive in the state: a long ridge of pinkish quartzite, scarcely 15 feet wide in some places, 1,700 feet high. The climb is lovely any day, whether by the Hickey or the Monument Trail. The hillside is covered with red pine and, in June, with flowering mountain laurel. A Bryant poem tells of a Native American maiden, disappointed in love, who hurled herself from Squaw Peak. Nathaniel Hawthorne, Herman Melville, and O. W. Holmes all picnicked here in 1850.

Tyringham Cobble, half a mile from Tyringham Center on Jerusalem Road. Open daily, year-round. The Appalachian Trail crosses a portion of this 206-acre

MONUMENT MOUNTAIN

property: steep upland pasture and woodland, including a part of Hop Brook, with views of the valley and village below.

Ashintully Gardens, Tyringham. Sodem Road, marked from the Main Road between Tyringham Center and Monterey. Open mid-June through mid-September, Wednesday and Saturday 1–5. Free to individual visitors; group tours by appointment. These elaborate gardens are sited on a 120-acre property below the ruins of the "Marble Palace," a pillared white mansion completed in 1912 as the centerpiece of 1,000-acre Ashintully Estate. This design of the garden is described as "episodic"—an artistic creation incorporating paths, fountains, bridges, stairs, gates, and lawns.

McLennan Reservation, Fenn Road, off Main Road south of Tyringham Center. Open daily, year-round. This 491-acre property adjoins Ashintully Gardens (see above) and was once part of the same 1,000-acre estate. Round Mountain and Long Mountain are the backdrop for paths through the woods, along brooks, and by a beaver pond.

Questing, New Marlborough. Open daily, year-round. From New Marlborough Center, take New Marlborough Hill Road for 0.6 mile. A 2-mile loop trail threads hardwood forest, upland field, pockets of wetlands, and the Leffigwell settlement where the first non–Native American children were born in Berkshire Country. The farmhouse remains private.

OTHER **Kennedy Park** in Lenox on Route 7. The grounds of the former Aspinwall Hotel offer trails for hiking, biking, and cross-country skiing.

Bowker Woods, Route 183 between Stockbridge and Chesterwood; drive in at the sign. There's a pine grove by a small pond, good for picnics.

Laurel Hill, Stockbridge. A path leads from the elementary school on Main Street to a stone seat designed by Daniel Chester French. Marked trails continue across the Housatonic to Ice Glen (a ravine) and to Laura's Tower (a steel tower); another trail leads along the crest of the spur of Beartown Mountain.

✿ **Berkshire Botanical Garden** (413-298-3926; www.berkshirebotanical.org), Stockbridge, junction of Routes 102 and 183. Gardens and gift shop open May through October, 10–5. Greenhouses open year-round. The 15 acres include a pond, woodland trail, and children's garden. There are shrubs, trees, perennial borders, greenhouses, herbs, and periodic lectures and workshops. Picnickers welcome. Admission charged mid-May to mid-October.

WATERFALLS Bash Bish Falls. The area's most famous and dramatic waterfall—a 60-foot cascade plunging through a sheer gorge (see also *State Parks and Forests*).

Race Brook Falls in Sheffield: a series of five cascades and a picnic area. From the turnout on Route 41 north of the Stagecoach Inn, follow red blazes for 1.5 miles.

Becket Falls, 0.2 mile up Brooker Hill from the Becket Arts Center (Route 8 and Pittsfield Road); there is a shallow turnout in which to park. It's a steep scramble down to view the 25-foot-high cascade.

Umpachenee Falls. At the New Marlborough Church in the village center, turn south; follow signs to Mill River. Just before the metal bridge there is a dirt road forking right; from here follow signs. While this is the least dramatic falls, it's the best swimming hole.

Campbell Falls State Park, accessible from Route 57 in New Marlborough, then a forest road to this site. The Whiting River pours over a split ledge and cascades 80 feet down a precipitous declivity. There are picnic tables, toilets, and foot trails.

Sages Ravine. A strikingly cut chasm with a series of falls, best accessed from Salisbury Road in Mount Washington and from Route 41 between Sheffield and Salisbury, Connecticut.

Also see *Birding*.

✴ Lodging

Note: We have tried to note the tax and service charges for lodging, but be sure to inquire when making a reservation. Most places also have a 2- or 3-day requirement for weekends July through October, and many inns offer midweek discounts, even in July and August. B&Bs with fewer than four rooms are not required to charge tax. Check with local chambers of commerce for seasonal B&Bs and apartments.

RESORTS

All resorts are in Lenox 01240.
&. **Blantyre** (413-637-3556; off-season, 413-298-3806; www.blantyre.com), Blantyre Road. Open mid-May through October. Built in 1902 to replicate an ancestral home in Scotland, this magnificent, Tudor-style mansion was lovingly restored to its original glory in 1980 by Jack and Jane Fitzpatrick, owners of the Red Lion

Inn in Stockbridge. There is a baronial entry hall and a truly graceful music room with crystal chandeliers, sofas covered in petit point, a piano, and a harp. Guests enjoy their meals in the paneled dining room, around the long formal table, or in the adjoining, smaller, octagonal room. (See *Dining Out.*) The 25 guest rooms are impeccably furnished with antiques, and most have a fireplace. There are 85 well-kept acres with four tennis courts, a swimming pool (with Jacuzzi hot tub and sauna), and competition croquet courts (grounds and buildings are not open to the public for viewing). Including continental breakfast, rates begin at $370 for a room and run to $1,350 per night for the two-bedroom Ice House Cottage.

⊗ ✎ **Cranwell Resort, Spa & Golf Club** (413-637-1364 or 1-800-272-6935; www.cranwell.com), Route 20. A 380-acre resort with 107 rooms scattered in five varied buildings. An imposing, Tudor-style 1890s summer mansion is the centerpiece, and both its common and guest rooms are large

and luxurious, furnished with period antiques. Less formal options in other buildings include family-friendly suites with large bedrooms, a living room with a sleeper sofa, and a galley kitchen. Buildings reflect the property's varied history, including its use for much of the 20th century as a famous Jesuit prep school. There are three restaurants, a lounge, meeting rooms, four claylike Har-Tru tennis courts, a heated outdoor pool, and snowmaking for cross-country skiing.

The big attractions, however, are the 18-hole, PGA championship golf course considered the Berkshires' most challenging (see *Golf*), and the resort's newest amenity: a luxurious spa complex, built at a cost of $9 million and one of the largest resort spas in the Northeast. The spa offers some 35 different treatments and has a 60-foot-long indoor heated pool, fitness room, sauna, whirlpool, and juice bar and café. Glass-enclosed heated passageways connect it with several resort buildings so that guests in about half the rooms can access the

CRANWELL RESORT, SPA & GOLF CLUB

Cranwell Resort, Spa & Golf Club

spa without going outdoors—a welcome convenience in winter. Rates are $165–415 a night depending on the season, time of the week, and type of room. Rates include full use of the spa, exclusive of spa and fitness services. The resort offers a number of packages, including golf and spa. Weddings and meetings are a specialty; before booking you might want to ask what else is booked for your stay.

Wheatleigh (413-637-0610; www.wheatleigh.com), Hawthorne Road. This yellow-brick palazzo was built in 1893 and set in 22 acres that now include a heated outdoor swimming pool and tennis courts. Tanglewood is around the corner. There are 19 large and elegantly decorated rooms, all with private bath, about half with fireplace. The restaurant is expensive (see *Dining Out*) and award winning. Rates are $425–1,450, without breakfast.

⊚ ✍ ☻ 㐂 **Seven Hills** (413-637-0060 or 1-800-869-6518; www.sevenhills.com), 40 Plunkett Street. Open year-round. This 1911 Tudor Revival mansion with its wonderfully ornate carved woodwork is set in 27 terraced and landscaped acres, next door to Edith Wharton's former home, the Mount. The manor itself has 15 various-sized bedrooms with flowery wallpaper, some with working fireplace and jet tub; a restored carriage house has six suites, all with fireplace, jet tub, and kitchenette; 37 more rooms (motel-style doubles) are in the adjoining Terrace building (several are handicapped accessible). Room 1 in the manor is a corner room with leaded-glass windows and sleigh bed, where we would read in front of the fireplace in the Victorian loveseat, and Room 4 is a pleasant suite with sitting

room and a sofa bed for children. The several dining rooms (see *Dining Out*) vary in size and function; one is known for its live entertainment, and weddings are a specialty here. Facilities include a new, landscaped pool and tennis courts; a path leads down to Laurel Lake. Pets and children are welcome. Rates with breakfast (continental only off-season) are $95–340 in the manor house and carriage house, $85–240 in the annex. Ask about MAP rates and packages.

✍ **Eastover** (413-637-0625 or 1-800-822-2386; www.eastover.com), 430 East Street. This 1,000-acre hilltop estate has been offering "old-fashioned fun" since 1947. There are 165 rooms, some in a turn-of-the-20th-century gilded "cottage," most in motel-style annexes. Facilities include a small ski slope with a chairlift, an ice rink, a driving range, a toboggan slide (the longest in New England), tennis courts, horseback riding and hayrides, archery, basketball, indoor and outdoor pools, sauna and exercise room, and a crenellated castle with swings for the kids. Other amenities include a huge dance hall, a Civil War museum, and a herd of buffalo! Weeks and weekends are tightly scheduled, with some programs geared exclusively to singles, others to families, still others to couples. Liquor is not served, but guests may bring their own. Weekends rates for couples are $245–364 per night with a minimum 2-night stay. Included are all meals and almost all activities except horseback riding. Special single and children's rates.

SPAS AND A YOGA CENTER Lenox is the spa center of the Northeast and said to have one masseuse for every

60 residents. Augmenting the residential centers described below are several day spas, a resource for all visitors, especially in the off-season when inn prices are so reasonable. Nowhere else in New England is it so possible to combine the comforts of an inn or B&B with so many services that improve the health of both body and spirit.

Canyon Ranch in the Berkshires (413-637-4100 or 1-800-326-7080; www.canyonranch.com), Bellefontaine, 165 Kemble Street, Lenox 01240. Sister to the famous spa in Arizona, this spectacularly deluxe, 150-acre fitness resort is blessed with a superb setting. The focal point is a grand 1890s manor house that is a replica of the Petit Trianon of Louis XVI. Guests sleep in the adjoining 120-room inn, a clapboard building in traditional New England style. Just about every health and fitness program imaginable is offered, and instruction and equipment are state of the art. The staff-to-guest ratio is about three to one. Meals are dietary but also gourmet and delicious. Canyon Ranch has been called "a cross between boot camp and heaven," but guests (who have included many celebrities) almost invariably depart glowing and enthusiastic. Three-night packages run $1,669.85 to $2,032.30 off-season, $2,187.64 to $2,666.59 in high season. Packages include meals and a wide variety of spa and sports services. Inquire about special deals such as the 10 to 15 percent discount for returning guests who bring a first-timer friend or relative with them, and off-season 1-day "Spa Renewal" programs.

☙ **Kripalu Center for Yoga and Health** (413-637-3280 or 1-800-741-7353; www.kripalu.org), Route 183, Lenox 01240. This yoga-based holistic health center offers a structured daily regimen and a variety of weekend, weeklong, and longer programs. A mecca for spiritual and physical renewal, nonprofit Kripalu is housed in a former Jesuit novitiate (once the estate of steel magnate Andrew Carnegie) on 300 acres overlooking Stockbridge Bowl and within walking distance of Tanglewood. Founded as a guru-centered yoga ashram, it is now staffed primarily by paid professionals, and the atmosphere is more relaxed and mainstream New Age than it was formerly. The country's largest holistic health center, Kripalu accommodates more than 300 guests and has a national reputation for training instructors in its own style of yoga. Facilities include whirlpools, saunas, hiking and cross-country trails, a beach, boats, and tennis; also

KRIPALU CENTER FOR YOGA AND HEALTH

a children's program during summer months. A variety of variously priced programs are offered, which include vegetarian meals and use of all facilities. The cost of a 2-night introduction to Kripalu yoga package ranges from $267 with dormitory accommodation to $562 in a single room with private bath. The price for a weeklong program of Tantric yoga, "the Yoga of Fulfillment"—open to anyone in good physical shape (many longer yoga programs are limited to certified instructors)—ranges from $973 in a dormitory to $1,687 in a private room. Kripalu also has a day-guest program priced at $30 weekdays and $40–45 on weekends, lunch and activities included.

Cranwell Resort, Spa & Golf Club (see *Resorts*) has an elaborate new spa facility that boasts a 60-foot-long heated indoor pool and offers more than 30 different spa treatments. Both day and overnight spa packages are available.

THE RED LION INN

Kim Grant

INNS

In Stockbridge

♂ ৬ **Red Lion Inn** (413-298-5545; www.redlioninn.com), Main Street, Stockbridge 01250. Probably the most famous inn in Massachusetts, the Red Lion is a rambling white-clapboard beauty built in 1897. Staying here is like stepping into a Norman Rockwell painting, and there isn't a musty or dusty corner anywhere. Even the cheapest, shared-bath rooms are carefully furnished with real and reproduction antiques and bright prints of Rockwell's *Saturday Evening Post* covers, and there are some splendid rooms with canopy beds. The inn's long porch, festooned with flowers and amply furnished with rockers in warm weather, is the true center of Stockbridge in summer, as is the hearth in its lobby in winter. There is a large, formal dining room, an inviting tavern, nightly entertainment in the Lion's Den (never a cover charge), and, in summer, a popular garden café. You now actually have a choice of 108 guest rooms (90 with private bath, 2 handicapped accessible) in the main inn and six annexes, one of them the old Stockbridge firehouse that Rockwell painted. $95–425 in summer, $85–385 in winter; children are free, but there's a $20 charge per cot. Inquire about **Meadowlark at Chesterwood,** a studio hideaway built by sculptor Daniel Chester French in 1905, off across the road and down a woods road from the present public part of his estate. The living and dining area features a big skylight and a view of Monument Mountain from its deck, and the cottage includes two bedrooms, a bath, and small kitchen. It's a graceful and comfortable as well as a historic space.

♪ **The Williamsville Inn** (413-274-6118; www.thewilliamsvilleinn.com), Route 41, West Stockbridge 01266. New owners Kandy and Erhard Wendt have completely renovated this old (1797) inn, among other improvements adding a new kitchen wing to house their culinary school. (He is a certified master chef.) The dining room, open to the public for dinner (see *Dining Out*), is a showcase for gourmet cuisine. There are 13 rooms in the main house, along with one suite and two cottages, all with private bath. The 10-acre grounds include flower and herb gardens, a tennis court, swimming pool, and seasonal sculpture garden. Very family-friendly with a playroom off the dining room and a fenced-in playground outside for young guests. Rates are $150–225 year-round and include a full breakfast and afternoon tea.

In Lee 01238
The Morgan House Inn (413-243-3661; www.morganhouseinn.com), 33 Main Street. Built in 1817 as a tavern and a stagecoach stop, Morgan House is conveniently sited in the center of town. Although better known as a restaurant (see *Dining Out*), it has 12 pleasant and comfortable rooms, 7 with private bath.

In Lenox 01240
♿ **The Village Inn** (413-637-0020 or 1-800-253-0917; www.villageinn-lenox.com), 16 Church Street. Dating from 1771 and the oldest house in Lenox, this is an authentic old New England inn but after many enlargements and renovations has all the modern conveniences. All of the 32 rooms have private bath (some with Jacuzzi tub) and are furnished, each differently, with antiques or reproductions, period prints, and country quilts. Many rooms have four-poster canopy bed, and some also have a working fireplace. The elegant dining room (see *Dining Out*) is open for breakfast and dinner but not lunch. British-style high tea is served on Saturday afternoon. $120–400 high season, $77–200 off-season, with continental breakfast.

Candlelight Inn (413-637-1555 or 1-800-428-0580; www.candlelightinn-lenox.com), 53 Walker Street. Open year-round. In the heart of the village, the Candlelight has eight attractive guest rooms upstairs, all with air-conditioning and private bath. There are four dining rooms plus a pub (see *Dining Out*). $125–205 with continental breakfast.

♪ **Apple Tree Inn** (413-637-1477; www.appletree-inn.com), 10 Richmond Mountain Road. This century-old house sits high on a hill overlooking the waters of the Stockbridge Bowl, near the main entrance to Tanglewood. The main house offers 12 rooms and two suites, four with working fireplace. The 21 rooms in the modern lodge are motel-style but pleasant and handy to the pool, which has the best view from any pool around. Landscaping includes a wide variety of roses that bloom from spring into fall, as well as apple trees. Well-behaved children are welcome. The circular, glass-walled dining room is open to the public in-season for dinner. Breakfast year-round and dinner off-season are served in the oak-beamed tavern (see *Dining Out*). $200–390 in the main house in high season, $100–235 in low season; in the guest house, $180–190 high season, $60–120 low season.

Gateways Inn (413-637-2532 or 1-888-492-9466; www.gateways.inn.

com), 51 Walker Street. Built by Harley Procter of Procter & Gamble in 1912, the inn has been said to resemble a cake of Ivory soap, but it is more elegant than that, with black shutters and central skylit mahogany staircase designed by the firm of McKim, Mead & White. Owners Fabrizio and Rosemary Chiariello have made many improvements. The 11 guest rooms all have private bath, telephone, television, and individually controlled central air-conditioning. Three are on the first floor, along with a restaurant (see *Dining Out*). Second-floor rooms include a suite with two fireplaces that was Arthur Fiedler's favorite place to stay when he conducted at Tanglewood; another room has a fireplace and wonderful Eastlake furnishings; and a third, named for Romeo and Juliet, features a king-sized sleigh bed under a small skylight. High-season rates are $120–425, low-season $100–330, with full breakfast.

Elsewhere

∞ ✿ 🐾 **The Old Inn on the Green and Gedney Farm** (413-229-3131 or 1-800-286-3139; www.oldinn.com), New Marlborough 01230. In the 1970s Bradford Wagstaff and Leslie Miller (now husband and wife) restored this vintage-1760 double-porched inn at the center of a beautiful village. Their nearby Norman-style barn at Gedney Farm now also houses fantasy guest rooms and suites, many with fireplace and tiled whirlpool, and, with the neighboring barn, a reception and banquet center. Two more village homes, the Hannah Stebbins House and the Thayer House, also offer elegant guest rooms or can be rented in toto; the nearby Gedney Manor, a vintage-1906 turret-ed brick mansion set in its own sweeping lawns, offers the most lavish, as well as some of the simplest, among the resort's 42 rooms. The property now totals more than 200 acres of fields and forest, webbed by walking paths. Frequently all rooms are reserved far ahead for weddings. Frequently, too, especially early in the week or off-season, you have your pick of rooms. On our most recent visit we walked out through fields full of buttercups and daisies and then sat down to a memorable dinner (see *Dining Out*), followed by a candlelit soak in the whirlpool tub with its view up into the barn's open rafters. The grounds also include a pool; at this writing, a spa at the manor is in the making. From $195–350, with continental breakfast. Add 5.7 percent tax, 10 percent service.

∞ 🐾 ✿ **The Egremont Inn** (413-528-2111), Old Sheffield Road, Box 418, South Egremont 01258. This four-story, double-porched landmark is in the middle of a classic crossroads village. The structure dates, in part, from 1780 but in the late 19th century expanded into a rambling country inn with wide and welcoming porches. Visitors enter a spacious reception area with an 18th-century fireplace and a settle; there are two more comfortable sitting rooms, each with a fireplace, stocked with books and board games. Innkeepers Steven and Karen Waller have totally renovated the inn, furnishing the 20 guest rooms with real and reproduction antiques, private baths (some Jacuzzis, some traditional claw-footers), and phones as well as new mattresses, most queen sized, and varied furnishings. Three rooms are family-geared suites. There's a tavern with its own menu as well as a delightfully old-fashioned dining room that features both a good reputation and music on Thursdays and Saturdays year-round (see *Dining Out*). Amenities include a pool and two tennis courts. Catamount ski area is just down the road. $90–225, more during foliage; weekend MAP packages available in July, August. Three-night minimum required on summer weekends. Add 10 percent tax and service.

Thornewood Inn (413-528-3828 or 1-800-854-1008), 453 Stockbridge Road (Route 7), north of Great Barrington, 01230. Terry and David Thorne are longtime owners of this large old inn that offers 15 guest rooms, all with private bath and furnished in antiques, many with gas fireplace. Common rooms ramble on and on, off away from Spencer's Restaurant (which, at this writing, may or may not move to an adjoining building). There's a landscaped garden with swimming pool on the quiet back side of the building, the side we suggest you request a room to face. Weekdays $105–235 year-round. Add 9.7 percent tax.

New Boston Inn (413-258-4477; www.newbostoninn.com), junction of Routes 8 and 57, Sandisfield 01255. This authentic 1737 inn is sited in the center of a minuscule village at the junction of two busy country roads. It's pleasant and informal. The former second-floor ballroom is now a Gathering Room, a great space with a billiards table, TV, piano, plenty of room to read and play games, and matching fireplaces at either end of the room. The seven upstairs guest rooms have wide floorboards, comfortable antiques, and private baths. Innkeepers Susan and Conrad Ringeisen offer lunch and dinner in the Tap Room (see *Eating Out*). Inquire about the

WILDFLOWER INN B&B IN GREAT BARRINGTON
Christina Tree

resident ghost. Rates begin at $115 double, $95 single. Add 5.7 percent tax. No children under age 12.

BED & BREAKFASTS

In Great Barrington 01230; add 9.7 percent tax

Windflower (413-528-2720 or 1-800-992-1993; www.windflower-inn.com), 684 South Egremont Road (Route 23). We keep returning to this gracious, turn-of-the-20th-century country mansion set in expansive grounds. The common rooms are just the right combination of elegance and comfort. All 13 guest rooms have private bath and queen-sized bed (most are canopy or four-poster), and 5 have a working fireplace. The bathrooms are fine, too; check out the deep clawfooted tub in Room 5 and the vintage, many-needled shower in Room 7—which is actually our favorite with its window seat, fireplace, and maple cottage furniture. Our second favorite is ground-floor Room 12 with its huge stone fireplace and easy access to the big screened porch and its wicker furniture. Several of the rooms have both queen and twin beds. But what really makes this place is the welcoming family that runs it: veteran innkeepers Gerry and Barbara Liebert and their daughter Claudia with her green-thumbed and handy husband, John Ryan. Whether you are traveling solo, as a family, or as a couple looking for a romantic getaway, this is one place that works for all—plus tunes you in to local dining and happenings. Facilities include a landscaped pool; golf and tennis are across the road at the Egremont Country Club. $100–200 with full country breakfast and afternoon tea featuring homemade cookies. The charge for an extra person in the room is $25, less for infants. Checks or AmEx please.

🐾 **Baldwin Hill Farm** (413-528-4092 or 1-888-528-4092), 121 Baldwin Hill Road N/S. This is a very special place: a Victorian farmhouse that commands a sweeping view of mountains. Dick Burdsall's grandfather bought the 450-acre hilltop farm as a summer place in 1912, adding touches like the mammoth fieldstone fireplace in one of the two living rooms. While Dick was growing up here (attending classes in the one-room schoolhouse), this was a serious dairy farm; now there are ducks and, every two years, sheep; the surrounding fields are still hayed.

AT BALDWIN HILL FARM IN SOUTH EGREMONT

Christina Tree

All four guest rooms (two with shared bath) are furnished with family antiques and have good views, but our favorite is the bay-windowed room with chairs positioned for enjoying the sight of Mount Everett to the south; it can be arranged with twin beds or a king. Inviting common spaces include a comfortably furnished screened-in porch and seats in the landscaped garden; there's also a pool in summer and cross-country skiing in winter. Guests choose from a full country breakfast menu. $99–130 in-season; $89–110, winter.

✒ **Seekonk Pines** (413-528-4192 or 1-800-292-4192; www.seekonk-pines.com), 142 Seekonk Cross Road (at Route 23). This is an expansive old home with spreading gardens, hammock, swimming pool, volleyball net, and picnic tables under the tall pines, and a large common room with a fireplace, VCR, and game table. Hosts Bruce, Roberta, and Rita Lefkowitz serve a full country breakfast; a guest pantry is stocked with complimentary soft drinks and teas. There are bikes for guests. Six guest rooms are furnished in antiques and collectibles, and there's a studio apartment, great for families, in the barn. Well-behaved children welcome. $135–250, less off-season.

⊙ ✒ 🐾 **Turning Point Inn** (413-528-4777; www.turningpointinn.com), corner of Route 23 and Lake Buel Road, RD 2, Box 140. Open year-round. Built as the Pixley Tavern in 1800, this striking brick inn, 3 miles west of downtown Great Barrington, has been nicely renovated, with six guest rooms (four with private bath) in the main house and a cottage. The wide-plank floors survive, and owners Rachel, Dennis, and Teva O'Rourke have enhanced the simple lines of the old inn with country charm, Shaker-plain but elegant furniture and quilts, and great colors (each room is different). While there's a pleasant sitting room, it's the old tavern room with its fireplace and long dining table that is the center of the house—appropriately, since the innkeepers are accomplished chefs who put their all into breakfast and are happy to rent and cook for the entire house. They also offer Saturday-night dinner by arrangement and cater. Pets are accepted in the neighboring two-story, two-bedroom cottage with its full kitchen, living room with cable TV, and heated sunporch. Children over age 3 are also accepted in the inn. Lake Buel is just down the road, and Butternut Basin ski area is a few minutes' drive. $105–255 per room May through October; inquire about cottage and off-season rates.

&. **Wainwright Inn** (413-528-2062; www.wainwrightinn.com), 518 South Main Street (Route 7), south of town. Said to date from 1766, this large, Victorian-looking house was expanded to its present shape by Franklin Pope, an electrical genius recognized for a number of inventions (a couple in partnership with Thomas Edison), but who died while tinkering with a transformer in his basement here. A place to stay for many decades, it's been thoroughly renovated and brightened by present innkeeper Marja Tepper. There's an attractive living room with an upright piano and fireplace, and a crisp, sunny breakfast room. The nine guest rooms vary, so we suggest asking for details when booking. You might want one in the quieter, rear wing of the building. $165–275 includes a three-course breakfast.

Christine's Bed & Breakfast (413-274-6149 or 1-800-536-1186; www.christinesinn.com), Route 41, Housatonic 01236. Christine and Steve Kelsey are Berkshire natives who know their way around. The house, which dates in part from the 18th century, is surrounded by gardens and farmland, off by itself but technically in Housatonic, the mill village within the town of Great Barrington. The four guest rooms have TV, phone, and air-conditioning. Common space includes a large sitting room and screened porch, with a special area reserved for tea. Inquire about dinner by arrangement in front of the old hearth. Children over 11 only please. $135–155 midweek, $165–190 Thursday through Sunday.

In Lee 01238

Historic Merrell Tavern Inn (413-243-1794 or 1-800-243-1794; www.merrell-inn.com), 1565 Pleasant Street (Route 102), South Lee 01260. This is a standout: a double-porched inn built in 1794 with a third-floor ballroom added in 1837. A stagecoach stop for much of the 19th century, it stood vacant for 75 years before previous owners Chuck and Faith Reynolds purchased it in 1981 and spent years restoring and furnishing it appropriately. Present owners George and Joanne Crockett appreciate what they have and maintain the place lovingly. All guest rooms have private bath and have been carefully decorated with an eye to comfort as well as style. All have TV. The Riverview Suite in a separate wing at the back has a king-sized bed, a wood-burning fireplace, and a private balcony overlooking the grounds and the Housatonic River. Guests breakfast in the old keeping room, and the taproom with its original birdcage bar in the corner is a cozy sitting room. Grounds slope gently in back to a gazebo beside the Housatonic. $95–255 in high season, $90–175 off-season with full breakfast. Children are $25 extra.

Applegate Bed and Breakfast (413-243-4451 or 1-800-691-9012; www.applegateinn.com), 279 West Park Street. This place is a winner: a 1920s mansion with a pillared portico that's spacious and comfortable. Gloria and Len Friedman, longtime Staten Island residents, bring people skills acquired in their previous careers to innkeeping. The living room is huge, bright, and comfortably furnished, with built-in bookcases and window seats, a fireplace, and space for reading or playing backgammon. Welcoming touches include flowers and chocolates in the rooms. The five rooms in the main house vary in size from huge (Room 1, with its king-sized four-poster, fireplace, and steam shower with two showerheads) to snug but cozy. There are also three suites in the house. Two more suites, along with a two-bedroom "cottage" apartment, are in the adjacent carriage house, all with patio and whirlpool tub. Amenities include a pool, a guest fridge, borrowable bicycles, and plenty of lawn. $140–310 in-season, $115–295 off. Inquire about winter and spring packages.

Federal House Inn (800-243-1824; www.federalhouseinn.com), 1560 Main Street (Route 102), South Lee 01260. This is a graceful Federal-era house, built in 1824, with 10 guest rooms all with private bath, three with gas fireplace, and most with four-poster bed. Guests have the use of a downstairs parlor. Owners Dick and

Sue Cody have lavished a lot of attention on the house, and the furnishings and decor reflect its era without detracting from the homey feeling. A very full breakfast is served, always with a hot entrée such as baked French toast with sausage patty, mushroom frittata and bacon, or scrambled eggs and salsa with sautéed breakfast ham. $150–250 high season, $100–125 off-season.

Devonfield (413-243-3298 or 1-800-664-0880; www.devonfield.com), 85 Stockbridge Road. A large, elegant house with an 18th-century core and turn-of-the-20th-century lines (it was landscaped and modernized by George Westinghouse Jr.). Rooms and suites are all furnished in antiques and have private bath; several have working fireplace and Jacuzzi, and a one-bedroom cottage by the large outdoor pool has kitchen facilities and a fireplace in the living room. There is a tennis court, and rates include full breakfast. Children over 10 welcome. $120–310 in-season, $90–225 the rest of the year. Inquire about midweek and off-season packages.

❦ **Parsonage on the Green** (413-243-4364), 20 Park Place. Built in 1851 to house the minister of the Congregational church next door, this comfortable house is set back on a quiet corner of the town green. It's furnished with the family history of its owners, the Mahonys (Barbara is a former history teacher, Don a retired businessman). Their collection of black-and-white and sepia photographs, antiques, china, and other mementos embraces an unusual span of generations, often with stories to match, and the effect is not at all overbearing. There is a library filled with books and games, and both a piano and a fireplace grace the parlor. All guest rooms have private bath. Breakfast is an event, a formal three-course meal served by candlelight in the dining room. Rates also include afternoon tea. $110–175 in-season, $80–125 off-season.

✐ 🐾 **The Inn at Laurel Lake** (413-243-9749; www.laurellakeinn.com), Route 20 West. This inn has served Berkshire travelers since 1900. One of its nicest features is the small private beach just 150 feet downhill from the house. Tom Fusco bought the inn in 1996 and has improved and brightened it considerably. Of the 19 rooms and suites, 17 have private bath. Facilities include a music room with over 1,000 classical recordings, tennis court and sauna, picnic tables on a bluff overlooking the lake, and a paddleboat and canoe. A well-behaved dog can be accommodated in the room with a separate entrance. The Cork 'n' Hearth restaurant is next door. Supervised children are welcome. Rates include continental breakfast. Picnics and dinner can be ordered. $95–225 in-season, $85–165 mid-October through June.

♿ **Chambery Inn** (413-243-2221 or 1-800-537-4321; www.berkshireinns.com), 199 Main Street. This unlikely lodging place, a parochial school built in 1885, was rescued from the wrecker's ball and moved to its present site by Joe Toole (whose grandfather was in the first class to attend the school). As you might suspect, the rooms are huge, with 13-foot-high tin ceilings, 8-foot-tall windows—and blackboards (chalk is supplied). Separate stairs are marked for girls and boys, but guests don't get their knuckles rapped with a ruler if they take the wrong one. A

continental breakfast is delivered to your room. $85–289, depending on the season and day.

Ashley Inn Bed and Breakfast (413-243-2746; www.ashleyinn.com), 182 West Park Street. This homey B&B has four simply but comfortably furnished rooms, all with private bath and themed to the colors blue, green, yellow, or mauve. The decor reflects the hobbies of innkeepers Dawn and Paul Borst: He collects antique clocks; she, Santa Claus figures. A full breakfast is served with the house specialty a large fruit-stuffed pancake called a "Dutch baby." Light afternoon tea is served on request. $90–135 high season, $65–95 off-season.

In Lenox 01240
Stonover Farm (413-637-9100; www.stonoverfarm.com), 169 Undermountain Road. The newest B&B in Lenox, Stonover Farm is a luxurious gem of a place with a setting to match: a quiet woods- and meadow-lined rural road just 0.6 mile from the entrance to Tanglewood. After spending more than 20 years in Los Angeles (where he was a successful rock record producer), Tom and Suky Werman moved to the Berkshires for a complete change of scene and lifestyle. They bought what had been the farmhouse of a former grand estate, a stone-and-shingle building built in the 1890s, and spent a year restoring and remodeling the house and its outbuildings. They also cleared and landscaped the 8-acre grounds, which include a spring-fed duck pond. The result is an elegant small B&B that has lots of character and tasteful touches and all the high-tech comforts. Walls are decorated with original paintings and prints, and

guests have the use of a library, a greenhouse solarium, and a computer with high-speed Internet access. Units are air-conditioned and have cable TV and phones with voice mail. There are three large suites in the main house. The adjacent Rock Cottage has a large, sunny living room (one wall is lined with windows), a kitchen, a master bedroom, and a smaller twin-bedded room in a turret, accessed by circular staircase, that makes an ideal children's room. The rate for suites is $325 a night in peak season, $225 at other times. The cottage is $450 a night in high season, $300 off-season. There is a 3-night minium over weekends at peak times, a 2-night weekend minimum the rest of the year. Rates include afternoon wine and cheese and a full, cooked-to-order breakfast.

✐ 🐾 ♿ **Rookwood** (413-637-9750 or 1-800-223-9750; www.rookwood-inn.com), 11 Old Stockbridge Road. A turreted, 21-room Victorian inn within walking distance of Tanglewood. All rooms have a private bath, some have a small private balcony, and 12 have a fireplace. We liked Victorian Dream on the second floor with its fainting couch, fireplace, and bath with both claw-footed tub and extra-large shower, but our favorite was Revels Retreat, a third-floor room with queen bed and an octagonal space with daybed four steps up in a turret with oval windows and incredible views. Suites have phone and TV. Well-behaved, supervised children are welcome, and two first-floor rooms are handicapped accessible (there's a ramp to the kitchen door). A three-room suite is available for rentals of a week or more. Rates, which include afternoon refreshments as well as a

full, "heart-healthy" breakfast, are $185–375 in summer, $100–250 the rest of the year, except holidays.

♿ **Hampton Terrace** (413-637-1773 or 1-800-203-0656; www.hamptonter-race.com), 91 Walker Street. Stan and Susan Rosen have completely renovated this handsome white frame turn-of-the-20th-century house, filling it with antiques, many family heir-looms. A 1929 Steinway grand piano graces the living room, for instance, and a hand-painted cabinet holds the family doll collection. The 11 rooms, 6 of which are in the restored carriage house, all have private bath. (Carriage house units have whirlpool tub.) Every room has TV, VCR, and CD player. High-speed DSL access is free. Guests can relax in the parlor of the main house; there is a separate lounge area in the carriage house. Breakfast is served in the dining room and sunporch of the house. $190–240 high season, $125–160 the rest of the year.

The Cornell Inn (413-637-0562 or 1-800-677-0562; www.cornellinn. com), 203 Main Street. This inn on the edge of the village has 28 rooms in three very different structures: a Gilded Age mansion built in 1888; the adjacent MacDonald House, dating from 1777; and a restored former carriage house. Most rooms have fireplace; all have a private bath and some, a Jacuzzi tub. The decor in the mansion is Victorian, but the decorative theme is colonial in MacDonald House and "country primitive" in the carriage house. Amenities include a pub-style guest lounge with access to a deck looking out on the Japanese rock garden. A continental breakfast is served Monday through Saturday, with a full breakfast buffet on Sunday.

$120 high season, $77–200 low season.

Garden Gables (413-637-0193 or 1-888-243-0193; www.lenoxinn.com), 135 Main Street (Route 7). Mario and Lynn Mekinda's inn, a triple-gabled, white-clapboard house dating in part from 1780, is set well back from the road but within walking distance of the village shops and restaurants. The 18 rooms are bright and comfortable, all with private bath, telephone (with answering machine), and air-conditioning, several with whirlpool, many with fireplace or private porch. Our favorites are in the back of the main house, but four suites in the garden cottages have cathedral ceilings and sitting areas. The ample grounds convey a sense of being out in the country, and the outdoor, guests-only pool is one of the biggest in Berkshire County. Breakfast, at a common table in the gracious dining room or at individual tables out on the porch, includes fresh fruit, yogurt, and cheeses as well as a hot dish. $130–265 in-season, $95–210 off-season.

🍴 ☗ **Walker House** (413-637-1271 or 1-800-235-3098; www.walker-house.com), 64 Walker Street. This expanded Federal-era (1804) house has a Victorian feel inside, nicely decorated with interesting art and inviting common rooms. A long flower-garnished and wicker-furnished veranda overlooks the expansive back garden. Five of the eight guest rooms, each named for a composer, have a fireplace, and all have charm. Innkeepers for more than 20 years, Peggy and Richard Houdek are art mavens and Richard remains a critic. We like to stay here for the same reason that we favor staying with skiing

innkeepers in Vermont: They know the scope of what's out there and the scoop on what's worth sampling because they do it all themselves. Ditto when it comes to eating out. If you stay in, there is a 12-foot screen in the library on which guests can view classic and current movies, operas, plays, and the large library of videos as well as TV specials. A continental breakfast with fruit, served at the dining room table, and afternoon tea are included in the rates. A new addition is a state-of-the-art cappuccino and espresso machine. $90–210 June through October, $90–160 the rest of the year.

Cliffwood Inn (413-637-3330 or 1-800-789-3331; www.cliffwood.com), 25 Cliffwood Street. On a quiet street just a block off Main, Cliffwood is the home of Joy and Scottie Farrelly, who speak four languages, and Valentina, a Yorkshire terrier. Built in 1888–89 as the summer home of a former American ambassador to France, the inn is airy and elegant with seven guest rooms, six with working fireplace. (You might ask for the third-floor room with skylight and king-sized bed from which you can enjoy the fireplace just inside the bathroom, with its oak floor and Oriental rug.) Only coffee and juice are served in the morning, but there are several good breakfast places nearby. Robes are supplied in winter to guests who wish to use the countercurrent indoor pool and spa in the basement with a glass wall looking onto the yard. Children from 11 years are welcome, but credit cards are not. $140–253 in-season, $95–172 the rest of the year.

♿ **Birchwood Inn** (413-637-2600 or 1-800-524-1646; www.birchwood-inn.com), 7 Hubbard Street. Ellen

Gutman Chenaux has brought many improvements to this grand old house (the oldest in Lenox), which dates, in part, back to 1767. There are nine rooms in the main house, all with private bath and telephone, and two in the carriage house. The library parlor is a gracious, welcoming room with window seats and a fireplace. The front porch, with its homey wicker furniture, is a popular gathering place in summer. Kennedy Park (good for walking and cross-country skiing) is across the street. You'll be able to spread out in Room 4, which has a big canopy bed and a fireplace. All rooms are nicely furnished. Rates are $100–275, with a full breakfast prepared by a trained chef.

Brook Farm Inn (413-637-3013; www.brookfarm.com), 15 Hawthorne Street. A handsome yellow Victorian house on a quiet byway south of the village, Brook Farm has been tastefully furnished to fit its period (1889) by owners Phil and Linda Halpern. There are 15 guest rooms, all with private bath, 6 with fireplace. The recently built carriage house annex has two rooms and a suite, all with whirlpool tub. Breakfast, featuring homemade baked goods, is buffet-style in the elegant green dining room overlooking the garden, and afternoon tea is served. There is a heated outdoor pool, a comfortable lounging parlor with fireplace, and a large library of poetry books and tapes. Poetry readings are a regular feature and Linda, a storyteller, often tells stories at tea time. $145–350 in-season, $100–300 in "quiet season."

🐾 **The Gables Inn** (413-637-3416; www.gableslenox.com), 81 Walker Street (Route 183). This gracious old home housed Edith Wharton while she was constructing the Mount. Central to everything in the village, it has 19 bedrooms with private bath. Some also have fireplace or TV and VCR. Pool, tennis court, gardens. Rates, with continental breakfast, are $125–250 in summer and fall, $99–160 the rest of the year.

&. **Harrison House** (413-637-1746; www.harrison-house.com), 174 Main Street. This handsome old house is on the northern fringe of Lenox village, across from Kennedy Park. Innkeeper Andrew Fishbein is an artist and also the breakfast chef. (Harrison is a dog.) The six guest rooms are nicely decorated with interesting art and a mix of antiques. All are air-conditioned and have private bath, cable TV, and fireplace, some original to the house. A suite offers a canopy bed, sitting room, and splendid Victorian bathroom. A first-floor room with fine views is also fully handicapped accessible. A wraparound porch and a combination sitting-breakfast room look out on the garden. $210–340 high season, $145–210 off-season with a full breakfast buffet.

&. **The Kemble Inn** (413-637-4113 or 1-800-353-4113; www.kemble-inn.com), 2 Kemble Street. This Georgian Revival mansion was built in 1881 by U.S. Secretary of State Frederick Freylinghuysen and is named for tart-tongued actress Fanny Kemble—a frequent Lenox visitor in the 19th century. All 14 guest rooms have private bath, telephone, and air-conditioning, and some have marble fireplace and Jacuzzi. Children over 12 are welcome. $110–315 with continental breakfast.

Whistler's Inn (413-637-0975; www.whistlersinnlenox.com), 5 Greenwood Street (corner of Route

7A). A mostly Tudor-style mansion with large, opulent common rooms including a ballroom, library, music room, and a baronial dining room. While it's across from the Church on the Hill and an easy walk from both village shops and Kennedy Park, the grounds include 7 acres of garden and woodland. The formal garden is Italianate. The 14 guest rooms all have private bath. In the carriage house, a very large room on the second floor has wide pine floors, two sitting areas, a NordicTrack, TV, small refrigerator, and lots of light, as well as interesting art, African artifacts, and books; the rustic suite on the first floor includes a queen bedroom with woodstove, a sitting/sleeping/TV room, and a private deck. Continental breakfast is served. The innkeepers, novelist Richard Mears and artist-writer Joan Mears, have been welcoming guests to their manor for more than 30 years. The library is well stocked, the walls hung with interesting art, and the atmosphere distinctly cultural. $110–275 in summer and fall, $90–190 off-season with breakfast.

In Sheffield 01257

Broken Hill Manor (877-535-6159; www.BrokenHillManor.com), 771 West Road. Many try but few are equal to the challenge of converting ponderous Edwardian mansions to truly inviting places to stay. Mike Farmer and Gaetan Lachance, however, have both the savvy and the furniture it takes. The colors and many details are authentically Edwardian, and while the furniture is comfortable, much of it is exotic, appropriate to the pervading sound and theme of opera music. The eight guest rooms are each named for an opera's heroine. Tosca, as you might suspect, is

the most elegant, featuring an Egyptian brass canopy bed, but our favorite is Violetta with its peach walls and coverlet and slightly less ornate (also Egyptian) bed. We could spend hours in the Great Room with its mix of comfortable and exotic furnishings (most rugs are also Egyptian) around the stone hearth. The dining room is formal, but there are also tables on the back terrace, beyond the totally revamped kitchen, surrounded by landscaped gardens. The house was built in 1900 and was previously home to the two writers of the radio soap opera *Young Doctor Malone.* Farmer and Lachance spent 4 years rewiring, plumbing (they installed five bathrooms), and landscaping. The 12 hilltop acres are just minutes from either Route 7 or Route 23 but seem totally removed. $125–185 includes a full breakfast.

Staveleigh House (413-229-2129; www.staveleigh.com), 59 Main Street (Route 7). Ali Winston continues to offer the exceptional hospitality for which this B&B was known under its previous owners, and she has spruced up this old (vintage-1818) parsonage just off the Sheffield village green, adding bright colors and well-chosen antiques to the seven guest rooms (five with private bath). Our favorite is a second-floor front room that's a symphony in blues and whites, but the ground-floor back rooms in the rear of the house are also appealing. Ali's green parrot Murray adds immeasurably to the parlor decor and conversation. We dropped by at teatime and the aroma of fresh-baked chocolate chip cookies was heady. We also liked the look of a quiche, presumably prepared for tea—which is included, along with a full breakfast, in rates of $85–125 off-season, $115–160 May through October.

The B&B at Howden Farm (413-229-8481; www.howdenfarm.com), 303 Ronnapo Road. When we first met artist Bruce Howden, he was operating the (then) only bed & breakfast in Burlington, Vermont. Howden has since inherited the family homestead, a Victorianized Greek Revival farmhouse and a big beautiful pumpkin farm, famous for having developed its own varieties and for its pick-your-own policy. It's all beautifully sited in Ashley Falls near Bartholomew's Cobble and the Colonel Ashley House. Guests can launch a canoe on the river and hike in the fields and woods. There are four rooms, two with private bath, two sharing. All are nicely furnished, but the beauty is Room 104, which offers a sitting room with bow windows overlooking fields. $99–149 includes a very full breakfast, perhaps featuring eggs from resident chickens.

❀ Birch Hill Bed & Breakfast (413-229-2143; www.birchhillbb.com), 254 South Undermountain Road (Route 41). Formerly Ivanhoe House, this gracious old country house is now owned by Wendy and Michael Advocate and is a real find for hikers or cross-country skiers and their dogs (subject to strict rules). Nearby hiking trails lead up to the five cascades along the Race Brook Trail, on up to a spectacular stretch of the Appalachian Trail across Mount Race; in winter you can poke around the inn's own 25 acres on skis. Guests are welcome to play games or the piano, watch TV, or dip into the library of the paneled Chestnut Room. The seven centrally air-conditioned rooms are nicely furnished, and all have private bath.

There is also a pool, and guests enjoy access to a small lake across the road. Children over 9 years only please. Memorial Day through Labor Day and October, from $130 weekdays to $195 on the weekends.

1802 House (413-229-2612; www.berkshire1802.com), P.O. Box 395, 48 South Main Street. This much-expanded early-19th-century house rambles back from Route 7 in the village of Sheffield. Nancy Hunter-Young and Rick Kowarek offer a choice of seven rooms with queen or double bed, five with private bath (two small rooms share). We love the screened porch, the long windows in the sitting room, and the spacious, nicely landscaped gardens in the rear. The full breakfast may include ice cream with your French toast. $100–145 single or double May 15 through November 1, from $90 off-season, $25 extra for a third person in a room.

In Stockbridge 01262

⚓ ♿ One Main Bed and Breakfast (413-298-5299; www.onemainbnb.com), 1 Main Street. This homey three-bedroom B&B is on the quiet end of Main Street, just beyond the point where heavily trafficked Route 102 diverges, and only a short walk or drive from the heart of Stockbridge. Innkeepers Marty Gottron and John Felton (a former National Public Radio foreign editor) owned a Lenox B&B, Amadeus House, for many years and delight in sharing their knowledge of the area with guests. The yellow-clapboard house, built in 1825, has a warm, old-fashioned, literary feel to it. The three bright and nicely decorated bedrooms, all with private bath and two with king-sized bed, are named for writers associated with the Berkshires: Edith Wharton, Herman Melville, and Nathaniel Hawthorne. Books by each are in their rooms, along with a selection of the works of other writers. The resident dog, a friendly Labrador, also has a literary link: He's called Tasso after a 16th-century Italian poet John admires. Guests can relax in the living room, the cozy parlor, or on the patio, where breakfast is served in good weather. In addition to fruits and cereals, breakfast always includes one main course such as "Felton's Flyaways," a tasty but low-fat pancake. Rates in midsummer and foliage season are $105–170; spring and early fall, $90–145. During peak periods there is a 3-night minimum stay on weekends and a 2-night minimum midweek.

Arbor Rose Bed and Breakfast (413-298-4744; www.arborrose.com), Yale Hill, Box 114. Some places have it and others don't. This does! Innkeeper Christina Alsop has a great sense of color and uncluttered, comfortable decor. The rose arbor is on the path to the front porch, while behind the pleasant old white house is a 19th-century millpond and raceway, filling the air with its pleasant sound. Nearby is a garden lush with flowers, herbs, and vegetables. Tucked away on a quiet road, this find is within walking distance of the Berkshire Theatre Festival complex and minutes from Stockbridge village. Twelve guests can gather around the harvest table for a full breakfast. The six guest rooms, split between the house and the rustic old mill building, have four-poster or canopy beds. We particularly like the meadow room and covet the room in the old mill right over the millrace. Rates are $110–175 in-season, $105–155 the rest of the year.

The Taggart House (413-298-4303; www.taggarthouse.com), 18 Main Street. The web site for this eccentrically grand B&B is the only one we've ever seen that includes a genealogy page. The family is that of W. Hinckley Waitt III, who—along with his artist wife, Susan—owns the place and runs it with patrician style. "We want guests to feel like they're staying at a friend's country estate," he says. The rambling mid-19th-century house, which includes a ballroom the size of a small airplane hangar, is stuffed with antiques—mostly Victoriana, but also oddities such as a billiards table that once belonged to heavyweight boxing champion Rocky Marciano. The four guest rooms are called the French, Russian, Willow Bough, and Clara Bow Rooms and themed accordingly. (The bed in Clara's has a carved ivory-and-ebony-wood headboard that belonged to the sexy silent film star.) Guest amenities include deep soaking tubs, a large library, and a complimentary beverage bar. Brunch is served at 9 AM by candlelight in the formal dining room. The 5-acre grounds have frontage on the Housatonic River. Rates are $199–399 in-season, $149–295 November through May.

Conroy's Bed & Breakfast (413-298-5188 or 1-888-298-4990; www.conroysinn.com), Route 7, P.O. Box 191. Set up and off Route 7 in 3 acres of lawn and woods, this 1830 brick farmhouse has a homey feel. There is a bright dining room and a small sitting area; the eight rooms—five in the main house (two with private bath) and three (all with private bathroom) in the old post-and-beam barn—are all country comfortable. Two of the barn rooms have decks, and the third offers a patio. The real treasure here, however, is the seasonal apartment in the barn with a deck, a sleeping loft, and a great downstairs space with fully equipped kitchen, great for families. $75–300 with full breakfast served in the dining room.

&. **The Inn at Stockbridge** (413-298-3337; www.stockbridgeinn.com), Route 7, Box 2033. This white-pillared mansion was built in 1906 and set on 12 acres with ample woods and meadow to tramp around in. Flowers, comfortable chairs, and books fill the living room, where afternoon wine and cheese are served and a fire is lit on rainy days. There's an attractive pool in the garden. Full breakfast is served in the formal dining room. In addition to the eight guest rooms in the main house—each different, most with king bed, and all with private bath—there are four large, new, well-appointed rooms in back near the pool. These have decorative touches of Kashmir, Scotland, Africa, or Provence, and one particularly attractive rose-colored room with a gas fireplace is fully handicapped accessible. A recently built annex, The Barn, has four deluxe suites with fireplace, large whirlpool tub, and decor to fit their names: Wharton, Rockwell, Shakespeare, and Shaker. All rooms have air-conditioning and telephone. $140–320 in-season, $140–415 off-season.

The Stockbridge Country Inn (413-298-4015; www.stockbridgecountryinn.com), Route 183, Box 525. Handy to Chesterwood and the Norman Rockwell Museum in the Glendale section of Stockbridge, this 1856 farmhouse (formerly known as Roeder House) offers an unusual amount of common space, including an elegant living room with fireplace, a less formal sitting room, and a sunporch overlooking the garden. The seven guest rooms all have private bath and are tastefully furnished with four-poster queen-sized bed, antiques, Laura Ashley fabrics and prints, bright chintzes, and hooked rugs. The walls are hung with original Audubon prints—which are for sale, as is much of the furniture, because innkeepers Diane and Vernon Reuss are antiques dealers. There is a large, heated outdoor pool. The full breakfast is cooked to order and in summer served on a screened porch looking out on the garden. $145–360, depending on the season.

Berkshire Thistle Bed & Breakfast (413-298-3188; www.berkshirethistle.com), P.O. Box 1227, Route 7. Gene Elling, a second-generation B&B host, and his wife, Diane, offer exceptional hospitality in this guest-friendly modern Colonial, which is set on 5 sloping acres with a spacious pool out back. Common space for guests overlooks a horse corral, and numerous bird feeders are visible from the breakfast table and the large deck. (We woke to a hummingbird hovering over our second-floor window box.) There are four guest rooms furnished simply but tastefully, with many pieces refinished by Gene. Breakfast is "expanded continental" midweek, but on weekends it's very full, all made from scratch. Children over 8 years. $145–185 in-season, $85–145 off.

Elsewhere
The Inn at Freeman Elms Farm (413-229-3700; www.vgernet.net/freeman), 566 Mill River, Great Barrington Road, New Marlborough 01230. This is a find: a handsome farmhouse

still in the same family that's owned it for nine generations. Obviously it was built very grandly in 1797. Later additions are limited to a spacious, screened front porch, furnished with plenty of rocking chairs, and a rear ell with a classic Mission-style dining room. The six guest rooms are furnished in family antiques and quilts, the kind most innkeepers covet. We especially like the "cottage" room with its mint-condition Cottage furniture. Breakfast is full, and the property totals 600 acres with fields, woods, gardens, orchard and cattle. Children must be 12 or older. $125–200 includes breakfast and private bath.

The Red Bird Inn (413-229-2349; www.theredbirdinn.com), Route 57, Great Barrington 01230. Never mind the mailing address, this vintage-1791 stagecoach stop sits at the junction of two country roads in New Marlborough. Owner (with his wife, Barbara) Doug Newman is a Culinary Institute of America–trained chef, so we assume the breakfast is good. When we stopped by in June rooms were still being readied for "the season," but the six centrally air-conditioned guest rooms all looked attractive, and new baths had been added. The house is a beauty, retaining many 18th-century features but with the addition of a spacious screened porch overlooking extensive gardens. May 15 through November 15 rates run $175–275 including breakfast.

❧ **The Silo B&B** (413-528-5195), 6 Boice Road, P.O. Box 5444, North Egremont 01252. What a great spot! This is an artfully designed home attached to an authentic silo, atop a knoll and surrounded by fields. The airy living room maximizes the view, beyond flowers and ever-popular bird feeders. Two guest rooms share an upstairs sitting area, and a third is on the ground floor. $115 midweek, $125 weekends, includes a full breakfast either in the breakfast room or on the screened porch. While there's an away-from-it-all feeling, The Silo is within walking distance of the North Egremont general store and of Elm Court Inn (see *Dining Out*). It's also handy to wading in the Green River and to swimming in Prospect Lake. No credit cards.

Linden-Valley (518-325-7100), P.O. Box 157, Hillsdale, NY 12529. Sited on the New York–Massachusetts border at Catamount Ski Area, but really in a landscaped world of its own. Linda Breen has created an exceptional hideaway: seven large, nicely designed and decorated rooms, the upper units with cathedral ceilings and those on the garden level with small terraces. Each has a TV, coffeemaker, and wet bar with icemaker. A full breakfast is served in the dining room, an inviting space with a fireplace, or, weather permitting, on the garden terrace. The magnificently landscaped grounds include a spring-fed pond with a sandy beach, a swimming pool, and two tennis courts. The previous owner of the nearby Swiss Hutte (see *Dining Out*), Linda is Bavarian, clearly a scrupulous housekeeper and an enthusiastic cook. $95–135 midweek, $145–175 on weekends includes a full breakfast.

Cobble View Bed and Breakfast (413-243-2463 or 1-800-914-7945; www.CobbleViewBandB.com), 123 Main Road, Tyringham 01264. Located across the road from Tyringham Cobble (hence the name), this B&B has four large rooms in the main house, all air-conditioned and all with private bath. Also in the house is a studio apartment with its own kitchen and a separate entrance. The large loft in the barn can accommodate four people. The house was built in the 1850s, and the decor is a pleasantly appropriate mix of antiques and reproductions. Guests have the use of two downstairs parlors. Rooms are $80–170, the loft $285, year-round. The enhanced continental breakfast is served by candlelight.

GROUPS

✔ ❄ **Race Brook Lodge** (413-229-2916; www.rblodge.com), 864 South Undermountain Road (Route 41), Sheffield 01257. Architect David Rothstein has transformed a 1790s barn into one of Berkshire County's more distinctive places to stay. "This is a chintz-free zone," Rothstein quips about the lack of antiques and frills in his 32 guest rooms (14 in the barn, many with private entry; 6 in the brick Federal-era Coach House; and the rest divided among cottages). The open beams and angles of the rustic old barn remain, but walls are white and stenciled; rooms are furnished with Native American rugs and quilts or spreads. As you would expect in a barn, the common room is large and multileveled, with some good artwork; a wine bar is in one corner. The lodge caters to hikers and walkers (as individuals and couples as well as groups), encouraging guests to climb the Race Brook Trail that measures 1.5 miles in distance and rises almost 2,000 feet in elevation—past a series of five cascades—to Mount Race. Abundant continental breakfast with one hot special. Children are welcome, as are well-behaved dogs (in certain rooms). $115–245 in high season; $95–175 low

season, lower midweek; 2-night minimum stay on high-season weekends.

⊚ ✔ **Seven Stones** (1-877-786-6307; www.thesevenstones.com), 103 Lake Buel Road, Great Barrington 01230. This is a former kids' summer camp and still looks like a summer camp, with lodging for 180 guests in a range of cottages, cabins, and bunkhouses. The most desirable (four-bedroom) cottages are pine paneled, with fireplaces, skylights, and decks overlooking the lake, but most of the buildings are grouped around the central green. Facilities include an airy dining pavilion and attractive gathering room with a stage. The food, we're told, is exceptional, prepared by a Culinary Institute–trained chef. Current owners cater to a variety of groups, ranging from theatrical and yoga to family reunions and weddings. The property features wooded trails (including a sampling of the AT), sports facilities (tennis, basketball, ropes, and more), and a lovely beach on Lake Buel, which is large by Berkshire standards, with no public swim access. While only groups of more than 20 people can reserve more than a few weeks in advance, there is frequently a cabin or two left over and available to families. $75–135 per person includes three meals.

Bucksteep Manor (413-623-5535 or 1-800-645-2825; www.bucksteep-manor.com), 885 Washington Mountain Road, Washington. The manor house at the heart of this 380-acre estate-turned-resort-and-conference-center is a grand Victorian mansion built in 1899. The eight upstairs bedrooms share three baths. The rooms vary in size, but are all pleasant and comfortably furnished. There is a tavern lounge and dining room on the first floor, as well as a living room with a large fireplace. Two separate lodge buildings have a total of 14 motel-style units, all with private bath. The campground has tent sites, RV hookups, and rustic (no plumbing or electricity) cabins. Recreational amenities include hiking and cross-country ski trails, two tennis courts, and a swimming pool. Bucksteep is a popular spot for conferences, family reunions, receptions, and other happenings; you might want to check ahead to see what's going on. $100–155, depending on season and time of week, including breakfast buffet. Campground rates are $10 per adult at campsites, $15 in the rustic cabins.

✳ Where to Eat

DINING OUT

In Great Barrington
Castle Street Café (413-528-5244; www.castlestreetcafe.com), 10 Castle Street. Open for dinner except Tuesday. Reservations advised. Next door to the Mahaiwe Performing Arts Center, Michael Ballon's casually elegant restaurant was the first high-end place to dine in Great Barrington, and it remains one of the best. Linen-draped tables and changing art set the tone for a frequently changing menu that features local farm products. More than a dozen entrée choices might include sautéed breast of duck with bok choy, water chestnuts, and ginger sauce ($21), or sautéed wild striped bass with fresh chanterelles ($23); pasta, burgers, and a vegetarian plate are also available. There is live music in the **Celestial Bar** (no cover charge).

&. **Pearl's** (413-528-7767; www.pearl-srestaurant.com), 47 Railroad Street.

Open for dinner and Sunday brunch. Reservations advised. A former auto parts store at the head of Railroad Street has been transformed into one of the most sophisticated restaurants around. Dark and richly paneled, it evokes the dining room on a vintage ocean liner. The original emphasis was on steaks but the menu is large and varied, ranging from pan-seared venison with sweet potato fritters, oven-roasted Vidalia onions, and pecan glaze to vegetarian ravioli (entrées $17–31). The bar is separate and features comfortable seating facing the plate-glass window overlooking the length of Railroad Street. Come evening, these are the most coveted seats in town. The bar menu includes a cheeseburger and chili as well as clams casino and fried calamari ($6–10).

&. **Bizen** (413-528-4343), 17 Railroad Street. Open for lunch and dinner daily. Michael Marcus opened this restaurant and sushi bar in 1997 to serve the food for which his pottery is intended. Marcus studied the distinctive pottery of Bizen in Japan for four years and has been creating it since 1982 in his Joyous Spring Pottery in Monterey. The restaurant has expanded several times and now includes a sake bar and an area of traditional tatami rooms specializing in "Kaiseki" cuisine with a prix fixe menu. The main menu features three dozen varieties of sushi, sashimi, and maki, all made from the freshest fish, seafood, and organic vegetables. Dinner entrées include seafood, chicken, vegetables, tempura, and noodles. Entrées $8.95–17.95.

Helsinki Café (413-528-3394), 284 Main Street. Open daily for lunch, dinner, and Sunday brunch. There's also a separate bar and nightclub, the area's hottest venue for live entertainment. "Colorful" is an understatement for the decor of this café that has, unfortunately, diluted its original Scandinavian and Russian menu with quasi-Thai and southern items. Happily, the "mad Russian" (crisp potato latkes headed with gravlax, sour cream, and caviar, served with berry compote, $17) survives, but we were disappointed in the "Finnish meat-balls"($16), and the wine list was overpriced. The lunch menu now includes "quesadilla of the day" and falafel as well as a Helsinki Salad.

Verdura Cucina Rustica (413-528-8969), 44 Railroad Street. Open for dinner. Reservations advised. Chef William Webber is an advocate of "slow food" and of local ingredients. The menu is theoretically northern Italian but varied. The "primi" course might include locally grown baby greens, roasted beets, chèvre, hazelnuts, and citrus balsamic vinaigrette ($9); "secondi" might be house gnocchi with asparagus, sweet peas, leeks, roasted mushroom, lemon, and basil. Entrées $21–27. At this writing Webber is expanding, turning the neighboring storefront into a wine bar. The plan is to be open for morning coffee and pastries and for light lunch.

Union Bar and Grill (413-528-6228), 293 Main Street. Open for dinner nightly, as well as Saturday lunch and Sunday brunch. Exposed pipes, stainless steel, and bleached tabletops with lime-green trim give this new storefront a loft-in-SoHo feel, but the ambience is relaxed and family-friendly, and the menu nouvelle country. Now owned by a Manhattan restaurateur, this remains a reliably good bet among the area's high-end

dining choices. The Caesar salad is excellent. Dining entrées might include pan-seared tuna with basmati rice, bok choy, and spicy soy wasabi sauce, or steak *au poivre* with sun-dried mashed potatoes, braised greens, and cognac Dijon shallot au jus. Entrées range from $11 for a grilled portobello sandwich to $24 for the tuna.

&. **Aegean Breeze** (43-528-4001), 327 Stockbridge Road (Route 7). Reservations advised. Open for lunch and dinner. The winning combination here is a light, bright, and airy decor and good service plus unusual Greek appetizers and a wide variety of very fresh fish entrées. You might begin with *prasopita* (baked stuffed filo with fresh leeks, feta cheese, dill, and scallions), and dine on the Aegean Breeze Platter (baked Chilean sea bass with Vidalia onions, tomato, feta, and fresh herbs, served in a clay pot). Dinner entrées $18.95–27.95.

Shiro (528-1898), 105 Stockbridge Road (at the junction of Routes 23 and 7). This is a local favorite with attention to presentation. Over 20 varieties of sushi are featured, along with hibachi-grilled steak and seafood, tempura dishes, and noodle dishes. Full bar.

In Lenox

Church Street Café (413-637-2745; www.churchstreetcafe.biz), 45 Church Street. Open daily for lunch and dinner May through February. Billing itself "An American Bistro," this lively, popular restaurant has an eclectic and always interesting menu. There is a pleasant dining patio and several connecting dining rooms, the walls of which are hung with paintings by local artists. Lunch on a quesadilla or the grilled pizza of the day and dine on sautéed Maine crabcakes or Spanish seafood stew. Entrées $18.50–26.50.

Bistro Zinc (413-637-8800), 56 Church Street. Open daily for lunch and dinner except Tuesday. Very popular, with a very contemporary decor and cuisine. Dine on porcini-encrusted chicken, pan-roasted Arctic char, or cassoulet. Entrées $19–25.

♿ **Café Lucia** (413-637-2460), 80 Church Street. Open for dinner daily except Monday, July through September; closed Sunday and Monday the rest of the year. A remodeled art gallery is the setting for appreciating fine regional Italian dishes such as *osso buco con risotto* and grilled paillard of chicken (thinly pounded breast of chicken, marinated in fresh lemon, olive oil, and herbs, grilled and topped with a fresh tomato, cucumber, and basil salsa, served on a bed of baby arugula). Try the tiramisu for dessert. Good wine list. The Caesar salad is rich and garlicky. Reservations recommended. Entrées $18–32.

Spigalina (413-637-4455; www.spigalina.com), 80 Main Street. Open for dinner daily in-season, closed Tuesday and Wednesday off-season. A very pleasant, popular presentation of the flavors and colors of the Mediterranean. Our mesclun salad with grilled shrimp was excellent, and the caramel chocolate mousse was light and satisfying. Grilled sea bass was perfection. Dinner entrées ($18.50–27) could be grilled Atlantic salmon with a lentil and vegetable Israeli couscous and saffron sauce, or rack of lamb with Provençal ratatouille.

Village Inn (413-637-0020; www.villageinn-lenox.com), 16 Church Street. The pleasant dining room of the inn is open to the public for breakfast and dinner but not lunch. (Afternoon tea is served Saturday 3:30–5.) Dinner entrées are $18.95–26.95 and include dishes such as Tropical Osso Buco (braised ham shank served with pineapple mango compote) and pistachio-encrusted rack of lamb.

Gateways Inn (413-637-2532), 751 Walker Street. Open daily for dinner, plus lunch and brunch on weekends (except Tuesday in winter). The warm colors and crisp settings of the formal dining room are the appropriate setting for excellent meals that might begin with roasted baby beet salad or Foie Gras Torchon and include pan-seared New England day-boat scallops with garlic mashed potatoes, asparagus, and truffle-infused olive oil; or braised lamb shank with polenta and roasted root vegetables. Entrées $22.50–27.

Blantyre (413-637-3556; www.blantyre.com), 16 Blantyre Road. Open May through November, Blantyre is a baronial mansion that epitomizes the Berkshires' Gilded Age glory; dining in its grand restaurant is a memorable (and expensive) experience. Diners are expected to dress appropriately;

VIEW OF RAILROAD STREET FROM PEARL'S IN GREAT BARRINGTON

Christina Tree

men must wear a jacket and tie. The cuisine is French (of course), prepared with care and served with flair. The wine list is vast and varied. The prix fixe menu is $80 per person, the five-course tasting menu $100, and the prix fixe with wine tasting $150. An 18 percent gratuity is added. Dinner is by reservation only. In July and August lunch is also served, on the terrace overlooking the splendid formal garden. The fixed price is $43, plus gratuity.

Wheatleigh (413-637-0610; www.wheatleigh.com), West Hawthorne Road. Open for lunch and dinner; check off-season. By reservation only, and jacket and tie required for men. The formal dining room in this Florentine palazzo, within walking distance of Tanglewood, features a contemporary American interpretation of the classic French kitchen serving dishes such as roasted guinea hen and Foie Gras Boudin with spring onion gnocchi and fiddlehead ferns. The prix fixe dinner menu (which includes a vegetarian option) is $85, and a fish tasting menu $115. The wine list is long and includes some superb (and very expensive) vintages.

Cranwell (413-637-1364; www.cranwell.com), Route 20. Breakfast, lunch, and dinner. "Wyndhurst," the main dining room of the baronial manor (Wyndhurst was its original name), is about as grand and richly appointed as it can be, and dining—orchestrated by executive chef Carl De Luce and chef de cuisine Christopher Bonniver—is fine indeed. Menu choices include the likes of seared soft-shell crabs, and duck confit with sweet-and-sour cabbage and warm peach and lemongrass stew. Entrées

$26.75–29.95. **Sloane's Tavern,** a seasonal English-style pub, is on the golf course; the **Music Room** offers live entertainment on weekends as well as a grill menu at lunch in winter. The spa also has a café serving light fare.

Lenox 218 Bar and Restaurant (413-637-4218; www.lenox218.com), Route 7A. Open for lunch, dinner, and Sunday brunch. The decor is hip and upbeat, and there's a menu to match. Dine on hot Sicilian sausage on polenta, Tuscan Italian meat loaf with onion rings and wine gravy, or "nutty chicken." Dinner entrées $15.95–24.95.

Apple Tree Inn (413-637-1477; www.appletree-inn.com), 10 Richmond Mountain Road. Open 7 days in July and August; the rest of the year dinner is served Thursday through Sunday in the large oak-beamed tavern. The round corner dining room, twinkling with myriad small white lights, seems suspended above the Stockbridge Bowl, which it overlooks. The menu might include chicken breast stuffed with goat cheese and served in a savory wine sauce, or filet mignon with rosemary sauce. Entrées are $17–28. Sunday brunch is served year-round.

Candlelight Inn (413-637-1555), 35 Walker Street. Open for dining in several small candlelit rooms—outdoor dining in summer—and a pub for lighter meals. Chef Aggie Ziemek is well known, and this is a perennial local favorite. The menu might range from wild rice with curried vegetables and summer pasta, to confit of duck and veal medallions with a lemon-caper butter sauce. Entrées $16–28.

Antonio's (413-637-8994), 15 Walker Street. A local fixture for many years,

Antonio's is a classic family-run restaurant with a loyal local clientele. (Proprietor Gennaro Gallo began working in the place when he was 8 years old.) The menu is basically mainstream Italian with such reliable dishes as chicken cacciatore, osso buco, and calamari marinara. House specialties include lobster risotto and "Melanzana alla Antonio" (eggplant layered with escarole, ricotta, and mozzarella, topped with tomato sauce). The long wine list, with more than 100 different vintages to choose from, is extraordinary for a small restaurant. There is an outside dining area as well as a main dining room. Entrées $17–26. Open daily for lunch and dinner in high season, closed Monday and Tuesday the rest of the year.

Firefly (413-637-2700), 83 Church Street. This cheery, popular place recently got a makeover that included a new name (it used to be the Roseborough Grill), an uncluttered contemporary decor, and an eclectic "world fusion" menu. Among the interesting choices are a Moroccan lamb, Merguez sausage, and Manchego cheese quesadilla; and Asian-barbecued ribs with wasabi mashed potatoes and braised baby bok choy. Open daily for dinner in summer; closed Tuesday and Wednesday off-season. Summer diners have the option of eating inside or outside on the porch. Tapas are served in the popular but often noisy bar, which also mixes high-octane drinks such as Tequila Cosmopolitans and Prickly Pear Margaritas, starting at 3 PM on Saturday and Sunday. Entrées $9–27.

Seven Hills (413-637-0060), 40 Plunkett Street. Open for dinner daily in-season; call for weekend hours off-season. The dining room of this grand, 1911 Tudor mansion is elegant, and the chef is well respected. You might choose sea bass topped with citrus-tarragon bread crumbs, or Muscovy duck breast stuffed with pineapple, dried cherries, and ginger. Entrées $16–27.

Trattoria il Vesuvio (413-637-4904), 242 Pittsfield Road (Routes 7/20). Though the exterior has little character (the building is a remodeled barn), this pleasant restaurant, owned and run by the Arace family, has a devoted following. The bread and pasta are homemade, and the menu features authentic Italian specialties such as roast breast of veal stuffed with prosciutto and spinach, or penne tossed in a sauce of tomato, basil, garlic, red peppers, and olive oil. Entrées $15–23.

In Lee

Ketchup to Caviar (413-243-6397; www.fromketchuptocaviar.com), 150 Main Street. Chef-owners Lynne and Christian Urbain, formerly of Once Upon A Table in Stockbridge, now run what is widely regarded as the best restaurant in Lee and among the very best in the Berkshires. Housed in large white mansion built in 1841, the restaurant has three comfortably intimate dining rooms and is open for lunch (11–2:30) and dinner (5–9). Lunch entrées are $6.95–13 and could be quiche of the day with a baby green salad mix, or Maine crabcakes with salad and horseradish beurre blanc. Dinner entrées are $9.50–24 and might include sautéed grouper with champagne-flavored sauerkraut, or slow-roasted Peking duck with rutabaga puree. The wine list is extensive. Closed Tuesdays in winter. Reservations are required in high season and a good idea the rest of the year.

Morgan House Inn (413-243-0181; www.morganhouseinn.com), 33 Main Street. The center of town since stagecoach days, this place is a sure bet for either lunch or dinner. It has been lucky over the years, regularly acquiring energetic owners who pour their all into the place. Both the tavern and more formal dining room are wood paneled, welcoming, and deservedly popular. Dine on blackened Atlantic salmon garnished with sun-dried tomato pesto or pan-seared pork paillards topped with caramelized apple brandy sauce. Open daily. Entrées $12.95–16.95.

Sullivan Station (413-243-2082), 189 Railroad Street. Housed in the old Lee railroad depot (still a stop on the Lenox-based Berkshire Scenic Railway), this has been a local institution for more than 20 years. Open for lunch and dinner, it's noted for stick-to-the-ribs fare such as burgers and roast beef sandwiches, baby back pork ribs with house barbecue sauce, and baked stuffed shrimp. Dinner entrées $14–21. Reservations suggested.

⌀ **Cork 'n' Hearth** (413-243-0535), Route 20. Open for dinner; call ahead in the off-season. Dine overlooking Laurel Lake if you can get a table near the large glass windows. This casual spot specializes in seafood, plus veal, chicken, duck, and beef; there's also a children's menu. Entrées are $19–25. Tavern food, along with homemade soups, salad, crab-stuffed mushrooms, and steamers, is served in the bar.

In Stockbridge

Red Lion Inn (413-298-5545; www.redlioninn.com), 30 Main Street. Breakfast, lunch, and dinner served daily. Reservations recommended. The formal and quite wonderful old main dining room bans blue jeans and shorts for dinner. You can lunch on salmon cakes or a grilled chicken salad and dine on brook trout, vegetable tart of artichokes and portobellos with frisée lettuce and chive oil, or sirloin of venison with wild mushrooms in red wine sauce. For dessert we recommend the Red Lion Indian pudding. The wine list is extensive, ranging from $24 for a young Pinot Grigio to $230 for a vintage French champagne. Entrées $20–36. Also see Widow Brigham's Tavern under *Eating Out.*

Rouge Restaurant and Bistro (413-232-4111), 3 Center Street, West Stockbridge. Up a side street in a small wooden building on the banks of the Williams River, Rouge draws diners by the droves with its Americanized international cuisine and elegantly casual atmosphere. Chef de cuisine William Merelle's moderately priced but imaginative menu includes dishes such as persillage of frog legs, pan-sautéed with sauce à la Rouge and polenta; and seared tuna encrusted with peppercorns and ginger with ratatouille. Tasting menus are available. The cozy bar serves memorable martinis, among other drinks. Open for dinner only Wednesday through Sunday 5–10. Entrées $19–22.

Once Upon a Table (413-298-3870), 36 Main Street. Tucked away in the Mews, around the corner from the Red Lion Inn, this popular place is open for lunch and dinner daily in July and August, variable days at other times. The menu changes with the seasons. Dinner entrées $18–22.

Williamsville Inn (413-274-6580; www.williamsvilleinn.com), Route 41, West Stockbridge. Owners Kandy and Erhard Wendt (he is a certified master chef and culinary instructor) also run a cooking school. Their dining room, open only for dinner Thursday through Sunday, is a showcase for gourmet cuisine. Meals are prix fixe, but diners have a choice of three, four, or five courses, priced at $38, $45, and $50, respectively. A typical five-course menu would be mixed greens with herbs and balsamic vinegar dressing, chilled creamy cucumber soup, free-range chicken breast braised in white wine and olive oil, a selection of international cheeses, and apple strudel with vanilla sauce for dessert. Seatings are at 6 and 8 PM. Reservations required.

Trúc Orient Express (413-232-4204), 3 Harris Street, West Stockbridge. In summer open daily for lunch (11–3) and dinner (5–9). Off-season open for dinner only, every day except Tuesday. A Vietnamese restaurant that's been here since 1979, offering an informal, pleasant, woven-straw and white-tablecloth decor, an extensive menu, and food that can be as spicy as you specify. Specialties include Trúc's special triangular shrimp rolls (with crab, pork, and vegetables surrounding a large shrimp, wrapped in crisp, golden rice paper) and many vegetarian selections. Dinner entrées range from $10.95 for Trúc's special fried rice (rice combined with peas, carrots, onions, shrimp, pork, chicken, and sausage) to $18.50 for lemongrass duck (crispy boneless duck topped with chopped lemongrass and chili sauce and served with fine rice noodles). A gift shop selling Vietnamese crafts is attached to the restaurant.

In Egremont
The Old Mill (413-528-1421), Route 23, South Egremont. Dining nightly; closed Monday off-season. Reservations a must. Chef-owner Kerry Morse has been creating some of most reliably superb fare in the county since 1978. The vintage-1797 gristmill by Hubbard Brook makes a simple, elegant setting for a meal that might begin with steamed mussels in light curry, or "soup of yesterday." Entrées might include grilled salmon with honey-mustard glaze over toasted orzo and tomato-zucchini gratin, grilled vegetable lasagna with goat cheese and marinara sauce, or grilled Angus New York steak with truffle butter, Cabernet demiglaze, and truffle fries. Entrées $16–26. It's first come, first served in the attractive tavern area, which has its own, more limited, similarly priced menu.

Elm Court Inn (413-528-0325), Route 71, North Egremont. Dinner Wednesday through Sunday (reserve). The large, low-ceilinged dining room of this 1790 inn gleams with polished wood. Chef-owner Urs Bieri serves mouthwatering fish and seafood along the lines of broiled striped bass with pecan crust and *pico de gallo,* or flash-seared scallops with garlic mashed potatoes and maple balsamic glaze; he also earns high praise for his classic German-Swiss dishes like Wiener schnitzel. The menu changes daily and might include venison scaloppine with green peppercorns and lingonberries, rack of lamb Provençal, or roast duckling. There is an extensive wine list. Entrées $18–27.

John Andrews (413-528-3469; www.jarestaurant.com), Route 23, South Egremont near the New York line. Open for dinner nightly; closed Wednesdays in winter. We love the warm, earth-toned walls and soft lighting, not to mention the menu that includes so many of our favorite foods: starters like lobster ravioli with lemon, pine nuts, and fried parsley ($10), followed by sautéed duck breast, crisp duck confit, mashed potatoes, braised greens, and balsamic maple syrup ($24). Leave room for dessert. Pastas such as fettuccine with mushrooms, parsley, and pine nuts begin at $17, and other entrées are $19–28.

The Egremont Inn (413-528-2111; www.egremontinn.com), 10 Old Sheffield Road, South Egremont. Open for dinner Wednesday through Sunday. Local residents vouch for the excellence of the food served in this classic old hotel dining room. You might begin with a summer vegetable risotto with fresh peas and a hint of lemongrass, and dine on pan-roasted grouper with shiitakes in a beurre blanc laced with spinach. Entrées $19–24. Live music Thursday and Saturday year-round. The reasonably priced tavern menu includes crispy fried scallops as well as burgers and grilled hanger steak ($9–17).

Swiss Hutte Inn & Restaurant (413-528-6200), Route 23 at Catamount ski area in South Egremont. Open in the winter and summer seasons for lunch and dinner. We should explain that "at Catamount" simply means within the grounds, which are delightfully green and landscaped in summer. The present chef-owner is Swiss, and entrée choices include Wiener schnitzel and "bundnerteller"—but it's a varied menu. Entrées may range from seafood curry to herb-crusted rack of lamb with a red wine glaze. The ambience is polished wood and linen with an outdoor patio, weather permitting. Entrées $23–28 at dinner, $12.50–18 at lunch.

Elsewhere
The Old Inn on the Green and Gedney Farm (413-229-3131), Route 57, Village Green, New Marlborough. Open for dinner in the 18th-century inn, either on the garden terrace or in the four small, candlelit (the only other light is from the hearth) dining rooms, daily except Tuesday July through October; weather permitting, you can also dine on the terrace in July and August. November through June it's also closed Monday. Reservations are required Saturday night, when only the $62 prix fixe menu (there are three choices per course) is served. On other nights it's an à la carte menu (entrées $22–35) that changes frequently and features locally grown produce. Executive chef Peter Platt is well known locally, having previously held the same position at Wheatleigh. A spring menu included Taft Farms asparagus with morels and truffle vinaigrette followed by a memorable seared pepper-crusted yellowfin tuna Niçoise with a tapenade beurre blanc ($28.50). Wish we had room for the chilled rhubarb soup. A $75 tasting menu is also available.

The Hillside (413-528-3123), Route 57, New Marlborough. Closed Monday year-round, Tuesday too in winter, otherwise open for dinner. Ask Berkshire residents what their favorite restaurants are, and this low-key but elegant place is always mentioned. Specialties are Continental classics like pâté maison and onion soup gratinée, filet of sole Oscar, melon and prosciutto, and veal dishes. Entrées $15–21.

EATING OUT

In Great Barrington
20 Railroad Street (413-528-9345),

20 Railroad Street. Open daily for lunch and dinner, also for Sunday brunch. Railroad Street was still dingy in 1977 when this friendly pub opened. Since then the side street has filled with boutiques and restaurants, but this one still stands out. The menu is huge, ranging through soups, chilis, nachos, salads, pocket sandwiches, burgers, and Reubens, and featuring daily specials like chicken Marbella. The ornate, 28-foot-long bar was moved from the Commodore Hotel in Manhattan to Great Barrington in 1919 and served as the centerpiece of a speakeasy until 1933—when it became one of the first legal bars in town.

✐ **Martin's** (413-528-5455), 49 Railroad Street. Open daily 6–3 for breakfast and lunch. Breakfast is an all-day affair, the omelets are a feast, and the burgers are outstanding, too. Beer and herbal teas are served, and crayons are at every table; inspired customers of all ages can design their own place mats. Martin Lewis worked in several of New York's most famous restaurants, but his wife is from Sandisfield and 15 years ago he opened this spotless, family-run diner-with-a-difference, good for a veggie sandwich or Berkshire Breeze (avocado, cucumber, tomato, sprouts, and Swiss or cheddar on farmer's bread) as well as a BLT or burger.

✐ **Cheesecake Charlie's** (413-528-7790), 271 Main Street. Open daily, Monday through Thursday 8–6, later Friday and Saturday, 10:30–5 Sunday. This spacious café is full of surprises: a juicer and an espresso machine, from-scratch muffins, breads, and soup, plus a wide choice of salads, many flavors of ice cream, and 55 kinds of cheesecake. There's wine and

beer, too, plus frequent "cabaret" performances ranging from afternoon skits and magic for kids to evening comics and concerts.

✐ **Baba Louie's Sourdough Pizza Restaurant** (413-528-8100), 286 Main Street. Open Tuesday through Sunday for lunch and dinner. Unusual wood-fired pizzas ("Pizza Festival" is topped with broccoli rabe, fresh tomatoes, roasted peppers, yellow squash, zucchini, mozzarella, and oregano) are the specialty, but there are also a surprising variety of salads and a hearty antipasto.

✐ **Siam Square** (413-644-9119), 290 Main Street. Lunch and dinner. This is a deep, deep storefront with a pleasant decor. No wine or beer at this writing, but BYOB. In addition to a choice of reasonably priced and quickly prepared curry and noodle dishes, you'll find an intriguing array of house specialties and Thai hot-and-sour salads. Try the Chicken Volcano: marinated Cornish hen with herbs, spices, and a sweet hot chili sauce.

Barrington Brewery & Restaurant (413-528-8282), 420 Stockbridge Road (Route 7) in Jennifer House Commons. Open for lunch and dinner. Both the brew and the food are good, and the scruffy barn atmosphere works. "Barn Brewed" is the original microbrew here; there are usually half a dozen on tap. The menu includes a plowman's lunch and hearty classics like shepherd's pie.

✐ **Four Brothers** (413-528-9684), Route 7. This restaurant is part of an upstate New York chain, but it doesn't seem that way. The decor is classic Greek, complete with plants and fake grape arbor. Generally regarded as having the best pizzas, Greek salads,

DOWNTOWN GREAT BARRINGTON

Kim Grant

and lasagna around; there's also fried fish and eggplant casserole. Dinners range from a small pizza to honey-dipped fried chicken.

The Great Barrington Bagel Company (413-528-9055), 777 South Main Street, Route 7 south, across from Guido's Market. Open 7–4 daily; Friday and Saturday until 5. Our New York friends tell us these are the best you can get north of Manhattan. We counted 19 varieties, from sesame to jalapeño to chocolate chip. This is a small, attractive deli with daily-made soups, eight kinds of smoked fish, and more than a dozen spreads, good for eat-in or take-out. Breakfasts served until 11 AM.

In South Egremont

Mom's Restaurant (413-528-2414), Route 23 in the village. A great little way stop that's open for breakfast, lunch, and dinner, with a shady deck in back overlooking a stream. A good

choice of burgers, sandwiches, soups, and salads for lunch. For dinner, 4–10, the chef and menu change entirely, to Italian classics like pasta, pizza, and veal scampi. Beer and wine are served.

In Lenox

Napa (413-637-3204), 30 Church Street. Open daily for lunch and dinner—and they deliver. A sensational addition to the village, with rotisseried chicken so good that half the town seems to order it nightly as take-out. No ordinary diner, this is the ground floor of a clapboard house, decorated with photos and art that changes. Our southwestern turkey taco salad with homemade guacamole salsa and a Mexican beer (served in a frosted glass with lime) hit the spot one warm evening, as did the Yankee pot roast in fall. Burritos and from-scratch soups are also specialties. Dinner entrées are all under $18.

✏ **Village Snack Shop** (413-637-4677), 27 Housatonic Street. Open for breakfast and lunch. Sandwiches, burgers, and luncheon specials. A time-warp local hangout and gossip exchange (if they don't know about it at the Village Snack Shop, it didn't happen).

Betty's Pizza Shack (413-637-8171), 26 Housatonic Street. A colorful addition to the Lenox fast-food scene, Betty's has a Hawaiian surfing theme with a neon color scheme and surfboards and surfing competition posters on the walls. The pizzas have names like Maui Mushroom, King Kamehameha, and Gidget's Veggie Pie; prices range from $8.75 for a small Plain Jane to $22 for a large Zuma Bay with a mound of toppings. Beer and wine are served.

Senor Chili's (413-637-2590), 9 Franklin Street. An unpretentious combination Mexican restaurant and pizzeria. Burritos, tacos, and fajitas are the menu mainstays, but you can also get "Mexican style" pizza—i.e., with lots of hot peppers.

In Lee

Cactus Café (413-243-4300), 54 Main Street. Open for lunch and dinner daily. A storefront, middle-of-town place that uses no lard and offers good fresh salsa. We had a fabulous chile relleno, brothy chowder overflowing with seafood, and a vegetable and three-cheese quesadilla. Beers include Carta Blanca, and there's sangria or wine by the glass. Dinner entrées $10–18.

✏ **51 Park Street** (413-243-2153), 51 Park Street. An informal eatery at one end of the Lee common, this restaurant and lounge offers wood-fired pizza ($7.50–10.50) and such wood-grilled entrées as salmon, steak, kielbasa, and barbecued chicken ($8.75–13.50), along with calzones, grinders, salads, and children's menu.

Joe's Diner (413-243-9756), 63 Center Street, South Lee. Open Monday through Saturday 5:30–9, Sunday 7–2. The scene of a famous Norman Rockwell *Saturday Evening Post* cover (the one where a burly but kindly state trooper counsels a runaway small boy sitting at the counter), this is still a local hangout. So, choose from a counter stool or a booth and watch the town saunter in and out. The food is good, and when particular specials are on the menu, such as corned beef or slow-roasted prime rib, there can be a line waiting to get in.

Paradise of India Restaurant (413-243-0500), 5 Railroad Street. Just off the main drag, a pleasant place for curries and tandoori dishes, a real bargain at lunch and dinner, too. Dinner entrées $9.25–18.95. BYOB.

Salmon Run Fish House (413-243-3900), 78 Main Street. The decor is minimal but the price is right and the seafood menu extensive. We enjoyed the fish-and-chips, but the specialty really is salmon, and it's served half a dozen different ways. Most entrées $8–20.

In Stockbridge

Theresa's Stockbridge Café (413-298-5465), 40 Main Street. Open 11–9. Closed Tuesday and Wednesday. Good for lunch. Anyone who knew the old Alice's Restaurant of Arlo Guthrie's song will do a double take at the present trompe l'oeil pillars and busts in this familiar space. The deli case is full of quiche, lemon chicken with couscous, and tasty Middle Eastern delicacies. There are also sandwiches, pizza, and two soups of the day. The marble tables are a bit small, the plates are paper, and the utensils are plastic, but there is a small patio and this is still an oasis of sorts.

Widow Brigham's Tavern at the Red Lion Inn (413-298-5545), Main Street. More casual and intimate than the formal dining room and good for lighter fare. The Red Lion burgers are legendary, and dinner stews are a good bet. In summer the garden itself is a pleasant café and the Lion's Den, opening at 4 on weekdays and noon on weekends, features live entertainment, no cover, and reasonable prices.

Elsewhere

Limey's (413-229-9000), 650 North Main (Route 7), Sheffield. Open Monday through Saturday 4:30–9, Sunday noon–9. A great roadhouse/family restaurant with deep booths and an English accent. Specialties include bangers and mash, shepherd's pie, and steak-and-kidney pie as well as BBQ spareribs and baked stuffed shrimp.

The New Boston Inn (413-258-4477), at the junction of Routes 8 and 57, New Boston. Open for lunch and dinner, also Sunday brunch June through September. An 18th-century taproom that's as good a way stop as ever. Dinner entrées range from $11 for meat loaf or fettuccine Alfredo to $19 for beef tenderloin. The New Boston Inn quesadilla stuffed with a choice of chicken, portobello, or shrimp ($12–14) is a favorite.

Jack's Grill & Restaurant (413-274-1000; www.jacksgrill.com), Main Street, Housatonic. Open for dinner except Monday. Owned by the Fitzpatricks of Red Lion Inn fame, this is

a former company store for workers at the textile mills in this classic mill village. It's decorated with nostalgia items like tube radios and a model railroad. The menu is self-consciously small town with chicken potpie and pot roast sandwich, "mac & cheese" and lumpy applesauce, even "mom's meatloaf dinner" and spaghetti with meatballs and sausages "like at home—except we do the dishes." Frankly, it all seems a bit much, including the prices ($5 for fries?).

SNACKS Bev's Homemade Ice Cream, 38 Housatonic Street, Lenox, and 5 Railroad Street, Great Barrington. Ice cream made daily in many flavors; the shops also sell sodas, malteds, egg creams, coffee, and pastries.

The Village Inn (413-637-0020), 16 Church Street, Lenox. A full English afternoon tea is served Saturday 3:30–5, with scones, strawberry preserves, clotted cream—the whole works.

PICNICS Perfect Picnics (413-637-3015; www.perfectpicnicsfortanglewood.com), 34A Main Street, Lenox. Specializes in elaborate picnics to be consumed in style on the lawn at Tanglewood. Options include grilled filet mignon basted in parsley-garlic butter, poached salmon, and chilled lobster tails with butter sauce. Besides plates, utensils, and napkins, picnic baskets come with after-dinner mints and a "romantic candle." Picnickers have to provide their own romance, however.

La Bruschetta (413-232-7141), 1 Harris Street, West Stockbridge. A take-out restaurant that is also a wine shop. Picnic choices include rotisserie-cooked chicken and duckling, osso buco, and "pocket symphonies": pita bread sandwiches with a choice of stuffings such as curried chicken or Scandinavian salmon salad. There are more than 600 different wines to choose from as a picnic accompaniment.

✳ Entertainment

MUSIC **Guthrie Center** (413-528-1955), 4 Van Deusenville Road, Great Barrington. This is the actual church immortalized as "Alice's Restaurant," and it now belongs to folksinger and writer Arlo Guthrie, who periodically performs here himself as well as staging other well-known performers.

Club Helsinki (413-528-3394), 284 Main Street, Great Barrington. South Berkshire's leading venue for live music, from reggae to folksingers to jazz, it gets the best, periodically staging big names at the Mahaiwe Performing Arts Center. The club itself is dark, narrow, and funky with a great bar and a bar menu from the same kitchen as the adjoining café (see *Dining Out*).

Celestial Bar at the Castle Street Café (413-528-5244; www.castle-streetcafe.com), 10 Castle Street. Live music nightly except Tuesday: piano, guitar, jazz groups. Check to see who's on. No cover. An attractive bar with its own menu. Also see *Dining Out*.

Egremont Inn (413-528-2111), 10 Old Sheffield Road. Live music Thursday and Saturday year-round. Also see *Dining Out*.

∞ **DeSisto Estate** (413-298-4032), Route 183, Stockbridge. A mansion housing a private school is the venue for summer theater, cabaret, and midweek dinner theater. Also a popular venue for weddings.

Dream Away Lodge (413-623-8725), 1342 County Road, Becket. An old roadhouse that once had a funky reputation, Dream Away has in recent years (under the ownership of Daniel Osman) become a very hip music and dining venue with a diverse and devoted clientele. The decor is eclectic, as is the music and also the cuisine, which Osman—a former Shakespeare & Company of Lenox actor—describes as "a daily happening." Name performers are booked on weekends, but the very popular Wednesday "open acoustic" night in the intimate music room attracts area musicians who can include, among others, local boy Arlo Guthrie. Open Wednesday through Sunday from Mother's Day to Halloween, weekends only from New Year's to Valentine's Day. Reservations are encouraged and often essential. Credit cards not accepted.

Cheesecake Charlie's (413-528-7790), 271 Main Street, Great Barrington. Frequent "cabaret" performances, ranging from afternoon skits and magic for kids to evening comics and concerts. Also see *Eating Out*.

FILM **Triplex Theater** (413-528-8886; www.thetriplex.com), 70 Railroad Street, Great Barrington. First-run and some art films, surround sound.

Also see *The Arts*.

✳ Selective Shopping

ANTIQUES SHOPS South Berkshire County is one of the antiques centers of New England. Log onto www.berkshireantiquesandart.com. A pamphlet listing Berkshire County antiques dealers is available from antiques stores and from the sources listed under *Guidance*. Sheffield alone has some two dozen dealers and is home to **Bradford Galleries** (413-339-6667; www.bradfordauctions.com), with monthly auctions of quality furniture and accessories and special rare-book and ephemera auctions five times a year.

The Buggy Whip Factory (413-229-3576; www.buggywhipantiques.com), Southfield. Open May through December, daily 10–5; January through April, closed Tuesday and Wednesday. This long, picturesque, sagging wooden tannery, said to date from 1792—it remained an ongoing business, producing the leather for buggy whips and other products, until 1973—now houses more than 70 antiques dealers, resulting in genuine variety. French Canadian antiques are the specialty, and there are also some reproductions. Even if you aren't looking for anything in particular, this is a great excuse to drive down some beautiful back roads. Displays now include a museum corner, with exhibits and video depicting the history of the factory.

Jenifer House Commons, Route 7,

a small shopping complex housed in old New England buildings north of downtown Great Barrington, is the site of 100-dealer **Coffman's Antiques Market** (www.coffmansantiques.com) and of **Carriage House Antiques** (413-528-6045), specializing in country French furniture, as well as garden and architectural elements.

Great Barrington Antiques Center (413-644-8848; www.greatbarringtonantiquescenter.com), 964 South Main Street (Route 7), Great Barrington. Some 50 dealers with a wide variety of furniture and furnishings.

ART AND ARTISANS Fellerman & Raabe Glassworks (413-229-8533; www.fellerman-raabe.com), South Main Street (Route 7), Sheffield. Open daily, Tuesday through Friday 8–6, Saturday through Monday 11–6 (closed Monday November through May). Don't miss this combination studio, gallery, and school. The showroom is a riot of brilliant colors and fascinating shapes: bowls, perfume bottles, dishes, jewelry. Visitors are welcome to watch Stephen Fellerman and other artists blow and shape these pieces of art.

DeVries Fine Art Gallery (413-637-3462; www.andrewdevries.com), 17 Franklin Street, Lenox. Just off Main Street, this gallery mainly displays sculptures, reliefs, sketches, watercolors, and pastels by Andrew DeVries. Other well-known artists, such as figurative painter Jonathon Nix and seascape and landscape painter Jay Connoway are also on view. This is a visitor friendly gallery where touching the sculptures, some outside in a garden setting, is actually encouraged. Open Saturday to Sun-

ANTIQUES SHOP IN SHEFFIELD

Kim Grant

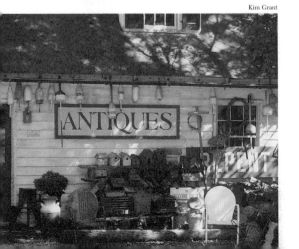

day, 12–4 in spring; daily in high season and by appointment the rest of the year.

Butler Sculpture Park (413-229-8924), 481 Shunpike Road, Sheffield. Open late May through October, daily 11–5; by appointment in winter. Turn left off Route 7 (3.7 miles south of the Sheffield Post Office) onto Hewins Street, then right onto Shunpike Road. Robert Butler fashions large, brightly colored abstract sculptures in his studio, which features a gallery with views over the Sheffield Valley. The building sits atop a hillside that's been landscaped with wooded paths into a truly remarkable sculpture garden.

Housatonic, Route 183, Housatonic. Within the town of Great Barrington but several miles north of downtown, this community centers on Monument Mills, which produced textiles from the 1890s until the late 1950s. The defunct brick mills have attracted artists since the 1970s and presently house a number of studios that hold periodic open houses. The **Tokonoma Gallery** (413-274-1166) at the bend by the bridge, with interesting photography, craft furniture, jewelry, prints, and fabric wares, is open year-round, Thursday through Monday 10–5 and Sunday noon–5. **Aberdale's** at 10 Depot Street (across from the post office) is the friendly general store, also good for ice cream and a remarkable wine selection.

Great Barrington Pottery (413-274-6259), Route 41, Housatonic. The handsome, nicely glazed pieces are fired in a Japanese wood-burning kiln. During July and August visitors are invited to view demonstrations of *ikebana* or the tea ceremony between 1 and 4 in the Kyoto-style teahouse;

DEVRIES FINE ART

Kim Grant

silk flowers are also sold.

October Mountain Stained Glass (413-528-6681), 343 Main Street, Great Barrington. Closed Monday. A variety of quality stained glass: lamp shades, bottles, jewelry, custom work.

Mill River Studio (413-528-9433), 8 Railroad Street. This long-established gallery specializes in fabulous vintage posters and other "vintage art" as well as archival framing.

Joyous Spring Pottery (413-528-4115), Art School Road, Monterey. Open daily 10–5 in summer; otherwise call ahead. Striking unglazed vases and other decorative pieces, fired once a year day and night for 12 days, an ancient Japanese technique called *yaki-shime.* At the same time, visit the neighboring Bidwell House; see *Historic Homes.*

Holsten Galleries (413-208-3044; www.holstengalleries.com), 3 Elm Street, Stockbridge, showcases some of the finest art glass around.

West Stockbridge is a cluster point for galleries and studios. These include **Hoffman Pottery** (413-232-4646), No. 103 on Route 41, featuring brightly patterned functional pieces; **Berkshire Center for Contemporary Glass** (413-232-4666), where the collection is large, varied, and stunning and where visitors may watch glassblowing or even try their hand; **Waterside Gallery** (413-232-7997), 30 Main Street, a large and diverse gallery, in business since 1980, with handcrafted jewelry, contemporary art, collectibles, and a seasonal sculpture garden; and **Antiqualia** (413-232-0040), 2 Main Street, with Mediterranean antiques and handmade quilts, including some superb vintage ones. **Clay Forms Studio** (413-232-4339; call ahead for hours), the source of Leslie Klein's ceramic visions, is on Austerlitz Road, about a 10-minute drive from the village on winding roads lined with farms and fields.

BOOKSTORES **The Bookloft** (413-528-1521), Barrington Plaza, Route 7, Great Barrington. A large, long-established, attractive independent bookstore with a knowledgeable staff.

The Bookstore (413-637-3390), 9 Housatonic Street, Lenox. An inviting bookstore with a large, well-chosen, and varied selection. Regional interest and authors with local connections are featured.

ANTIQUARIAN BOOKS **Farshaw's Bookshop** (413-528-1890), 13 Railroad Street, Great Barrington. An

TOKONOMA GALLERY IN HOUSATONIC

Christina Tree

inviting shop, specializing in the rare and unusual. Michael and Helen Selzer founded www.bibliofind.com, the Internet's largest marketplace for old and used books, when they sold out a few years back. Now they operate only in the summer and Christmas seasons, spending the remainder of their time in Carefree, Arizona.

North Star Rare Books (413-644-9595), 684 South Main Street (Route 7), Great Barrington, specializing in 18th- through 20th-century historical and literary manuscripts and rare volumes. Sited unexpectedly in a mini shopping mall next to Housatonic River Outfitters, Randy Weinstein's shop seems as much gallery as bookshop, a serene space displaying valuable vintage manuscripts and illustrations, all said to come from local collections.

Yellow House Books (413-528-8227), 252 Main Street, Great Barrington. Open Monday through Saturday 10:30–5:30, Sunday noon–5. Bonnie and Bob Benson's store fills several rooms in a house, with a cat. They specialize in rare books, photographs, children's illustrated books, and folklore and encourage browsing. We always come away with something we never meant to buy but are grateful we did.

Berkshire Book Company (413-229-0122), 510 South Main Street (Route 7), Sheffield. A broad range of titles but emphasizing children's books, cookbooks, first editions, history, and military.

SPECIAL SHOPS Country Curtains (413-298-5565; www.countrycurtains. com), at the Red Lion Inn, Stockbridge (see *Lodging*). A phenomenon rather than just a store, nationally known through its catalog, Country Curtains is a source of a wide variety of matching curtains, bedding, and pillows, beautifully displayed in the rear of the inn. Open daily.

Yankee Candle (413-499-3626; www.yankeecandle.com), 475 Pittsfield Road, Lenox, and 34 Main Street, Stockbridge (413-298-3004; www.yankeecandle.com). Candles (including dip-your-own), gifts, and bath accessories. More than 100 candle fragrances to choose from, with one always discounted 25 percent.

Charles H. Baldwin & Sons (413-232-7785; www.baldwinextracts.com), 1 Center Street, West Stockbridge. This wonderful, aromatic emporium has been in the same family since 1888 and on the same spot since 1912, making and selling its own "table syrup" (a blend of maple and cane sugar syrup) and pure vanilla extract and other cooking extracts and flavorings. The cluttered little shop sells some gifts and souvenirs, but most customers are looking for extracts, particularly the hard-to-find pure vanilla. Even if extracts aren't

your thing, we recommend a visit just to smell the delicious compounded aroma of the place.

Kenver, Ltd. (413-538-2330), Route 23, South Egremont. Housed in an 18th-century tavern, a long-established source of skiwear.

Guido's Fresh Marketplace in Pittsfield (413-442-9909), 1020 South Street, and in Great Barrington (413-528-9255), 760 South Main Street. The standout places to shop for a full line of vegetables, health food, and deli items as well as seafood and meat; great baked goods, too.

The Snap Shop (413-528-4725), 14 Railroad Street. Open Tuesday through Friday 9–5:30, Saturday 8:30–4. Steve Carlotta and his

FARSHAW'S BOOKSHOP ON RAILROAD STREET IN GREAT BARRINGTON

Kim Grant

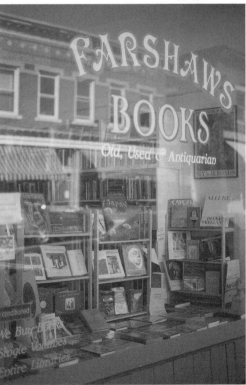

nephew Tony Carlotto have been running this friendly camera shop since 1972. We tried to buy an expensive new card for our digital camera and instead were given a lesson in how to work with what we had.

Byzantium (413-528-9496), 32 Railroad Street, Great Barrington. Our favorite for women's clothing and accessories.

Gatsby's (413-528-9455), 25 Railroad Street. The neon HOTPOINT sign suggests that this was recently an appliance store, but this emporium, selling everything from bras to lawn chairs, has been here since the 1970s. It's still fun to browse, though prices have risen steeply in recent years.

OUTLET MALLS Prime Outlets at Lee (413-243-8186 or 1-800-866-5900; www.primeoutlets.com) at Mass Pike exit 2 in Lee. A nicely grouped array of more than five dozen outlets offering upscale and everyday wares, from Liz Claiborne and Polo Ralph Lauren to Reebok and OshKosh B'Gosh. There is a central food court and plenty of parking. In summer a shuttle bus runs to and from downtown Lee.

✳ Farms

Note: **Berkshire Grown** (www.berkshiregrown.org) is the community group promoting locally grown food, flowers, and plants. Look for their tabloid *Buyer's Guide* in information centers and at farm stands.

In Great Barrington
Farmer's Market, Old Train Station, corner of Castle Street and Taconic Avenue (behind town hall). Early May through October, Saturday 9–1. Organic vegetables, fruit, dairy products, pasta, flowers, prepared foods, special events.

Windy Hill Farm (413-298-3217), 686 Stockbridge Road, Great Barrington. Open April through Christmas, daily 9–5. Pick-your-own apples (more than 25 varieties), pies and fresh-pressed cider in fall, extensive container-grown nursery stock, and hardy perennials; staff are very knowledgeable.

Taft Farms (413-528-1515 or 1-800-528-1015; www.taftfarms.com), corner of Division Street and Route 183. Over 400 produce items, baked goods, and free-range chickens. Call to find out what is in season in the way of PYO fruits and vegetables.

In Monterey
Gould Farm and Roadside Store (413-528-1804), Route 23. Farm stand with Gould Farm produce, maple syrup, salad dressing, eggs, wood products, and yarn. Also serving whole-food breakfast and lunch with farm eggs and meats.

Lowland Farm (413-528-0728), 128 New Marlborough Road. Open year-round daily, mulch hay, maple syrup, PYO raspberries in-season.

🍴 **Rawson Brook Farm** (413-528-2138), off New Marlborough Road, 2 miles from Route 23 in Monterey. Getting there is half the fun, since the back roads to the farm are beautiful. Wayne Dunlop and Susan Sellew have chosen to supply local restaurants and customers rather than go big time—an option that is very real given the quality of their **Monterey Chèvre** goat cheese, in five varieties (plain, with chives and garlic, no salt, with thyme and olive oil, and a peppered log). The cheese is available in various sizes from the fridge at the dairy at prices well below what you pay in local stores. Children will love seeing the baby goats, but adult supervision is a must.

In Sheffield

Farmer's Market, Old Parish Church, Route 7, early May through Columbus Day weekend, Friday 4-7. Produce, baked goods, cut flowers, pasta, perennials, bedding plants, soups, maple syrup, etc.

Bob Kelly's Farm (413-229-8307), 1647 Hewins Street, Ashley Falls (from Route 7 south, turn left onto Hewins Street, then go right at the sign). Open June through October, Tuesday through Sunday and holidays 10–4. Vegetables and herbs, melons, tomatoes, peppers, strawberries, shell beans, and flowers.

Howden Farm (413-229-8481; www.howdenfarm.com), 303 Rannopo Road. From Route 7 in Ashley Falls, follow signs for Bartholomew's Cobble and the Ashley House. Rannopo Road runs north between these two sites. Also off Route 7A south of Sheffield. Home of the Howden Pumpkins, two varieties developed by John A. Howden. Family run since 1937; PYO pumpkins on weekends and holidays starting in late September. PYO blueberries and raspberries in July and August. Good for sweet corn and eggs, too. Also see *Lodging*.

Equinox Farm (413-229-3366), 489 Bow Wow Road. Open daylight hours, Memorial Day through Labor Day. From Route 7 south, turn right onto Cook Road, then right onto Bow Wow. A variety of greens, mesclun, salad greens, herbs, heirloom tomatoes.

Elsewhere

Blueberry Hill Farm (413-528-1479; www.austinfarm.com), Mount Washington Road, Mount Washington. If you don't happen to have your own blueberry patch, this is the next best thing: pick-your-own wild blueberries (late July through frost, 9–5 except Wednesday) in one of the Berkshires' most beautiful settings (see Mount Washington under *Villages*).

High Lawn Farm (413-243-0672), 535 Summer Street, Lee, is a source of the creamiest milk around. Visitors are welcome.

✳ Special Events

May: **Chesterwood Antique Auto Show,** Stockbridge. **Memorial Day Parade,** Great Barrington.

June: **Summerfest** in Great Barrington—music, dancing, food, games (a mid-June Saturday).

July: **Fireworks** and Independence Day music at Tanglewood. **Independence Day** parade and celebrations, Pittsfield.

August: **Berkshire Crafts Fair,** at the high school, Great Barrington. **Annual Antiques Show,** midmonth at Berkshire Botanical Garden. **Berkshire Jazz Festival** at the Butternut Ski Basin, Great Barrington (413-499-0856; www.jazzforumarts.org).

September: **Barrington Fair** at the Great Barrington Fairgrounds. The **Tub Parade** in Lenox is a re-creation of the Gilded Age end-of-summer procession in which carriages and carts were decked with flowers (late September).

October: **Berkshire Botanical Garden Harvest Festival,** Stockbridge. **Halloween Walk through Ice Glen** (a Stockbridge tradition), usually followed by a bonfire. **Spirits of**

Sheffield Rise Again—a dramatized tour of the town's 14 cemeteries on Halloween weekend.

December: **Stockbridge Main Street at Christmas** is decorated to re-create the way it looked in Norman Rockwell's famous painting (first weekend). **Naumkeag** is also decorated for Christmas (see *Historic Homes*). **Lenox Holly Fair.**

CENTRAL AND NORTH BERKSHIRE

North Berkshire is its own ruggedly beautiful landscape of steep-sided, wooded valleys cut by the rushing Hoosic River, divided and dominated by Mount Greylock. In 1800 Timothy Dwight, president of Yale University, described the view from Greylock's 3,491-foot summit as "immense and of amazing grandeur." Dwight's widely read guidebook may have inspired many subsequent visitors, including Nathaniel Hawthorne, who compared the "high mountain swells" of the Taconics on the west to "immense, subsiding waves," and Henry David Thoreau, who bushwhacked up and spent the night on top, waking to "an ocean of mist . . . and undulating country of clouds." The view from the summit, now accessible by paved road, extends 70 to 100 miles on a clear day.

Mount Greylock isn't an isolated peak but part of a range that includes three of the highest mountains in Massachusetts, rising steeply from the countryside on four sides. It's said that Herman Melville, gazing at Mount Greylock from his home in Pittsfield, was inspired to write about a whale. The range divides the north–south flow of traffic in this region the way a big boulder divides the flow of a narrow stream. Route 7, running from Williamstown down to Pittsfield on the western side of the range, is the main road, while Route 8, from North Adams south through Adams and Cheshire, is the road less taken.

Greylock, topped by Massachusetts's official war monument, is the only New England mountain that still has a place to stay on the summit. Massively built of fieldstone in the 1930s by the Civilian Conservation Corps, Bascom Lodge continues to welcome patrons who hike, bike, or drive up. The surrounding 12,500-acre state reservation offers excellent hiking and some of the finest views in New England.

Given what it has to offer, the reservation is underused. Even in foliage season, when the mountain and the countryside colors are spectacular, relatively few visitors take the trouble to drive to the summit (it's accessible from both the region's major highways, Route 2 and Route 7), let alone hike up.

Everyone visits Williamstown, the area's "village beautiful." Sited at the junction of Route 2 and Route 7 and home of prestigious Williams College, Williamstown is the quintessential gracious old college town. It is also home to the Sterling and Francine Clark Art Institute, internationally known for its collection of paintings by French impressionists and 19th-century American masters. The Williams College Museum of Art also displays several icons of American art, and in summer the Williamstown Theater Festival is a destination in its own right.

It's neighboring North Adams, however, that's been making news lately. In 1999 the brick mill town became home to MASS MoCA (the Massachusetts

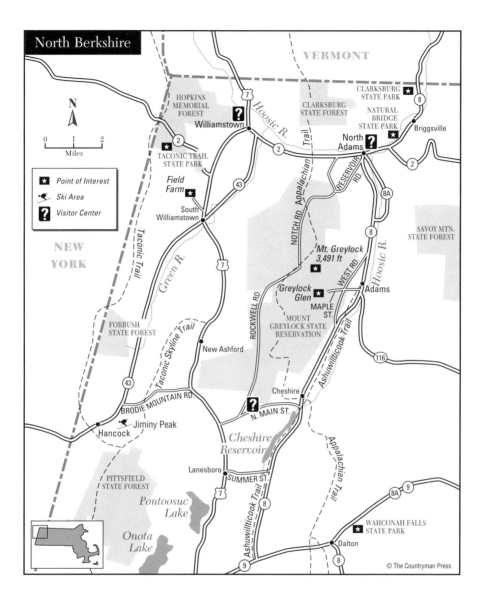

Museum of Contemporary Art). One of the world's largest contemporary art and performance centers, it's sited at the confluence of the north and south branches of the Hoosic River, housed in a vast mill complex originally built to produce and print textiles (old-timers still remember the river turning purple on Thursdays). It was subsequently home for more than 40 years to Sprague Electric Company, employing more than 4,000 people during World War II to produce high-quality electrical components. Sprague closed in 1985, and the museum was conceived—but still took 13 years in the making. MASS MoCA is also the venue for numerous and varied live performances and an outdoor film series. It has sparked a genuine renaissance in this proudly gritty little city, which now offers as many dining choices as Williamstown, plus an upscale inn or two.

North Adams was once part of Adams, now its smaller sister town. In Adams old textile mills remain imposing examples of late-19th-century industrial architecture, and some house discount outlets.

Mount Greylock towers over Adams, visible everywhere. The high plateau above the town, known as Greylock Glen, a high shelf of woods and meadow, has been proposed for a series of aborted developments over the years. The entire mountain is webbed with hiking trails, and the new Ashuwillticook Rail Trail runs south along Cheshire Reservoir (from which the Hoosic River flows north).

Below Cheshire and Lanesboro the landscape opens expansively into a broad valley with Pittsfield at its center. The two branches of the Housatonic River and all roads meet in Pittsfield, Berkshire's only real metropolis and its county seat. As travel writers have politely observed for several decades, Pittsfield is "in transition." The Berkshire Mall, just north of town, has drained business from its Main Street, and its traditional industries are not what they used to be. Still, Park Square, laid out in 1752 at the heart of this proud community, is well worth a stop to visit the lively Berkshire Museum. Increasingly, too, Pittsfield is an inviting place to stay. Hancock Shaker Village, 5 miles west of town, represents the largest collection of Shaker artifacts on any original Shaker site and evokes a sense of the rare and beautiful places (not just things) that Shakers created.

AREA CODE 413.

GUIDANCE Discover the Berkshires Visitor Center (413-743-4500 or 1-866-444-1815), Berkshire Visitors Bureau, 3 Hoosac Street, Adams. Open daily; hours vary seasonally. This new center is attached to Berkshire Visitor Bureau offices.

North Adams. Phone inquiries: **Mayor's Office of Tourism** (413-664-6180; tourist@bcn.net); the office at 6 West Main Street is open year-round, weekdays 9–5, and stocked with brochures. **Western Gateway Heritage State Park** (413-663-6312), sited in the railyard just off Main Street, is accessible from State Street (Route 8 south). It's open year-round, daily 10–5, offers plenty of parking, and doubles as an information center. A seasonal information booth, staffed by volunteers, is on your right as you enter the city on Route 2 (Union Street) from the east at **Windsor Mill;** it's open seasonally 11–4. Local historian Paul W. Marino (413-663-3809; historyman@fiam.net) offers free, seasonal tours of downtown.

Pittsfield Visitors Center (413-395-0105), 121 South Street. Look for this new facility, with parking, just south of the Capitol Theater. Open Monday through Thursday 9–5, Friday 9–8, Saturday 9–5, Sunday 11–3. Also see www.pittsfield-ma.org.

Williamstown Chamber of Commerce (413-458-9077 or 1-800-214-3799; www.williamstownchamber.com) maintains a well-stocked unstaffed information booth at the junction of Routes 2 and 7.

Also see *Guidance* in the "Berkshire County" introduction. Useful web sites: www.berkshires.org; www.masscountryroads.com; www.iBerkshires.com.

or 1-800-292-2782), corner of Columbus Avenue and North Street in downtown
Pittsfield, due to open in 2004, serves local and long-distance buses as well as
Amtrak under one roof.

By bus: From New York City, **Bonanza** (1-800-556-3815) serves Williamstown
via Pittsfield (413-442-4451); **Peter Pan/Trailways** (1-800-343-9999; www.
peterpanbus.com) serves Pittsfield via Lenox, Lee, and Springfield. *From
Albany,* Bonanza and **Greyhound** both offer service to Pittsfield. *From Boston,*
Peter Pan/Trailways serves Pittsfield.

By train: Amtrak (1-800-USA-RAIL) stops in Pittsfield en route from Boston to
Chicago.

By car: From Boston, Route 2 (see "Along the Mohawk Trail") is a half-hour
shorter and far more scenic way to north Berkshire County than the Mass Pike.

GETTING AROUND Williamstown, North Adams, Adams, Cheshire, and Lanesboro are all served by buses of **BRTA,** the **Berkshire Regional Transit
Authority** (413-499-2782 or 1-800-292-BRTA).

MEDICAL EMERGENCY **911** reaches police, fire departments, and ambulances
throughout this area.

Berkshire Medical Center (413-447-2834), 725 North Street, Pittsfield.

North Adams Regional Hospital (413-664-5256), Hospital Avenue.

✳ To See

TOWNS AND CITIES **Adams** (population: 9,213). In McKinley Square at the
center of Adams stands a bronze statue of President William McKinley, arms
outstretched pleadingly as they were when he asked Congress to pass a tariff
protecting American textile manufacturers from foreign competition. The pro-
tective tariff was responsible for Adams's period of greatest prosperity and
directly benefited a local industrialist and longtime friend of McKinley, William
Plunkett, owner of the Berkshire Cotton Manufacturing Company. A grateful
and grieving Plunkett erected the statue after McKinley's assassination in 1901.

Adams was founded by Quakers, and their 1782 meetinghouse still stands on
Friend Street. The town's most famous daughter is Susan B. Anthony
(1820–1906), the daughter of Quakers who became a leading suffragist, instrumental in passing legislation that gave married women legal right over their children, property, and wages. A plaque at the southern end of Main Street
commemorates her as the only woman to have ever graced the face of an American (silver) dollar.

Approaching Adams from the North on Route 8, you pass an unsightly operation
mining calcium carbonate from Mount Greylock—but persevere. At the McKinley Statue turn onto Hoosac Street to find the town's prime outlet and a major
new visitors center. Or head up Maple Street through orchards to Greylock Glen
with its trails and views. Note the new Ashuwillticook Rail Trail running south
through Cheshire.

North Adams (population: 15,038). Few communities in Massachusetts have had a more dramatic death and rebirth than its smallest city. A 1939 guide, *The Berkshire Hills* (American Guide Series), notes that "No city of twenty-five thousand people in New England has a greater variety of retail establishments." Main Street is lined with "mid-Victorian blocks, small drygoods stores, taverns, colorful fruit stands and markets, and ten-cent stores." It adds: "There is a constant hum of noise and a confusion of tongues: French-Canadian, Italian, nasal Yankee. . . . North Adams is nervous with the energy of twentieth century America."

The energy that powered North Adams—the railway, the Arnold and Windsor Print Works and other textile mills, along with a variety of small manufacturing industries—all ebbed with surprising rapidity. Arnold Print Works closed in 1942, and its vast space was filled by Sprague Electric Company, which flourished during World War II and came to dominate the economy, producing circuitry that, among other things, was used to detonate atomic bombs and later helped launch systems for Gemini and moon missions. As noted in this chapter's introduction, Sprague finally closed completely in 1985, but it had atrophied long before and the downtown had already been decimated by "urban renewal." One entire side of Main Street was razed. At the time—and for a decade thereafter—the idea that a contemporary art museum could revive this city full of vacant mills and sagging mill housing seemed scarcely believable. Luckily both MASS MoCA director Joseph Thompson and North Adams mayor John Barrett III believed in it deeply enough to hang on through thick and thin. Aside from the museum itself, the former Sprague complex now houses a growing number of enterprises. Other burgeoning enterprises in the city's former mill buildings range from artists' studios and high-tech firms to a major shiitake mushroom producer.

While North Adams remains funky and rough around the edges, especially off-season, MASS MoCA has made a palpable difference, confirming their pride in

NORTH ADAMS, "CITY OF STEEPLES"

Kim Grant

place for natives and attracting enthusiastic newcomers. Facades along Main and Eagle Streets have been restored and half a dozen quality restaurants have opened along with specialty shops, complementing long-established eateries, bakeries, and stores. Now the first Friday of each month is celebrated with evening gallery receptions, store sales, and music; seasonal guided downtown and cemetery walks are offered on alternate Saturdays; and in the railyard volunteers have opened a North Adams Museum of History and Science, filling three floors of an old coal storage shed with displays about the city's railroad and industrial history.

Much of the old railyard is now the **Western Gateway Heritage State Park,** with sophisticated displays dramatizing construction of the Hoosac Tunnel—the phenomenon that created this brick city in the first place. Because the Hoosac Range, just east of North Adams, is so steep, early locomotives were unable to climb it, which meant a railroad couldn't run directly westward from Boston. Massachusetts's industries were handicapped, and Boston's future as a major port was in doubt until 1875, when—after 25 years of nonstop work, at a cost of nearly 200 lives—a 4.75-mile-long railroad tunnel was finally blasted through the Hoosac Range.

Beyond the narrow downtown, North Adams's streets climb steeply up the hills. At the foot of Main Street, turn at the Blackinton Mansion (now the public library) onto Church Street, lined with turn-of-the-20th-century mansions. Follow it up by the Massachusetts College of Liberal Arts and turn onto Kemp Avenue to find Windsor Lake, the scene of outdoor band concerts on Wednesday evenings in summer. Local musicians perform Thursday nights at the Western Gateway Heritage State Park.

Pittsfield (population: 41,482). Berkshire County's only real city has a proud industrial history that has been dominated for many years by General Electric. GE first opened here in 1907, absorbing the Stanley Electric Manufacturing Company (Berkshire native William Stanley invented the electric transformer and first lit up stores along Great Barrington's Main Street in 1886). This remains headquarters for GE's Plastics Division, which has, in turn, spawned a number of local plastics companies. The industrial area lies primarily east of the downtown—for which Park Square forms a centerpiece at the intersection of four wide streets aptly named North, South, East, and West. It was in Park Square in 1807 that Elkanah Watson introduced the first Merino sheep to New England, marking the beginning of an era in which this particular breed of sheep became a significant part of the landscape (clearing it in the process), along with mills to process their wool. Watson also founded the Berkshire Agricultural Society and in 1811 held one of the country's first agricultural fairs on the square.

In the second half of the 19th century the arrival of the railroad changed Pittsfield, transporting its burgeoning products, principally textiles and paper, and bringing visitors to stay in its hotels and build summer homes. The arrival of General Electric changed it yet again, almost doubling its population in 30 years. For a sense of the city's Gilded Era, walk up quiet, gracious Wendell Avenue (visitors are welcome in the Women's Club of Pittsfield at No. 42) and around the common, noting the Victorian Gothic Athenaeum (now the registry of

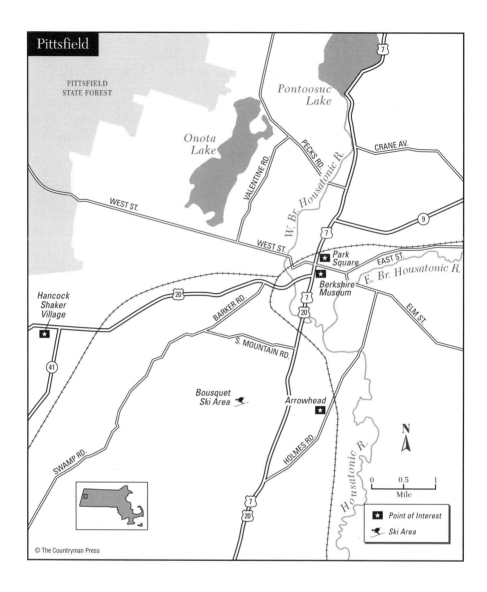

Pittsfield

PITTSFIELD
STATE FOREST

*Pontoosuc
Lake*

*Onota
Lake*

PECKS RD.

VALENTINE RD.

CRANE AV.

WEST ST.

W. Br. Housatonic R.

WEST ST.

7

9

7

Park
Square

EAST ST.

E. Br. Housatonic R.

Berkshire
Museum

20

7

20

Hancock
Shaker
Village

41

BARKER RD.

S. MOUNTAIN RD.

ELM ST.

*Bousquet
Ski Area*

Arrowhead

N

SWAMP RD.

HOLMES RD.

Housatonic R.

0   0.5   1
Mile

7
20

★ Point of Interest
🎿 Ski Area

© The Countryman Press

deeds), the courthouse built of Sheffield marble, and St. Stephen's Church with
its stained-glass windows by Louis Comfort Tiffany. Step around the corner to
the Berkshire Museum with its fine art and many family-friendly exhibits.

Williamstown (population: c. 8,400). From its earliest years Williamstown has
been an orderly, elegantly planned, and education-minded community. It was
founded in 1753 as West Hoosac, and at their first meeting the seven original pro-
prietors passed what would now be called zoning laws. Meadows and uplands were
divided, and settlers were required to clear a minimum of 5 acres of land and
build a house at least 15 by 18 feet—a substantial dwelling by frontier standards.
An exact replica of one of these "regulation" houses, built as a town bicentennial

project using mid-18th-century tools and methods, stands in **Field Park,** a remnant of the original town green. Two years after the settlement was founded, Colonel Ephraim Williams Jr.—who had commanded the local fort and first surveyed the area—wrote a will endowing "a free school forever," provided that the township fell within Massachusetts (New York claimed it) and was renamed Williamstown. Shortly after making his will, Williams was killed in upstate New York fighting the French, but the conditions of his will weren't met for many years.

Because the border between Massachusetts and New York was long disputed, the school, now **Williams College,** couldn't be founded until 1791. It quickly became central to town life, however. In 1815, when finances were shaky and the trustees considered moving the school to a less isolated location, local people pledged enough money to keep it in town. **Williams College** (413-597-3131; www.Williams.edu) presently enrolls some 2,000 students, almost equally divided between men and women and drawn from throughout the United States and more than 40 countries. Tours of the 450-acre campus are available at the admissions office (next to the Adams Memorial Theater). Few other colleges are as entwined with their communities. Be sure to pick up the *Guide to the Campus*, with a map that covers half of town. Buildings of interest to the general public (in addition to the art museum) include **Chapin Library** (413-597-2462) of rare

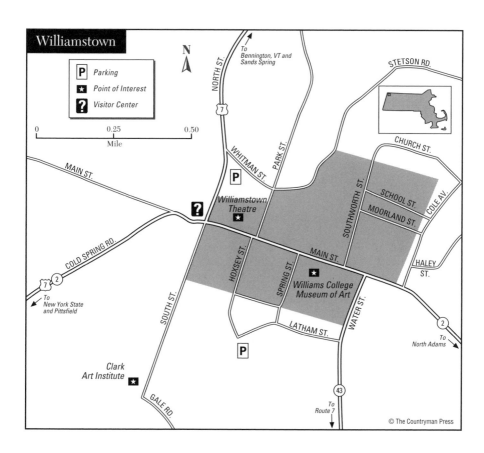

& **STERLING AND FRANCINE CLARK ART INSTITUTE** (413-458-2303; www.clarkart.edu), 225 South Street, Williamstown. Open daily July through Labor Day 10–5; otherwise closed Monday. Free November through May and but otherwise $10 per adult June through October; also free under age 18 and students with ID. Inquire about the combination ticket with MASS MoCA. The increase in price in recent years reflects the quality of special exhibits. The permanent collection rivals those of many city museums. There are medieval works like a 15th-century panel painting by Piero della Francesca and works by such masters as Fragonard, Turner, and Goya. The museum is best known for its French impressionist paintings (Monet, Degas, Pissarro, and more than 30 Renoirs) and for its American period pieces by Winslow Homer, John Singer Sargent, and Frederic Remington. R. S. Clark (1877–1956), grandson to a founding partner in the Singer Sewing Machine Company, settled in Paris and began collecting art in 1912. When he met Francine (1876–1960), she was an actress with the Comedie Française. The couple collected avidly for their own pleasure but considered donating everything to the Metropolitan Muse-

um of Art before determining in 1950 to build a museum to house it in this serene, safe town, far from the threat of nuclear war then felt in New York City. The white-marble building at the center of the present museum was opened in 1955. It has since been substantially expanded, and another major expansion by the Japanese architect Tadao Ando is planned. The Clark Art Institute is set in 140 acres of lawns, mead-ows, and walking trails, spotted with picnic tables and benches. Inquire about concerts and other special programs, including a series of films and lectures.

PIERRE-AUGUSTE RENOIR'S *THE CONCERT* (1880), AT THE STERLING AND FRANCINE CLARK ART INSTITUTE

Sterling and Francine Clark Art Institute

& **WILLIAMS COLLEGE MUSEUM OF ART** (413-597-2429; www.wcma.org), Route 2. Open Tuesday through Sat-urday 10–5, Sunday 1–5. Free. This is one of the finest college art museums in the country, too often overlooked by visitors. It's easily accessible from Spring Street (Williamstown's shopping drag) as well as from Main Street (Route 2).

Kim Grant

MASSACHUSETTS MUSEUM OF CONTEMPORARY ART (MASS MOCA)

The striking building combines a vintage-1846, two-story octagon with a major three-story addition designed by Charles Moore, filled with unconventional spaces. The museum has an outstanding permanent collection of American 19th- and 20th-century works by Eakins, Hassam, Feininger, Rivers, and Hopper, and represents the world's largest collection of works by Charles and Maurice Prendergast. Exhibits change frequently.

✒ ♿ **MASSACHUSETTS MUSEUM OF CONTEMPORARY ART** (MASS MoCA; 413-662-2111; www.massmoca.org), 87 Marshall Street, North Adams. Open daily 11–5, closed Tuesday except in July and August when it's open every day 10–6. $9 per adult, $3 children 6–16. November through May rates for students and seniors drop to $7. Inquire about Kidspace, an interactive area with special exhibits for kids, open varying hours to the public but in summer months usually Thursday through Monday noon–5 and weekends off-season (but call to check). Also inquire about the seasonal combination ticket with the Clark Art Institute. Check the schedule of upcoming programs, which might include weekend films, Saturday-night Dance Parties, and varied special exhibits and events. "MASS MoCA" stands for "Massachusetts Museum of Contemporary Art." So what's it like? It's fun. Exhibits change so constantly that it's pointless to describe what we last saw here, but one thing we notice consistently is that as we wander

EDWARD HOPPER'S *MORNING IN THE CITY* (1994), AT THE WILLIAMS COLLEGE MUSEUM OF ART

from gallery to gallery, our perceptions alter. In contrast to a traditional museum in which you focus on one painting or sculpture after another, here the size of the viewing space itself changes constantly: One moment you are in a small blackened room mesmerized by a computer-composed choreography, and the next you are faced with a gallery as big as a football field, its walls stamped and streamed with myriad shapes and colors. Finally stepping outside, you may see actors filming while in another millyard workers may be installing a stage for the night's performance. The mill's old bell tower tolls the quarter hour in muted tones (the volume of this "sound art" varies with the intensity of the sun) and in front of it upside-down trees, presented by the Clark Art Institute as a welcoming present, appear to thrive. If conventional museums are boxes, MASS MoCA is more of an open platform. The lines between the exterior and interior of the building, between art and urban reality, blur. The 15 galleries fill four large buildings in this 25-building complex connected by the courtyards, viaducts, and elevated walkways that evolved to house Arnold Print Works (1860–1942), one of the world's leading textile producers. Sprague Electric Company occupied the complex from 1942 to 1985, at its height employing 4,137 workers. In 1986, when Williams College Museum of Art director Thomas Krens was searching for a space to display large modern art pieces, North Adams mayor John Barrett III showed him the vacant

Sprague mill buildings. (Krens went on to direct the Solomon R. Guggenheim Museum, which is devoted primarily to modern art.) The ups and downs of the project, shepherded by MASS MoCA's present director Joseph Thompson over the next dozen years, easily fill a book. **Lickety Split,** the museum's café, is open for breakfast (you can come in before the museum opens) and lunch as well as during after arts events; Eleven (see *Dining Out*) is next door. Inquire about guided tours and audio guides.

Christina Tree

UPSIDE-DOWN TREE EXHIBIT AT MASS MOCA

WILLIAMS COLLEGE IN
WILLIAMSTOWN

Kim Grant

books in Stetson Hall, which sits behind Thompson Memorial Chapel, across Main Street from the Museum of Art. It's worth visiting to see the college's priceless collection of documents from the American Revolution. Original copies of the Declaration of Independence, the Articles of Confederation, two early versions of the Bill of Rights, and a draft of the Constitution are exhibited. Closed Saturday and Sunday. **Hopkins Observatory** (413-597-2188), dedicated in 1838, is one of the first observatories in the country. Free shows are offered here in the Milham Planetarium most Fridays; since space is limited, make reservations.

The town has been a tourist destination since the mid–19th century. As early as the 1830s, local mineral springs began attracting visitors, and by the Civil War, Williamstown was an established resort with some large hotels and palatial summer homes. The old resort hotels are long gone, but there are many appealing places to stay. Bucolic South Williamstown still has a number of gentlemen's farms, some quite grand. **Sterling and Francine Clark Art Institute** alone is worth a trip to Williamstown, and its world-class collection is complemented by that of the first-rate **Williams College Museum of Art.**

The **Williamstown Theatre Festival** is one of the best of its kind in the country. Also check out the **Williamstown House of Local History** in the Elizabeth S. Botsford Memorial Library (413-458-2160), 1095 Main Street (open Monday through Friday 10–12, Monday and Wednesday until 1, or by appointment: nancywb947@aol.com). Built in 1815 as a residence for the college treasurer, this homey library building retains many original features, including a curved staircase and graceful fireplace mantels. The House of Local History wing contains an extensive and eclectic collection that includes spinning wheels, Civil War uniforms, old ice skates, photos, and much more.

All in all, Williamstown, a jewel of a village set within a circle of mountains, deserves more than a quick stop.

MUSEUMS Contemporary Artists Center (413-663-9555; www.thecac.org), Historic Beaver Mill, 189 Beaver Street (Route 8 north), North Adams. This building near the entrance to the Natural Bridge State Park is a nonprofit artists' studio facility with extensive floor-level galleries theoretically open May through

October, Wednesday through Saturday 11–5, Sunday noon–5. Check the web site or call for current exhibits.

& **Dark Ride Project** (413-664-9550), Historic Beaver Mill (Route 8 north), North Adams. Open in summer, Wednesday through Sunday noon–5, weekends in fall noon–5. $10. Call first to make sure it's running. The creation of multimedia sculptor-artist Eric Rudd, this is a 10-minute ride on the "sensory integrator" during which hooded passengers view abstract imagery. After the ride they enter a cavernous "Space Sculpture garden."

A Chapel for Humanity (413-664-9550), 82 Summer Street, Post Office Square, North Adams. Donation suggested. Open in summer Wednesday through Sunday noon–5, fall weekends noon–5. A former 1890s church now houses an installaton of 150 life-sized figures and more than 50 ceiling panels by Eric Rudd.

✔ **Berkshire Museum** (413-443-7171; www.berkshiremuseum.org), 39 South Main Street (Route 7, just south of Park Square), Pittsfield. Open Monday through Saturday 10–5, Sunday noon–5; $7.50 adults, $6 seniors and students, $4.50 age 5–18. An example of what a regional museum should be. Founded in 1903 by Dalton philanthropist Zenas Crane, its no less than 18 galleries display both permanent and changing exhibits. There are frequent films, performances, lectures, and concerts in the **Little Cinema,** a 300-seat theater. The permanent collection includes American and European paintings, 15th- to 18th-century European works, and ancient artifacts, including a 2,000-year-old mummy. There are also interactive exhibits based on toys by Alexander Calder, and children love the "Dino Dig" in the Gallery of Dinosaurs; the natural history collection of shells, gemstones, and fossils; and the aquarium featuring fish from throughout the world, as well as reptiles, spiders, local animals, and birds.

✔ **Western Gateway Heritage State Park,** Furnace Street, North Adams. This is the city's rehabbed former railyard, with ample parking, a block south (off Route 8) from the corner of downtown Main and Marshall Streets. There are now two museums here. The big draw is the **Western Gateway Heritage State Park museum** (413-663-6312), open year-round, daily 10–5. Housed in a former railroad freight shed, its sophisticated displays tells the epic story of the construction of the 4.75-mile-long Hoosac Tunnel, one of 19th-century America's greatest engineering feats. The tunnel took 25 years to build, from 1850 to 1875, claimed nearly 200 lives, pioneered use of the explosive nitroglycerine, and cost $20 million—a vast sum for the time. An audiovisual presentation takes visitors back in time with the sounds of dripping water, pickaxes striking stone, nitroglycerine explosions, and a political debate about the

WESTERN GATEWAY HERITAGE STATE PARK

©DCR/John Crispin

✎ **HANCOCK SHAKER VILLAGE** (413-443-0188; www.hancockshaker-village.org), 5 miles west of Pittsfield on Route 20, at its junction with Route 41; use the Mass Pike West Stockbridge exit (take Route 41 north to Route 20 west). Open daily, year-round. Winter hours are 10–3 until Memorial Day weekend, then 9:30–5 through Columbus Day weekend. Closed Thanksgiving, Christmas, and New Year's Day. Admission: $15 adults in summer, $12 late October until the Friday before Memorial Day weekend when tours are all guided, free year-round for those under 18. Inquire about frequent special events.

Founded in 1783, this "City of Peace" was the third of what would eventually number 19 Shaker communities stretching from Maine to Kentucky (see *Shakers* in *What's Where*). In the mid–19th century it numbered some 250 brethren divided among six "families," farming 3,000 acres. It survived until 1959.

In 1961 the village's buildings were about to be sold to a neighboring racetrack when a group of Pittsfield residents rallied and bought the entire community—including 1,000 acres—from its last Shaker sisters. Since then it has evolved into a 20-building museum housing the largest collection of Shaker artifacts on any original Shaker site. The buildings have been restored, including the much-copied and -photographed round stone barn, and the five-story Brick Dwelling House, built in 1830 to house 100 Shaker brethren and sisters.

A scattering of tidy buildings surrounded by its own orchards and meadows, the village looks like some primitive painter's vision of the heavenly king-

HANCOCK SHAKER VILLAGE

CLOAK ROOM IN THE 1830 BRICK DWELLING

dom. The guides, craftsmen, and furnishings all tell about the dancing monks and nuns who turned farming, craftsmanship, and invention into visible prayers. Note the frequent special events staged throughout the year. During fall and on holiday weekends Shaker dinners are served in the brick building (call for reservations). The visitors center includes a Center for Shaker Studies and a gallery displaying the village's spirit drawing collection as well as an orientation theater, a changing

exhibit gallery, and a gift shop selling yarn, herbs, and baked goods made on the premises. It also includes a café with a children's menu. Families should take care not to miss the hands-on Discovery Room in the 1910 barn: Visitors can weave and spin, try on Shaker-style clothes, milk MaryJane (a life-sized replica cow), sample 19th-century toys and games, and check out the beehive and newly hatched chickens. Inquire about the **Shaker Trail** leading to the adjacent **Pittsfield State Forest** (see *Green Space*), traveling past the sites of old Shaker dwellings and religious ceremonies. During summer months inquire about the day's schedule of thematic tours and crafts demonstrations.

OVAL BOX MAKING DEMONSTRATION

merits of the massive project. Displays also depict other aspects of North Adams's history and include a miniature railroad with a precise diorama of the city in its heyday. There are changing arts and crafts exhibits, too. Other buildings in the "Park" contain the Freight Yard Pub, shops, and the new, volunteer-operated **North Adams Museum of History and Science** (413-664-4700). Open April through December, Thursday through Saturday 10–4; off-season, Sunday 1–4. Free. This fascinating museum fills three floors of a former coal storage shed with exhibits on North Adams history and industry. Hands-on history and science discovery rooms are geared to children, and working model trains will delight rail buffs. Donations requested.

Crane Museum of Papermaking (413-684-6481; www.crane.com), off East Housatonic Street (Routes 8/90), 30 South Street, Dalton. Open June through mid-October, weekdays 2–5. Free and worth a stop. Housed in the rag room of the **Old Stone Mill** (1846) in a garden by the Housatonic, the displays and a video tell the story of papermaking from rags and include a fascinating variety of paper money. Crane Paper is the sole supplier of "money paper" to the U.S. Mint; the company has been in the family for five generations.

THE ARTS Williamstown Theatre Festival (413-597-34399; www.WTFestival.org), P.O. Box 517, Williamstown. Since 1955 this festival has offered some of the best theater in the Northeast from the last week of June through August. Both new and classic plays are presented, featuring top actors and actresses. Most performances (some 200 each July and August) are on the main stage of the 521-seat **Adams Memorial Theatre,** but other venues are also used.

Berkshire Opera Company (413-442-9955; www.berkshireopera.org). The year 2004 marks the 20th anniversary of the company and the 15th of summer performances under the artistic direction of Joel Revzen. Venues for productions include the Mahaiwe Performing Arts Center in Great Barrington, the Koussevitzky Arts Center at Berkshire Community College in Pittsfield, Chapin Hall at Williams College in Williamstown, and Lee High School in Lee.

Albany-Berkshire Ballet (413-445-5382; www.berkshireballet.org), 51 North Street, Pittsfield. Performances are staged periodically year-round at the Berkshire Community College Koussevitzky Arts Center and other venues, reviewed respectfully in New York and Boston.

South Mountain Concerts (413-442-2106), Routes 7/20, 2 miles south of downtown Pittsfield. A series of five Sunday-afternoon concerts September to early October, featuring internationally known chamber ensembles, performed in an acoustically fine music hall. Top performers and serious patrons characterize the series, and performances frequently sell out.

Massachusetts Museum of Contemporary Art (MASS MoCA; 413-662-2111; www.massmoca.org), 87 Marshall Street, North Adams. See *Museums.* MASS MoCA sponsors a year-round series of live concerts and other performances.

Concerts at Tannery Pond (1-888-820-1696), P.O. Box 446, New Lebanon, NY 12125. The setting for these outdoor chamber music concerts, staged on selective Saturday evenings late May through mid-October, is beautiful: the

ERMAN MELVILLE (1819–91) spent 13 of his happiest, most productive years at Arrowhead, a farm on the southern edge of Pittsfield that's now headquarters for the Berkshire County Historical Society. Forced to work after his father's bankruptcy and death, Melville held a number of jobs, joined the merchant marines, and—at age 22—set sail on the whaler *Acushnet.* He jumped ship in the Marquesas Islands and spent time in Hawaii before returning to Boston, where he wrote *Typee,* followed by several more South Seas–based novels. Established as a writer, he married and in 1850 brought his wife, Lizzie, and baby son Malcolm to spend the summer at his uncle's fine house (now the Pittsfield Country Club) on Route 7.

It was on a famous rainy picnic atop Monument Mountain that he met Nathaniel Hawthorne (then living at Tanglewood in Lenox). The two young writers bonded instantly, and Melville was influenced by Hawthorne to become a year-round Berkshire resident. He bought a farm just up the road from his uncle, one commanding the same splendid view of Mount Greylock—which is said to have inspired his grandly conceived story of the great white whale and the mad sea captain. Melville penned *Moby-Dick* in a study overlooking the mountain. In all he wrote four novels, a collection of short stories, and 10 magazine pieces as well as beginning a book of poetry in this wonderfully rambling 18th-century house with its central hearth (described in the short story "I and My Chimney"). Unlike his far more famous neighbor, Oliver Wendell Holmes, Melville seems to have kept somewhat aloof, preferring to farm and write rather than to party.

Arrowhead, which is furnished with many original pieces, evokes Melville the author and father—who had difficulty supporting his wife and four children despite his prodigious literary output. Melville eventually sold the farm to his brother and moved to New York, where he worked in the Customs House for more than 20 years, earning $4 per hour and finding time to write only poetry and, eventually, *Billy Budd,* published in 1924, 33 years after his death.

Arrowhead (413-442-1793; www.mobydick.org), 789 Holmes Road (off Routes 7/20), Pittsfield, is open daily Memorial Day through October, tours on the hour 10–4; otherwise by appointment. $8 adults, $4 students, $2 children. A 20-minute film on Berkshire cultural history is shown. The 40-acre grounds include a walking trail.

Note: Melville buffs should also find the **Herman Melville Memorial Room** in the **Berkshire Athenaeum** (413-499-9486), Pittsfield's public library at 1 Wendell Avenue on Park Square. It contains every book about as well as by the author and such artifacts as the desk on which he wrote *Billy Budd.* **Canoe Meadows,** the former property of Oliver Wendell Homes (see *Birding*), is just up Holmes Road.

861 PHOTO PORTRAIT OF HERMAN MELVILLE

pond on the grounds of the former Mount Lebanon Shaker Village, now the Darrow School, a coed boarding school with a campus that occupies and sensitively enhances the former Shaker Village, just over the New York line from Hancock and off Route 20.

Main Street Stage (413-663-3240; www.mainstreetstage.com), 57 Main Street, North Adams. Year-round performances are given in a storefront theater.

SCENIC DRIVES **Mohawk Trail.** Even if you don't drive to the northern Berkshires via Route 2, better known as the Mohawk Trail (see "Along the Mohawk Trail"), be sure to drive from North Adams up along Route 2 to the Western Summit and park at the Wigwam Gift Shop to take in "the three-state view" before plunging back down the well-named Hairpin Turn as it zigs and zags its way into North Adams.

Williamstown to Pittsfield. Along Route 7 south through South Williamstown, the views are of high meadows and mountains. Turn at the Five Corners Store onto Route 43 and follow it through the steep, mostly wooded Jericho Valley to the village of Hancock; continue on into New York State and turn south onto Route 22. At the high school in New Lebanon make a sharp left east onto Route 20 and continue over Lebanon Mountain. Stop by **Hancock Shaker Village** (see *Museums*), then continue east to Pittsfield.

The Notch Road up Mount Greylock from Route 2 in North Adams is one of the most dramatic roads in New England. Usually traffic-free, it spirals up and up, 9 miles from Route 2 until, as you near the summit, single trees seem outlined against endless sky. Drive up early in the morning or at sunset. You can eat and sleep at the top (see Bascom Lodge under *Green Space*), or at least wander off down a trail long enough to stretch your legs.

Greylock Glen, Adams. Route 8 is the main north–south drag through Adams, but find your way up to parallel West Road and then Gould Road. This quiet old road climbs up and up to the glorious high meadow that's been the object of a series of development schemes, including a ski area, a gambling casino, then a high-altitude cross-country resort. At present, however, Gould Street ends at the Gould farmhouse, and while the area is webbed with hiking and biking trails, few are marked. A Department of Conservation and Recreation (DCR) pavilion by a small pond (good for a dip) is the site of periodic educational programs. It's a magical spot.

✳ To Do

BIKING **Ashuwillticook Rail Trail** (www.berkshirebikepath.org) is an 11-mile bike path with the first 5 miles, from Berkshire Mall Road in Lanesboro to Cheshire, now paved. The remaining 6 miles exist as a path, and plans call for paving it. The currently completed portion is unusually scenic, paralleling Route 8 but also following the shores of Berkshire Pond and Cheshire Reservoir for several miles. It replaces tracks first laid in 1845 and used until 1990. Rental bikes are available at **Berkshire Outfitters** (413-743-5900; www.Berkshireoutfitters.com) on Route 8 south of Adams.

The Mountain Goat (413-458-8445; www.themountaingoat.com), 130 Water Street in Williamstown, is an excellent source of biking information in the Williamstown area. Recommended: Route 43 along the Green River. **Plaines Bike & Ski** (413-499-0294; www.plaines.com), 55 West Housatonic Street (Route 20) in Pittsfield, rents bikes.

Jiminy Peak (413-738-5500; www.jiminypeak.com) rents mountain bikes in summer, along with use of lifts and 14 trails, some singletrack and some downhill cruises. Helmets are required. An all-day trail and lift access pass is $20 (bikes and helmets not included).

Berkshire Cycling Association (www.berkshirecycling.org), based in Pittsfield, schedules frequent rides.

Rubel Western Massachusetts Bicycle and Road Map (Rubel Bike Maps) is highly recommended for its in-depth coverage of the area. At this writing an excellent, free *Berkshire Bike Touring* map/guide, based on Rubel, is available from the regional information sources listed under *Guidance*. *Bike Rides in the Berkshire Hills* by Lewis C. Cuyler (Berkshire House Publishers) is a tried-and-true guide to local cycling, available at local book and sports stores.

BIRDING Canoe Meadows Wildlife Sanctuary, Holmes Road off Route 7, south of Pittsfield. This 290-acre Massachusetts Audubon sanctuary offers a mix of wetlands and croplands with 5 miles of trails. A great place to jog. No restrooms.

Dorothy Frances Rice Wildlife Refuge in Peru, on South Road off Route 143 from the town center. Three hundred acres, walking trails, and self-guiding trails owned by the New England Forestry Foundation.

CAMPING

State forests and parks

The Massachusetts Department of Conservation and Recreation (DCR) publishes a handy map and guide and maintains a visitor-friendly regional office on Route 7 south of Pittsfield (413-442-8928; www.massparks.org). For reservations, phone 1-877-422-6762. Campsites are sited in **Clarksburg State Park** (50 campsites near Mauserts Pond; flush toilets and showers but no hookups), in the **Mount Greylock State Reservation** (34 wooded campsites, 5 group campsites, 5 backpacker shelters; no flush toilets, showers, or hookups), and in **Pittsfield State Forest** (13 rustic campsites on Berry Pond at the top of Berry Mountain, 18 at the Parker Brook campground at the mountain's base; flush and nonflush toilets, no

ASHUWILLTICOOK RAIL TRAIL

A. Blake Gardner/Berkshire Visitors Bureau

showers or hookups). See *Green Space* for details about these preserves; also see **Savoy Mountain State Forest** in "Along the Mohawk Trail."

Historic Valley Park Campground at Windsor Lake in North Adams (413-662-3198), 10 Main Street, North Adams, open May 15 through October 15, a city-operated facility on a quiet lake, minutes from downtown North Adams and Route 2, offers 100 campsites ranging from water and electric hookup sites to "wilderness," tent-only sites; some wilderness (walk-in) tent sites and some lakeside. Even in August there are usually vacancies midweek. No motorcycles permitted.

For other private campgrounds, contact the **Massachusetts Association of Campground Owners** (781-544-3475; www.campmass.com).

CANOEING AND KAYAKING The **Hoosic River** flows north from Cheshire Lake, offering some good kayaking and canoeing along the way. Check in with **Berkshire Outfitters** (413-743-5900; www.berkshireoutfitter.com), Route 8 south of Adams, for canoe and kayak rentals as well as sales and guidance (closed Monday).

Canoes and boats can also be rented at **Windsor Lake** (413-662-3198) in North Adams.

Cheshire Reservoir (also known as Hoosac Lake) on Route 8 in Cheshire offers a good launch area, as does **Richmond Pond,** Swamp Road in Richmond. **Berry Pond** in **Pittsfield State Forest** (see *Green Space*), one of the highest ponds in the state, is also accessible for kayaks and canoes.

Berkshire Rowing and Sculling Association (413-496-7769; www.berkshire-sculling.com), Pittsfield. Lew Cuyler rents and offers instruction in an unusually lightweight and stable scull for use on Onota Lake.

On Pontoosuc Lake, Route 7 in Pittsfield, **Wild'N'West Snow & Water** (413-445-5211) offers a variety of boat rentals. On neighboring **Onota Lake, Onota Boat Livery** (413-442-1724) rents motor and pontoon boats as well as sailboats, kayaks, and canoes.

FISHING Licenses for fishing (currently $11.50 age 15–17, otherwise $12.50 for a resident and $23.50 for a nonresident for 3 days) are required for everyone age 15 or over. They are available at local sporting stores and by contacting the Division of Fisheries and Wildlife (413-447-9789), 400 Hubbard Avenue, Pittsfield. Log onto www.state.ma.us/dfwele or www.masswildlife.org. The **Green River** is a famous trout stream. Anglers should also check out **Cheshire Reservoir** in Cheshire, **Mauserts Pond** in Clarksburg, **Windsor Lake** in North Adams (where you can rent a boat), **Onota** and **Pontoosuc Lakes** in Pittsfield, and **Richmond Pond** in Richmond. **Points North Outfitters** (413-743-4030), 111 Forest Park, Adams, sells fly-fishing gear, runs fly-fishing schools, and offers guided trips on the Deerfield River. Also see **Savoy Mountain State Park** in "Berkshire Hilltowns"; it's accessible from Route 2 just east of North Adams.

FOR FAMILIES *♂* **The Pittsfield Astros** (413-499-6387; www.pittsfield-astros.com) play in Wahconah Park, 105 Waconah Street, Pittsfield. Mid-June through mid-September this professional minor team (Class A) plays more than three dozen home games in their classic ballpark. The ticket price is right and it's serious baseball, the way baseball used to be.

🖉 **Alpine Slide at Jiminy Peak** (413-738-5500; www.jimminypeak.com), Corey Road (between Route 7 and Route 43), Hancock. Open daily Memorial Day through Labor Day, weekends in May and September, 10:30 AM–9 PM. An Alpine Slide offers a 5-minute ride down, accessible via a 15-minute chairlift ride up the mountain. Miniature golf, trout fishing, a rock climbing wall, and tennis program are also part of the summer scene here.

PONTOOSUC LAKE OFFERS EXCELLENT BOATING AND FISHING

Kim Grant

🖉 **Play Bousquet** (413-442-8316; www.bousquets.com), Dan Fox Drive, Pittsfield. Open Memorial Day through Columbus Day. This small ski area is a summer family fun park with water slides and activity pool, a miniature golf and a driving range, a go-cart track, a climbing wall, and chairlift rides.

🖉 **Family Fun Center** (413-499-0051), 10 Williamstown Road (Route 7), Lanesboro. Go-carts, bumper boats, miniature batting cages, and a snack bar.

🖉 **Buster's Entertainment Center** (413-499-7500; www.bustersforfun.com), 457 Dalton Avenue, Pittsfield. More than 100 games for kids of all ages.

Also see *Museums, Farms,* and *Special Events.*

GOLF **Bas-Ridge Golf Course** (413-655-2605), 151 Plunkett Avenue (off Route 8), Hinsdale. 18 holes, challenging but user-friendly.

North Adams Country Club (413-663-7887), River Road, Clarksburg. Nine holes.

Pontoosuc Lake Country Club (413-4217), Kirkwood Drive, Pittsfield. 18 holes, reasonable rates, snacks, beverages.

Skyline Country Club (413-445-5584), Route 7, Lanesboro. 18 holes. Dining area with pub menu.

Taconic Golf Club (413-458-3997), Meachem Street, Williamstown. Open daily mid-April to mid-November but only Tuesday through Friday to the public.

Waubeeka Springs Golf Links (413-458-8355), Route 7, South Williamstown. Open daily April to mid-November.

Wahconah Country Club (413-684-1333), Orchard Road in Dalton. 18 holes, after 2 PM on weekends.

132

HIKING AND WALKING Mount

Greylock. The 60 miles of trails in the Mount Greylock Reservation include more than 11 miles of the Appalachian Trail. The (literally) top hike in North Berkshire is from the summit of Mount Greylock (accessible by road; see *Green Space*), which has been newly landscaped with trailheads clearly marked and quotes from literary and historic figures who walked this way inscribed on "interpretive stones" scattered along the trails. Wear sensible shoes and clothing and enjoy the views. *Note:* Food and lodging are available at Bascom Lodge at the summit.

Kim Grant

TRAILS IN THE MOUNT GREYLOCK RESERVATION

Hopkins Memorial Forest (413-597-2346), Northwest Hill Road, Williamstown, is a 2,050-acre preserve owned by Williams College with a network of hiking (and, in winter, cross-country skiing) and nature trails. The **Hopkins Farm Museum** and a botanical garden are also here.

Field Farm (413-458-3135; www.thetrustees.org), Sloan Road, South Williamstown. Foot trails (more than 3 miles) wander through meadows, cropland, marsh, and forest with spectacular views of Mount Greylock to the east. Waterfowl frequent the pond, and the lime-rich soil nurtures an abundance of wildflowers. There are two buildings on the property, an outstanding 1950s home (see the Field Farm Guest House in *Lodging*) and "The Folly," a small house designed by noted architect Ulrich Franzen and open to the public by appointment. From the intersection of Routes 43 and 7, take Route 43 west and then make an immediate right onto Sloan Road; the reservation is 1 mile down the road. This is also a favorite local cross-country skiing venue.

A GREAT SPOT FOR PICNICKING AT THE TOP OF MOUNT GREYLOCK

Christina Tree

Taconic Crest Trail. The 35-mile ridgeline trail along the western rim of Berkshire County is accessible from Hopkins Memorial Forest, from Field Farm, and several other trailheads in North Berkshire, but it should not be attempted without a trail map. Serious hikers should pick up a copy of the *North Berkshire Outdoor Guide* published by the Williams

Outing Club and available at the Mountain Goat (see *Bicycling*). *Nature Walks in the Berkshire Hills* by Charles W. G. Smith (AMC) and *Hikes & Walks in the Berkshire Hills* by Lauren Stevens (Berkshire House) are both very useful.

Also see *Green Space*.

HORSEBACK RIDING DeMayo's Bonnie Lea Farm (413-458-3149), Route 7, Williamstown. Guided cross-country trail rides for riders over 13 and by appointment only.

SWIMMING ✔ Sands Spring Pool and Spa (413-458-5202), Sands Spring Road (off Route 7, north of Williamstown; turn at the Cozy Corner Motel and Restaurant). Open May through September, 11–7. This attractive 50-by-75-foot pool is fed year-round by mineral springs that were well known to the Native Americans for centuries. It's surrounded by lawn on which patrons spread their towels; there are picnic tables and some lawn sports. Billed as the oldest spa in the United States, it was formally established in 1813 and in 1842 became the centerpiece for a resort hotel. The century-old pavilion survives, and includes a snack bar, changing rooms, and whirlpool. The pool is sparkling clean, 74 degrees, and genuinely exhilarating. There's a separate wading pool for preswimmers, and a sauna. Inquire about fitness classes and swim lessons.

Windsor Lake (413-662-3198), off Kemp Avenue, North Adams. This pleasant city-run beach is set in a 180-acre preserve and seems miles from the mills that are just blocks away. There's a pavilion, lifeguards, and, just off the lake, 100 campsites (see *Camping*). Nonresidents pay a nominal fee per car.

Margaret Lindley Park (Route 2 and Route 7), Williamstown, is a well-kept town pool with changing rooms and picnic tables; daily charge for nonresidents. Open summer and school vacation, daily 11–7.

See also **Clarksburg State Park** and **Pittsfield State Park** under *Green Space*, and **North Pond** in **Savoy Mountain State Park** under "Berkshire Hilltowns."

SANDS SPRING POOL AND SPA, WILLIAMSTOWN

Christina Tree

TENNIS There is a free town court off Main Street, across from the **Maple Terrace Motel,** Williamstown. **Williams College** (413-597-3131) maintains 12 clay and 12 hard-topped tennis courts (fee and reservations). **Berkshire West Athletic Club** (413-499-4600), Dan Fox Drive, Pittsfield, has four outdoor and five indoor courts. **Ponterril/YMCA** (413-499-0687), Route 7, Pontoosuc Lake, Pittsfield, offers six clay courts; fee for nonmembers.

✳ Winter Sports

DOWNHILL SKIING *Note:* Jiminy Peak and Brodie Mountain are under the same ownership and just 3.2 miles apart. Inquire about reciprocal tickets.

⚲ **Jiminy Peak** (413-738-5500 or 1-888-4-JIMINY; www.jiminypeak.com), Corey Road, Hancock, open mid-November to mid-April. Set high in the Jericho Valley, a narrow corridor that runs east–west between Route 43 and Route 7. Jiminy Peak is a self-contained four-season resort—the largest ski resort in southern New England—with rental two- to four-bedroom condos and a 105-suite inn (see *Lodging*); Founder's Grill, a gracious restaurant; and new Hendricks Lodge on the summit. For the 2003–04 season Jiminy Peak's Village Center was completed, featuring a Children's Center and a Welcome Center. *Vertical drop:* 1,200 feet. *Terrain:* 40 slopes and trails. *Lifts:* 1 six-passenger, 2 quads, 3 triples, 2 double chairs, 1 Mighty-Mite (a carpetlift). *Snowmaking:* 95 percent of area. *Facilities:* The new Children's Center accommodates up to 350 SKIwee and Explorer program participants with their own rental shop and cafeteria; it also offers a playroom for children not skiing. *Rates:* $52 adults, $46 teens, $35 seniors on weekends; $39/30 during the week; less for 4 hours and younger kids. Lodging-skiing packages. *Note:* Condo-style accommodations have increased substantially for the 2003–04 season.

⚲ **Bousquet** (413-442-8316; www.bousquets.com), Pittsfield. Marked from Routes 7/20 south of town. The Berkshires' oldest ski area, founded in 1932, and the one that pioneered both the ski train and night skiing. Noted for friendly slopes ideal for beginning and intermediate skiers. Two surface lifts, one rope tow, snow tubing. Open daily in winter, also nightly except Sunday. *Vertical drop:* 750 feet. *Terrain:* 21 trails. *Rates:* $25 skiing, $15 tubing; night: $15 skiing, no tubing.

JIMINY PEAK

Jiminy Peak

⚲ **Brodie Mountain Ski Area** (413-443-4752; www.skibrodie.com), Route 7, New Ashford.

CROSS-COUNTRY SKIING Brodie Mountain Ski Area (413-443-4752), Route 7, New Ashford, maintains roughly 16 miles of trails with a good deal of variety. Wide, tracked trails are lit at night (used by the Williams College Ski Team), and less formal trails run through pastures and up into the wooded **Mount Greylock State Reservation.** Rentals are available here and also in Williamstown at the **Mountain Goat** (413-458-8445) and **Goff's Sports** (413-458-3605). Cross-country skiers are also welcome on the **Taconic Golf Course,** in Hopkins Memorial Forest, and on the **Stone Hill** trails. Also see *Green Space*.

SNOWMOBILING Snowmobiling is permitted in many local state parks. Check with the Pittsfield office of the DCR (see below). Guided snowmobile tours are offered by Wild'N'Wet Snow & Water, Inc. (413-445-5211; caseycare@peo-plepc.com).

SNOW TUBING Snow tubing is featured at Brodie Mountain (413-443-4752).

✳ Green Space

STATE PARKS AND FORESTS *Note:* The Massachusetts Department of Conservation and Recreation (DCR) publishes a handy map and guide and maintains a visitor-friendly regional office on Route 7 south of Pittsfield (413-442-8928; www.massparks.org).

Natural Bridge State Park (413-663-6312), Route 8, North Adams. The centerpiece of this 49-acre park is an unusual natural formation, a white-marble bridge spanning a steep gorge that's attracted tourists since the 1830s, when Nathaniel Hawthorne compared the stream churning through its depths to "a heart that has been rent asunder by a torrent." There are picnic tables, nature trails, and restrooms; in summer a park interpreter is on hand to explain the geological forces that created the bridge. It's also a popular local fishing spot.

Clarksburg State Park and **Clarksburg State Forest** (413-664-8345), 1199 Middle Road, Clarksburg. Off Route 8 north from Route 2. Together, the park and forest cover 3,250 wooded acres that are particularly beautiful in foliage season. The park's **Mauserts Pond** has a day-use area with swimming, picnic facilities, and a pavilion. There is a scenic nature trail around the pond and 50 campsites nearby (nominal fee). (In "West County," also see **Savoy Mountain State Forest,** with its beautiful **Tannery Falls,** swimming in North Pond, and camping at South Pond, all not far from Adams.)

&. **Pittsfield State Forest** (413-442-8992) totals 9,695 acres. From the corner of Route 20 and Route 7 in Pittsfield, drive west on West Street, north on Churchill Street, and west on Cascade to the entrance. A 5-mile circular paved road follows Lulu Brook to high, scenic **Berry Pond,** good for boating (no motors); swimming, however, is in smaller **Lulu Pond.** A pavilion that can be rented by groups in summer serves as a warming hut in winter. **Tranquillity Trail,** a paved, three-quarter-mile loop through spruce woods, has been designed for wheelchair access. There are taped descriptions of flora and fauna. In June the forest harbors 40 acres of azaleas. **Balance Rock**—a 165-ton boulder poised on another rock—is accessible via Balance Rock Road from Route 7 in Lanesboro.

Wahconah Falls State Park (413-442-8992), off Route 9 in Dalton, 3 miles east of the town center. A 2-minute walk brings you from the parking area down

Mount Greylock State Reservation (413-499-4262). Open from sunrise until half an hour before sunset year-round—but the road, subject to weather conditions, is open only May through October. Snowmobiling permitted.

In 1898, 8,000 acres on Mount Greylock was the first property acquired by the state's forest and park department. The reservation now numbers 12,500 acres with 60 miles of trails. The drive to the top is itself an adventure, winding and dramatic, literally the top of any sight to see in North Berkshire. On the early-June day we last drove it, we began in summer, with fully leafed-out trees, and drove back up into spring, with buds, blossoms, and a sharp drop in temperature.

The 3,491-foot summit has been recently landscaped with a topographic diorama added. The **Summit Veterans Memorial Tower** is now (theoretically) open daily mid-May through mid-October, but it's frequently closed Wednesday. You can climb the stairs inside this 92-foot-high granite tower built in 1933 as a war memorial. On a clear day, five states can be seen from both the top and bottom of the tower. The Appalachian Trail crosses the summit, and several other trails beckon. Note the Thunderbolt Ski Shelter, which has been restored. It was built in the 1930s at the top of a ski trail by the Civilian Conservation Corps (CCC), which also built the handsome, fieldstone **Bascom**

MOUNT GREYLOCK IN WINTER

Berkshire Visitors Bureau

Lodge (413-743-0591; Mount Greylock Reservation, Lanesboro 01237) here at the summit. It's open mid-May through late October, serving snacks and light meals as well as full meals and lodging by reservation. Now operated by Nature's Classroom (www.naturesclassroom.org), it offers a pleasant sitting room and accommodates guests in four double-occupancy rooms, two family rooms, and two bunk rooms, each sleeping nine. All baths are shared, but there are individual shower closets. Sheets, blankets, and towels are provided. The entire lodge can be rented, and it's a great place for weddings. A shop sells trail snacks, maps, and guides, and there is a snack bar with a gourmet view.

Note the new "interpretive stones" scattered along trails near the summit recalling the experiences here of notables who have come this way in the past. Our favorite remains the description by Henry David Thoreau, who spent a July night up here in 1844 when only a "rude

Kim Grant

SUMMIT VETERANS MEMORIAL TOWER AT THE SUMMIT OF MOUNT GREYLOCK

observatory," built by Williams College students, stood on the summit. In *A Week on the Concord and Merrimack Rivers,* Thoreau describes the way he built a fire and "encased" himself in boards to keep warm. At dawn he found himself above the clouds, which he described as: "floating on this fragment of the wreck of the world, on my carved plank, in a cloud land." Imagine the novelty of sitting above the clouds before the era of airplane windows, high-rise buildings, or even the summit hotels built after the Civil War atop New England's highest mountains. All these are, incidentally, gone, leaving Bascom Lodge as the region's only mountaintop lodging.

There are two main approaches to the 3,491-foot-high summit—one from Lanesboro and the other from North Adams—neither of them well marked.

Driving north on Route 7 from Pittsfield, look for the small brown MOUNT GREY-LOCK RESERVATION sign in Lanesboro. If you pass "Vacation Village," you've gone too far. Turn up North Main Street, which becomes Rockwell Road. Stop in at the **Mount Greylock Visitors Center** (413-499-4262; open mid-May to mid-October, daily 9–4) and continue another 9 miles. From North Adams, one road to the summit begins at the Western Gateway Heritage State Park, connecting with the Notch Road, which begins off Route 2 (look for the small brown-and-white sign).

The Cascades, a waterfall formed by Notch Brook as it tumbles into a pool below, is a popular 1-hour hike from Route 2: Park on Marion Avenue and pick up the path at the end of the street. Cross the footbridge and follow the trail.

Stony Ledge, a picnic area with one of the most dramatic overlooks in the state, is at the far end of the camping area.

Also see **Greylock Glen** under *Scenic Drives*.

BASCOM LODGE

to picnic tables, scattered among the smooth rocks above the falls; **swimming** is permitted in the small pool at their base.

Peru State Forest (413-442-8992), off Route 143 in Peru; south on Curtin Road, 1 mile from Peru Center. Garnet Hill (2,178 feet) yields a good view of the surrounding country, and there is fishing in **Garnet Lake.**

PICNICKING **Stone Hill.** A 55-acre town park, accessible from Stone Hill Road off South Street, Williamstown, offers wooded trails and a stone seat with a view. Also see **Stony Ledge** on Mount Greylock.

✳ Lodging

INNS

In Williamstown 01267

✑ ♿ **The Williams Inn** (413-458-9371 or 1-800-828-0133; www.williamsinn.com), Main Street (junction of Route 2 and Route 7). Carl and Marilyn Faulkner are thoroughly capable innkeepers, and their 125-room hostelry serves as the heart of town. At first glance you might wonder how such a prominent site—across from the green, at the junction of Routes 2 and 7—came to be filled by a boxy motor lodge. In fact, a white-pillared mansion built with the Proctor & Gamble fortune stood here and served for decades as a fraternity house until one bitter-cold night in 1979 when it burned to the ground. Its picture hangs in the lobby, a spacious, comfortable space with the feel of a country campus hotel. Rooms are comfortable, motel-style, crisply, attractively furnished in reproduction antiques, with full bath, TV, phone, computer hookup, and air-conditioning; the 24 "premier rooms" in the new wing are better than comfortable. Request a corner room. Amenities include an indoor swimming pool, sauna, and hot tub. The dining room is open for breakfast, lunch, and dinner, and lighter fare is served in the tavern lounge, known for its burgers. This is, incidentally, the ideal place to stay without a car—it's a short walk from the museums and steps from the Adams Memorial Theater (venue for the Williamstown Theater Festival), and its outer lobby (open 24 hours) doubles as the Bonanza bus stop. Rooms are $165–290 per couple; junior suites, from $165. No charge for children 14 and under in the same room.

♿ **The Orchards** (413-458-9611; www.orchardshotel.com), 222 Adams Road (off Route 2). Walled away from a commercial strip on the eastern edge of town, the Orchards faces inward, on a flowery, inner courtyard with a patio dining by a reflecting pool. The feel is of a small, elegant country hotel, and tea is served in a spacious sitting room fitted with Oriental rugs, crystal chandeliers, and antiques. The tone is formal. There are 45 rooms and two suites, each different, many with fireplace and window seat, all furnished with English antiques, goosefeather and down pillows. Amenities include a fridge, full bath, and separate dressing area. The restaurant is highly rated (see *Dining Out*). Innkeeper Sayed Saleh is obviously devoted to creating one of the best inns anywhere. One complaint: Staff are drawn from foreign countries and are understandably unaware of the locale. Amenities include a pool and an exercise center with a sauna and whirlpool. Rates $195–375 Memorial Day weekend through early November. Less off-season.

⊗ **Buxton Brook Farm** (413-458-3621; www.buxtonbrookfarm.com), 9 Northwest Hill Road. Open weekends only, year-round. Nancy Alden's Federal home is set among tall pines on 70 acres abutting Hopkins Memorial Forest. It's both comfortable and gracious, with more common space ranging from a formal, antiques-furnished sitting room with a fireplace and a big formal dining room to the totally laid-back den between the patio and open kitchen. The Greylock Suite is immense: a master bedroom with a big four-poster bed; a full sitting room with a TV, plenty of books, and a fold-out couch; and a full bath with a deep soaking tub. The other two substantial rooms have private bath. The spacious grounds include a pool. $125–195.

⊗ **Steep Acres Farm** (413-458-3774; jmgangemi@adelphia.net), 520 White Oaks Road. High on a hill with splendid views and bird life, this handsome, spacious, vintage-1900 home, set in 50 acres, has been home to Mary and Marvin Gangemi since 1978, one that they have shared with guests since 1983. Special features include the ample sunporch filled with white wicker and flowers, from which you can watch birds feeding just outside, and the 2-acre pond down in back, good for swimming, fishing, and boating. Over the years the Gangemis have obviously merged smaller rooms into flowing downstairs spaces. Our favorite guest room, upstairs in back, features an Eastlake bed handed down through the family. There are four rooms all told, three baths. $70–110 includes a full breakfast and taxes. **The Birches** (413-458-8134), a new home built along traditional lines by Mary and Marvin's son Daniel, is just downhill and also part of the property. It offers three more rooms, including one with a king-sized bed, fireplace, and whirlpool. $100–175 includes a full breakfast and afternoon refreshments.

Williamstown Bed and Breakfast (413-458-9202; www.williamstown-bandb.com), 30 Cold Spring Road. A spacious 1880s house nicely but unfussily furnished in period style, steps from Field Park (the town green) and within walking distance of downtown shops. There's a sitting room opening onto the oak-furnished dining room, the setting for a full breakfast that always includes a hot entrée and home-baked breads. The four good-sized guest rooms each have private bath. Full breakfast is included. Children over 12 please. $90–180 double.

The House on Main Street (413-458-3031; www.houseonmainst.com), 1120 Main Street. Built in the early 1700s, this house was moved to its present site in the 1830s, enlarged and Victorianized in the 1870s, and began taking in "guests" in the 1930s. Chris is among the generations of female undergraduates who were "put up" here by their Williams College dates. Thoroughly remodeled and modernized by the Riley family, it now offers six large, sunny, and cheerfully decorated guest rooms, three with private bath and the others sharing a bath and a half. A full breakfast is served in the country-style kitchen. Guests have the use of a parlor and a large screened porch. $85–10 double, $25 extra person, includes a full breakfast. Two-night

minimum in summer, fall, and holiday weekends.

Upland Meadow House (413-458-
3990), 1249 Northwest Hill Road.
This contemporary house is set in 160
acres, high on a hill beyond Hopkins
Forest but less than 3 miles from the
middle of town. It's very much Pan
Whitman's home, but the two adjacent rooms (sharing one bath) are
very private, with their own sitting
room and a splendid view west to the
Green Mountains. It's a great spot for
birders, cross-country skiers, and hikers as well as anyone who savors
mountain meadows and views. Pan is,
incidentally, known for her blueberry
and raspberry jams. $90 includes
breakfast served, when possible, on
the big deck. Two-night minimum
only on major weekends.

In North Adams 01247
Jae's Inn (413-664-0100; www.
jaesinn.com), 1111 South State Street.
At the end of a long driveway south of
town, off Route 8, this old inn (formerly Two Sisters) has been thoroughly revamped. Jae Chung grew up
in North Adams and owns several
highly rated restaurants in Boston.
His attractive, informal restaurant
here (see *Dining Out*) is also justly
popular. The 11 rooms are nicely furnished and air-conditioned, with gas
fireplace, Jacuzzi, and TV with DVD.
Facilities include a tennis court, heated swimming pool, basketball court,
and spa. $95 includes continental
breakfast. The attached spa offers a
full menu of body treatments: mas-
sage, manicure, etc.

In Pittsfield 01201
♾ **Thaddeus Clapp House** (413-
499-6840 or 1-888-499-6840;
www.clapphouse.com), 74 Wendell
Avenue. Just a block off South Street

(Route 7) and a leafy stroll from Park
Square, this 1871 mansion evokes a
sense of what Pittsfield once was and
may yet again be. A dilapidated apartment house when Rebecca Smith
began renovations in 2001, it is now
an elegant B&B with eight suites.
Each has a fireplace, cable TV, fridge,
AC, and data port; all are spacious
and airy, furnished in handsome
antiques. Several have whirlpool bath
as well as shower. Decor throughout
is predominantly Arts and Crafts,
which, Smith likes to point out, was a
reaction to heavy Victorian clutter.
Woodwork is extraordinary throughout, set off by dozens of Oriental rugs.
Thaddeus Clapp was superintendent
and then president of the Pontoosuc
Woolen Mill, one of the city's economic engines, but his passion was
acting (his stage name was "Thaddeus
Clappertino") and the spacious public
rooms were designed as venues for
musical performances, poetry, and
theatrical readings as well as elaborate
dinner parties. An enthusiastic historian, Smith has named each room for
local notables of the era. Our favorite
is the third-floor Thomas Colt Suite
with its sunny, separate sitting area.
Breakfast and tea are served in the
dining room, and there are occasionally theatrical presentations in the
parlor. July through October, Thursday through Sunday $195–250, Mon-
day through Wednesday $149–175;
off-season $125–195; breakfast and
tea included.

♪ **White Horse Inn** (413-442-2512;
www.whitehorsebb.com), 378 South
Street (Routes 7/20). Linda and Joe
Kalisz dislike words like "elegant" (as
in B&B) and "gourmet" (as in restaurant). They pride themselves on offering eight comfortable guest rooms in

Christina Tree

RIVERBEND FARM

TWO HISTORIC WILLIAMSTOWN B&BS Riverbend Farm (413-458-3121), 643 Simonds Road (Route 7), Williamstown 01267. Open late April through October. Many B&Bs try to cultivate a colonial ambience, but Riverbend Farm doesn't have to try: It's an authentic 1770 former tavern listed on the National Register of Historic Places. The present parlor was originally the tavern tap-room, where the Battle of Bennington was planned and where Colonel Ephraim Williams signed his will endowing Williams College. Owners David and Judy Loomis have lovingly restored the place, preserving the wood paneling, wide floorboards, and massive central chimney serving five working fireplaces. Breakfast is served at a long table by the hearth in the old "keeping room" or kitchen. The two common rooms are as comfortable as they are historic, and there is a fridge for guest use. Each of the four guest rooms reflects careful, scholarly restoration: Period lighting fixtures, latch doors, and exposed original wallpaper lend authenticity. One of the two shared baths has a claw-footed tub; the other, downstairs, has a shower and shelves filled with antique glass bottles, pottery, and jugs. A substantial continental breakfast featuring homemade bread and granola is served in front of the hearth. Because the house accommodates just 10 people max, it's a great place to rent as a whole for reunions. $100 per room; $20 for third person in a room

The Guest House at Field Farm (413-458-3135; www.guesthouseatfield-farm.org), 554 Sloan Road (off Route 43, near the intersection with Route 7),

Williamstown 01267. Owned and maintained by the Trustees of Reservations. In more than 250 upland acres, with a spectacular view of Mount Greylock, Lawrence Bloedel had a house built in 1948 by Edward Goodell that represents, both inside and out, the best of 1950s design. He filled it with furniture to match and with a priceless collection of modern art. Many of the artists were, however, little known at time they were patronized by Bloedel, a 1923 graduate of Williams College and heir to a fortune earned in the Pacific Northwest and Canada. Bloedel himself designed and made furniture, some of which survives in the house. Bloedel died in 1976 and on the death of his wife, Eleanor, the most valuable paintings found their way into museums. Most went to the Whitney in Manhattan, but one of the most moving—*Morning in the City* by Edward Hopper—usually hangs in the Williams College Museum of Art. The property was donated to the Trustees, but without funds to maintain the house. Initially the idea was to tear it down, but preservationists David and Judy Loomis, who had meticulously restored Williamstown's 18th-century tavern as a bed & breakfast, suggested that this exceptional home might do the same. Luckily they prevailed, serving as its initial hosts.

Guests will appreciate the enormity of the loss this house would have been. Field Farm's meadows and woods are beautiful, webbed with 4 miles of trails, good for cross-country skiing as well as walking (see *Green Space*), but to stay in this house is a gift. We sat mesmerized at the dining room table, facing the picture window through which clouds quickly shaped and reshaped above Mount Greylock, drifting toward us above the pond and landscaped lawns below the house. Beside the living room picture window, which commands the same view, there's a telescope with an Eames chair beside it. The room is sparely, comfortably furnished with cleanly lined, bright, and comfortable pieces, some sculpture and paintings. The simple hearth here, as in other rooms, features unusual hand-painted tiles. The cork floors are warmed by copper pipes, corners are rounded, and lighting is recessed. In all there are five guest rooms, and at this writing all except the ground-floor room (a former study, with its own balcony) retain their original furnishings. The large master bedroom with its balcony and glass-faced hearth is the indisputable gem. $145–225 includes a full breakfast and use of the guest pantry to store a picnic and drinks. While weekends are booked far in advance, midweek nights are frequently wide open.

THE GUEST HOUSE AT FIELD FARM

Trustees of Reservations

THE PORCHES INN

(413-664-0400; www.porches.com), 231 River Street, North Adams 01247. These six wooden row houses, each containing four apartments, were built facing the vast brick Arnold Print Works around 1900. With slate roofs, some shingle detailing under their sharply peaked gables, and distinctive, continuous porches, they were a cut above the city's typical, no-frills workers' housing. The mill across the river (then Sprague Electric) closed in 1985, and the by-then dilapidated row houses continued to deteriorate. Luckily, however, they remained clearly visible from a major gallery in the mill, which reopened in 1999 as MASS MoCA (see *Museums*). Thanks to foresight and funding ($6 million) by Williams College graduate Jack Wadsworth and Berkshire hotelier Nancy Fitzpatrick, the wooden row houses were thoroughly but sensitively renovated to form one of New England's most unusual lodging places. Each building is now painted a different, tasteful color (red, yellow, sage, gray, and blue); together they house 52 guest rooms, including 25 suites.

In contrast to the other Fitzpatrick family properties (the Red Lion Inn in Stockbridge and Blantyre Castle in Lenox), the decor is a combination of sleek contemporary and 1950s funky. Specially designed steel cupboards hiding TVs, DVD players, and mini bars resemble mill lockers; windows are bare except for natural linen ingeniously hung. In the luxurious bathrooms large mirrors, set into the original, battered window frames, hang above marble sinks. Furnishings are simple and comfortable, hung with paint-by-the-number oils, and bedside tables are topped with 1950s futuristic lamps. Top-floor rooms as well as suites feature skylights; suites have a Jacuzzi tub and separate living room; two-bedroom suites feature two baths with Jacuzzis as well as bedrooms, connected by a spiral staircase, plus a sitting room.

Halls throughout the inn are hung with vintage souvenir plates and memorabilia from the Mohawk Trail. Guests check in at a central reception desk in their turn-of-the-20th-century house, all with private bath, phone, and air-conditioning. Some rooms have two double beds; fax and laundry service are also available. A full breakfast in summer is served in the glass-walled dining room or on the deck, both of which overlook a lovely yard; breakfast is usually continental off-season. Children are welcome. June through Labor Day weekend: Weekend rates $170–190, weekdays $120–140, less off-season.

🐾 🦮 **Country Hearts** (413-499-7671; www.countryheartsbnb.com), 52 Broad Street. This Carpenter Gothic "painted lady" is just off South Street in a quiet neighborhood of older homes, within easy walking distance of the Berkshire Museum. The welcome is warm, though the eclectic decor of the common rooms is rather

a row house that also offers two comfortable sitting rooms, one with a fireplace stocked with local reading material, and a large, sunny breakfast room. There's a sauna in the small 1850s River Street house out back, beside the landscaped lap pool that's usable year-round. River Street itself has not been rehabbed, but it's a short, safe walk to downtown restaurants, shorter still to MASS MoCA with its many evening performances. Frankly, however, enthusiastic as we are about MASS MoCA, we wearied of looking at its vast brick presence and will request a room with a

ROW-HOUSE EXTERIOR OF THE PORCHES INN

Nicholas Whitman

view of the green hill right behind the inn on our next visit. $160–285 for rooms, $225–305 for suites, and $295–495 for two-bedroom suites Memorial Day through November 11; slightly less off-season.

sparse (a nice alternative, perhaps, to chintz and knickknacks). There are four guest rooms, each with private bath. The one in front has two brass beds (double and queen); we liked the one at the other end of the hall with lots of original wainscoting in the bath. Enjoy the perennial gardens in spring and summer from the deck, with barbecue grill; there's a jungle gym for the kids. $160 weekends in-

season and $99 weekdays; less off-season; includes continental breakfast. No minimum-stay requirement!

Elsewhere

∞ **The Inn at Richmond** (413-698-2566 or 1-888-968-4748; www.inna-trichmond.com), 802 State Road 9 (Route 41), Richmond 01254. Away from other inns but handy to Hancock Shaker Village and a pleasant ride from North and South Berkshire attractions, this is a gem of an inn. Jeri and Dan Buehler offer three comfortable, elegant guest rooms, three suites, and three cottages on this gentleman's farm, dating in part from the 18th century. All rooms have air-conditioning and phone as well as private bath and queen- or king-sized bed. Landscaped grounds include perennial gardens and woodland trails; inside there's an attractive parlor and library. Cottages have fully equipped kitchens, and some suites and cottages have fireplaces and whirlpools. High-season rates are $165– 275 for rooms and suites on weekends, $125–225 midweek; cottages are $1,300–1,500 per week or $195–265 per day. All rates except weekly cottage rentals include a full breakfast.

☼ **Harbour House Inn** (413-743-8959; www.harbourhouseinn.com), 725 North State Road (Route 8), Cheshire 01225. Eva and Sam Amuso are warm and welcoming hosts to this mansion-sized country house in the shadow of Mount Greylock. As a stop on the Albany–Springfield stage, it first welcomed guests in 1793, but it was substantially expanded in the 1880s as the manor of a 500-acre gentleman's farm. The name "harbour" refers to safety—this was a known stop for fleeing slaves on the Underground Railroad. With its immense, long sitting room and six guest rooms, it works well as a B&B. The master suite with its fireplace, many windows, and paneling (it was the former library) is beloved by brides, and there is a two-room suite with fireplace and balcony on the third floor. We thoroughly enjoyed a night in "Country Sunshine," a comfortable room cleverly decorated in

lemon yellow and Wedgwood blue. A full breakfast is served at the long dining room table. The Ashuwillticook Rail Trail, just down the road, runs along Cheshire Reservoir, and the main access road up Mount Greylock and hiking trails in Greylock Glen are both handy. Come to think of it, while it's quite far from anywhere else to stay, Harbour House is handy (because of the way the roads run) to most of Berkshire County and to much of the Berkshire Hilltown area as well. $110–250 in summer and fall; less off-season.

MOTOR INNS AND MOTELS Crown Plaza Hotel (413-499-2000 or 1-800-2-CROWNE; www.berkshire inns. com), Berkshire Common at West Street, Pittsfield. This is the Berkshires' only high-rise and very much a part of the county seat. There are 179 rooms, an attractive indoor pool, and Dewey's Restaurant (see *Dining Out*). Rooms: $159–289 in summer and fall, off-season $139–169.

🍴 ♫ **North Adams Holiday Inn** (413-663-6500 or 1-800-HOLIDAY; www.holidayinnberkshires.com), 40 Main Street, North Adams. This seven-floor, 87-room hotel, the only place to stay during North Adams's darkest era, has risen to the city's change in status. It's been thoroughly, tastefully renovated. On a downtown site that has been occupied by a hotel since the city's inception, it continues to serve as the heart of town. Rooms vary in configuration, with king beds or two queens. Steeples (see *Eating Out*) serves three meals a day, and there's an indoor pool, sauna, game room, and weight room in the basement. No minimum 2-day stay on weekends except during college grad-

uations. $89–129. Some smokers'
rooms.

🦆 *⚲* **Northside Motel** (413-458-
8107; www.northsidemotel.com), 45
North Street (Route 7), Williamstown
01267. On a prime location in the
heart of Williamstown, this family-run
motel rambles back from the handsome home in which Fred Nagy's
mother began accommodating
"House Party girls" (weekend dates at
then all-male Williams College fraternity houses) more than 40 years ago.
The motel offers 30 clean, individually controlled heat and air-conditioned
units with direct-dial phone and cable
TV; there's a swimming pool. Rooms
from $90, including a continental
breakfast, served in the original
house. No pets, but children under 10
are free; cribs and cots, available.

The 1896 House Inn & Motels
(413-458-1896 or 1-888-999-1896;
www.1896house.com), Route 7,
Williamstown 01267. Brookside
Motel, the neighboring red barn that's
housed a restaurant for many decades
but has been expanded to include lux-
ury suites, and the Pondside Motel
across Route 2 are now all under the
same ownership. The six "Barnside"
suites are elaborately decorated, each
evoking a different era or theme. All
have a sitting area, gas fireplace, spacious bath with dual whirlpool tubs,
TV, DVD/CD player, data port, and
more. They are, however, all rather
dark, with windows only at the
entrance (June through August,
$229–249 on weekends, $179–199
Sunday through Thursday; off-season
from $149). Rooms in the neighbor-
ing Brookside Motel are crisp and
cheerful ($139–169 in high season,
from $89 off-season with breakfast).
Across the road, Pondside units have

been decorated to look more like
B&B than motel rooms; the "Sweetheart Room" has a canopy bed and
whirlpool, and a three-room suite has
a full kitchen and whirlpool bath
($189–209 in high season, from $109
off-season). Check special packages
and current offerings on the web site.

Other lodging

⚲ **The Country Inn at Jiminy Peak**
(413-738-5500; outside Massachusetts, 1-800-882-8859; www.jiminy-
peak.com), Jiminy Peak, Corey Road,
Hancock 01237. At the base of the ski
mountain, this facility offers one-bedroom efficiency suites, also a restaurant and lounge, an outdoor pool,
indoor and outdoor whirlpools, and
exercise and game room. Each suite
has a master bedroom with a king-
sized bed, a living room with a queen-
sized sleep sofa, two cable TVs, a
bath, a powder room, and a fully
equipped kitchen. Two- and three-
bedroom condominiums are also
available. Units are nicely laid out and
furnished. $159–229; larger units,
$229–599; rates are based on double
occupancy; children 13 and younger
stay free. See *Skiing, Biking,* and *For
Families.*

Also see **Bascomb Lodge** in *Green
Space.*

✳ Where to Eat

DINING OUT

In Williamstown

Mezze Bistro & Bar (413-458-0123;
www.mezzeinc.com), 16 Water Street.
Open for dinner except Wednesday.
"Mezze" as in "middle"—in between
a restaurant and bar. Nancy Thomas's
popular bistro has a seasonal deck
overlooking the Green River, and the
decor in both the new restaurant and

bar (the original burned in 2000) is sophisticated and appealing. You might begin with yellowfin tuna tartare with celery, fresh horseradish, and chive crackers, then dine on asparagus and ricotta ravioli with toasted asparagus and truffle oil, or on confit of salmon in olive oil with ragout of morels and Jacob's ramps. Entrées $20–26. The bistro menu might include tomato and garlic bread soup, or fried pork with Vidalia onion and grapefruit ($6–14).

♠ ✿ **Hobson's Choice** (413-458-9101), 159 Water Street. Open 5–9:30 for dinner. A friendly, unpretentious roadhouse-style restaurant with old-fashioned wooden booths. The ground floor of an 1830s house is the setting for the most popular, moderately priced place to dine in town. Recently expanded, it's now easier to get into than in years past and just as good. The menu is vast, ranging from vegetarian pasta to prime rib, with plenty of seafood and chicken options. All dinners include the big salad bar as well as starch and vegetable. Beers and specialty drinks. Entrées are $11–20.

Yasmin's Restaurant at The Orchards (413-458-9611), 222 Adams Road (Route 2). Open for lunch and dinner; Sunday brunch. An elegant formal dining room serving basically Continental cuisine. Tables are set with Irish linen and decorated with fresh flowers; there is also patio dining in the garden, weather permitting. The menu changes frequently but might include quails stuffed with sweet potatoes and cashews on mango-chili chutney, or mustard-crusted rack of lamb. Dinner entrées $19–31.

The Williams Inn (413-458-9371), Main Street. The formal inn dining

room remains a favorite with many. It's a traditional American menu with such entrées as roast pork tenderloin Shaker-style ($17.25), New England scrod baked with tomatoes and smothered leeks topped with choron sauce ($17.50), and roast rack of lamb ($24.95).

In North Adams

Dora's Fine Dining (413-664-9449), 34 Holden Street. Open Monday through Saturday 4:30–9:30, Sunday noon–9. Closed Tuesday. Reservations accepted on weekends. Andreas Karampatsos acquired a loyal following during 25 years as chef at the Taconic Restaurant in Williamstown and this new, smaller venture has met with only good reviews. The brick-walled, nicely lit space seats just 75 at a time but the menu is large, ranging from filet mignon and rack of lamb through classic Italian veal dishes to "Mango Tango" (a vegan dish of garlic, ginger-marinated tofu, seasonal vegetables, toasted nuts, and mango), from "Andy's 'Original' Chicken Vermont" to Gorgonzola pasta (shrimp, chicken, or vegetables and roasted fennel sautéed with onion, plum tomato, and fresh herbs on rigatoni, topped with grated tomato). Entrées $15.95–19.95, including bread, house salad, starch, and vegetable.

♠ **Jae's Inn** (413-664-0100), 1111 South Street (Route 8 south). Open for lunch Monday through Saturday and for dinner nightly. Jae Chung is a North Adams native who established a reputation as a restaurateur in Boston. Jae's Inn is another of the great new dining additions to North Adams: brightly, sleekly decorated, and featuring broadly Oriental dishes, spicy Korean beef stew, pad Thai, even an udon soup wih shrimp tempura, as well as a wide choice of sushi. You can also order grilled chicken, baked salmon, or filet mignon. Entrées $8.95–16.95.

Gramercy Bistro (413-663-5300), 24 Marshall Street. Open Monday through Thursday 5–9, until 10 Friday through Sunday. Also open for breakfast on weekends (8–1). Closed Tuesday. Alex Smith's storefront restaurant sits invitingly across from MASS MoCA. We have heard good things about it but must have just hit it on a bad night. The fettuccine was below par, and the grilled sea bass—and the rice that went with it—was cold. The bread and herb olive oil was, however, delicious, as were the olives and a salad. We liked the atmosphere and are eager to give it a second chance. It's known for a great Sunday brunch.

Milan Restaurant (413-664-9955), 55 Main Street. Open for dinner Tuesday through Saturday, lunch Tuesday through Friday (noon–1:30). Closed Sunday and Monday. Another welcome, trendy, and upscale addition to the North Adams dining scene: It's an à la carte northern Italian menu with antipasto and a choice of "insalata," many pastas, and some veal and steak entrées. You might dine on *fusilli di Milan* (with prosciutto, roasted red peppers, and fresh tomato) for $15.95, or try veal scaloppine with grilled eggplant, roasted red pepper, and Fontina, served with fresh spinach ($17.95).

& **Eleven at MASS MoCa** (413-662-2004), 1111 MASS MoCA Way. Open for dinner Tuesday through Saturday 5–9; for lunch daily 11:30–4. Dinner reservations recommended. In the museum courtyard but a separate entity, this sleek bistro is under the same ownership as popular Mezze in

Williamstown. A choice of salads and sandwiches for lunch, also a good burger—which is available at dinner, too, along with tuna *au poivre,* seared and served with French lentils and green beans, or you can dine on pad Thai. Local ingredients are featured. Dinner entrées $10–20.

In Pittsfield

Kim's Dragon Restaurant (413-442-5594), 1231 West Housatonic Street. Open daily 4–10; closed Monday in winter. What Kim Van Huynh's modest Vietnamese restaurant lacks in atmosphere, it makes up for with the quality of its food. The ingredients are fresh and local, and the flavors are distinct. You might begin with Saigon noodle soup or a bowl of lemongrass soup, then dine on scrod crisped with fresh tomatoes, onions, and nuoc mam on a crêpe filled with seasonal vegetables, or on shrimp sautéed with curry, onions, noodles, coconut milk, and peanuts. Entrées $11.95–19.95. Beer and wine are served.

Trattoria Rustica (413-499-1192), 75 McKay Street. Open for lunch

GRAMERCY BISTRO

Kim Grant

Wednesday, Thursday, Friday (noon–2); for dinner daily except Thursday (5–9). Reservations suggested. Plenty of atmosphere and fresh-made pasta combine to make this a welcome addition to the downtown Park Square area. The half a dozen choices of pasta might include linguine with New Zealand baby clams sautéed in white wine with garlic, or fresh ricotta-stuffed ravioli tossed in a *filetto di pomorini* with fresh basil. Dinner entrées $14-19.

Mazzeo's (413-448-2095), 7 Winter Street. Open for dinner Wednesday through Sunday. Reservations suggested. A local favorite, secreted just off the main drag. To find it, turn off East Street at Wendy's. An old-fashioned Italian restaurant with many antipasti and house specialties that include eggplant Parmesan and vegetable lasagna. Entrées $13.95–21.95.

Dewey's Restaurant & Lounge (413-499-2000), Crown Plaza Hotel, second floor, 1 West Street. Open for all three meals. No surprises here, but a big dinner menu ranging from turkey potpie ($6.95) to crab-stuffed filet mignon ($23.50).

Elizabeth's Café Pizzeria (413-448-8244), 1264 East Street (across from the GE plant). Open Wednesday through Sunday for dinner. Expanded from its original modest beginnings, still an interesting eatery. Soups are great; real Italian polenta is a specialty. There are marvelous salads. Complete dinners are $16.50.

✐ **Dakota** (413-499-7900), Route 7, Lenox–Pittsfield line. Open for dinner daily and Sunday brunch. There is a large fieldstone fireplace in the dining room, which is supposed to resemble an Adirondack lodge. Specialties include seafood, hand-cut steaks, and mesquite-grilled fish, along with some heart-healthy choices. Dinner entrées range from $10.95 for ground sirloin to 20.95 for prime rib.

Elsewhere

Mill and the Floss (413-458-9123), Route 7, New Ashford. Dinner nightly except Monday. A long-established favorite among Berkshire regulars. An 18th-century farmhouse with an open kitchen, specializing in French country cuisine. Entrées might include crabcakes in Dijon sauce, tournedos béarnaise, and rack of lamb; $23–28.

The Silvia Inn (413-749-0009), 17 Commercial Street (Route 8), Adams. Closed Monday. Argentinian Silvia Biurrun has created a totally unlikely and inviting restaurant in the former parlors of her vast former mill owner's mansion. You might dine on *osso buco de la casa* with a port wine demiglaze, or Chilean sea bass with lemon and herbs. Prices are surprisingly reasonable, from $10.95 for pesto pastas handmade by Silvia to $17.95 for roast rack of lamb.

EATING OUT

In Williamstown

See **Hobson's Choice** under *Dining Out*. It's the best dinner value.

Papa Charlie's Deli and Sandwich Shop (413-458-5969), 28 Spring Street. Open from breakfast through dinner. Overstuffed sandwiches and bagels, many named for actors at the Williamstown Theatre Festival and other notables, are what this place is about, and in off-hours it's a great place to play student, even if you aren't one, sipping slowly and reading a book in a deep wooden booth. The overflow basement area is less inviting.

Helen's (413-458-1360), 60 Spring Street. Open Tuesday through Friday 11–6:30, Saturday 11–4; open summer Sundays 11–4 but otherwise closed Sunday and Monday. A spacious, friendly haven specializing in Boar's Head deli sandwiches, a variety of salads, and a vegetable and juice bar.

Thai Garden (413-458-0004), 27 Spring Street. Open for lunch and dinner daily. An attractive atmosphere and reasonably priced, tasty food are an irresistible combination. The only problem is quantity. Dine on duck in a Shoo Shee curry. Dinner entrées $8.95–11.95.

✓ **Chef's Hat** (413-458-5120), 905 Simonds Road (Route 7, north of town). Open for breakfast from 6:30 (7 on Sunday) and lunch until 3; closed Monday. Bob and Amy Pudvar will tell you that if you know where to look, the original diner car is still here, but they have expanded, adding knotty pine and booths. Locals crowd in on weekends to breakfast on hash and eggs (steak and eggs is also on the menu) and a wide choice of omelets or pancakes. There's actually a wide choice of everything, and it includes diner classics like a hot turkey sandwich, and liver and onions; also salads, stir-fries, and a surprising variety of fish and seafood. The children's menu includes a foot-long hot dog with fries.

Cozy Corner Restaurant (413-458-3854), 850 Simonds Road (Route 7). Breakfast, lunch, and dinner daily. An unpretentious roadhouse with low prices and a loyal following. Fish-and-chips and pizza; also Greek and Mexican specialties. A selection of beers.

Tavern Menu at the Williams Inn (413-458-9371), 1090 Main Street. Served 11:30 AM–10 PM, Sunday until 9:30. The large tavern area is known for its "Berkshire burger"; also good for tavern stew, the plowman's plate, and soups and sandwiches.

Purple Pub (413-458-3306), Bank Street (just off Spring Street). Open for lunch and dinner, until 1 AM weekends. This hospitable little place really feels like a pub. You'll get good sandwiches and burgers, daily specials, and fast and friendly service. There is a small outdoor dining area.

✓ **Misty Moonlight Diner** (413-458-3305), 408 Main Street (Route 2). A family restaurant with a contrived but pleasant 1950s atmosphere with a jukebox. Open 7 AM–10 PM, and serves breakfast all day as well as a large choice of burgers, sandwiches, vegetarian dishes, BBQ ribs and chicken, pastas, and fried seafood, also daily specials. Fancy rum as well as nonalcoholic smoothies and margaritas are also house specialties, and there's a choice of beer on tap.

Lickety Split (413-458-1818), 69 Spring Street. This lunch place offers good soups, sandwiches, and salads. Eat inside or across the street in warm weather at the café tables in front of The Library.

Chopsticks (413-458-5750), 412 Main Street (Route 2). Open daily for lunch and dinner. An established and popular restaurant with a large menu featuring Japanese, Chinese, and Korean dishes. The lounge specializes in "exotic tropical drinks" and also carries imported Chinese beers. Lunch specials are $5.35.

Water Street Grill (413-458-2175), 123 Water Street. Open for lunch and dinner. A more formal Grill and an informal Tavern. There's a weekday lunch buffet in the Grill as well as sandwiches, salads, and burgers. Dine on grilled chicken, or a grilled eggplant dinner in the Tavern. We had a bad experience, however, on our last visit and found that no one we mentioned it to was surprised. Hopefully this old standby will rebound.

Also see **The Store at Five Corners** under *Selective Shopping*.

In North Adams
Freight Yard Pub (413-663-6547), Western Gateway Heritage State Park. Open 1:30–11. An informal place, this pub has something of a sports-bar atmosphere. Burgers, ribs, seafood, and Italian dishes are always on the menu. Locally made kielbasa is a specialty, and there is an outdoor dining patio.

*Appalachian Bean** (413-663-7543), 67 Main Street. Open for breakfast and lunch. This place is a winner, a deep, high-ceilinged former store with brick walls and a great choice of specialty sandwiches, freshly made soups, and a big salad bar. Try the Richmond roll (grilled eggplant, sun-dried tomatoes, and mozzarella on sourdough).

*Jack's Hot Dogs** (413-664-9006), 12 Eagle Street (off Main Street). Lunch, dinner, and noshing in between. A local institution that's been in the same family for more than seven decades. If you like hot dogs with all the trimmings (including sauerkraut), Jack's is the place.

*Joga Café** (413-664-0126), 23 Eagle Street. Open for lunch and dinner; music and dancing Thursday through Saturday until 2 AM. Not inviting from the street, but step inside to brick walls, pleasing light wood tables and bar, muted colors, and good art. The lunch menu is a

winner: a wide choice of panini, bruschetta, and "tramezini"—crustless white-bread sandwiches with fillings such as avocado and shaved Parmesan with sliced tomato and lemon aioli. Leave room for dessert. The bar here boasts one of the biggest selections of beer in the Berkshires. Kids' menu.

*Steeples** (413-664-6581), 40 Main Street (the Holiday Inn). Open for all three meals. A big, cheerful dining room with terrace tables in summer, checked tablecloths, friendly wait staff. The menu is family geared and priced, from tenderloin tips to baked stuffed shrimp. All entrées include pasta fasoli, house salad, vegetable, and starch.

Also see **Bascomb Lodge** under *Green Space—Mount Greylock*.

In Pittsfield
See **Kim's Dragon Restaurant** under *Dining Out*.

Court Square (413-442-9896), 95 East Street, Pittsfield. Open daily for breakfast, lunch, and Sunday brunch. Full breakfast menu and many salads and sandwiches; also known for pies.

Patrick's Pub (413-499-1994), 26 Bank Row. Open for lunch and dinner; closed Sunday. Dark, pubby

JACK'S HOT DOGS, ADAMS

Kim Grant

atmosphere. Sandwiches and wraps at lunch, reasonably priced staples such as baked stuffed sole and honey-Dijon chicken at dinner.

The Highland (413-442-2457), 100 Fenn Street. An oasis for the frugal diner since 1936. Open for lunch and dinner; closed Monday. Reasonably priced road food, fully licensed. No credit cards, no reservations, no pretensions.

The Brewery (413-442-5072), 34 Depot Street. Open for lunch and dinner. Handy to the Berkshire Museum; good for soups, burgers, specialty sandwiches, pastas, and brews.

Elsewhere

✧ **Jack's Hot Dog Stand** (413-743-3630; www.jackshotdogstand.com), 53 Park Street (Route 8), Adams. Open weekdays 10–7, Saturday 10–4; closed Sunday. The former Miss Adams Diner, a 1940s classic (Worcester lunch car No. 821), is now owned by the same family that has been selling hot dogs on Eagle Street in North Adams for 80 years. The menu is limited to hot dogs, hamburgers, sausages, and fries, with all the trimmings.

✧ **Lakeside** (413-743-7399), 178 South State Road (Route 8), Cheshire. Across from Cheshire Reservoir, this is a cheerful roadhouse with deep booths and friendly waitresses. Burgers, scallop dinners, homemade meat loaf, honey-mustard chicken dinner, foot-long hot dogs, whatever, reasonable prices. Fully licensed.

✳ Entertainment

Also see *The Arts.*

Williamstown Community Theatre and the college's **Williams Theater** perform during winter months.

Sterling and Francine Clark Art Institute presents a variety of films, lectures, and plays throughout the year.

Little Cinema (413-443-7171), 39 South Street, Pittsfield. This 300-seat theater in the Berkshire Museum features art and classic films.

Images Cinema (413-458-5612), 40 Spring Street, Williamstown. A classic college-town movie house showing foreign films and interesting domestic ones.

La Choza (413-448-6100), 75 North Street, Pittsfield. This informal "cantina Americana" is the setting for live bands and other performances Thursday through Saturday nights. $5 cover.

Also see **Joga Café** under *Eating Out.*

The Women's Club of the Berkshires (413-447-7641), 42 Wendell Avenue, Pittsfield, stages periodic plays and other live performances at the Thomas Colt House.

✳ Selective Shopping

ANTIQUES SHOPS **The Library Antiques** (413-458-3436 or 1-800-294-4798), 70 Spring Street, Williamstown. Open daily. An ever-expanding series of spaces filled with fine antiques of all sorts, as well as many unusual gifts. Browsers welcome.

Saddleback Antiques Center (413-458-5852), 1395 Cold Spring Road (Route 7), Williamstown. Closed Wednesdays in winter. A dealers' group shop in an old schoolhouse. All manner of antiques, including furniture, pottery, and posters.

Collector's Warehouse (413-458-9686), 105 North Street (Route 7), Williamstown. Open Wednesday through Friday 10–3, Saturday 10–5.

Miscellaneous antiques and collectibles, including glassware, jewelry, frames, dolls, linen, and furniture.

BOOKSTORES Water Street Books (413-458-8071), 26 Water Street, Williamstown. The town's independent, full-service bookstore.

Barnes & Noble (413-496-9051), Berkshire Crossing Mall, Route 9, Pittsfield. A superstore and a Starbucks.

Papyri Books (413-662-2099; www.papyribooks.com), 49 Main Street, North Adams. Karen Kane's shop is an oasis for book lovers: mostly used books but some new titles with inviting seating, coffee and a fridge in the back, and a full schedule of readings, signings, music, and art on the first Friday and open mike on the second Saturday of every month. Also check out literary events sponsored by neighboring Inkberry (www.inkberry.org).

GALLERIES

In North Adams
Contemporary Artists Center (413-663-9555; www.thecac.org), Historic

PAPYRI BOOKS, NORTH ADAMS

Kim Grant

Beaver Mill, 189 Beaver Street. A nonprofit studio and workshop facility. On the way to the Natural Bridge, the gallery is theoretically open May through October, Wednesday through Saturday 11–5, Sunday noon–5, and displays are usually worth checking out. Also check out Abbie Hatton's upstairs weaving studio (413-664-8056) with striking monoprints by Grandon Graving in the adjoining gallery.

Joel Rudnick (413-458-4791), 5 Holden Street. A studio-gallery open intermittently. Rudnick is a skilled painter and sculptor, specializing in the figure. Call ahead.

Stonewood Artisans (413-664-6244), 107 Main Street, showcases the work of primarily local arts and craftspeople.

In Pittsfield
Berkshire Artisans (413-499-9348), 28 Renne Avenue, Pittsfield. Open Monday through Friday 11–5, Saturday from noon. Just behind the vest-pocket park on Main Street, a handsome gallery hosting exhibitions by nationally known professionals; also the setting for performances and concerts.

In Williamstown
The Harrison Gallery (413-458-1700), 39 Spring Street. Changing exhibits.

Plum Gallery (413-458-3389 www.plumgallery.com), 112 Water Street. Changing exhibits featuring contemporary art and ceramics.

FACTORY OUTLETS Old Stone Mill (413-743-1042), 2A Grove Street (Route 8, south of town), Adams. Save up to 75 percent on a wide variety of wallpapers, some matching fabrics, comforters.

Interior Alternatives Outlet (413-743-1986), 5 Hoosac Street, Adams. A wide selection of Waverly fabrics, also some wallpaper, bedding, Oriental and area rugs.

Berkshire Sportswear (413-664-4931), 121 Union Street, Windsor Mill. Factory firsts and seconds of women's sportswear, specialty knits. A genuine outlet with genuine bargains upstairs where it's made. Cash only.

FARMS AND FLOWERS

In Cheshire

Lightwing Farms (743-4425). Route 8, site of Saturday Farmer's Market, 10–4. Also open July through early October for vegetables, flowers, and honey.

ᵔ **Whitney's Farm Stand** (413-442-4749) Route 8, 2.5 miles north of Berkshire Mall. Open Easter to Christmas, home-grown fruits and vegetables including melons, sweet corn, and apples; also bedding plants, perennials, a deli, a bakery, a dairy bar, and a petting zoo. PYO blueberries and pumpkins in-season.

In Dalton

Holiday Farm (413-684-94444; www.holidayfarm.com), Holiday Cottage Road, off Route 9 east. Pumpkins, maple products, mountain bike races Wednesday evenings.

In Hancock

ᵔ **Ioka Valley Farm** (413-738-5915; www.berkshireeagle.com/iokafarm), 3475 Route 43, not far from Jiminy Peak. Uncle Don's Barnyard is the big attraction here (call ahead for seasonal hours); also maple syrup and a pancake café. PYO strawberries mid-June through mid-July, pumpkins in fall, cider and apples, farm-theme playground, picnic area,

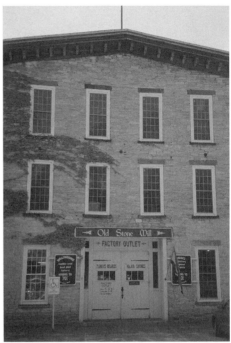

OLD STONE MILL, ADAMS
Christina Tree

special events.

In Lanesboro

Lakeview Orchard (413-448-6009; www.lakevieworchard.com), 34 Old Cheshire Road. Open early July through Thanksgiving. From Route 8, take Old State Road to Summer Street to Old Cheshire Road; from Route 7, take Summer Street to Old Cheshire. Sixteen varieties of apples, sweet cherries, peaches, plums, blueberries, shallots, onions, homemade doughnuts, pies and turnovers, jams, apple butter, sweet cider pressed in-season. A beautiful location.

Mountain View Farm (413-445-7642), Old Cheshire Road (see directions above). Open mid-June through October. Sweet corn, PYO tomatoes and strawberries in-season. Another beautiful location.

In Williamstown

ᵔ **Green River Produce** (413-458-2470), on Route 43 at its junction with Route 7. PYO strawberries, blueberries, tomatoes, and peppers. Full greenhouse and nursery. Corn, summer squash, tomatoes, winter squash, Indian corn, pumpkins, and cider press in-season. Petting farm and hayrides.

In Richmond
Bartlett's Orchard (413-698-2559; www.Bartlettsorchard.com), 575 Swamp Road, Richmond. Four miles south on Barker Road from Route 20. Open daily mid-August to late spring. Generations of Bartletts have grown, sold, and shipped apples from these 52 hillside acres. There are 18 varieties of apples plus a full bakery (try the cider doughnuts) and specialty foods; also milk, bread, ice cream, and more.

Furnace Brook Winery at Hilltop Orchards (413-698-3301; www.Hilltoporchards.com), Route 295 between

IOKA VALLEY FARM, HANCOCK

Berkshire Visitors Bureau

Routes 41 and 22 (look for sign). Free wine tasting. Varietal grape and specialty wines and Johnny Mash Hard Cider. PYO apples, pears, plums in summer and fall, picnics encouraged, special events. Also apple brandy, preserves, vegetables in-season, sweet corn, eggs, and dairy products. Johnny Mash (www.Johnnymash.com) is oak-aged and well-respected hard cider.

SPECIAL STORES

In Williamstown
❧ **Where'd You Get That?** (413-458-2206), 20 Spring Street. Open daily. Ken and Michele Gietz are enthusiastic purveyors of some wild toys geared to children of all ages: strategy games, gizmos, gadgets. Also chocolates and gourmet candy.

The Mountain Goat (413-458-8445), 130 Water Street. The founding store in what's become an upcountry chain specializing in outdoor clothing, equipment, and bicycles (rentals, too); also local books and plenty of advice about where to do whatever you do outdoors. Inquire about special events including rock climbing and mountain bike camp.

The Store at Five Corners (413-458-3176 or 1-800-261-4245), in South Williamstown at the junction of Routes 7 and 43. This hip general store has a good deli (and café tables); specializes in gifts, gift baskets, and specialty foods.

In Pittsfield
The Cottage (413-447-9643), 31 South Street, Pittsfield. A stylish shop with tableware, baskets, gourmet foods, soaps, clothing, jewelry, and more.

Greystone Gardens (413-442-9291), 436 North Street. Antique, really antique (as in 19th century) clothing, as well as jewelry, linens, greeting cards, and gifts.

In North Adams

Eziba Gallery (413-664-6888 or 1-888-404-5108), 46 Eagle Street, North Adams. Known for its catalog, Eziba features handmade artifacts from throughout the world.

Galabriel's (413-664-0026), 105 Main Street. Closed Monday. Comfortable, wearable, reasonably priced women's clothing, mostly natural fibers; also beaded and sterling-silver jewelry.

Tala's Quilt Shop (413-664-8200), Heritage State Park. A full line of quilting supplies and finished quilts.

❋ Special Events

February: **Winter Weekend at Hancock Shaker Village**—hands-on ice harvesting and special activities for children (www.hancockshakervillage. org).

April: **Williamstown Jazz Festival** features world-class performers, college jazz bands, jazz dance, lectures, and more (www.williamstownjazz. com).

April–mid-June: **New Life on the Farm**—a barn is filled with baby sheep, hatching chicks, kids, piglets, and other new livestock with mothers. Exhibition organized by New England Heritage Breeds Conservancy.

May: **Memorial Day Parade** in North Adams.

June–December: **First Friday Art Walks** with music and food, late-night shopping (413-664-6180).

Late June: **North Berkshire Food Festival,** North Adams (413-664-6180). **Sheep Shearing Weekend** at

Hancock Shaker Village illustrates the entire sheep-to-shawl process with hand spinning, shearing, weaving and dyeing, sheep show, ice cream socials.

July 4: Pittsfield boasts one of the biggest **Fourth of July parades** in the country, nationally televised.

Mid-July: **Eagle Street Beach Wednesday,** North Adams—the length of Eagle Street is turned into a beach, sand from curb to curb. Sand sculpting competition (413-664-6180).

July–August: **Concerts** Tuesday evenings at the Clark Art Institute in Williamstown; every Wednesday at 7 in North Adams by Windsor Lake (rain date the following Sunday); and Thursdays at 7 at the Western Gateway Heritage State Park.

Late July–early August: **Susan B. Anthony Days** commemorate the suffragette, who was born in Adams. Main Street is closed off and filled with booths, games, and food stalls.

Mid- to late August: **Adams Agricultural Fair. Hancock Shaker Village Antiques Show**—a major array of Shaker, American, and European antiques displayed in the Round Stone Barn.

Late August: **Berkshire Children's Circus,** Patterson Field House, Berkshire Community College, North Adams. A one-ring circus culminates the summer camp's skill building: tumbling, cycling, juggling, trapeze skills, etc., by performers age 8–15 (413-499-4660).

Late September: **Country Fair and Crafts Festival at Hancock Shaker Village,** featuring New England Heritage Breeds Conservancy Exhibition of Heritage Livestock, crafts, lawn games, daily parade of animals.

First weekend in October: **Northern**

Berkshire Fall Foliage Festival in North Adams. Includes races, games, suppers, and sales, and culminates with a big parade that traditionally coincides with peak foliage colors.

Columbus Day weekend: **Mount Greylock Ramble**—a traditional mass climb of "their" mountain by Adams residents.

Mid- to late October: **Williamstown Film Festival** honors major figures in American cinema (wwww.williams-townfilmfest.com).

First weekend in December: **Christmas at Hancock Shaker Village**— free afternoon oxen- and horse-drawn wagon and sleigh rides, demonstrations, make-your-own toys.

ALONG THE MOHAWK TRAIL

Beyond North Adams the Berkshire Hills rise steeply on the east, traversed by one of the country's first roads designed specifically for auto touring.

The Mohawk Trail, as this stretch of Route 2 is known, loosely (very loosely) shadows an ancient Indian trail that ran from the Hoosac Valley up over the Hoosac Range and along a wooded ridge, then dropped down into the wide Deerfield River valley and followed the Deerfield to the Connecticut River valley. In the late 18th century both a toll road and a "shunpike" traversed this high country, an era evoked by the fine old houses along the Deerfeld in Charlemont and by the Charlemont Inn, built in 1787 to accommodate stagecoach traffic.

"Peaks of one or two thousand feet rush up either bank of the river in ranges, thrusting out their shoulders side by side . . . I have never driven through such romantic scenery, where there was such a variety and boldness of mountain shapes as this," Nathaniel Hawthorne wrote in 1850.

For all practical purposes, however, north Berkshire County continued to be isolated from eastern Massachusetts until the opening of the 4.75-mile-long Hoosac Tunnel in 1875. In the first decades of the 20th century the speediest, safest way from Boston to North Adams was still by train through the Hoosac Tunnel. By then, however, rail travel was old hat.

Everyone wanted to escape the narrow dictates of the rails and to get off on their own four wheels. Cars could drive from Greenfield to Charlemont and then along the Deerfield River, but there they met the same mountain that had stumped railroad builders for so long. Already motor traffic (almost all recreational at the time) was flowing along "Jacob's Ladder" (present Route 20) and into South Berkshire instead. The city fathers of North Adams rose to the challenge and on October 22, 1914, 15 miles of carefully graded (no more than 7 percent), unpaved but well-oiled road over Hoosac Mountain was formally dedicated and hailed by the *North Adams Transcript* as a "symphony of sylvan delight." In 1921 the eastern end of this "Mohawk Trail" was rerouted from less dramatic Shelburne Road to climb over a high shoulder of Greenfield Mountain. Given the absence of official route numbers (the U.S. Highway System was adopted in 1926), white-and-red-striped markings for the Mohawk Trail extended east much of the way to Boston. The present Mohawk Trail officially extends from Williamstown to Millers Falls.

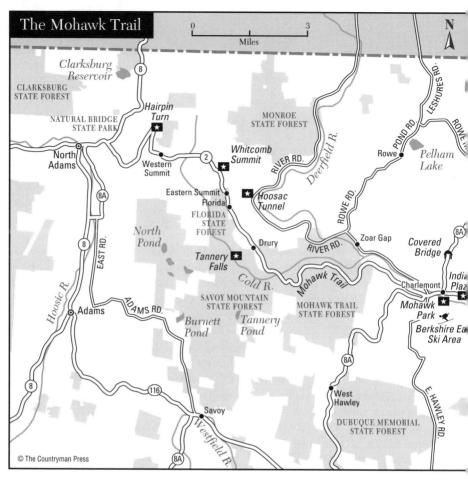

It's the 38 miles between North Adams and Greenfield, however, that we focus on here. This was the stretch of the trail recognized as a destination in its own right from the 1920s through 1950s, a period during which it sprouted tea shops and gift shops, motor courts, motels, and campgrounds (both private and state), and seasonally accommodated more than 1,000 tourists.

Take its very name and theme. Ignoring the century in which this route evolved as an 18th- and 19th-century way west, "Mohawk Trail" conjures up the narrow path blazed by Indians, not even local Indians (the Mahicans on the western side and Pocumtucks on the eastern side of the Hoosac Range) but the more famous marauders from (present) upstate New York who used it as a warpath.

In 1914 America's first affordable cars were just beginning to transform the way ordinary folks vacationed (between 1908 and 1927, 15 million Model Ts were produced). In the 1920s motor touring along the Mohawk Trail increased dramatically, and many of the surviving trading posts were built. "Tourists" drove their first cars over the trail and returned year after year.

Over the years the road broadened and was further rerouted, and cars picked

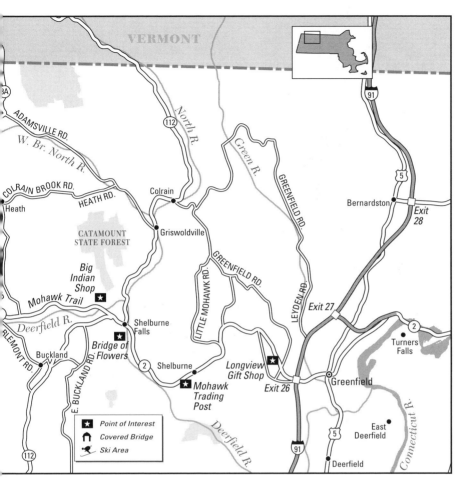

up speed. Always to some degree a day trip, the Mohawk Trail gradually lost its status as a destination, and today it's promoted primarily as a foliage route. Several of the old motor courts were replaced by motels but many simply disappeared, along with vintage restaurants and tearooms. Attractions along the Trail are small, family-owned businesses, and in many cases they have just been hanging on.

In the 1990s the tourist tide once more began turning. White-water rafting on the Deerfield River began once more to fill motels and cabins as well as a burgeoning number of B&Bs and the revived 18th-century Charlemont Inn. About the same time the village of Shelburne Falls, known since the 1920s for its "Bridge of Flowers"—a major attraction on the Trail (which went straight through the middle of the village until the 1950s)—was evolving into one of the liveliest arts centers in New England.

At this writing the Mohawk Trail is once more in transition. With its long-overdue recognition as a "scenic corridor" has come funding for a visitors center–museum in Charlemont (still far from a reality). Hopefully, too, the signage will improve. At present anyone who is not reading this chapter has no

BRONZE SCULPTURE ON
MOHAWK TRAIL IN CHARLEMONT

Kim Grant

warning of where to turn off for the best views or how to find Tannery Falls.

Like the Mohawk Trail, this chapter links Berkshire and Franklin Counties, describing what's to be found on and just off the Trail. Our description runs from west to east, but obviously you can come the other way—and in practice it's frequently difficult to cross from the eastbound to westbound sides of the road. Frankly, we prefer to drive it east to west. Either way it remains one of the most scenic drives in New England.

GUIDANCE Mohawk Trail Association (www.mowhawktrail.com), P.O. Box 1044, North Adams 01247, publishes a free brochure to the attractions along its length.

Also see **Shelburne Falls Village Information Center** and **Franklin Country Chamber of Commerce** in "West County." And check out www.MassCountryRoads.com and www.shelburnefalls.com.

Note: The Mohawk Trail Historic Auto Trail Guide by Clint Richmond (Muddy River Press, Brookline, $9; inquiries@muddyriverpress.com) is illustrated with many vintage postcards and photos of the Trail.

DEERFIELD RIVER

Kim Grant

In 1914 the Mohawk Trail officially began in **North Adams** at the intersection (now marked by Dunkin' Donuts and McDonald's) of Union and Eagle Streets.

Natural Bridge State Park (www.massparks.org) is the first sight to see, just a few minutes' detour off Route 2 westbound, marked from Route 8A beyond the Beaver Mill with its **Contemporary Artists Center and Gallery.**

The Hairpin Turn, the most dramatic reverse curve in all New England, zigs and zags its way up to the **Western Summit** (2,020 feet), where there are turnouts at the **Golden Eagle Restaurant** and the **Wigwam & Western Summit Gift Shop & Cottages** (413-663-3205), 2350 Mohawk Trail. The shop and cottages with a "three-state view" date from 1914, when a tearoom and a (long-gone) observation tower opened. At this writing the shop has been owned for 40 years by Inna and Werner Gertje. Open March through December, it specializes in Minnetonka Moccasins, Anheuser-Busch beer steins, and Fenton glass, among many other souvenirs and collectibles. The five cottages (most have a double bed) are open May through October ($60–70 in summer, $70–80 in fall).

In **Florida,** one of the coldest towns in the state (it was named in 1805 just as the United States was purchasing Florida from Spain), the road levels out.

Savoy Mountain State Forest (413-663-8469; www.massparks.org) is accessed by Central Shaft Road (it angles off to the right). The forest's 11,118 acres harbor some fascinating history and evocative places. A Shaker colony was among the early-19th-century settlements for which now only cellar holes exist. The most developed corner of the park, around North and South Ponds, was later the Haskins Club, a private resort. You can **swim** and **fish** for trout in **North Pond,** which offers changing rooms and restrooms. There's also a **boat** ramp, and there are 45 **campsites** (open Memorial Day through Columbus Day) in a former apple orchard along with four **cabins** (open year-round) by South Pond. The forest offers 24 miles of **hiking** trails, two **ski touring** loops, and a "crooked forest" of deformed trees. The waters are stocked with fish.

Whitcomb Summit, Florida, is the highest point on the trail (2,173 feet). The spectacular "100 mile view" is west over wave upon wave of hills and mountains; a steel (and lower) version of the vintage-1915 tower survives. The bronze elk, placed here by the Massachusetts Elks in 1923, is magnificent. At its dedication, speakers included Boston's Mayor Curley.

♂ ☃ **Whitcomb Summit Motel, Cabins and Cafe** (413-662-2625 or 1-800-547-0944; www.whitcombsummit.com), 229 Mohawk Trail, Florida. Open mid-May to mid-November. Ed

"FAMOUS HAIRPIN TURN" POSTCARD

Muddy River Press

LIFE'S A PICNIC ON THE MOHAWK TRAIL

Muddy River Press

THIS POSTCARD DEPICTS A VERMONT FAMILY ENJOYING A PICNIC ON WHITCOMB SUMMIT SOON AFTER THE 1914 OPENING OF THE MOHAWK TRAIL

and Carol Drummond have given this historic property a fresh lease on life. They have salvaged eight of the cabins (which once probably numbered three times as many) and are in the process of refurbishing the 18 units in the two-story motel, room by room ($55–110 in summer, depending on the room, which includes a suite; $45–75 in cabins, more in foliage season; children 12 and under are free; extra charge for pets, which are allowed only in the cabins). The cabins are rustic, accommodating from three to six people, each with a heater, shower, and TV. One began life as "the Hairpin turn tourist shop" and was hauled the 5 miles uphill one winter in the 1920s. The grounds include a pool, but the big attraction here is the view. The café is open (same season as the motel) for breakfast and lunch. This once housed the "largest souvenir and gift shop in America," and a small shop is planned, along with a tower (much reduced in height), from which you look back down the narrow Deerfield Valley. A path leads off to **Moore's Summit** (2,250 feet), the highest point on the Mohawk Trail.

THE TOWER ON WHITCOMB SUMMIT WHERE YOU CAN SEE THE "100 MILE VIEW"

Kim Grant

Scenic detour: **Whitcomb Hill Road/The Eastern Portal and River Road.** East of the elk statue, **Whitcomb Hill Road** plunges off to the north, corkscrewing downhill at a grade that vintage-1912 cars simply could not handle. This is the old road up (and down) Hoosac Mountain, the one the Mohawk Trail was designed to replace. At the bottom of the hill turn left and drive a mile or so to the railroad tracks. Park just beyond them to see the "Eastern Portal" of the Hoosac Tunnel.

If you continue on this road a little more than 3 miles, passing a series of fishing and boating access points, until you reach the Fife Brook Dam, in another mile you will see the **Bear Swamp Visitors Center** (closed at this writing; for information, call 413-424-7219). The **Dunbar Picnic Area** with restrooms and swings is another mile up the road, across from the trailheads for hiking in the **Monroe State Forest** (413-339-5504; www.massparks.org). You can loop back on Monroe Hill Road past the decommissioned Yankee Rowe Nuclear Power Plant, into the village of **Rowe** and on back down the Zoar Road to Route 2.

If you return to the bottom of Whitcomb Hill, you can follow the Deerfield River east (chances are you will see trout fishermen) to the lovely, pine-shaded, riverside **Zoar Picnic Area** and on through mountain-walled **Zoar Gap** to Charlemont. This makes a nice loop from the east if you only want to drive as far west as Whitcomb Summit.

The **Eastern Summit Gift Shop**

(413-663-6996), 367 Mohawk Trail, is the next Mohawk Trail landmark (westbound lane, but worth the crossover). The view, north and west over tier on tier of mountains, is similar to that from Whitcomb Summit. The shop has been owned by the Deveney family for more than 30 years, and the complex, which began with a shop and now defunct cabins across the road, dates back at least another 40.

Dead Man's Curve is just beyond Brown's Garage ("no gas") in the village of Drury. The overhead warning sign with its flashing lights suggests many fatal accidents over the years. It marks the beginning of the descent down the "Eastern Slope" of the Hoosac Range, following the Cold River.

Detour: **Tannery Falls.** It's more difficult to catch the turnoff traveling eastbound than it is west, but just east of the bridge that marks the Florida–Savoy line, make a right turn onto Black Brook Road and drive for about 10 minutes; take a left onto unpaved

VIEW FROM PORCH OF EASTERN SUMMIT GIFT SHOP

Kim Grant

Tannery Road, which, after another 10 minutes or so, brings you to the parking area for Tannery Falls (the sign may be down because it's a local collectors' item, but the path from one end of the parking area is well marked). Just be sure not to go alone (it's steep), and don't try to climb the falls itself (it looks so tempting that people try, and several have died in the process).

The trail follows a narrow stream that rushes steeply downward beneath fir and spruce trees to a lookout at the top of the falls, fenced with wire cable. What you see below is a glorious cascade, swirling through variously shaped rock pools, a pattern repeated again and again. In spring or after a big rain this series of cascades is replaced by a thunderous, continuous rush of water. The path continues steeply downward, but instead of shadowing the cascade it now follows another stream that suddenly appears, plunging down through a rocky gorge. New, broad steps, fashioned from rail ties, ease the descent, and more massive old granite steps lead to an islandlike promontory at the confluence of the two brooks, the floor of the hollow and end of the trail. A circle of stone seats suggest a picnic spot fashioned by and for druids, and the view back up the waterfall is spellbinding.

TANNERY FALLS IN SAVOY
MOUNTAIN STATE FOREST

©Kindra Clineff/DCR

⚓ ♿ **Mohawk Trail State Forest** (413-339-5504; www.massparks.org), Route 2, Charlemont, covers 6,457 acres, and offers 56 **campsites** and seven log **cabins** (one wheelchair accessible). There's **swimming** in a human-made pool in the Cold River, complete with bathhouse, scattered picnic tables, and many miles of hiking trails, including a portion of the original Indian path. Camping here is permitted year-round; in winter there are snowshoeing and cross-county ski trails. The remnants of the original Mohawk Trail can be seen as a hiking trail with a series of switchbacks ascending Lookout Mountain from the west end of the camping area.

Mohawk Park in West Charlemont is the official centerpiece of the trail. A bronze statue with its arms raised, the unofficial symbol of the trail, was placed here in 1932 by the Improved Order of Red Men. The arrowhead-shaped tablet at the base of the statue reads: HAIL TO THE SUNRISE—IN MEMORY OF THE MOHAWK INDIAN. There is a wishing pool with 100 inscribed stones from the various tribes and councils from throughout the country. Note the Mohawk Park Cabins across the way, a vestige of what once was.

Note: The **Rowe Road** is a left off Route 2 here, and the next left puts you on River Road leading back along the Deerfield River to **Zoar Gap.** We have described it coming from the other direction from Whitcomb Summit. If you continue north (instead of turning left), you come to **Rowe** (see "West County").

The Shunpike Marker by the river is dedicated to "the thrifty travelers of the Mohawk Trail who in 1797 here forded the Deerfield River rather than pay the toll at the Turnpike Bridge and who in 1810 won the battle for free travel on all Massachusetts roads." It's worth noting that the marker was placed here in 1957 as construction of the Massachusetts Turnpike was getting under way. The Mass Pike has substantially reduced traffic on Route 2.

Shelburne Falls Area Business Association

"HAIL TO THE SUNRISE"
STATUE IN MOHAWK PARK

✒ **Zoar Outdoor** (www.zaroutdoor.com). This is home base for the area's oldest, most diversified white-water sports company. See *White-Water Rafting* in "West County."

⊗ *✒* 🏨 **Charlemont Inn** (413-339-5796), Main Street, Charlemont. This is the landmark inn along the Mohawk Trail and continues to offers three daily meals as well as spirits and lodging. See *Lodging* in "West County."

The Federated Church in Charlemont has excellent acoustics and for almost 35 years has been the venue for the **Mohawk Trail Concerts** (413-625-9511 or 1-800-MTC-MUSE; www.mohawktrailconcerts.org).

✒ **Indian Plaza Gift Shop & Pow Wow Grounds** (413-339-4096), 1475 Mohawk Trail. Dating from 1933 and site of the tragic death of the owner's wife during the Hurricane of 1938, which flooded the Deerfield River. It has been in Harold Roberts's family for more than 37 years and is open daily 10–6, best known as the site of periodic powwows from early May through the Columbus Day weekend.

✒ **The East Charlemont Picnic Area** (eastbound) along the Deerfield River is a charmed spot with tables and a view of fields across the river and the venerable Hall Tavern Farm down the road. (The original Hall Tavern now serves as the reception center for Historic Deerfield.)

Several motels—the **Red Rose** (formerly cabins), the **Olde Willow Motel and Restaurant,** the **Oxbow Resort Motel** (see *Lodging* in "West County") and

Hilltop Motel (formerly Rio Vista)—are holdovers from the Trail's glory days. For more about Stillwaters Restaurant, see *Dining Out* in "West County."

Crabapple Whitewater (www.crabappleinc.com) has renovated and expanded what's left of a vintage cabin complex. Inquire about "funyaks." See *White-Water Rafting* in "West County."

❧ **Tubing** (floating downriver in rubber tire tubes) is a popular summer pastime on this stretch. Look for seasonal signs for TUBES.

❧ **Big Indian Shop** (413-625-6817), 2217 Mohawk Trail. Open year-round daily, 9-5 May through December, shorter hours off-season. Named for the 28-foot-tall Indian that guards its door, this is an old-fashioned souvenir shop and proud to be one. It's been in Jon Estes's family for 69 years, and Kim Estes is usually behind the counter to sell you a rubber drum or tomahawk, a cowboy hat, maple products, or moccasins. It's a must-stop for kids, with live goats, a covered wagon, and a tepee.

Shelburne Falls (www.shelburne-falls.com). The trail no longer passes through the middle of town as it once did, but this unusual village is now the hub of the trail, offering the only visitors center (with restrooms) along the trail and most of its places to eat. Eastbound you turn onto State Street and follow it to the **Bridge of Flowers.** Park and walk. Note the **Sweetheart Restaurant** on Route 2A just off Route 2. Its name recalls the heart-shaped maple sugar candies Alice Brown began selling from her home here in 1915. The spot went on to become The Sweet Heart Tea Room and eventually a full-service restaurant that served as a driving destination for generations of families.

Gould's Sugar House (413-625-6170), Route 2, Shelburne. Open in sugaring season (March and April) and during foliage (September and October), daily 8:30–2. A great roadside stop that's been in the family for generations; specialties include pancakes, waffles, and fritters laced with the family's maple syrup.

The Mahican-Mohawk Trail runs for 7.5 miles between Shelburne Falls and Deerfield. Several years ago the

JON ESTES, OWNER OF THE BIG INDIAN SHOP, WITH THE GIANT 28-FOOT-TALL WOODEN INDIAN THAT MADE HIS STORE FAMOUS

Christina Tree

Berkshire writer and naturalist Lauren Stevens initiated a study that revealed not only the location of the old riverside path but also the fact that it was still roughly maintained by the New England Power Company to access a series of hydroelectric dams. Thanks to the concerted efforts of local environmental groups, this trail is now accessible to sturdily shod hikers. The entire hike takes at least 4 hours, but the most impressive and rugged few miles are at the Shelburne Falls end. Details are in the "West County" chapter; see *Green Space*.

The **Mohawk Trading Post** (413-625-2412; www.Mohawk-trading-post.com), 874 Mohawk Trail, Shelburne. Open all year. The easternmost Indian-themed shop on the Trail, this is less dramatic on the exterior than others (the fiberglass buffalo is smallish but big enough for a small boy to sit on), though inside there's plenty to please: a wide selection of books about Native Americans and quality soapstone carvings and pottery, sterling Indian jewelry and moccasins. Laurie York is the current owner, and it's been in her family since 1985. The stuffed bear by the entrance, she explains, evokes the memory of the live bears for which the trading post was long known, and the genuine fossil by the counter was "liberated" from the Connecticut River by the son of the previous owners.

Wovenwood's Baskets & More (413-625-9226), eastbound side. We're not sure how far back Bill and Bev Neeley's "Little Log store" dates, but the large stocks of baskets, wooden bowls, nesting dolls, and the like are in keeping with the Trail traditions. Note that the Shelburne Country Store next door was once the central building of a motor court.

Goodnow's Chip'n'Putt (413-625-6107), 1211 Mohawk Trail, Shelburne. Open seasonally, 7:30–dusk. Fun for beginners and advanced players.

Mohawk Orchards (413-625-2874) maintains a seasonal farm stand on the westbound side of the road. PYO apples Labor Day through Columbus Day at the orchards themselves, less than a mile north on the Colrain Road.

The Outpost (413-625-6806 or 1-800-541-5086), 1385 Mohawk Trail, Shelburne. Open year-round, daily

YOU CAN'T MISS THIS SIGN TO LONGVIEW TOWER SPECIALTY SHOPS

Christina Tree

10–5. Looks can be deceptive. This shop (eastbound) looks both smallish and new. It was originally "Indian Park" but is now substantially expanded and specializes totally in sheepskin products (car seats, slippers, mittens, and more); also fine leather products. Beware. We left with a pair of gloves.

Longview Tower Specialty Shops (413-772-6976), 497 Mohawk Trail. Opened in 1923 as the "Long Vue" by the same the Misses Mansfield who also owned the Western Summit observation and gift shop. It's on the westbound side and frequently difficult to stop either way—but worth the effort. Locals bring their picnics up (there are benches) and regularly visit the petting zoo. There is also a serious leather shop here (Ron Rowe makes much of what he sells), plus souvenirs and fudge. What it's still about, however, is the "three-state view" (New Hampshire, Vermont, and Massachusetts). Rebuilt in steel in 1952, this five-story observation tower is the only one left along the Trail that's still its original height.

Old Greenfield Village (413-774-7138; www.crocker.com/Greenfield/ogv.html), 368 Mohawk Trail. Open mid-May to mid-October, Saturday and holidays 10–4, Sunday noon–4; weekdays by appointment. $5 adult, $4 seniors, $3 students (6–16), free under age 6. This is a genuine, Yankee kind of phenomenon, a collection of thousands of artifacts formerly found in stores, in dental offices, churches, barbershops, and tool shops around the turn of the 20th century, all collected over 30 years by retired schoolteacher Waine Morse.

THE BERKSHIRE HILLTOWNS

WEST COUNTY

THE HIDDEN HILLS

T he 500 square miles of rolling farm and forest between the Connecticut River valley and Berkshire County is known, among other things, as the "Berkshire Hilltowns." Its glacially rounded hills and river-sculpted valleys are, in topographical fact, as much a part of the Berkshire Hills as Berkshire County to the west.

Early settlers dubbed it the "Berkshire Barrier," but Native Americans knew how to traverse the region. They followed its two major rivers—the Deerfield and the Westfield—which have cut three parallel east–west valleys, now obvious traffic conduits. Route 2 (the "Mohawk Trail"), the northernmost east–west high road ("highway" would be an overstatement) shadows the ancient Mohawk Trail along the Deerfield River. Route 9 (the "Berkshire Trail") follows the main stem of the Westfield River across the middle of the state, while Route 20 ("Jacob's Ladder"), now shadowed by I-90 (the Mass Pike), hugs the west branch of the Westfield. This high ground is also the watershed between the two major north–south valleys in the Northeast. It's said that raindrops falling on the western slant of the Congregational church roof in hilltop Peru ultimately flow into the Hudson, while those on the eastern slant fall into the Connecticut.

Much of this area looks the way Vermont did a couple of decades ago: Valleys are steep, alternately wooded and patched with open fields. In winter cross-country skiers, snowshoers, and snowmobilers drive from Boston and Hartford to take advantage of the highest, most dependably snow-covered trails south of Vermont. Early spring brings sit-down breakfasts in sugarhouses and tours of the sugarbush (there are more maple producers here than in all the rest of the state put together). In late spring white-water rafters begin converging on the Deerfield River, and nationally ranked white-water canoeists compete on the Westfield. Anglers find trout in both rivers. In summer back roads beckon bicyclists, and hikers follow trails to hilltop lookouts and deep-in-the-woods waterfalls. In fall the Mohawk Trail is thronged with leaf-peepers, but back roads receive surprisingly little use.

Despite the fertile bottomland along the Deerfield and Westfield Rivers, this area was very sparsely settled until the end of the French and Indian Wars in

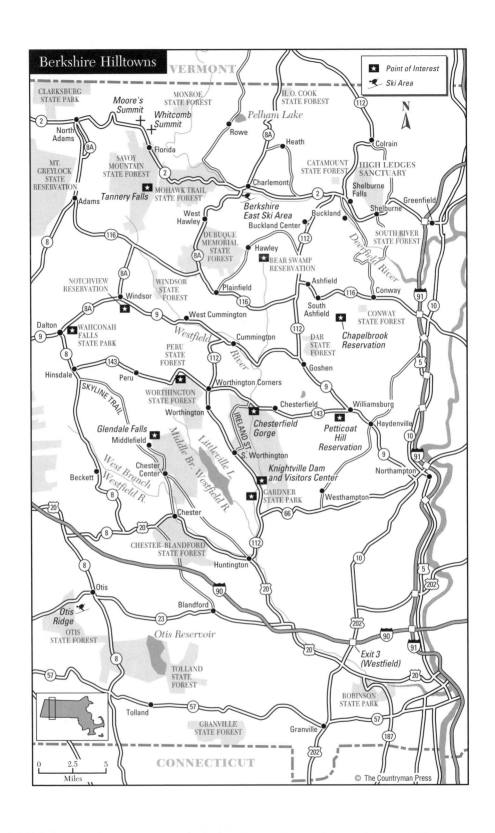

Berkshire Hilltowns

VERMONT

CONNECTICUT

Point of Interest

Ski Area

N

CLARKSBURG STATE PARK

Moore's Summit

MONROE STATE FOREST

H. O. COOK STATE FOREST

Pelham Lake

112

North Adams

2

8A

Whitcomb Summit

Florida

Rowe

8A

Heath

Colrain

MT. GREYLOCK STATE RESERVATION

SAVOY MOUNTAIN STATE FOREST

2

CATAMOUNT STATE FOREST

HIGH LEDGES SANCTUARY

Shelburne Falls

Tannery Falls

MOHAWK TRAIL STATE FOREST

Charlemont

2

Greenfield

Adams

West Hawley

Berkshire East Ski Area

Buckland

Shelburne

116

DUBUQUE MEMORIAL STATE FOREST

Buckland Center

112

SOUTH RIVER STATE FOREST

8

8A

Hawley

BEAR SWAMP RESERVATION

Deerfield River

NOTCHVIEW RESERVATION

8A

WINDSOR STATE FOREST

Plainfield

Ashfield

116

Conway

91

Windsor

116

South Ashfield

CONWAY STATE FOREST

10

Dalton

8A

9

West Cummington

Westfield

112

Chapelbrook Reservation

5

WAHCONAH FALLS STATE PARK

Cummington

DAR STATE FOREST

9

8

PERU STATE FOREST

River

Goshen

Hinsdale

143

Peru

112

Worthington Corners

9

WORTHINGTON STATE FOREST

Chesterfield

143

Williamsburg

10

SKYLINE TRAIL

Worthington

IRELAND ST.

Chesterfield Gorge

Petticoat Hill Reservation

Haydenville

91

Glendale Falls

Middlefield

Littleville L.

S. Worthington

9

West Branch Westfield R.

Chester Center

Middle Br. Westfield R.

Knightville Dam and Visitors Center

Northampton

Beckett

20

8

Chester

GARDNER STATE PARK

Westhampton

10

8

20

66

CHESTER–BLANDFORD STATE FOREST

112

5

8

Huntington

202

90

20

Otis

Blandford

10

90

Otis Ridge

23

202

91

OTIS STATE FOREST

Otis Reservoir

20

Exit 3 (Westfield)

20

57

8

TOLLAND STATE FOREST

ROBINSON STATE PARK

57

Tolland

57

GRANVILLE STATE FOREST

Granville

187

0   2.5   5

Miles

202

CONNECTICUT

© The Countryman Press

1756. Most towns were incorporated shortly before the Revolution, and many hill farms were deserted as early as the 1820s, when the Erie Canal opened the way to greener, less stony, western pastures. The stone walls pioneers built now lie deep in the area's many state parks and forests. Currently the Hilltowns are home to an unusual number of artists, craftspeople, and musicians. The biggest events are still country fairs.

Berkshire Hilltown residents cherish the elusive, firefly-like quality of the area's attractions, a quality that, admittedly, can be frustrating to casual visitors who may not be in the right place at the right time on the right day. A former Colrain Center church is, for instance, filled with live jazz and satisfied dinner patrons—but only on summer Saturday evenings and special occasions. Internationally famed musicians perform in an old church in Charlemont—but only Saturday evenings in July and August. And world-class pianists perform in a defunct 19th-century academy building in South Worthington, but only Friday evenings and Sunday afternoons in July and August.

On the other hand, lodging prices are well below those in Berkshire County. Berkshire County's museums, summer theater, music, and dance are, moreover, just a short drive to the west, as are the museums and restaurants of the Five-College Area to the east. The Hilltowns have a long tradition of welcoming summer people (witness William Cullen Bryant's summer home and several former 19th-century hotels), and throughout the past century many farms took in summer boarders.

Though the Hilltown area may all look much the same to visitors, locals will tell you that the region is clearly divided along county lines. Conway, Ashfield, Hawley, and the towns to the north all fall into "West (Franklin) County," whereas Plainfield, Windsor, and the towns along Route 9 and south consider themselves the "Hidden Hills," a name coined by the area's bed & breakfast association.

Christina Tree

Present lodging options in the Hilltowns include roughly three dozen widely scattered B&Bs, including several farms. At present the only staffed information center in this entire area is in Shelburne Falls, the obvious way stop on the Mohawk Trail and one of the liveliest dining and crafts towns in New England.

Few regions this beautiful and accessible are this unspoiled, a situation that may not last forever.

WEST COUNTY

West Franklin County, better known as "West County," has been attracting artists, craftspeople, and musicians for many decades and now also harbors a fair share of contemplative communities. Locals speak of a special energy emanating from this particular roll of hill and valley. One thing's certain: Wherever creative and questing spirits gather, you are sure to find exceptional peace and beauty.

"Everything that I do and make is interconnected, influenced by this view," internationally respected glass artist Josh Simpson once told us, spreading his arms to the hills that circle his studio.

Simpson's deeply colored "planets" and other art pieces are featured in the Salmon Falls Artisans Showroom, a former granary in Shelburne Falls, a village formed by the centers of two towns, linked by the two bridges pictured on our book's cover.

Nothing in Shelburne Falls works quite the way it does in other places. Its old trolley bridge is now a walkway awash with colorful flowers, and its vintage-1913 iron bridge, the main thoroughfare, is the venue of an annual community banquet. An old trolley has been rehabbed and again rumbles back and forth up at the old depot, restored by volunteers.

Always a modest shopping and dining hub for the surrounding hilltowns, Shelburne Falls is evolving as a restaurant and gallery town, but with a difference. The several "upscale" restaurants are heavy on greens and grains rather than your wallet, and galleries are artist and artisan owned. Shelburne Falls is also still a mill village with a cutlery factory dating back to 1837, a family-owned grocery store, an independently owned pharmacy with a soda fountain, and an old-fashioned news store.

Just north of Shelburne Falls, hills hump abruptly and roads climb steeply through Heath and Colrain and on to Vermont. West of the village the Mohawk Trail follows a stunning stretch of the Deerfield River to Charlemont; to the south Route 112 leads south through Buckland's magnificent farmland to Ashfield. Back roads wind up into hills to classic clapboard villages, 50-mile views, and unexpected finds: here a farm with yaks and camels, there a woodworker's or weaver's studio, a winery or waterfall, and always a river or brook. Hiking trails abound and lodging places, while frequently hard to find, are equally hard to leave.

"It's what you don't see here that's striking," an Ashfield resident observes. Over the past 17 years the Ashfield-based Franklin Land Trust has alone has preserved some 10,000 acres (more than 15 square miles), just one sign of the ways local residents, few of them wealthy, feel about the look of this land.

AREA CODE 413.

GUIDANCE **Shelburne Falls Village Information Center** (413-625-2544; www.shelburnefalls.com), 75 Bridge Street, P.O. Box 42, Shelburne Falls 01370. The visitors center is open May through October, daily 10–4, Sunday noon–4; catch as can the rest of the year. A friendly, well-stocked information source (with restrooms) for the surrounding area as well as the village, in a former fire station at the center of town.

Franklin County Chamber of Commerce (413-773-5463, daily, 24 hours; www.franklincc.org) operates the **Upper Pioneer Valley Visitor Information Center** just off I-91 (exit 26) at the Route 2 rotary behind Appleby's on Route 2A east, open daily 9–5 (until 8 on Friday), with restrooms and local products as well as information. You can also request a helpful map and guide from the chamber at P.O. Box 898, 395 Main Street, Greenfield 01302.

GETTING THERE *From Boston:* There is no bus or train service. The obvious way by car is Route 2, which technically becomes the Mohawk Trail in Orange but really begins looking like a tourist route west of Greenfield. From points north and south, take exit 26 off I-91 at Greenfield. From Amherst, take Route 116 north; from Northampton, Route 9 north to Route 112.

GETTING AROUND A good map is a necessity because the state map and larger New England maps will leave you assuming that many of the most beautiful roads in this region don't exist. Franklin County publishes an excellent free, detailed map, and the *Rubel Western Massachusetts Bicycle and Road Map* covers the territory well.

MEDICAL EMERGENCY Dial **911.**

✳ Villages

Ashfield. This unusually spirited town of some 1,900 people publishes its own newspaper. A large, former summer hotel still stands in the middle of the village, but most traffic now stops at Ashfield Hardware and Countrypie Pizza. The pride of Ashfield remains the Wren-style steeple on its town hall (built as a church in 1814) and its unusual number of both maple producers and craftspeople, most of whom exhibit at the annual fall festival on Columbus Day weekend. Ashfield is the birthplace of movie director Cecil B. DeMille (his parents happened to be staying at the hotel) and has been home for a number of artists and writers, making for an unusually interesting **Ashfield Historical Society** (open Fridays 11–4 in July and August, or call 413-628-4541; www.ashfield-museum.org). Ten rooms of exhibits include the glass-plate photos of New England towns and working people taken by the two Howes brothers of Ashfield around the turn of the 20th century. In summer there is swimming at the small town beach (transients discouraged), right in the village on Ashfield Lake, and there are two outstanding Trustees of Reservations properties (see *Green Space*). The Ashfield Fall Foliage Festival, always held Columbus Day weekend, is one of the most colorful in New England.

Buckland (population: c. 2000). Buckland's town hall stands just across the

Bridge of Flowers in the heart of Shelburne Falls (the town's northern boundary is the Deerfield River). The village center of Buckland is, however, a gathering of a classic little church, a historical society, a small brick library, and aristocratic, 18th-century homes (one of them now a bed & breakfast), all set high on a hill a dozen miles south and off Route 112. The **Buckland Historical Society Museum** (413-625-9763; open on the second and fourth Sundays in July and August, 2–4, as well as for special programs) is housed in a historic building near the Mary Lyon Church in Buckland Center. Inquire about special events at its **Wilder Homestead** on Route 112, a 1775 saltbox with five working fireplaces and a barn filled with equipment, weaving looms, and a shoemaker's shop. The society's collection features exhibits about Mary Lyon, the Buckland woman who pioneered education for women in the early 19th century and is remembered as the founder of both Mount Holyoke College in South Hadley and Wheaton College in Norton. It was in the ballroom of the four-square, four-chimneyed **Major Joseph Griswold House** on Upper Street that Mary Lyon opened her first academy in 1823, teaching the family and neighborhood children (open by appointment through the Mary Lyon Foundation: 413-625-2555). The way to the site of Mary Lyon's birthplace is marked from Route 112 (East Buckland Street).

Charlemont (population: 1,358). The Deerfield River rushes down from Vermont, then slows, widens, and turns east in Charlemont, creating fertile floodplains that clearly have been farmed since the mid–18th century, judging from the age of several proud farmhouses. The 18th-century Charlemont Inn's tavern and restaurant mark the heart of town, along with A. L. Avery & Son General Merchandise, now run by the fifth generation of the family that opened it, still

SCENIC VIEW OF ASHFIELD

Kim Grant

stocking everything from cheese to hardware, boots to beef. This town is the only one in New England known for both alpine skiing (Berkshire East) and white-water rafting. Rafting has introduced many visitors to the high backcountry north of Route 2. **Bissell Covered Bridge** spans Mill Brook just off Route 2 on Route 8A (currently just pedestrian traffic). The **Charlemont Historical Society Museum** in the town hall is open by appointment: 413-339-6633. In July and August the **Mohawk Trail Concerts** in the Federated Church draw a sophisticated audience from throughout the Northeast.

CHURCH IN VILLAGE OF COLRAIN   Kim Grant

Charlemont **Yankee Doodle Days** in July commemorate the fact that it was here at a local muster in the 1750s that America's first famous song was written—by a British doctor who was part of a British regiment, poking fun at the local militia.

Colrain (population: 1,813). This hilly town boomed with sheep raising, cotton mills, and an iron foundry in the mid–19th century, all linked to the train at Shelburne Falls by trolley. The old foundry is still in Foundry Hollow, and a covered bridge sits by the North River (waiting to be put back on its pilings). Catamount Hill is said to be the site of the first schoolhouse to fly the American flag, so it's appropriate that the town now harbors "Glowing Glory"(www.glowingglory.com), the country's largest neon American flag, designed by local neon artist Pacifico Palumbo and set on a hilltop across from Pine Hill Orchards on the Greenfield Road soon after 9/11 to honor U.S. veterans. The **Colrain Historical Society** (413-624-3710) is housed in the **G. William Pitt House** on Main Street. The village center with its three churches (one is now the popular **Green Emporium;** see *Dining Out*) and common is at the junction of four scenic routes, including Route 112 north to Vermont. Colrain lists a dozen sugarhouses, and **West County Winery** welcomes visitors on the way to the center from Route 2 (see *Selective Shopping*). The annual village fair, held the third Saturday in September, showcases local crafts. Colrain now harbors several unusual B&Bs.

Conway. Turn off Route 116 and stop long enough at the triangular green to admire the domed **Marshall Field Memorial Library** (413-369-4646), gift of the native son who founded a Chicago department store. There's a marble rotunda and elaborate detailing within; the historical collection is open selected days. The heart of town is easy to miss: **Baker's Store** serves lunch, great pie, and all the local news you need. Note the covered bridge across the South River off Route 116. A Main Street (Route 116) storefront now houses the **Conway Historical Society,** open July through Labor Day, Sunday 1–4.

Heath (population: 805). Heath is worth finding, just for the fun of it: a classic hilltown with a common surrounded by the usual white-clapboard buildings. What's amazing (going and coming) are the long views. Heath is known for its wild blueberries, and the **Heath Fair,** held two weekends before Labor Day, features horse pulling, music, and food.

Shelburne Falls. Usually rivers divide towns, but in this case the Deerfield has united the 19th-century dining and shopping areas of two towns (Buckland and Shelburne) to form Shelburne Falls, one of the most unusual and lively villages in New England. Instead of a common, there's the Bridge of Flowers (see *To See*). An iron bridge, which the community has restored rather than replacing the way most communities do (claiming that they will be rarer than covered bridges in a couple of decades), also links the main streets on both sides of the river. An aberration from its rural setting, this totally Victorian shopping center has become a showcase for art and crafts work produced in the surrounding hills. The **Glacial Potholes** at the foot of Salmon Falls (Deerfield Avenue, off Bridge Street) are a many-colored and unusually shaped phenomenon, worth a look. The **Shelburne Historical Society** (413-625-6150), in the Arms Academy Building (corner of Maple and Church Streets), is open Wednesday 10–4 and Sunday 2–5 from July through October, and **Lamson & Goodnow Cutlery,** "the oldest continuously sited cutlery company in the country" (founded 1837), maintains a gift shop. The second-floor Opera House in vintage-1897 **Memorial Hall** has been restored and once more serves as the town's movie house (Pothole Pictures) as well as the stage for live entertainment. A **Riverwalk** runs along the Buckland side of the river. Also see the **Mahican-Mohawk Trail** along the Deerfield under *Green Space.*

DOWNTOWN SHELBURNE FALLS

Kim Grant

Rowe (population: 380) is known chiefly as the former home of New England's first atomic energy plant (1961–93), which has had obvious effects on the town's budget for civil amenities. Instead of the usual town dump, Rowe has a landscaped "Refuse Garden." Plaques label the sites of buildings that stood in town when it bustled: the Foliated Talc Mill (1908–22) and Eddy's Casket Shop (1846–1948), for example. The Browning Bench Tool Factory has been restored and moved to the shore of Pelham Lake, where it serves as an arts and community center. There are picnic tables in 1,000-acre **Pelham Lake Park,** and a gazebo ornaments the common. The **Rowe Historical Society Museum** (open July through third weekend of October, Sunday

2–5, otherwise by appointment; call Alan Bjork: 413-339-4700) collection includes records and artifacts from 18th-century Fort Pelham (the site is marked). The Rowe Conference Center, originally a Unitarian Church summer camp, features workshops led by authorities on a broad spectrum of subjects.

✳ To See

⏿ **The Bridge of Flowers.** Local garden clubs began planting this concrete, multiarched bridge with flowers as a war memorial in 1919. Now meticulously tended by the Shelburne Falls Women's Club and reserved for foot traffic, it may well be the world's floweriest bridge, abloom from April through October with 500 varieties of plantings, including a number of trees. It's especially beautiful at dusk with the reflections in the quiet river on its western side.

Shelburne Falls Trolley Museum (413-625-9443; www.sfm.org), 14 Depot Street, Buckland (in the railyard). Open weekends May through October, also Mondays July through October 1–5. There is memorabilia in the visitors center, with model trains for "young folks" to operate. The big attraction here is a vintage-1896 trolley, which for 20 years carried passengers and freight the 7 uphill miles to Colrain and back down. It's up and running at the depot, having been restored by volunteers—after serving as Marshall Johnson's chicken coop for 70 years, which everyone agrees saved it, both because it was up off the ground and because the chicken manure kept the wood lubricated. The present ride may be short, but it's enlivened by conductor Sam Bartlett's narration. Passengers learn that they are en route to visit relatives in Colrain, having come in on the B&M (freight trains still use the adjacent tracks). They hear about passing factories, picking up schoolkids and shoppers on the way to "Colrain City" and its four-story (long since vanished) inn.

THE BRIDGE OF FLOWERS IN SHELBURNE FALLS

Kim Grant

✎ Also see **Tregellys Fiber Farm** under *Selective Shopping*. The farm features a menagerie of some 200 animals, including two-humped camels, llamas, yaks, and rare and heritage breeds of many other animals.

SCENIC DRIVES Along the Mohawk Trail. See the previous chapter.

River Road to Whitcomb Summit is a worthwhile deviation from the Mohawk Trail. Take the road marked ROWE just west of the village of Charlemont, but bear left almost immediately at the fork (marked by a dead tree with numerous signs tacked to it) along **River Road.** Follow it along the river, by the **Zoar Picnic Area** in a pine grove. Continue along the river as the valley walls steepen, past Whitcomb Summit Road, over the railroad tracks. Look here for the eastern portal of the Hoosac Tunnel, opened in the 1870s by blasting through granite.

Shelburne to Conway. There are two scenic ways from Shelburne to Conway, both good bicycle routes. The first is simply to take the Conway Road south along the river from the Buckland side; the second is to go south from Route 2 at the sign for Shelburne Center, where you pick up Bardwell's Ferry Road, one of the prettiest roads we know anywhere. At one high point you can see Mount Tom in Holyoke off across hills. Just beyond comedian Bill Cosby's house (it's easy to spot because the sign warns: IF YOU ARE NOT INVITED DO NOT PASS THROUGH THESE GATES), the road dips across the railroad tracks and crosses the Bardwell Ferry Bridge. Wiry and graceful, it's one of the most unusual little bridges in Massachusetts and a popular fishing spot. The Conway stretch of the road is also beautiful and joins the Shelburne Falls Road not far north of Conway Village.

Peckville Road from Route 2 up to the Apex Orchards offers a spectacular view of the hills.

Other suggested routes

Circle through Colrain Village. Take Greenfield Road to Colrain Center, then back down to Route 2 on the Shelburne Falls Road, or vice versa.

Route 112 between Buckland and Ashfield threads a beautiful valley.

Get lost. There are so many beautiful roads in this area that you really can't lose—and the best way is to get lost. Again we recommend the *Rubel Western Massachusetts Bicycle and Road Map,* as well as the free map published by Franklin County.

ARTISTS OFTEN ENJOY THE INSPIRATIONAL VIEW FROM THE BRIDGE OF FLOWERS

Kim Grant

✳ To Do

BICYCLING **Bicycles Unlimited** (413-772-2700), 322 High Street, Greenfield. During the summer season this shop rents mountain bikes (selling most of them around Labor Day) and can advise about good routes through this region's maze of back roads. Also see *Rubel Bicycle and Road Map* in *What's Where.*

Zoar Outdoor (see below) in Charlemont has begun renting mountain bikes, suggesting routes, and mapping self-guiding tours. All the

Scenic Drives described above are good for bicycling, and many more are scenic, curving, and little trafficked.

CANOEING AND KAYAKING Zoar Outdoor (1-800-532-7483; www.zoaroutdoor.com), Route 2 in Charlemont, rents canoes and kayaks for use on several stretches of the Deerfield. Shuttle service, canoeing and white-water clinics, and sit-on-top kayaks for the calmer reaches of the river are also offered. Inquire about "family trips."

Crab Apple (1-800-553-7238; www.crabpplewhitewater.com/deerfield) offers inflatable kayak ("funyak") rentals with a shuttle to the put-in point.

FISHING The 12-mile stretch of the Deerfield River in Charlemont lures anglers from across the Northeast. There is a catch-and-release section in the village of Hoosac Tunnel. Beware of the changing depth of the water throughout this area due to releases from the dam. The **Catamount State Forest** (413-339-5504) harbors a 27-acre trout-stocked lake. **Davenport's Mobil** (413-625-9544), Route 2 in Shelburne Falls, stocks fishing supplies.

GOLF Edge Hill Golf Course (413-628-6018), Barnes Road in Ashfield. This former dairy farm is now a nine-hole course with the golf shop, snack bar, and lounge in the former barn overlooking a pond.

Goodnow's Chip'n'Putt (413-625-6107), 1211 Mohawk Trail (Route 2), Shelburne. Open seasonally, 7:30–dusk. Fun for beginners and advanced players.

HORSEBACK RIDING See **High Pocket B&B** under *Lodging.*

Flames Stables (802-464-8329), Route 100 South, Wilmington, Vermont. Western saddle trail rides, pony rides for young children (just over the border from Rowe).

ROCK CLIMBING ❧ **Zoar Outdoor** (www.zoaroutdoor.com), Route 2, Charlemont, runs a rock climbing school that emphasizes toprope climbing with the rope anchored by an instructor; there is a low student–instructor ratio. One- and 2-day novice and intermediate clinics are

ZOAR OUTDOOR OFFERS WHITE-WATER CLINICS ON THE DEERFIELD RIVER

Zoar Outdoor

offered, including special parent–child clinics and climbs geared to kids age 10–15.

SWIMMING See *Green Space* for the **Mohawk Trail** and **Savoy Mountain State Forests;** ask locally about swimming holes in the Deerfield River.

TUBING Bring your own, or pick up an inner tube at **Davenport's Mobil** (413-625-9544) on Route 2 in Shelburne Falls, and coast down the Deerfield River (Charlemont is the local hub for tubing).

WHITE-WATER RAFTING "When I first approached New England Electric they said 'No. You can't raft the river,'" Bruce Lessels recalls, adding that over the next few years, the power company became increasingly cooperative. In 1989 the company began releasing water from Fife Brook Dam with a regularity that makes rafting possible on most days April through October on a 10-mile stretch of Class II and III whitewater—from Florida, through steep, green-walled, boulder-strewn Zoar Gap, and on down to Charlemont. Admittedly not as visually and viscerally exciting as parts of Maine's Kennebec or Penobscot Rivers, it offers a great introduction to rafting. The day we ran it, a third of our group was under age 16 (minimum weight: 50 pounds). The Upper Deerfield Dryway, a stretch of Class IV whitewater above the Fife Field Dam, is also now rafted on specific days (adding up to more than 30 each season). The lower river is great for family float trips, canoeing, and recreational kayaking and tubing.

✔ **Zoar Outdoor** (1-800-532-7483; www.zoaroutdoor.com), based in a 1750s house with 80 acres on Route 2 in Charlemont, is headed by Bruce Lessels, a former member of the U.S. Olympic white-water team. The complex presently includes a bathhouse with changing rooms and hot showers, an orientation pavilion, cabin tents, primitive tent sites, and (promised for 2004) a guest lodge. Trips range from challenging rides down the Dryway and clinics for expert white-water kayakers to family float trips. Rates run $38–99, depending on day, trip, and age of the person involved. Also see *Canoeing and Kayaking*, *Bicycling*, and *Rock Climbing*.

Crab Apple (1-413-625-2288 or 1-800-553-7238; www.crabapplewhite-water.com), Route 2, Charlemont. A well-established family-owned outfitter with a home base on Maine's Kennebec River, Crab Apple has been offering raft trips on the Deerfield since 1989. It offers the full range of rafting trips and rents "funyaks" (inflatable kayaks). Its base is a former Mohawk Trail restaurant. $78 per

LEARN HOW TO ROCK CLIMB AT ZOAR OUTDOOR'S CLIMBING SCHOOL

Zoar Outdoor

adult on weekends, $73 midweek for the 10-mile Zoar Gap trip. Inquire about 2-day packages.

Moxie (1-800-866-6943; www.wild-rivers.com), with its home base on Maine's Kennebec, is based here at Berkshire East ski area in Charlemont. It offers both Dryway (Class IV whitewater, $95, minimum age 14) and Zoar Gap ($70 weekdays, $85 weekends) runs.

✳ Winter Sports

CROSS-COUNTRY SKIING **Stump Sprouts** (413-339-4265; www.stumpsprouts. com), West Hill Road, West Hawley. High on the side of a mountain, this 450-acre tract offers some memorable cross-country skiing on wooded trails at 1,500-to 2,000-foot elevations. Snacks and rentals are available in the warming hut, which is part of Lloyd and Suzanne Crawford's home (see *Lodging*). There are 25 km of trails, lessons, and guided tours.

Also see *Green Space* for trails in the **Savoy Mountain** and **Kenneth Dubuque Memorial State Forests.**

DOWNHILL SKIING **Berkshire East** (413-339-6617), South River Road, Charlemont. Known affectionately as "Berkshire beast," this is an unusually challenging mountain for its size. *Vertical drop:* 1,180 feet. *Terrain:* 45 trails, 40 percent expert, 40 percent intermediate. *Lifts:* Five lifts, including a quad that's new for the 2003–04 season. *Snowmaking:* 100 percent of terrain. *Facilities:* Nursery, two base lodges, ski school, shop; open daily; night skiing Wednesday through Saturday; snowboarding.

SNOWMOBILING **The Snowmobiling Association of Massachusetts** (413-369-8092; www.sledmass.com) happens to be headquarted in Conway, but the web site offers guidance to some 500 miles of trail throughout the state, a little more than half on private and the remainder on state land. There are no rentals in the Hilltowns, but there's no doubt that this area offers some of the best sledding in the state. Snowmobilers are advised to check the web site and contact local clubs.

✳ Green Space

STATE FORESTS *Note:* See www.massparks.org for details about all the following:

Monroe State Forest (413-339-5504) covers 4,000 acres in the towns of Florida and Monroe. Access is on Monroe Road off Route 2 (just east of Whitcomb Summit; see River Road under *Scenic Drives*). Nine miles of hiking trails and several "pack-in" campsites are on the **Dunbar Brook Trail;** about 2 miles in is one of the last stands of old-growth forest, with a beautiful stand of red spruce and a 300-year old hemlock. The Roycroft Lookout takes in a panorama of the Deerfield River valley. Watch out for the many moose droppings.

Mohawk Trail State Forest (413-339-5504), Route 2, Charlemont. See "Along the Mohawk Trail" for details.

Catamount State Forest (413-339-5504), Route 112, Colrain. Fishing is the big attraction in this 1,125-acre forest in southwestern Colrain and eastern Charlemont. Streams and a 27-acre lake are stocked. There are also hiking and riding trails.

H. O. Cook State Forest (413-258-4774), Route 8A, Heath. The lure here is fishing for trout in more than 5 miles of streams. There are also hiking and riding trails. Access is off Route 8A on State Farm Road in northeastern Heath, 1 mile south of the Vermont line.

Kenneth Dubuque Memorial State Forest, also known as **Hawley State Forest** (413-339-5504), northwest of Plainfield on Route 8A, offers a fine loop hike starting at Moody Spring, a genuine mineral spring with a metal pipe spouting water. A sign proclaims: THIS WATER HAS PROVEN HELPFUL IN CASES OF SORE THROAT, STOMACHACHE, INTESTINAL DISORDERS, RHEUMATISM AND ALL SCROFULA DISEASES. Not far from the spring, just off East Hawley Road, stands a well-preserved charcoal kiln. The forest's many miles of dirt roads make for fine winter ski touring and summer dirt biking.

HIKING AND WALKING Bear Swamp Reservation, maintained by the Trustees of Reservations (www.thetrustees.org), is in Ashfield on Hawley Road (less than 2 miles west of the junction of Routes 116 and 112). It has 171 acres with roads and trails and is known for wildflowers: lady's slipper, painted trillium, cowslip, marsh marigold, blue gentian, wild azalea, and flowering dogwood.

High Ledges, Shelburne. A 300-acre preserve with superb views of the surrounding countryside. This Massachusetts Audubon Sanctuary is still maintained by the family that donated it. From Route 2 in Shelburne, turn onto Little Mohawk Road, then follow Audubon Society signs.

The Mahican-Mohawk Trail runs for 7.5 miles between Shelburne Falls and Deerfield. Based on a recent study and the work of local volunteers, a stretch of the ancient Indian path (now roughly maintained by a power company to access a series of hydroelectric dams) is now accessible to sturdily shod hikers. The entire hike takes at least 4 hours, but the most impressive and rugged few miles are at the Shelburne Falls end—and just 1 mile can feel like a satisfying outing. The trailhead is marked on Route 2 just east of the police station; there is also limited parking in Wilcox Hollow (also marked a bit farther east). Visitors are advised to ask directions and pick up a trail map at the **Shelburne Falls Village Information Center** (see *Guidance*). Another segment of this trail can be hiked in the **Mohawk State Forest** in Charlemont.

The stone tower on Massamett Mountain was built by the town of Shelburne. You can climb the stairs inside to some wonderful views through big open windows. The view encompasses Mount Greylock on the west, Mount Snow and Stratton Mountain in Vermont, Mount Monadnock in New Hampshire, and the Holyoke Range to the southwest. The easiest way to get there from Route 2 is up Cooper Lane behind Gould's Sugarhouse, through Gould Farm to Davenport's Sugar Farm at the end. Be warned that although this looks like a one-way road, it definitely is not. You can park at Davenport's Sugarhouse and walk the fire road the mile to the tower.

Riverwalk, Shelburne Falls. This pleasant walkway begins on the Buckland side of the Deerfield River opposite McCusker's Market and offers a view of the Salmon Falls and Potholes on its way to the Lamson & Goodnow outlet.

Also see **Dunbar Brook Trail,** described under **Monroe State Forest,** above.

PICNICKING Gardner Falls, Shelburne Falls Recreation Area. Follow North Street along the river until you see the sign. The old power canal here is a great fishing spot, and it's also a fine place for a picnic (go past the picnic tables, down by the river).

South River State Forest (413-268-7098 or 413-339-5504; www.massparks. org), north from Conway Village on the Shelburne Falls and Bardwell's Ferry Roads (see *Scenic Drives*), **South River Station** offers picnic tables and grills scattered along the gorge of the South River to its confluence with the Deerfield. Near the parking area, notice the South River Dam, once used to power the trolley line.

Malley Park on the Buckland side of the Deerfield River (near the Lamson & Goodnow factory) offers a good view of the potholes.

Also see **High Ledges,** above.

WATERFALLS Chapelbrook Reservation (www.thetrustees.org), maintained by the Trustees, is in South Ashfield. (Where Route 116 doglegs east, continue south on the Williamsburg Road for 2.25 miles.) Turn left to find the series of shallow falls that spill into a deep pool, perfect for sliding down. Across the road, the Chapelbrook Ledges offer long views.

Tannery Falls. Take Black Brook Road off Route 2 just east of the bridge that marks the Florida–Savoy line. One of the most spectatular waterfalls in the state. For directions and description, see "Along the Mohawk Trail."

✳ Lodging
INNS AND BED & BREAKFASTS

In Ashfield 01330
🛏 **Bull Frog Bed & Breakfast** (413-628-4493), Route 116. Open year-round unless Lucille Thibault is in Australia. Lucille's 200-year-old Cape sits back from Route 116 with a lovely back garden, a frog pond, and five kinds of berry bushes. The organically grown blueberries, strawberries, blackberries, several kinds of raspberries, gooseberries, and currants are the ingredients for the homemade jams that are part of the full country breakfast. The big country kitchen with its antique, wood-fired Glenwood stove (in constant use) is the gathering place for the house; there's also an upstairs TV room. There are four guest rooms and two baths, but the baths are only rented for the use of one room, unless it's family or friends who share. One former parlor now features a round, king-sized bed and fireplace. Lucille irons the sheets. $115 double, $75 single year-round.

🛏 **Corner Porches B&B** (413-628-4592), 82 Baptist Corner Road. Jean Silver is a craftsperson whose comfortable, informal 19th-century house is on a quiet side street near the center of this interesting town. She offers two to four cheerful rooms (depending on season and need) with handmade quilts and shared baths. Cats and dogs in residence. Families welcome. $75–80 double.

In Buckland 01338

Johnson Homestead Bed & Breakfast (413-625-6603; thejohnsonhomestead@msn.com), 79 East Buckland Road, Shelburne Falls 01370. Susan Grader's grandparents took in boarders for a full 40 years in this gracious 1890s farmhouse; now Susan and her husband, David, have revived the tradition. Sited on a quiet road, this is a gracious, pleasant place with a big inviting country kitchen and two more comfortable common rooms. The three guest rooms (we like the one with the 1805 maple bed and hand-loomed coverlet) share two baths. Breakfast is an event, seated with a clear view of the garden bird feeders—and the hummingbirds, goldfinches, and woodpeckers. You may feast on a mushroom and basil omelet in puff pastry, fresh fruit cup including home-grown peaches, and walnut-pumpkin muffins with home-made jam. Susan is an exceptionally hospitable host, also a writer with a flair for rhyme. $65–110 double, $20 per extra person; children 12 and over welcome. The house features an unusual outdoor fireplace and flower gardens and is set in 80 acres with a brook. A ways off Route 112, it's on the way to nowhere except Mary Lyon's birthplace.

Bird's Nest Bed & Breakfast (413-625-9523), 2 Charlemont Road. This hospitable house was built in 1797 at the head of Buckland Center's handsome street, across the road from the striking, white Mary Lyon Church, known for its carillon. Mary Lyon, who founded Mount Holyoke and Wheaton Colleges, taught a Winter School for Young Ladies here 1830–32. Guests enter the house through a comfortable brick-floored room, and common space includes the original keeping room and a big, sunny dining room. Cindy Weeks is a sculptor and painter who gives workshops, Edith Dolby is a weaver, and three generations of this family are represented in the furniture, rugs, paintings, pottery, and other decorations in the house. There are three upstairs guest rooms, each with private bath. Rooms vary in size and ambience but all are pleasant. $80–95 includes a full breakfast. Well-behaved children over 10 are welcome.

Restful Crow (413-625-9507; www.therestfulcrow.com), 6 Cross Street. Diane Poland has furnished an 1820 house on a quiet street with appropriate antiques and offers three guest rooms with handmade quilts and full baths. Common space includes a screened porch, sunroom, library, and parlor. $95–125 includes an expanded continental breakfast. Well-behaved children over 10 are welcome.

In Charlemont 01339

ⓘ ✆ ☎ **Charlemont Inn** (413-339-5796; www.charlemontinn.com), Route 2 (Mohawk Trail). Hospitality here dates back to a decade or so before 1787, the year Ephraim Brown formally declared his house an inn. Hats off to Charlotte Dewey and Linda Shimandle for rescuing and preserving (as their brochure proclaims) "a place with character." There's a kayak above the porch and a suit of armor by the check-in desk; the Full Moon Tavern offers local brews and a pool table. The inn serves all three meals (in several venues) every day of the year (see *Where to Eat*). A dozen or so crisp and clean, antiques-furnished upstairs guest rooms (some permit smoking) flank a narrow hall; eight rooms share semiprivate baths, and five others share two hall baths. There are also two suites in the adjoining "Cottage," one with kitchen facilities. Past guests have included Benedict Arnold, General John Burgoyne, Mark Twain, and President Calvin Coolidge. Present guests tend to be fishermen, white-water rafters, history buffs, snowmobilers, and skiers as opposed to the Jacuzzi-and-gas-fireplace crowd. From $35 single, $75–100 double.

∞ **The Warfield House Inn at Valley View Farm** (1-888-339-VIEW; www.warfieldhouseinn.com), 200 Warfield House Road. The two guest facilities here are a white-clapboard country house with green awnings and a smaller country cottage. Together they accommodate a total of 23 people; some baths are private, others shared. Both offer fireplaces in living rooms, hot tubs on porches, with front rooms overlooking the valley and the ski area, Berkshire East, on the opposite slope. The 540-acre hillside spread set high above Route 2 includes a barnyard with llamas, goats, bunnies, and chickens, but the centerpiece of the property is a restaurant (see *Dining Out*), and the complex lends itself to reunions and weddings. $115–125, $150 for a suite, includes a full breakfast.

In Conway 01341
⌁ **The Merriams** (413-369-4052), 39 Marshall Road. This 1767 center-chimney classic house could easily fit into the lineup in Old Deerfield. Its paneling is exquisite, and a formal parlor is hung with family portraits.

The upstairs former ballroom is still used as common space. A full breakfast is served in the formal dining room. Guest rooms include two spacious doubles ($90) and one single ($75), divided between the main house and the just-slightly-more-rustic "barn." Bob Merriam taught English at Deerfield Academy for 25 years and now maintains an antiquarian bookshop here. Mary Merriam is a noted quilter.

In Colrain 01340
❧ **Penfrydd Farm B&B** (413-624-5516; www.penfrydd.com), 105 Hillman Road. Thom Griffin, an opera singer and farmer, is your host at this 160-acre hilltop farm, ringed by more hills. Resident animals include llamas and horses; guests are invited to hike along paths through woods and meadows. There are four guest rooms, three sharing a bath ($75 per couple); one, far larger and more attractive than the others, has a whirlpool tub ($90). Plans call for reducing the number of bedrooms and increasing the number of baths. Common space is informal and attractive. There's a baby grand piano, a Franklin fireplace, many plants and books; rates include breakfast.

High Pocket B&B (413-624-8988; www.highpocket.com), 38 Adams Place Road. Sarah and Mark McKusick live down the road from this 160-year old clapboard house with three guest rooms (all with private bath), a game room in the barn, and a hot tub on the porch with a 50-mile view. On the day we visited, dozens of goats were lazing in a neighboring field, but the specialty of this house is horseback riding. The McKusicks have more than a dozen steeds and offer trail rides, but only to their guests.

Beginners are welcome (it's $50 for 2 hours), as are more accomplished riders, and guests are invited to bring their own mounts. The adjoining properties add up to 650 acres; single-track trails traverse surrounding fields and woods as well. This is a full house with a living room (with TV and woodstove), laundry room, and full kitchen, but breakfast is included in $90 per couple ($30 extra for a 1-night stay on Friday and Saturday); horses are boarded for $25 per night.

Keldahus (413-634-3090; www.keldaby.com), 12 Heath Road. Cynthia Herbert is a weaver (see *Selective Shopping*), and Bob Ramirez has incorporated some amazing pieces from other places into this sunflower-yellow house, set in its gardens. During the summer months the couple move out to the attached studio and invite guests to use the big upstairs double or small single room (available separately or as a suite) and the colorful bath with leaded windows around the whirlpool tub. Similar windows are found in master bedroom and along the breezeway between the big country kitchen and the studio; they all were formerly installed in the library at Columbia University. The house is filled with imaginative touches, and the garden offers more places to relax under two big box elders. It's $60 for the single room, $95 for the double, and $120 for both; rates include a full breakfast.

✍ ☙ **Olde Carey House** (413-624-0062; www.oldecaryhouse.com), 7 York Road, P.O. Box 313. An 1846 house on 12 acres, up an unpaved road but near the village. Anneliese Zinn offers four guest rooms (two with king-sized bed) and two shared baths with a dining and common room and 12 wooded acres beyond an inviting porch and yard. $65–85 includes a full breakfast featuring delicacies like stuffed French toast. No credit cards. Children and pets are accepted by special arrangement.

In Rowe 01367
✍ **Maple House Bed and Breakfast** (413-339-0107; www.maplehousebb.com), 51 Middletown Hill Road. A 200-year-old farmhouse that took in summer boarders a century ago, Maple House sits high on a hill surrounded by fields. Becky and Michael Bradley have teenagers of their own and welcome families. Common rooms are comfortable any time of year, and the sunroom has a brick oven fireplace. The five guest rooms feature pine floors, exposed posts and beams, and bright quilts; they range from a king with private bath to a two-room family suite. Full breakfasts feature homemade syrups (blueberry and raspberry as well as maple) and locally grown produce. Guests can swim in Pelham Lake, fish or raft, canoe or kayak on the Deerfield River, ski at nearby Berkshire East, or cross-country out the back door, around the lake, and into Rowe Forest. There's also year-round trail riding 4 miles up the road in Vermont—sleigh rides, too. $50–70 single, $80–100 double; dinner is available for groups of eight or more. Inquire about special packages.

In Shelburne 01370
Kenburn Orchards B&B (413-625-6116 or 1-877-KENBURN; www.kenburnorchards.com), 1394 Mohawk Trail. Susan Flaccus's father and grandfather planted the apple trees in the 40-acre orchard on the 160-acre farm, but Susan and her husband, Larry, moved up here relatively

recently and have transformed the old homestead into a delightful B&B. The three guest rooms (with private bath), the dining room, and the sitting room are all sparely, nicely furnished. Nothing froufrou but everything in keeping with the character of the house: a pencil-point canopy bed in the Isadore Pratt Room upstairs and a cherry king-sized bed in the downstairs bedroom, quilts and Oriental carpets, wood and gas Vermont Castings stoves (air-conditioning in summer), lovely new baths, plenty of light, and exceptional views. $125–155 per couple includes a full, candlelit breakfast served at the formal dining room table. For slightly more, the Isadore Pratt Room can be rented as a suite with a sleep sofa in an adjoining room.

Six Maple Street (413-625-6807), 6 Maple Street, Shelburne Falls. Open weekends May to November. Judy Hoyt grew up in this 18th-century house, the oldest standing home in the village of Shelburne Falls. It's been in her family since the late 19th century, and the two upstairs guest rooms (sharing one and a half baths) are furnished in family antiques. The larger one retains a marble sink. There's a gracious living room with a fireplace and a big kitchen and yard. Given the superb restaurants in Shelburne Falls, it's nice to stay somewhere you can walk home to. $90–100 includes a continental breakfast.

OTHER LODGING ∞ ♨ ♪ **Stump Sprouts Guest Lodge** (413-339-4265; www.stumpsprouts.com), West Hill Road, Hawley 01339. Lloyd Crawford has built this modern, hilltop lodge almost entirely with his own hands, from timbers he found standing on this 450-acre spread. He also built the bunks and much of the furniture inside. There are 10 rooms, sleeping from two to five, and the common spaces are on many levels (there are lofts and corners to sit in with skylights and stained glass). Windows maximize the view of tier upon tier of wooded hills. The former barn is a great rec room with table tennis, pool, and a piano; the ceiling drops down for warmth in winter and can be raised to allow even more space (the old silo is a great aerie) in summer. There's a wonderful view from the sauna, too. Vegetable gardens supply the table, which Suzanne Crawford sets family-style, or you can cook for yourself. It's possible to come singly or in couples, but it's most fun to come as a group. In winter there are the cross-country ski trails for which this place is well known, and in summer the trails are still there to walk or bike. In winter $139 per person per weekend includes six meals; from $199 on 3-day holiday weekends includes six meals. Spring through fall a 2-night weekend with three meals is $109, and if you cook and clean for yourself rates begin at $29 midweek, $59 on weekends.

♪ **Rowe Camp & Conference Center** (413-339-4954; www.rowe-center.org), Kings Highway Road, Box 273, Rowe 01367. The Unitarian-Universalist center consists of a farmhouse and assorted camp buildings on a quiet back road. There are 18 private and semiprivate rooms with a total of 125 beds, mostly dorm-style. On most weekends throughout the year there are speakers (many of them well known) on topics ranging from "Writing from the Heart," to "Herbs, Holiness, and Menopause," to "Gardening: Making and Keeping a Private Eden." Seven summer weeks are also reserved for school-age, adult, and family camps. There are two costs for each conference: the first is housing, which includes six meals and ranges from $80 for 2 nights' camping to $190 for single occupancy in a private room; the second is the program cost, which is based on family income and runs $160–240. Bill fondly remembers his wake-up call here: "'Tis a gift to be simple" played at his door on a recorder.

✍ ♿ **Blue Heron Farm** (413-339-4045; www.blueheronfarm.com), Warner Hill Road, Charlemont 01339. Bill and Norma Coli offer a choice of lodging options on their 140-acre organic farm with a swimmable and skiable pond. Open year-round. Four rentals: a self-contained cottage (two bedrooms, two baths, fireplace, sleeps up to seven), a log cabin (sleeps up to four, one bedroom), an attractive apartment attached to the sugarhouse (sleeps up to three), and The Maples, a post-and-beam Cape that includes a king-bedded bedroom, an upstairs bedroom with twins, and a loft with a sleep sofa, plus a living room with fireplace, dining room, and full kitchen. Overall this place is great for families; pony-cart rides, berry picking, and helping with the horses and goats are encouraged. $95–250 per night, 2-night minimum; cheaper by the week and month.

✍ **The Oxbow** (413-625-6011; www.oxbowresortmotel.com), 1741 Mohawk Trail, Charlemont 01339. A one-story motel with 25 rooms (19 with two double beds), grouped around a swimming pool. All have air-conditioning and TV, and the property includes tennis courts. Stillwaters Restaurant (see *Dining Out*) is next door, and the Deerfield River is just across Route 2. Rooms in the front have river views, but those in the rear are quieter. $49–79 double. No charge for children under 16.

Zoar Outdoor (1-800-532-7482; www.zoaroutdoor.com), Route 2, Charlemont. At this writing the area's oldest rafting company has bought a house adjoining its present property; plans call for a guest lodge with four to six rooms, shared and private baths.

CAMPGROUNDS

State parks and forests
See www.massparks.com. For camping reservations, call 1-877-422-6762 or reserve online through www. ReserveAmerica.com. For detailed fees, see *Camping* in "What's Where." For details on camping in the Mohawk Trail State Forest and Savoy Mountain State Forest, see "Along the Mohawk Trail."

Private
Zoar Outdoor (1-800-532-7483; www.zoaroutdoor.com), Route 2, Charlemont. Set in a wooded area surrounded by 80 acres of woods and offering 10 cabin tents, each with a wooden deck, four cots, a gas lantern, a gas grill, and a porch; there are also several primitive tent sites. (See *White-Water Rafting*.)

✳ Where to Eat
DINING OUT

In Charlemont
∞ **The Warfield House at Valley View Farm** (413-339-6600 or 1-888-339-VIEW), 200 Warfield Road, off Route 2. Dinner Thursday through Sunday, lunch Friday, and Sunday

brunch. This is the most spectacularly positioned restaurant in the Hill-towns. Perched on a hill, its walls of windows overlooks the slopes of Berk-shire East ski area. The barnyard is home to exotic as well as farm ani-mals; inquire about llama trek picnics and buggy rides. Weddings and spe-cial functions are a specialty. Dinner might begin with pan-fried crabcakes topped with shaved fennel, or Bermu-da onion salad with lemon-caper sauce. Entrées might range from maple-glazed chicken to filet mignon with roasted garlic mashed potatoes and fresh vegetables with thyme but-ter. Entrées $12.95–17.95. The **Hawk's Nest Pub** here offers less formal dining. Weddings are a special-ty (see *Lodging*).

🍴 **Stillwaters Restaurant** (413-625-6200), 1745 Mohawk Trail (Route 2). Open for breakfast Saturday and Sun-day and for dinner nightly except Tuesday. Under ownership by Michael Phelps, this Mohawk Trail landmark (formerly attached to the Oxbow Motel) has gained a solid rep-utation. It's a big old dining room set high above the road, with a view of the river across the way. The big menu ranges from a burger or soup (with bread and salad bar) through several steak dishes. You might dine on sea scallops and shrimp sautéed with garlic butter and wine, chicken piccata, or eggplant Parmesan. The children's menu includes a hot dog with choice of potato and vegetable of the day ($3.95). Entrées $12.95–17.95. Full liquor license.

In Colrain
∞ **Green Emporium** (413-624-5122; www.greenemporium.com), Route 112. Open summer Saturdays 6–9 with live jazz and "country fusion

cuisine," and also for many special events (ranging from Valentine's Day to a Basil Festival, for instance); check out the web site. Reservations required. Michael Collins, a New York chef, and Pacifico "Tony" Palumbo, a well-known neon artist, have transformed a 150-year-old for-mer Methodist church into an excep-tional space filled with round tables, neon, fresh flowers, and aromas. Entrées run $19–25 including salad and fresh bread. Beer and wine are served. Because this is a former church with a garden in back and a chef in residence, it's a popular venue both for weddings and receptions.

In Shelburne Falls
Café Martin (413-625-2795), 24 Bridge Street. Open for lunch Tues-day through Sunday, dinner Tuesday through Saturday, and breakfast on weekends. This gets top local reviews. It's an informal storefront restaurant with a varied menu that might include grilled eggplant (with goat cheese, roasted red pepper, and sautéed mushrooms) sandwich at lunch, and ranges for dinner from "the ultimate blue burger" or a Niçoise salad to grilled Ahi tuna with wasabi dressing, a vegetable paella, or steak with Gor-gonzola butter. Breakfast might be a red and green scramble melt (eggs with artichoke hearts and roasted red pepper on toast, topped with melted cheddar). Dinner entrées $6.95–18.95, averaging around $12. Full liquor license.

Tusk'n'Rattle (413-625-0200), 10 Bridge Street. Open Monday through Thursday 5–9, Sunday 10–2, bar 4–11. Margaritas are a specialty, along with "Indian-Latin" cuisine. You might begin with ginger carrot soup, then feast on curried lamb patties with a red lentil mango salad and minted yogurt. A lively atmosphere, microbrews on tap, entrées $8.95–16.95.

A Bottle of Bread (413-625-6502), 18 Water Street. Open Wednesday through Saturday for dinner, lunch on Friday and Saturday, and Sunday brunch (11–3) and dinner. Nicely sited in an old house near the Shelburne entrance to the Bridge of Flowers; the best views are from the porch (screened in summer, glass paneled in winter). The menu ranges from sandwiches and a French tart with seasonal vegetables and cheese to sirloin tips with sweet potato fries. Specialties include bouillabaisse and salmon in parchment, and even vegans are well served. Dinner entrées $8.50–15.

The Shire Restaurant (413-625-2727), 2 State Street. Open for lunch and dinner daily. Overhanging the Deerfield with a front-and-center view of the Bridge of Flowers, the sunporch is the place to eat here. The food gets mixed reviews, but both atmosphere and service are fine. Dinner entrées $7.50–18.

EATING OUT

In Ashfield
☙ **Countrypie Pizza Company** (413-628-4488), 343 Main Street. Open Monday through Saturday 11:30–9. Good pizza with plenty of veggie varieties, including eggplant, broccoli, artichoke hearts, feta, and Garden Delight, featuring fresh spinach, mushrooms, and so forth. Also Sicilian wraps and grinders.

In Charlemont
☙ **Charlemont Inn** (413-339-5796;

www.charlemontinn.com), Main Street. Open daily 6 AM through dinner, best known for live entertainment on weekends. The Full Moon Tavern is the apt name of the inn's big, informal dining room with its friendly bar and pool table; dining is also available on the sunporch, and in summer there's a patio. Anything goes here, from burgers to vegetarian dishes; specialties include home fries, Zoar steak, and BBQ ribs, and may include roast duck. There's also a children's menu.

Charlemont Pizza (413-339-4472), Main Street. Open at 11 daily, noon Sunday, until at least 9. Try the kielbasa pizza with extra cheese.

In Colrain
☙ **Café at Pine Hill Orchards** (413-624-3325), Greenfield Road. Closed as we write but due to open in 2004 for all three meals. The rebuilt (after a fire) oasis serves home-baked items, as well as soups and sandwiches. The property also includes a petting zoo, picnic tables, and West County Winery (see *Selective Shopping*). Come after dark to see "Glowing Glory" (see Colrain under *Villages*) on a hillside across the way.

In Shelburne Falls
McCusker's Market & Deli (413-625-9411), 3 State Street. Open Monday through Saturday 7 AM–8 PM, weekends 7 AM–7 PM. Michael McCusker's brightly painted (in its original colors) former Odd Fellows Hall (built in 1877) is on the Buckland side of the two bridges, stage center on our book's cover. Since 1979, the market has specialized in natural foods, vitamins, and much more. The deli is good for a "vegiwich," "turkeyberry," or variety of roll-

ups and wraps as well as an OatsCream softserve. There are booths in back and in the adjoining bookstore; also outside tables in-season. A favorite place to catch up on the news, especially if it's local.

Mother's (413-625-6300), 43 Bridge Street. Open daily 7 AM; closes at varying hours. The original Mother's has moved up Bridge Street, enlarged, and changed hands, and at this writing the reviews are mixed: good breakfasts and chilis but fewer (and smaller) sandwiches. Still a good source for a picnic up at High Ledges.

Shelburne Falls Coffee Roasters (413-625-6474), Roasters Café, 35 Bridge Street. Open 6–6 daily, this pleasant café is the original in a coffeehouse that's good enough to have sprouted an expanded version out on Route 2 and other offshoots in the valley. Coffees and baked-from-scratch pastries are the draw, as well as blended frozen drinks.

Gould's Sugar House (413-625-6170), Route 2, Shelburne. Open in sugaring season (March and April) and during foliage (September and October), daily 8:30–2. A great roadside stop that's been in the family for generations; specialties include pancakes, waffles, and fritters laced with the family's maple syrup.

Bridge Street Café (413-625-6345), 65 Bridge Street. Open except Wednesday at 7:30 for breakfast and Sunday brunch with a varied menu of eggs, pancakes, and baked goods; also for lunch basics (sandwiches and burgers, salads and melts). A pleasant space with seasonal backyard tables. Inquire about dinner on selected nights.

✷ Entertainment

CONCERTS Mohawk Trail Concerts (413-625-9511 or 1-800-MTC-MUSE; www.mohawktrailconcerts.org), 75 Bridge Street, Charlemont. After almost 35 years, this series of chamber and choral music concerts only seems to get better. Concerts are Saturdays at 8, late June through mid-August, in the 225-seat, acoustically fine Federated Church on Route 2.

The Charlemont Inn (www.charlemontinn.com). Saturday-night music ranges from bluegrass and folk through jazz.

Hilltown Folk Concerts (413-625-2580; www.hilltownfolk.org) are held frequently in Memorial Hall, Shelburne Falls.

Shelburne Falls Military Band. Billed as the country's oldest military band. Concerts are held on Wednesdays from mid-June through August at various locations in Shelburne Falls.

FILM Pothole Pictures (413-625-2526), Memorial Hall Theater, Shelburne Falls. A series of spring and fall classic and art films shown Friday and Saturday at 7:30, May through June and October through December, in the 400-seat restored theater that's upstairs in the town hall. The current movie schedule is posted on www.shelburnefalls.com.

Zoar Outdoor (1-800-532-7483; www.zoaroutdoor.com), Route 2 in Charlemont (see *White-Water Rafting*), schedules a summer series of films, free and usually depicting paddling adventures. A nominally priced barbecue usually precedes the films.

PERFORMANCE Ashfield Community Theater (413-628-3336). Year-round program of community theater and performing arts education.

Also see **Green Emporium** under *Where to Eat*.

✳ Selective Shopping

ANTIQUES SHOPS The **Shelburne Falls Village Information Center** (see *Guidance*) publishes a list of local dealers. Our local favorite is Strawberryfield Collectables (413-625-2039), 1204 Mohawk Trail (Route 2), on the corner of the road to Colrain.

APPLE WINERY AND ORCHARDS **West County Winery** (413-624-3481; westcountycider.com) at Pine Hill Orchards, on the Shelburne–Colrain Road (3.4 miles west on Route 2 from the Greenfield traffic circle at I-91, exit 26). Open June through December, Thursday through Sunday 11–5; otherwise please call first. Since 1984 this family-owned winery has been producing wines that steadily earn wider recognition and distribution. The showroom is a cottage behind the farm stand at **Pine Hill Orchards** (413-625-2874; open year-round daily), by a duck pond with some barnyard animals fenced in beside. Judith Maloney proffers hard cider and apple wine in tiny cups. We recommend the West County Extra Dry, a blend of McIntosh, Northern Spy, Red Delicious, and other West County apples with a crisp, rich taste. Eight hard ciders, dry to sweet, with alcohol 5 to 7 percent, also several combination fruit wines, are produced from local fruit, available for sampling. PYO at Pine Hill in-season; also see *Eating Out*.

Mohawk Orchards (413-625-2874), farm stand on Route 2, orchard just north on the Colrain–Shelburne

Road. Open May through October daily. Pick-your-own apples in-season; picnic tables, small farm animals for petting.

CRAFTS SHOPS

In Shelburne Falls

Note: **Gallery Walks** promote village galleries and studios the third Friday of every month, 5–8 PM.

Salmon Falls Artisans Showroom (413-625-9833), 1 Ashfield Street. Open April through December, daily 10–5, Sunday noon–5; January through March, Wednesday through Saturday 10–5, Sunday noon–5. Housed in a former granary. This is an exceptional gallery showcasing some 185 local craftspeople and artists and featuring the distinctive, widely acclaimed glass orbs by Shelburne-based Josh Simpson. On our last visit it was easy to miss the entrance to this major gallery, well worth finding.

Shelburne Artisans Cooperative (413-625-9324), 26 Bridge Street, closed Tuesday, open Thursday through Saturday 11–7 and otherwise noon–4. A shop filled with striking work by 50 mostly local members.

Bald Mountain Pottery (413-625-8110), 28 State Street. Open except Tuesday 11–5; also closed Monday off-season. The distinctive, functional pottery by Sarah Hettinger and James Gleason includes striking vases and lamps made in this riverside studio overlooking the Bridge of Flowers.

Laurie Goddard Studios (413-625-0201; www.lauriegoddard.com), 9 Bridge Street. Open year-round. Laurie Goddard is best known for her museum-quality translucent bowls, but more recently she has been creating striking abstract designs on gessoed Masonite panels, gilded with combinations of semiprecious leaf such as copper, Dutch metal, and metallic powders, then overpainted and finally varnished.

North River Glass Studio (413-625-6322; www.ycglass.com), Deerfield Avenue. Watch glass being blown; the resulting deeply colored vases, bowls, perfume bottles, and art glass are displayed in the adjacent Young & Constantin Gallery, which also carries glass jewelry.

Art Inside (413-625-2870), Deerfield Avenue. Open Wednesday through Sunday 11–5, longer in summer and fall. The name may change for this artist-run gallery (there's been an ongoing discussion with Intel, which claims it), but whatever it's called, it's an interesting place.

Textile Arts (413-625-8241), 16 Water Street. Open Wednesday through Sunday, until 7 on Thursday. A weaving studio at the Bridge of Flowers in which Susie Robbins displays locally woven wool blankets and shawls, cotton place mats and tablecloths, local wools; also books.

Ann Brauer Quilt Studio (413-625-8605), 2 Conway Street. Open Wednesday through Saturday 10–5, Sunday noon–5. This nationally known quilter is usually to be found in her small, pink shop on the Buckland side of the river, frequently stitching away on stunning quilts, wall hangings, pot holders, shoulder bags, place mats, and other creations.

Dick Muller & Co. Leather (413-625-6205), 6 Bridge Street. Diane and Dick Muller have been working together for more than 36 years, crafting custom sandals and lovely wallets, bags, and belts in their Ashfield studio.

Mole Hollow Candles (413-625-6337), Deerfield Avenue. Open daily 10–5, later in summer. Overlooks the potholes along the Deerfield River; candles are made on weekdays. The shop also sells gifts and cards.

Wings of Light (413-625-0144 or 1-877-440-8444; www.clearangel.com), 20 Bridge Street. Andree Clearwater is known for her guardian angel paintings. Her "Angel Gallery" and gift shop is dedicated to archangel Michael and features her paintings, prints, cards, postcards, and other gift items.

Elsewhere

Mike Purington Wood Bowls (413-624-0036; www.naturalturnedwoodbowls.com), 285 Thompson Road, Colrain. Open Sunday 2–6 and by appointment. Purington turns bowls in his shop facing north toward the Green Mountains. Each piece of wood is turned to a shape that suits its character, then set to dry for several months before being finished with oils and beeswax.

Eddie's Wheels (413-625-0033 or 1-888-211-2700; www.eddieswheels.com), 347 Little Mohawk Road,

NORTH RIVER GLASS STUDIO

Kim Grant

Shelburne Falls. On the way to High Ledges (see *Green Space*), this unusual studio-showroom in the Patten Hill section of Shelburne is dedicated to making custom carts for dogs that have lost mobility in their hind legs. They are sold throughout the world.

SPECIAL SHOPS

In Shelburne Falls
Lamson & Goodnow Mfg. Co. (413-625-6331 or 1-800-872-6504), 45 Conway Street. This venerable complex of classic mostly 19th-century wood and brick mill buildings dates from 1837 and claims to be "the longest continually sited cutlery manufactury in the country." During the Civil War it was also one of the country's biggest, producing tableware and professional and agricultural cutlery and becoming known for its variety of ivory-, horn-, and exotic-wood-handled items. Today it simply claims to be one of the best, still known for a full line of professional cutlery and specialized tools such as putty knives, scrapers, laboratory spoons, scoops, and spatulas. It's a combination outlet and classy kitchen store. There are usually buys to be had on superb kitchen knives.

McCusker's Market (413-625-9411), 3 State Street. A combination health food store and deli (see *Eating Out*) in a picturesque 1877 former Odd Fellows Hall, the heart of the village.

The Whistling Crow (413-625-2595), 10 Bridge Street. Open Wednesday through Sunday 11–5. A combination nature store and candy shop geared to wildlife lovers (books, birding supplies) with proceeds benefiting CROW, a wildlife rehabilitation center in nearby Hawley.

Lapis Mountain (413-625-9399), 55 Bridge Street. Jake Mayers's apothecary/acupuncture shop is all about tea, including many rare teas. The "tea and tonic bar" features more than 40 unusual teas available by the cup, pot, or in bulk. Tonics and herbal beverages designed to provide strength and energy are another specialty. We recommend "Tame the Elements Elixir."

Boswell's Books (413-625-9362), 1 State Street. Open daily. A full-service bookshop with new and used books, audio and video rentals, pleasant reading corners.

Nancy L. Dole Books & Ephemera (413-625-9850; ndole@crocker.com), 32 Bridge Street, second floor. Open Tuesday through Friday from 11, Saturday and Sunday no later than 1. This is a find, an upstairs cache of some 25,000 books plus old prints, photos, postcards.

Elsewhere
Ashfield Hardware & Supply (413-628-3299), 343 Main Street, Ashfield. A store that's housed many enterprises over the years, but none more varied and useful than at present under its female owners. An exceptional independent hardware store specializing in hard-to-find items and those with natural ingredients, plus soaps and toys, hand-forged items, plants, and 50-cent ice cream cones.

Note: See "Along the Mohawk Trail" for more information on the trading posts and gift shops along Route 2.

✳ Farms
Tregellys Fiber Farm (413-625-6448; www.tregellysfibers.com), 15 Dodge Branch Road, Hawley. Open Wednesday through Sunday 10:30–5.

A suggested donation of $6 per person is appreciated. In back of beyond, accessible from Route 112 on the Ashfield–Buckland line. Spreading for some 138 acres across Hog Mountain in the Dodge Corner area of Hawley, this farm is well named. "Tregelly" means "hidden homestead" in Cornish, whence Ed Cothey originally came. Ed and wife Jody envisioned a few animals and a garden when they moved here just a decade ago, but their passion for animals and fiber arts took on a life of its own. The animals now number around 200 and include unusual heritage breeds such as Galloway cattle, yaks, camels, Icelandic sheep, Navajo Churro sheep, llamas, and Bactrian (two-humped) camels from Mongolia, not to mention peacocks and an assortment of birds. Many visitors come just for the raw

fibers in an array of natural colors and a rainbow of processed fibers, also hand-dyed using only botanical dye extracts. The base for the yarns comes from the Angora goats, blended with wool and other fibers before spinning. Needless to say this is a mecca for knitters and weavers—but it's also just a fascinating all-around place to visit. The shop carries shawls and other finished products. Turn off Route 112 onto Chesson Brook Road and follow the camels.

Keldaby Farm and Moonshine Design (413-624-3090; www.keldaby.com), 12 Heath Road, Colrain. Open May through October. Visitors are welcome in the barn and fields with the Angora goats. Cynthia Herbert-Ramirez dyes the yarn from their soft fleece (blended with fine wool) here in her studio, then designs and weaves it into shawls, scarves, and other striking designs. Also see Keldahus under *Lodging*.

Apex Orchards (413-625-2744), 153 Pecksville Road, Shelburne. PYO apples in September and October. Also available: peaches, Asian pears, blueberries, honey, cider vinegar, and one of the region's more amazing views.

Donovan Farm (413-339-4213), Forget Road, Hawley. The state's largest organically certified farm, with sweeping views and five kinds of potatoes, produces its own hand-cooked, organic potato chips.

Hall Tavern Farm (413-625-9008; jayhealy6387@aol.com), Route 2, East Charlemont. The state's oldest privately owned tree farm produces timbers and lumber for its sawmill and offers a variety of kiln-dried wood products, including wide pine flooring, paneling, and wainscoting as well

ASHFIELD HARDWARE AND SUPPLY

Christina Tree

as ash, cherry, maple, and oak flooring from its 500 acres. The property includes a 4-mile hiking and snow-shoeing trail.

Burnt Hill Farm (413-337-4454), Burnt Hill, Heath. Pick-your-own blueberries in-season on top of a mountain with a 50-mile view.

The Benson Place (413-337-5340), 182 Flag Hill Road, Heath. Unsprayed, wild, lowbush blueberries. PYO late July through late August; the farmstand is also open 9–5 daily.

Walnut Hill Farm (413-625-9002), 104 Ashfield Road, Shelburne Falls. Open daily 7:30–7. A dairy farm and vegetable stand welcome visitors. The world's largest ox, weighing 4,700 pounds, was raised here at the turn of the 20th century.

SUGARHOUSES Sugaring season can begin as early as late February and extend well into April. A brochure detailing information about the sugaring process and each producer is available from the **Massachusetts Maple Producers Association** (www.massmaple.org), Watson-Spruce Corner Road, Ashfield 01330. During sugaring season you can call the **Massachusetts Maple Phone** (413-628-3912) to get an overall view on whether the sap is flowing and producers are "boiling off." The following sugarhouses (a partial list) are geared toward visitors more than most, but it's still a good idea to call before coming. All also sell their syrup from their farms year-round.

In Ashfield
South Face Farm (413-628-3268; www.southfacefarm.com). Tom McCrumm and Judy Haupt offer a sit-down dining room during sugaring

season, as well as exhibits of antique maple-sugaring equipment. This has been a working farm for 150 years, and some of the maples along the road are probably that old. The present sugarhouse dates back 50 years, recycled from a 19th-century barn. **Gray's Sugarhouse** (413-625-6559; www.grayssugarhouse.com) also has a long-established, visitor-geared sugarhouse in another corner of town.

In Charlemont
Blue Heron Farm (413-339-4045) welcomes visitors with rental units attached to its sugarhouse (see *Lodging*); the farm also features dairy goats, Norwegian Fjord horses, and organic produce.

In Conway
Boyden Brothers, right on Route 116, is the big producer here, but a number of other producers using wood-burning evaporators are scattered through the hills.

In Hawley
Clarks Sugarhouse (413-337-5788). Call for directions. It's not far from Berkshire East.

In Heath
Girard's Sugarhouse (413-337-5788) has been operating for more than 100 years. **Maple Ledge Farm** (413-337-4705), 107 Branch Hill Road, is just beyond the Heath Fairgrounds heading north toward Route 8A; **Berkshire Sweet Gold Maple Farm** (1-888-57-MAPLE) bottles single-batch high-grade syrups in imported glass.

In Shelburne
Gould's Sugar House (413-625-6170), right on Route 2, features locally made syrup on waffles; also homemade sausage and sugar-on-

snow among its other items (see *Eating Out*). **Davenport Maple Farm** (413-625-2866), set high above the valley with a splendid view, operates a restaurant during sugaring season and sells syrup from the house year-round (a good excuse to drive up). **Graves Sugarhouse** (413-625-6174), 104 Wilson Graves Road on the Greenfield–Colrain Road, is an old-fashioned wood-burning operation with an open barn.

✳ Special Events

Note: Check www.shelburnefalls.com for current Shelburne Falls–area events, and www.mafa.org for dates and details on agricultural fairs.

March: **Art on Sunday,** a major auction of work by juried artists and artisans, benefits the Franklin Land Trust (413-628-4696).

May: **Indian Powwow** at Indian Plaza, Charlemont. **Memorial Day Parade,** Shelburne Falls.

June: **Riverfest**—daylong festival along the street and river in Shelburne Falls.

July: July 4 **Indian Pow Wow,** Charlemont; **July 4 parade** in Shelburne Falls; **Rowe Old Home Day** (first weekend). **Franklin Land Trust Annual Farm and Garden Tour** is a great excuse to explore back roads leading to some amazing properties (midmonth; 413-628-4696). **Charlemont Yankee Doodle Days** at the Charlemont Fair Grounds—3 days of music and games, square dancing, fireworks, BBQ (third weekend).

August: **Bridge of Flowers 10K road race** and **Bridge Dinner,** Shelburne Falls. **Heath Fair**—one of the state's most colorful country fairs

SOUTH FACE FARM

Tom McCrumm

(midmonth; 413-337-5716). **Shelburne Grange Fair** (last weekend).

September: The big event comes the last weekend with the **Conway Festival of the Hills,** one of New England's most colorful foliage festivals—arts and crafts, skillet toss, weaving, ox-driving, and more (413-369-4631). The **Colrain Fair** is midmonth.

October: **Ashfield Fall Festival** on Columbus Day weekend is not to be missed—art and crafts exhibits, music, games, antiques sales, demonstrations, all kinds of food, farm products, and more.

November: **Annual Hard and Sweet Cider Tour** of orchards, hard-cider-making demos, apple pie tasting, crafts fair, lunch and supper (first weekend; 413-773-5463). **Moonlight Madness**—tree lighting, caroling, and special sales in Shelburne Falls (the day after Thanksgiving).

December: **Tuba Christmas** concert in Shelburne Falls.

ANNUAL BRIDGE DINNER ON THE IRON BRIDGE IN SHELBURNE FALLS

Shelburne Falls Area Business Association

This 225-square-mile spread of rolling hill and woodland is so far off the tourist map that it's called "the Hidden Hills." It's been bypassed by the Massachusetts Turnpike—there are no exits in the 33 miles between Westfield and Lee—which suits most of its residents just fine. Along the meandering Westfield River and its branches, these fertile valleys between wooded hills remain profoundly Yankee.

During the decades before income taxes, when wealthy Americans were building themselves summer palaces in Stockbridge and Lenox, a number of farms around Worthington and Cummington were gentrified; the William Cullen Bryant Homestead in Cummington is the most obvious surviving example. For much of the 20th century, however, this area was just a nameless region to pass through.

It was in 1982 that the Hilltown Community Development Corporation placed an ad in local papers asking people with spare rooms to consider the bed & breakfast business. A dozen or so households responded, forming the Hampshire Hills Bed & Breakfast Association and publishing a descriptive brochure. Their towns became known as the Hampshire Hills, a name that still applies generally to this area, despite the fact that some of the B&Bs as well as the swimming holes, craftspeople, fishing spots, waterfalls, and otherwise hard-to-find gems are actually in Hampden County to the south. This area offers few restaurants, but many, many likely picnic spots and sources.

Jacob's Pillow Dance Festival in Becket, the Miniature Theatre of Chester, and the Sevenars concerts in South Worthington are all widely acclaimed, but most events—such as auctions, agricultural fairs, and town homecomings—are only promoted locally, usually with flyers tacked up on general store bulletin boards and other public places. March is the time to sample this region's true culinary specialty: maple syrup, served up on pancakes or snow, at the sugar-houses in which it's just been made. April brings fishing and one of the country's most famous white-water races. All summer is prime time, highlighted by August's old-fashioned agricultural fairs. September brings PYO apples and fresh cider throughout the area, and during foliage season its high, maple-lined roads rival any in Vermont.

AREA CODE 413.

GUIDANCE The Jacob's Ladder Business Association (1-888-838-2474; www.jlba.org), P.O. Box 19, Huntington 01050, is a source of a variety of helpful material about towns on and off Jacob's Ladder, the 33 miles of Route 20 between Russell and Lee.

For a free map and guide, visit www.hidden-hills.com; another useful web site is www.hilltowns.com. Also see *Lodging*.

GETTING THERE Part of the beauty of this area is in its approach. Few places in this region are much more than half an hour's drive from I-91 or the Mass Pike, but you are quickly on back roads. The principal east–west roads—Route 9, Route 20, and Route 23—follow the river valleys, while Route 57 to the south is a high old byway. The major north–south routes, Route 112 and Route 8, also follow rivers. If you are coming from the east via the Mass Pike, take exit 3 in Westfield.

MEDICAL EMERGENCY Dial **911.**

✳ Villages

Chester (population: c. 1,200; www.chestermass.com) is a town with a split personality: Chester Village, down on Route 20, and Chester Center up on Chester Hill. **Chester Village** boomed with the mining and grinding of emery (as in emery boards and sandpaper) and with the advent of the railroad, which heads northwest out of town, all uphill. It's still the way Amtrak goes from Boston to Chicago, and it was a huge engineering feat to snake tracks up these ridges in the 1840s. The **Chester Railroad Museum** (413-354-7778) in the vintage-1841 depot at the head of Main Street (off Route 20) was originally built as a place to eat (dining cars had yet to be invented) midway between Springfield and Pittsfield. The museum is open July through September, Saturday and Sunday 11–3.

WORTHINGTON FARM

Kim Grant

The **Chester Historical Society Museum** (open the first Wednesday of each month and by appointment: 413-354-7829) is headquartered in the former small brick jailhouse on Route 20. The town hall is seasonal home to the distinguished **Miniature Theater of Chester.** On Route 20 in the middle of the village a sign for Middlefield points the way up to the Skyline Trail. Turn off onto Johnson Hill Road to find **Chester Center,** the picturesque 18th-century heart of town with its church and graveyard. Signs steer you to **Chester Hill Winery.** Ask locally about how to kind the **Keystone Arch Bridges** off Route 20.

Chesterfield. A white-clapboard village with an 1835 Congregational church, 1848 town hall, and the **Edward Memorial** (historical) **Museum** near the library. But the big attraction is **Chesterfield Gorge.** The town stages a rousing July 4 parade. The **Bisbee Mill Museum** (413-296-4750) on East Street is open June to October, Sunday 2–5 and by appointment; inquire about special events. It includes a working 19th-century gristmill as well as a rare collection of tools, equipment, and photographs of the town's past industries, including buggy whips, granite blocks, and maple sugar.

Cummington. The classic village center is posted from Route 9 and worth a stop to see the **Kingman Tavern** (open Saturdays 2–5 in July and August), a lovingly restored combination tavern, fully stocked general store, and post office. There are a dozen period rooms filled with town mementos like the palm-leaf hats and cigars once made here. There is also a barn full of tools and a shed full of horse-drawn vehicles. The big annual event is the **Hillside Agricultural Society Fair,** the last weekend in August. Cummington has nurtured a number of poets over the years and is the longtime home of America's former poet laureate Richard Wilbur. The **William Cullen Bryant Homestead** offers one of the best views of the town and its valley.

Middlefield (population: 542), a town in which the main road (one of the few that's paved) is known as the Skyline Trail because it follows the edge of a 1,650-foot-high plateau, offers long views west to the Berkshires. The only specific site to visit here is **Glendale Falls,** but everywhere you walk or drive is rewarding. The **Middlefield Fair** (second week in August) is one of the oldest (since 1856) and most colorful (horse and oxen draws, a sheep show, country bands, and plenty of food).

Plainfield. This beautiful old farming town has a population of 589, which swells to 2,000 in summer. Roads are lined with stone walls and avenues of maples, and the center has its mid-19th-century white Congregational church and town hall. The **Shaw-Hudson House** (413-634-5417), open by appointment, was built in 1833 by Dr. Samuel Shaw, medical partner and brother-in-law of William Cullen Bryant. Note the post office in the back of the white house across Route 116.

Williamsburg. The easternmost of the Hilltowns, this village is something of a bedroom town for Northampton 8 miles to the east. The village center straddles the Mill River and invites you to stroll, munching something you've bought at the **Williamsburg General Store,** the source of a "Walking Guide" published by the **Williamsburg Historical Society** (413-268-7733), which is housed in the 1841 town hall. Exhibits include photographs of the 1874 flood that burst a dam 3 miles above the village, killing 136 residents, collapsing buildings, and wiping out most of the mills. The museum also includes the Olde Grist Mill with its collection of farm tools and equipment and the one-room Nash Hill School (the buildings are open summer Sundays). **Snow Farm** (see *Arts and Crafts Programs*) attracts participants from around the country.

Worthington. The village at the heart of this town, known locally as Worthington Corners, is a classic, mid-19th-century crossroads with its general store and surrounding old homes, along roads that radiate in every direction. Note the grocery, golf course (vintage 1904), B&Bs, cross-country ski center, and hot-air ballooning. Turn off Route 112 in South Worthington to see the 19th-century academy building that now houses the **Sevenars Music Festival.** Continue on Ireland Street to farms and orchards spread along a high ridge.

✳ **To See**

HISTORIC HOMES ♿ **William Cullen Bryant Homestead** (413-634-2244) in Cummington, south of Route 9 off Route 112. Open for guided tours from the last week in June through Labor Day, Friday, Saturday, Sunday, and holidays 1–5; until Columbus Day, weekends and holidays. $5 adults; $2.50 age 6–12. This graceful mansion is filled with the spirit of an obviously tough-minded and original individual and with a sense of the era in which he was thoroughly involved. William Cullen Bryant was born in Cummington in 1794 and is remembered for his early nature poems—"Thanatopsis" and "To a Waterfowl," for example—and for his impact as editor and part owner for half a century (1829–78) of the *New York Evening Post.* Bryant successfully advocated causes ranging from abolitionism to free trade to the creation of Central Park. He returned to his boyhood home at age 72, buying back the family homestead, adding another floor, and totally transforming it into a 23-room Victorian summer manse set atop 246 acres of farmland. The land has since been reduced to 189 acres, but the expansive view remains. The house has been preserved (painted in its original chocolate browns) by the Trustees of Reservations to look as it did during Bryant's last summer here, in 1878. In 1999 a new visitors center was added, including a video tour of the house for those who cannot physically make one.

INTERIOR OF WILLIAM
CULLEN BRYANT HOMESTEAD
Trustees of Reservations

SCENIC DRIVES In the Hilltowns the drive that is not scenic is the exception. You almost can't lose, especially if you turn off the main roads in search of the waterfalls, swimming holes, crafts studios, and maple producers described in this chapter. Several drives, however, are particularly noteworthy.

The Skyline Trail, accessible from Route 143 in Hinsdale and from Route 20 in Chester, follows the edge of the Berkshire plateau through the middle of Middlefield. It's possible to make a loop from Chesterfield through Middlefield, stopping at Glendale Falls and the River Studio and returning via Chester Hill (another high point), but it's best to ask directions locally.

Ireland Street, Chesterfield to South Worthington. A mile or so west of the village of Chesterfield, turn left off Route 143 at the bridge. This is Ireland Street and best known as the way to **Chesterfield Gorge** (0.8 mile from Route 143 at River Road). Be sure to stop there. Then continue along Ireland Street, which is a straight, high ridge road. Stop at **Ireland Street Orchards** for the view, if for nothing else. Continue on to South Worthington. If you feel like a swim, **Gardner State Park** is just down Route 112.

Jacob's Ladder Trail Scenic Byway. The 33 miles of Route 20 between Russell and Becket are now promoted as "Jacob's Ladder," an early auto route (long since backroaded by the Mass Pike) that takes its name from the Becket farmer who is said to have hauled autos up the steepest pitch with oxen. This route actually predated the Mohawk Trail as a motorway between the Pioneer Valley and Berkshire County. The Ladder crests in Becket at a ridge billed variously as 1,781 and 2,100 feet high. Whichever it is, the view of the Berkshire Valley is splendid. Note "Jacob's Well," the spring used to cool the radiators of early cars, still in use beside a rest area.

General Knox Trail (Route 23) forks off from Route 20 in Blanford heading west through Otis. The Otis Reservoir, with swimming and boating (see "South Berkshire"), is just over the line. This route got its name (which actually applies to much of Route 20, too) because it was the path over which Boston book dealer Henry Knox mounted a successful winter effort to drag the cannons captured by Benedict Arnold and Ethan Allen at Fort Ticonderoga back to Boston, where they played a crucial role in liberating the city.

Route 57 from Westfield through Tolland and Granville. This route is well known to South Berkshire residents as a shortcut to Bradley International Airport in Connecticut, but it's otherwise one of the most obscure and backroaded of the state's historic east–west highways. It's the most southerly and one of the highest, obviously the reason why the railroad chose to follow the Westfield

FARM STAND ON IRELAND STREET BETWEEN WEST CHESTERFIELD AND SOUTH WORTHINGTON

Kim Grant

River instead. These villages—which clearly prospered in the late 18th and early 19th centuries, judging from the buildings along the road—were left to fade away. Tolland today is known chiefly for the Tolland State Forest, with some of the best campsites in the state. West Granville is worth pausing to note its early-18th-century meetinghouse; Granville is a must-stop to buy the cheese that's been sold at the general store here since the 1850s. The road then spirals down out of the Berkshire Hills into the Connecticut River valley at Southwick, notable for its many tobacco sheds and farm stands.

Get lost. Seriously. This is high, largely open countryside that was far more populated a couple of hundred years ago than it is now. If we try to direct you from Plainfield to Buckland via the web of back roads that begin with Union Street north from the middle of Plainfield, you will have us to blame. So, bring a camera, a map, and a compass and explore.

✳ To Do

BALLOONING Worthington Hot Air Ballooning (413-238-5514), Buffington Hill Road, Worthington. Paul Sena offers champagne flights year-round. He will pick up passengers almost anywhere in the Berkshires, but prefers to fly from Worthington and neighboring Cummington, over the hills and down into the Connecticut River valley. Request the multicolored "Thunderbuster" balloon: yellow, red, and orange on one side, blue and purple on the other. $200 per person for a 1-hour champagne flight.

BICYCLING Mountain bikers enthuse about the unpaved **River Road** south from Chesterfield Gorge in Worthington (see *Green Space*) to Knightville Dam. The *Rubel Western Massachusetts Bicycle and Road Map* is an excellent guide to biking throughout this area. See *Special Events* for the **Great River Ride** on the Columbus Day weekend.

CAMPING To reserve campsites in state forests, phone 1-877-422-6762 and check out what we say under *Camping* in "What's Where." The web site of the Department of Conservation and Recreation (formerly Department of Environmental Management) describes each park: www.massparks.org. **DAR State Forest** (413-268-7098), Goshen, provides 50 campsites, each with a table and fireplace. **Windsor State Forest** (413-663-8469), marked from Route 9 in West Cummington, offers 24 campsites; also see **Savoy Mountain State Forest** in "Along the Mohawk Trail"; all three areas offer swimming.

ARTS AND CRAFTS PROGRAMS Snow Farm (413-268-3101; www.snowfarm. org), 5 Clary Road, Williamsburg 01096. For more than 15 years this crafts center was known as "Horizons," but in 2001, when its founder determined to sell the property, longtime staffers Mary Colwell and her husband A. J. LaFluer realized that they couldn't bear to see the "New England Craft Program," as it's otherwise known, dissolve. So they sold their Northampton home, and with some help from glassblower Josh Simpson, the area's best-known local artisan, they continue to offer a full and varied program of weekend and weeklong workshops taught by dozens of skilled craftspeople, most of whom already have a long association with this special place. Check out the web site or request a catalog for a sense of current courses, which typically include ceramics, glassblowing, silk screening, wood sculpture, basket making, and photography. The setting is a 50-acre farm with lodging in dormitories and doubles (gender-specific shared baths), a common room, and a dining hall in which the meals served are all made from scratch. A sale featuring the work of craftspeople from around the country is held in November.

Becket Arts Center (413-623-6635; BerkshireArts@aol.com). A former wooden schoolhouse offers seasonal arts and crafts programs as well as workshops in writing and music.

FISHING The **Little River** and all three branches of the **Westfield River** are recognized throughout the country for the quality of their fishing.

GOLF **Beaver Brook Golf Club** (413-268-7229), 191 Haydenville Road (Route 9), Williamsburg, and the **Worthington Golf Club** (413-238-4464), Worthington, are both nine holes.

Whippernon Country Club (413-862-3606), 490 Westfield Road, Russell. A nine-hole course, challenging for beginners, with nice views and terrain.

SWIMMING The **West Branch, Middle Branch,** and **Westfield River** proper all weave their way through this area, offering countless swimming holes to which B&B hosts can direct you. More formal, public swimming spots like Plainfield Pond tend to be restricted to residents.

DAR State Forest (413-268-7098; www.massparks.com), Goshen, maintains a swimming area on Upper Highland Lake (see *Green Space*).

Windsor State Forest (413-684-9760; www.massparks.com), River Road, West Cummington, has a swimming area on a dammed portion of the river (see *Green Space*).

✎ **Gardner State Park** (www.massparks.com), Route 112, Huntington. Probably the best-known swimming hole on the Westfield River. A great spot to bring small children; there's an old-fashioned picnic pavilion in the pines.

✱ Winter Sports

CROSS-COUNTRY SKIING **Hickory Hill Ski Touring Center** (413-238-5813; www.xcskimass.com/HickoryHill/), Buffington Hill Road, Worthington. Open Friday through Monday in-season. The lodge is an old potato barn with a bar and snack bar. Trails climb through maples, birches, beeches, and firs, skirting a large field or two, and follow several streams to an altitude of more than 1,800 feet. Although a track is carefully groomed with a snowcat for skating and free-style skiing, more than half the trails are tracked for traditional recreational skiing.

Notchview Reservation (413-684-0148; www.thetrustees.org), Route 9, Windsor. The highest cross-country trails in Massachusetts are found on this 3,000-

acre Trustees of Reservations property. Admittedly, it takes a new snowfall to work your way up to the summit of 2,297-foot-high Judges Hill, but frequently there is snow on the former lawns of the General Budd Homesite. The panoramic view from this open area includes the notch in the hills cut by the Westfield River, for which the preserve is named. Adults $9, children $2.

Maple Corner Farm (413-357-8829; snow phone, 413-357-6697; www.xcski-mass.com/MapleCorner/). On a 500-acre working farm at an elevation of 1,400 feet, the Maple Corner cross-country center has 20 km of groomed trail over varied terrain. There is a rental shop and a lodge with a fireplace and snack bar. Open 10–5 weekdays, 9–5 weekends.

DOWNHILL SKIING **Blandford Ski Area** (413-848-2860; snow phone, 413-568-4341; www.skiblandford.org), Blandford. Call for directions. A small ski area that's been owned and operated by the Springfield Ski Club since 1936: 26 trails and slopes, two chairlifts, a T-bar and multilift. Snowmaking. Open late December to mid-March, 8:30–4 Friday through Sunday, and daily during school vacations. Night skiing Monday and Wednesday through Saturday. $19 Friday and $28 weekends, holidays, and school vacations.

✳ Green Space

STATE FORESTS *Note:* All state parks and forests are detailed at www.mass-parks.com.

DAR State Forest (413-268-7098), Goshen, provides 50 campsites, each with a table and fireplace. The swimming area at Upper Highland Lake, complete with bathhouses and lifeguards, also has a boat ramp (no motors allowed). Trails lead to Moore's Hill, just 1,697 feet high but with an extensive view.

Windsor State Forest. Marked from Route 9 in West Cummington. You can swim in the dammed section of the river; there are campsites, bathhouses, picnic tables, and grills here. Also see Windsor Jambs under *Waterfalls.*

East Branch State Forest (413-268-7098), River Road, Chesterfield, offers some good fishing.

Chester-Blandford State Forest (413-354-6347), Route 20, Chester, offers camping, fishing, as well as extensive hiking trails and easy access (a half-mile walk over a cement and then two steel-grate bridges) to the picnic site by 100-foot **Sanderson Brook Falls.**

HIKING AND WALKING **Notchview Reservation** (413-684-0148; www.the-trustees.org). The **Budd Visitor Center** on Route 9 in Windsor (1 mile east of the junction with Route 8A) is open daily year-round. There are picnic tables and trail maps for the 25 miles of hiking and cross-country trails (see *Winter Sports*) on this former 3,000-acre estate maintained by the Trustees of Reservations. This is a good place for birding.

Windsor State Park (www.massparks.com) is a quarter-mile-long gorge with sheer cliffs, topped with hemlocks above the rushing water. A trail leads along the edge. Unfortunately, picnicking is not permitted at the edge of the gorge, but it's a beautiful walk (there's a railing). The state dams the river for swimming, and there are bathhouses, 80 picnic tables, and grills. This stretch of the Westfield River is a popular spot for white-water canoeing. There are also many miles of hiking trails.

Petticoat Hill Reservation (www.thetrustees.org) in Williamsburg (up Petticoat Hill Road from the village). A trail leads to the summit of Scott Hill. Stone walls and cellar holes hint that this spot was the most populated part of town in the 1700s, but it's now forested, a good spot for wildflowers.

Devil's Den Brook in Williamsburg is a rocky gorge off Old Goshen Road (turn right onto Hemenway Road at the western fringe of the center, then branch left onto Old Goshen). If you take the next left, up Brier Hill Road, you come to 70 acres of wooded trails, good for cross-country skiing and hiking. Ask locally about **Rheena's Cave.**

WATERFALLS **Glendale Falls,** Middlefield (www.thetrustees.org). Turn off the Skyline Trail Road onto Clark Wright Road—which is closed in winter—some 3.5 miles southeast of the village. Glendale Brook drops more than 150 feet over rocky ledges. There are 60 surrounding acres.

Chesterfield Gorge (www.thetrustees.org). Turn off Route 143 at the West Chesterfield Bridge; the gorge turnoff is marked 1 mile south on River Road. Open daily 8 AM–sunset. $2 per adult, free under age 12. A deep canyon was carved by the Westfield River and walled by sheer granite cliffs topped with hemlock, ash, and yellow birch. Swimming is not allowed, but the Trustees of Reservations provide picnic tables.

Salmon Brook Falls. A drop of 50 feet in the Chester-Blandford State Forest, south of Chester, marked from Route 20; a good spot for a picnic.

Windsor Jambs in Windsor State Forest, marked from Route 9, West Cummington. A quarter-mile-long gorge with sheer cliffs, topped by hemlocks above rushing water. A quiet, beautiful place.

Also see **Sanderson Brook Falls** under *State Forests.*

✳ Lodging

BED & BREAKFASTS *Note:* Most of the B&Bs described below are members of the **Hampshire Hills Bed & Breakfast Association** (1-888-414-7664 or 1-888-527-0570; www.hamphillsbandb.com), P.O. Box 553, Worthington 01908, and are pictured on the web site.

✎ **The Worthington Inn** (413-238-4441), at Four Corners Farm, Old North Road (Route 143), Worthington 01098. Debi and Joe Shaw's striking, 1780 house has wide floorboards,

five fireplaces, and fine paneling, restored in 1942 by the architect responsible for much of the Old Deerfield restoration. There are horses in the horse barn and 60 surrounding acres on the edge of a picturesque village, really someplace special. The three bedrooms are sparely, tastefully furnished with antiques and down comforters; all have a private bath and wonderful light. Common space is elegant and comfortable, lived in by a real family. As appealing in winter as summer: Hickory Hill Ski Touring

Center is less than a mile away. Children and horses are welcome. The Shaws are hospitable, helpful hosts. $110–130 includes a full breakfast.

Upland Meadows Farm (413-634-8884), 338 West Cummington Road (Route 112), Cummington 01026. A beautifully restored 18th-century house on 200 acres looking over rolling countryside. Owner Judy Bogart has given her B&B an uncluttered modern feeling while respecting the house's character. The three nicely furnished bedrooms, all with private bath, are bright and sunny and made even cheerier by floral wallpaper and prints. Animals in residence on the farm include sheep, goats, a horse—and a llama. $90 year-round with full breakfast.

🐾 **Seven Hearths** (413-296-4312), 412 Main Road, Chesterfield 01012. An 1890s house that has been renovated to look older, set in the middle of the village historic district. Doc and Denise LeDuc serve memorable multicourse breakfasts (maybe stuffed French toast prefaced by a fruit-stuffed melon) in the formal dining room. The common rooms and three of the four guest rooms have working fireplaces; the larger guest room offers sitting and writing space and a private bath, while the fourth room is reserved for guests traveling together. Facilities include a hot tub. $80–130.

🐾 **Twin Maples** (413-268-7925), 106 South Street, Williamsburg 01096. This vintage-1806 house is set in its own 27 acres and surrounding farmland on a back road not far from the center of town. It's been home to Eleanor and Martin Hebert for more than 40 years. The three bedrooms and shared bath are clean and crisp (we like the blue room with the

antique iron-and-brass bed), and the welcome is genuine. During March you can watch sap turn into syrup in the sugarhouse, and any season you can meet the farm animals, which included—at latest count—a dozen Hereford heifers, two calves, a flock of Rhode Island Red hens and roosters, a number of sheep, and two dogs. $70–80.

🐾 🐾 **Cumworth Farm** (413-634-5529), 472 West Cummington Road (Route 112), Cummington 01026. Open May through November only. Home of the McColgan family, this is still a working farm growing berries, raising sheep, and producing maple syrup. Eileen McColgan continues the hospitable tradition of her parents, who were among the first B&B operators in the area. There are six guest rooms in the handsome 18th-century, hip-roofed farmhouse all furnished with antiques. Shared baths, but a hot tub is also available. Full farm-style breakfast. $65–85.

🐾 **Baird Tavern** (413-848-2096; www.bairdtavern.com), 2 Old Chester Road, Blandford 01008. This 1768 house retains its original wide paneling and floorboards and conveys a sense of comfort as well as history. Host Carolyn Taylor has carefully preserved the authentic look of the house, originally a tavern catering to travelers on the old Boston-to-Albany turnpike. (The Massachusetts Turnpike follows the same approximate route but is out of sight of the house—although not quite out of hearing.) A settle sits next to the big old fireplace in the original kitchen, and the onetime taproom is now a comfortable but uncluttered sitting room. Guest rooms are up the stairs built around the central chimney; one room retains its original walls and has a spinning wheel and period decor, but again nothing is cluttered. In all there are three guest rooms, the largest with four beds, sharing one and a half baths. A cot and crib are available, and a couple of Persian Angora cats (which Carolyn raises) are usually in residence. There is a beautiful perennial flower garden. Carolyn is a local caterer, and breakfasts can as easily be quiche or omelets as blueberry pancakes, although the berry-packed latter is the house specialty. $70–110 with a 2-night minimum on holiday and peak-season weekends.

The Hill Gallery (413-238-5914), 137 East Windsor Road, Worthington 01098. In his country contemporary multilevel home, which he designed and built himself, Walter Korzec has been welcoming guests since 1982. The Windsor Suite, on two levels apart from the rest of the house, has its own entrance, a rec room (with pool table, fridge, and phone), an exercise bike, a working fireplace, and plenty of space; the bedroom has a four-poster double bed, wide floorboards, mirrored closet doors, and a private bath. The Worthington Room set high with a Palladian window overlooking the two ponds and hills beyond, also has a mini fridge and a phone. Guests are welcome to use the living room with its working fieldstone fireplace. $65–90 includes a full breakfast. Korzec is an artist whose paintings and often whimsical constructions decorate the house and are displayed in the barn (which he also designed and built) that functions as an art gallery. A cottage is available, too.

✒ **Flower Hill Farm** (413-268-7481; www.caroldukeflowers.com), P.O. Box 454, Williamsburg 01096. Carol Duke has created 5 acres of flower gardens

ENJOY THE TRANQUIL BACKYARD OF BAIRD TAVERN

Christina Tree

on the slope below her vintage-1790 home, which sits high on a back road. While she promotes herself primarily as a place to stay within easy striking distance of Northampton, the location and feel are very much up-in-the-hills and away-from-it-all. Carol offers two suites, both unusually large and attractive. Downstairs there's a bedroom with queen-sized bed, fireplace, and bath adjoining a beautiful sitting room with a large fireplace. Upstairs is a bright bedroom with a queen bed, bath, small sitting and dining area, kitchen facilities, and a balcony. Both suites enjoy a view across the gardens to the mountains. Furnishings are appropriate to the age of the house and include many antiques. The dining room doubles as an art gallery. Floors are all gleaming hardwood, and guests are asked to bring slippers. The 20-acre property includes blueberries as well as flowers. $125–145, depending on room and time. Snow Farm is minutes away. Rates include an organic vegetarian/vegan breakfast (organic fruit salad, muffins, juice, tea, and coffee).

East Windsor Guest House (413-684-3191), 565 Worthington Road, Windsor 01270. A mile off Route 9. Open year-round. Susan and Richard Jacob's Colonial-style house offers three guest rooms (one is a single) that share two baths.

1886 House (413-296-0223 or 1-800-893-2425), 202 East Street, Chesterfield 01012. Located at the top of a scenic ridgeline, the house has three guest rooms, two with private bath. $95–125 with full breakfast.

OTHER LODGING Capen Farmhouse Guest Cottage (413-238-5304), 2 Capen Street, Worthington 01098. Open June through October. A rustic one-room cottage built as an artist's studio around 1900. The setting is romantic, in an old orchard beside a burbling trout stream, but while it's charming, the cottage is quite small (the antique four-poster bed is handsome but takes up a chunk of available space) and has a tiny bathroom. Guests have the run of the 100-acre property and use of a gazebo and the large swimming pool. The rate is $95 with a continental breakfast, self-served in the cottage, that includes "gourmet" muffins. Two-night minimum on weekends.

Also see **Blue Heaven Farm** in *Selective Shopping—Farms.*

✳ Where to Eat

DINING OUT Abijah Willard's (413-354-2200), 30 Main Street, Chester. Open for lunch and dinner Tuesday through Saturday, Sunday for brunch. This is a welcome addition to an area that doesn't have a surfeit of good restaurants. The atmosphere is elegant with crisp white tableclothes and good service, although the bar just off the dining room can get a bit noisy. Owner-chef Kim Jaslics prepares international dishes such as ginger soy stir-fry, spinach ravioli in red pepper cream sauce, and rack of lamb with peanut butter dipping sauce. Entrées $14–22.

Williams House (413-268-7300), Route 9, Williamsburg. Closed Monday; otherwise open daily for lunch and dinner. This old landmark, with its low-beamed dining room and large hearth, is a welcoming oasis. Lunch on sandwiches or more interesting fare such as herb-crusted brook trout. Entrées run $14.95–24.95. There are daily specials and full wine and liquor lists.

EATING OUT Woodside Restaurant
(413-268-3685), Main Street (Route
9), Williamsburg. Open 6 AM–8 PM;
until 2 PM Monday, until 9 PM Friday
and Saturday. Clean, welcoming, a
counter as well as several tables,
homemade soups, daily specials.

The Creamery (413-634-5560), corner of Route 9 and Route 112, Cummington. Open daily 7 AM–7:30 PM
weekdays, from 7:30 Saturday, 9 on
Sunday. This expanded general store
with its deli and hot food items, fabulous baked goods, crafts, and wine
selection is an oasis in these hills. The
tables are limited but round, and
strangers share—although it's true
that most patrons know each other.
The blackboard menu features soups
and sandwiches. Bread is freshly
baked.

Spruce Corner Restaurant (413-
268-3188), Route 9, Goshen. Jerry
Bird is the chef-owner of this cheery
way stop. Open for breakfast, lunch,
and dinner. This is pickup truck and
Harley-Davidson country, which does-
n't mean the food isn't fine. Everyone
feels welcome.

✳ Entertainment

Jacob's Pillow Dance Festival (413-
243-0745; www.jacobspillow.org),
George Carter Road, Becket (off
Route 20, 8 miles east of Lee). America's oldest dance festival and still its
most prestigious, Jacob's Pillow presents a 10-week summer program of
classic and experimental dance. For
more details, see "South Berkshire."

Miniature Theatre of Chester
(413-354-7771; www.miniaturethe-
atre.org), P.O. Box 722, Chester
01011-0722. The season runs 5 nights
a week from the last week of June to
the first week in October. Vincent

Dowling, a former artistic director at
Dublin's famed Abbey Theatre, first
came to Chester to fish and swim in
the Westfield River and has since
built himself a house while staging a
summer program of plays—a mix of
lesser-known classics and original
works, performed in Chester's town
hall (150 seats). Casts members are
professional actors and generally outstanding. Tickets are $20 Wednesday
and Thursday, $24 Friday through
Sunday.

Sevenars Music Festival (413-238-
5854), Route 112 between Huntington and Worthington. Concerts are
Friday evenings (at 7:30) and Sunday
afternoons (at 5), early July through
Labor Day. The seven Rs stand for
the seven Schrades, who include
Robert (longtime soloist with orchestras and a member of the faculty at
the Manhattan School of Music), his
wife Rolande (a concert pianist in her
own right and composer of more than
1,000 songs), Robelyn, Rorianne, and
Randolf Schrade (all with impressive
degrees and concert careers). The
twins Rhonda-Lee and Rolisa don't
perform, but Robelyn's husband, well-
known New Zealand pianist David
James, and their daughter, Lynelle,
do. Concerts are staged in the tongue-
and-groove paneled hall of a double-
porched, 19th-century academy just
off Route 112 by the South Worthington Cascade. Door donation $20
adults, $15 seniors and students.

Dream Away Lodge (413-623-8725)
1342 County Road, Becket. An old
roadhouse that once had a funky reputation; see "South Berkshire."

Bel Canto Opera Concerts (413-
848-2052), at the Historic White
Church, North Street, Blanford. Arias
and ensembles held in August.

Note: Tanglewood Music Festival and the many other Lenox- and Stockbridge-area summer music and theater events are an easy drive from most parts of this region. See "South Berkshire."

✳ Selective Shopping

ANTIQUES SHOPS Sena's Auctions (413-238-5813), Buffington Hill Road, Worthington. Since the 1950s, auctions have taken place on Tuesdays, but check to make sure. Held in the former potato barn that serves in winter as a ski touring center.

Chesterfield Antiques (413-296-4252), Route 143, Chesterfield, has a good selection.

CRAFTS The Basket Shop (413-296-4278), 513 Main Road (Route 143), Chesterfield. The shop itself is special, built by hand by Ben Higgins with an open basket-weave ceiling, woven cabinet doors, dovetailed drawers, and a variety of timeworn tools. Ben specialized in the rare art of weaving ash baskets, a skill his son-in-law Milton Lafond carries on using a variety of wooden molds, some 100 years old. The baskets are striking and unusually durable. Call before making a special trip; inquire about Open Days.

Sheepgate Handwovens (413-848-0990), Otis Stage Road, Blandford. Open Thursday through Sunday 11–5. The sheep are at the door, and the weaver is working her hand looms, selling one-of-a-kind clothing, shawls, bedding, pillows, sheepskin, buttons, and jewelry.

Stonepool Pottery (413-238-5362), Conwell Road, Worthington, just up Ireland Street from the old academy in South Worthington (take the next left). Open by chance or appointment year-round. Distinctive. Functional work by potter Mark Shapiro and his apprentices is displayed in a small gallery above Shapiro's home an old homestead in which the Reverend Russell Conwell was born. Conwell later added an unusual "stone pool" and built the nearby academy, but he is better known as the founder of Philadelphia's Temple University.

Judy Tavener Artoli (413-623-6481), Skyline Trail, Middlefield. The bright oils, acrylics, pastels, hand-painted floor cloths, and clothes displayed in the artist's own studio here are all highly original. No fixed hours, but there is usually someone around on weekends.

River Studio (413-238-7755), 36 East River Road, Middlefield. Open Friday and Saturday 11–3, by appointment at other times. The internationally acclaimed dancing statues of Andrew deVries are a find in their own right—especially set as they are on a meadow stage in a particularly obscure and lovely corner of Middlefield.

Quilts by Jane (413-634-5703; www.quiltsbyjane.com), Route 116, Plainfield. Jane Neri's eye-catching quilts festoon her front porch; visitors are welcome. Neri enjoys coming out to escort you into her studio (alias garage), hung with dozens of bright quilts, all made from castoff materials friends and neighbors bring her. Quilts are priced reasonably.

Snow Farm (413-268-3101; www.snowfarm.org), 5 Clary Road, Williamsburg 01096. Operated by the New England Craft Program, Snow Farm offers workshops and classes year-round in a variety of crafts including ceramics, glassblowing, silk screening, wood sculpture, basket making, and photography. A sale featuring the work of craftspeople from around the country is held all through November.

✳ Farms

Ireland Street Orchards (413-296-4024), Ireland Street, Chesterfield. April through November, open 10–6. Pick-your-own apples and flowers; a farm stand with local produce and crafts; horse-drawn hayrides on weekends during harvest season. Annual apple festival the first weekend in October.

Splendorview Farm (413-634-5528), 160 Bryant Road, Worthington. A sheep farm with a nice view. Tours offered.

✐ Gran-Val Scoop (413-357-6632 or 413-357-6632; www.gran-valscoop. com), 233 Granby Road (Route 189), Granville. This century-old family farm has a large dairy herd (along with sheep, goats, chickens, and rabbits) and makes more than two dozen flavors of gourmet ice cream using locally produced maple syrup, wild blueberries, peaches, and other fruits and berries.

Maple Corner Farm (413-357-8829), 794 Beech Hill Road, Granville. A working farm since 1840, Maple Corner sells maple syrup and products along with jams and jellies year-round. Pick-your-own blueberries daily July through mid-September. A sugarhouse and pancake restaurant is open late February to early April; in winter the farm is a cross-country ski center with rental equipment and 20 km of groomed trail.

Robert's Hillside Orchards (413-357-6690), South Lane Road,

Granville. Open July 15 through December 24, 9 AM–dark. Pick-your-own blueberries, peaches, and apples; a cider mill, hiking trails.

Mountain Orchard (413-357-8877), 668 Main Road, Granville. Pick-your-own apples (eight varieties), nectarines, and peaches. Open August through November, daily 8–8.

Nestrovich Fruit Farm (413-357-8520), 561 Main Street (Route 57), Granville. Apples, peaches, nectarines, plums, sweet cider, and honey. Open July 15 through April, daily 9–6.

Pathways Farm Perennials (413-357-6631), 62 Water Street, Granville. Wide selection of perennials and hardy garden plants. Open April through October, daily 9–6.

Blue Heaven Blueberry Farm (413-623-5519), 246 Skyline Trail, Middlefield. Daily in August, 9–4. PYO blueberries and raspberries. A furnished apartment is also available by the night, week, or month.

Waryjasz's Potato Farm (413-634-5336), 166 East Main Street (Route 116), Plainfield. It's difficult to miss this hilltop barn with its painted people and many signs. Potato lovers can choose from white, red-skinned, table stock, and rye seed potatoes; browsers will find a flea market's worth of trash and treasure in the barn.

Outlook Farm (413-529-9338), Route 66, Westhampton. Open weekdays 6 AM–7 PM, weekends 6–6. You can pick your own apples and find seasonal fruit and produce here, but the real specialties of the roadside store are homemade sausage, smoked hams, bacon, and ribs (although the pigs are no longer raised here the way they used to be, the USDA-certified slaughterhouse and smokehouse continue to operate). Sandwiches and daily specials are served. Hayrides available.

Cumworth Farm (413-634-5529), Route 112, Worthington. Pick-your-own blueberries and raspberries; the farm also sells jam and syrup.

WINERY **Chester Hill Winery** (413-354-2340; www.blueberrywine.com), 47 Lyon Hill Road, Chester. Joe and Mary Ann Sullivan make three kinds of blueberry wine—semidry New Blue, full-bodied Best Blue, and the sweet, brandy-enhanced Bay Blue—using local blueberries from nearby Kelso Homestead. They also make a white wine with grapes from upstate New York. The winery, which has a gift shop and tasting room, is open June through December, Saturday and Sunday 1–5, or by appointment. A blueberry festival, "Blueberry Days of Summer," is held the second week of August.

GENERAL STORES **Granville Country Store** (1-800-356-3141; www.granvillestore.com), Granville, just off Route 57. Open daily 7–6:30, Sunday 7:30–5:30. A typical village store but with a difference: a store cheese called Granville Cellar Aged Cheddar has been sold here since 1851; will ship anywhere. Current owner Ernie Hodur still uses the original recipe and aging method, producing a cheddar that's sharper and tastier than most. Hodur asks that it be kept at room temperature. We had no choice, given the fact that we were on the road without a cooler when we picked up a piece, and can attest that it kept surprisingly well and made for several memorable picnics.

High Country General Store (413-258-4200), Route 57, Tolland. Open daily 7–7, Sunday 9–5. Not particularly picturesque, but claims to be "the biggest little store in the country" and serves breakfast and lunch.

Huntington Country Store (413-667-3232; www.hcstore.com), Route 112 north of the village, Huntington. Known for its baked goods and candy; 20 flavors of ice cream and jams, mustards and herbs, also greeting cards, specialty foods, gifts, gadgets, and local crafts.

Williamsburg General Store (413-268-3036; www.wgstore.com), 3 Main Street, Williamsburg. Local maple products, daily-made breads and pastries, candy, handcrafted jewelry and many local crafts, 32 flavors of real ice cream, coffees, teas, cheese, jams, jellies, mustards, herbs, spices, and more.

The Corners Grocery (413-238-5531), Worthington Center. A double-porched, extremely photogenic store in the middle of a matching village; good picnic makings.

Also see **The Creamery** in Cummington under *Eating Out.*

SUGARHOUSES As already noted, the Hilltowns are the prime source of Massachusetts's maple sugar. Sugaring season can begin as early as late February and extend well into April. Locals and visitors alike are drawn to sugarhouses and pancake breakfasts featuring the new syrup. A brochure detailing the sugaring process and listing each producer is available from the **Massachusetts Maple Producers Association** (413-628-3912), Watson–Spruce Corner Road, Ashfield 01330, to which most area producers belong. The association web site, www.massmaple.org, lists

WILLIAMSBURG GENERAL STORE

Kim Grant

producers and sugarhouses open to the public and has a map showing where they are. It also has links to some 30 sites where you can learn just about all there is to know about maple syrup—including how to make it and cook with it. The following sugarhouses welcome visitors during sugaring-off, but call before coming. All also sell their syrup from their farms year-round:

In Chester
High Meadow Sugar Shack (413-667-3640) on the Skyline Trail offers spectacular views. **Roaring Brook Farm** (413-667-3692), 190 Skyline Trail, is a traditional operation that still uses a wood-fired evaporator to make syrup.

In Chesterfield
Bisbee Family Maple (413-296-4717) has a hand-built sugarhouse sited in the apple orchard; hot coffee and picnic tables; maple creams a specialty. **Krug Sugarbush** (413-268-

7098), South Street, offers nature walks through the sugarbush.

In Cummington
Cumworth Farm (413-634-5529) is between Worthington and Cummington on Route 112; the McColgan family has been making maple syrup for a long time, and the 200-year-old farmhouse is also a B&B (see *Lodging*). **Tessiers Sugarhouse** (413-634-5022), 60 Fairgrounds Road, is half a mile south of Route 9. **Temple's Sugar House** (413-634-2194), 115 Dodwell Road, is located a mile off Route 9.

In Granville
Maple Corner Farm (413-357-8829), 794 Beech Hill Road. Maple museum, sugarhouse tours, and a restaurant open weekends March to mid-April.

In Hawley
Clark's Sugar House (413-339-5517), 7 Bozrah Road. From Route 2,

take the East Hawley Road toward Berkshire East ski area.

In Heath
Girard's Sugarhouse (413-337-5788), 57 Number Nine Road. An old-fashioned sugarhouse in operation for more than a century.

In Huntington
Norwich Lake Farm (413-667-8830), 87 Searle Road. A traditional, wood-burning sugarhouse with eating facilities.

In Plainfield
Bob's Sugar House (413-634-5399), Route 16. A wood-burning sugar shack just a mile west of Plainfield center.

Thatcher's Sugar House (413-634-5582), 12 Broom Street. A traditional operation half a mile south of Route 16 and 3.5 miles north of Route 9.

In Williamsburg
Paul's Sugar House (413-268-3544 or 1-800-499-3544), Route 9, a mile west of Williamsburg center. Antique equipment on display; maple candies, and also apple, cherry, and blackberry syrups. **Lawton Family Sugar House** (413-268-3145), 47 Goshen Road. A family tradition for six generations. **Dufresne Sugar House** (413-268-7509; www.berkshire-maple.com), 113 Goshen Road. A large-scale (4,000 maple trees) family operation. Most of the boiling is done in the late afternoon or at night. Call ahead.

In Worthington
High Hopes Sugarshack (413-238-5919) displays work by local artists and features an "all-you-can-eat" pancake buffet. **The Red Bucket Sugar Shack** (413-238-7710) features pancakes, French toast, wagon rides, and snowshoeing. **Windy Hill Farm** (413-238-5869), the oldest sugarhouse in town, offers a dining room with a full maple menu in-season.

✳ Special Events
March: **Chester Hill Maplefest,** Chester Hill on Skyline Drive—pancake breakfast, tractor-pulled hayrides to a local sugar shack, music, crafts (third Saturday; 413-354-6315).

April: **Westfield River Wildwater Canoe Races,** Huntington, is billed as the oldest continuously run whitewater race in America (third weekend; 413-354-9684).

May–October: **Hilltown Farmers' Market,** Huntington town common, Saturday 9–1 (mid-May through Columbus Day weekend).

May: **Chester on Track** commemorates that town's railroading history with a parade, live music, and antique car show and open house at the Railroad Museum (413-354-6570).

July: **Independence Day,** Chesterfield—parade, fireworks, much more (413-296-4049). **Bryant Homestead Craft Festival,** a 2-day weekend (10–5) superlative happening at the William Cullen Bryant Homestead in Cummington, with more than 100 juried artisans, live bands, food, pony rides and petting zoo, classic autos, and tea on the veranda (midmonth; 413-634-2244). **Scottish Festival** in Blandford (third weekend).

August: Some of the state's oldest and most colorful fairs are held in this area; visit www.mafa.org for exact dates. Check out the **Littleville Fair** at the Littleville Fairgrounds, Chester (first weekend; 413-667-8738); the **Middlefield Fair,** Bell Road (second weekend; 413- 623-6423); and the **Hillside Agricultural Society Fair** (Cummington Fair) in Cummington (last weekend; 413-634-5091).

September: **Blandford Fair,** held since 1867 on Labor Day weekend, is big (www.theblandfordfair.com). **The** **Williamsburg Grange Fair** is the following weekend.

Columbus Day weekend: **Great River Ride**—a 100-mile bicycle tour of the Hilltowns (413-562-5237; www.newhorizonsbikes.com).

The Pioneer Valley

SPRINGFIELD AREA

UPPER PIONEER VALLEY

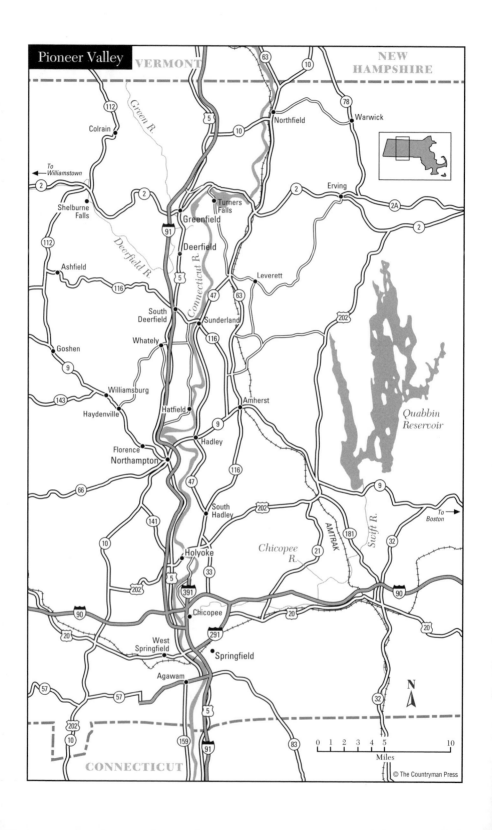

THE PIONEER VALLEY

T his valley seems to have been a Yankee version of the Garden of Eden: rich soil bordering a waterway to the ocean. It was farmed for thousands of years before the first English colonists arrived in the 17th century, "settling" here almost a full century before moving into the flanking hills.

The valley was carved by a series of glaciers, the last leaving 2-mile-deep Lake Hitchcock in its wake. Geologists have found that the lake was suddenly released, rushing to the sea all in one day—some 10,000 years ago. Just 5 miles wide up around the Vermont–New Hampshire line, the valley widens to 20 miles down around Springfield. Improbably, an abrupt chain of mountains marches east–west across the middle of the valley (do they suggest a mammoth herd of dinosaurs to anyone else?), yielding views from ridge paths and from two especially famous peaks—Mount Tom and Mount Holyoke—on opposite sides of the Connecticut. Both peaks are accessible by car, and both overlook the Oxbow and river loop.

New England's longest river, the Connecticut plays a far more obvious role as the boundary between New Hampshire and Vermont and is commemorated in the name of another state, for which it serves as centerpiece. Still, in its 69-mile passage through Western Massachusetts the Connecticut River has created a region as distinctive as any. The problem has always been what to call it.

In 1939 the Western Massachusetts Visitors Association sponsored a contest for a name to promote the area. The winner was "King Philip's Realm," a reference to the 17th-century Indian chief who unquestionably visited here but received a far-from-warm welcome. Instead "the Pioneer Valley" was adopted, and the name has come to apply to the three counties—Hampden, Hampshire, and Franklin—that flank as well as include the valley. We like the name to the extent it underscores its early settlement. What we don't like is the way it suggests that the entire area is a flat valley when, in fact, these counties include some of the hilliest country in the state (see "Berkshire Hilltowns"). At any rate "Pioneer Valley" is the only name that's stuck.

Perhaps the valley's most striking feature is the way in which its many layers of history—from dinosaurs to diners—are visible, far more than in most places. The dinosaurs left tracks, lots of them. Many were unearthed during construction of I-91 in the 1960s and can be viewed in half a dozen places, from science museums to the ground at Smith's Ferry.

In the 18th and early 19th centuries Massachusetts's communities along the Connecticut—isolated from the state's coastal capital and population centers— developed their own distinctive, valley-centered society, architecture, and religion. In the 1730s and 1740s the Northampton-based Reverend Jonathan Edwards challenged the theology of Boston-based Congregationalism, trumpeting instead the message that everyone (not just the "elect") could be saved. Edwards's emotionally charged revival meetings launched a "Great Awakening" that rippled throughout New England.

In the valley itself this fire-and-brimstone brand of Calvinism lingered on well into the 19th century, long after Boston had forgotten its Puritan horror of sin and embraced a more permissive Unitarianism. Puzzling on the themes of death and eternity in Amherst in the 1850s through 1870s, the poet Emily Dickinson was more a part of her time and place than is generally understood.

The valley's stern religion bred a concern for proper schooling. Deerfield Academy, founded in 1797, quickly attracted female as well as male students from throughout the area. Amherst College was founded in 1821 by town patriarchs, and in 1837 all-female Mount Holyoke College opened in South Hadley. Both contributed more than their share of Protestant missionaries.

Subtly but surely, education became a religion in its own right, and today it represents one of the valley's leading industries. Its heart is the Five-College Area, home to Smith, Hampshire, Amherst, and Mount Holyoke Colleges and the University of Massachusetts at Amherst. It represents one of the country's largest rural concentrations of students and certainly one of its liveliest rural music, crafts, art, and dining scenes.

The Connecticut served as a highway on which new settlers continuously arrived and crops were exported. Flat-bottomed, square-rigged boats plied this thoroughfare, deftly negotiating half a dozen patches of "quick water." In 1794 Springfield was chosen for the site of a federal armory. Skilled workmen flocked to the spot and began turning out muskets that went downriver, too.

Today it is difficult to grasp the former importance of this waterway. In the 1790s transportation canals were built around the falls at Holyoke and at Turners Falls. A number of vessels were built on West Springfield's common around 1800, and at the height of the subsequent canal-building craze, a canal system linked Northampton with New Haven.

With the dawn of the industrial revolution in the 1820s, the waterfalls that had been obstacles in the canal era were viewed as the valley's biggest assets. In the 1820s Boston developers began to build textile mills at Chicopee Falls, and in the 1830s and 1840s developed Holyoke from scratch—a planned, brick town, complete with factories, 4.5 miles of power canals, workers' housing, and mill owners' mansions. Meanwhile, Springfield was booming, thanks to its own home-bred inventors and investors, a breed initially drawn to the area by the armory.

The 1890s through 1920—the period from which most buildings in its towns and cities still date—was obviously the valley's most colorful and exuberant era. In Springfield public buildings like the magnificent City Hall and Symphony Hall, the soaring Florentine-style campanile, and the quadrangle of museums all conjure up this era. Trolley lines webbed the valley, transporting mill workers to mountaintops and parks. Also during this period, volleyball was invented in

VIEW FROM MOUNT HOLYOKE, BY WILLIAM HENRY BARTLETT, IS IN THE COLLECTION OF SPRINGFIELD'S CONNECTICUT VALLEY HISTORICAL MUSEUM.

Holyoke (look for exhibits in the Children's Museum complex), and basketball (the spectacular Hall of Fame tells the story) in Springfield.

The valley today is distinguished by its number of extensive, manicured parks, its elaborate stone and brick public buildings, and its private school and institutional buildings designed in every conceivable "Revival" style—all gifts of 19th-century philanthropists who refused to be forgotten (each bears the donor's name). Mount Holyoke itself now stands in vast Skinner Park, donated by a family that made its fortune producing satin in the country's largest silk mill. Northampton's 200-acre Look and 22-acre Childs Parks were both donated by the industrialists whose names they bear, and Stanley Park in Westfield was created by Stanley Home Products founder Frank Stanley Bevridge. Although Springfield's 795-acre Forest Park isn't named for its principal benefactor, it does harbor New England's most elaborate mausoleum, built by ice-skate tycoon Everett H. Barney.

As early as the 1820s, sophisticated tourists came to view the valley's peculiar mix of factory and farmscape, bottomland and abrupt mountains. In 1836 Thomas Cole, one of America's most celebrated landscape artists, painted the mammoth work *The Oxbow: View from Mt. Holyoke, Northampton, Massachusetts, after a Thunderstorm*, now owned by New York's Metropolitan Museum. The Oxbow subsequently became the "motif number one" of Western Massachusetts, and the small Mountain House on the summit of Mount Holyoke was soon replaced with a more elaborate hotel (a portion of which still survives), accessed from riverboats and a riverside train station by a perpendicular cog-and-cable-driven railway. Other hotels appeared on Mount Tom and atop Sugarloaf Mountain in South Deerfield.

Still linked both physically (by I-91, which superseded old north–south highways Routes 5/10, which in turn had upstaged the railway, which had replaced the river) and culturally with Connecticut's cities and with Brattleboro, Vermont, more than with Boston, the valley remains a place unto itself.

A case can be made that this Massachusetts stretch of the Connecticut Valley is the cultural heart of New England. The distance from Springfield's quadrangle of art, science, and heritage museums on the south to Old Deerfield's house and town museums on the north is little more than 40 miles, a straight scenic shot up I-91. Midway between these destinations lies the Five-College Area, with its extraordinary art museums at Smith, Amherst, and Mount Holyoke Colleges; the illustrations to be seen at the Eric Carle Museum; two house museums devoted to Emily Dickinson; and the National Yiddish Book Center—all within an 11-mile radius.

These cultural attractions are unusually accessible, set in one of New England's most intensely cultivated agricultural pockets, a distinctive landscape in which paved roads climb to hilltop lookouts, hiking trails follow ridgelines, and bike paths trace old trolley and rail lines.

The Connecticut itself is recapturing some of its old status as the region's focal point. It has made a dramatic comeback since the federally mandated Clean Water Act began to take effect in the 1970s. Now swimmable and fishable, it has been further improved through the protection of more than 4,000 riparian acres in Massachusetts. Underpromoted, a 52-mile Riverway State Park is now a reality.

On summer weekends hundreds of powerboats emerge from marinas sited on the deep lakelike stretches of the river above the power dams at Holyoke and Turners Falls, but two particularly beautiful stretches of the river—the dozen miles below Turners Falls and above French King Gorge—are too shallow for powerboating and particularly appealing to canoeists. The easiest way onto the river is aboard snappy riverboats: The *Quinnetukut II* cruises back and forth through French King Gorge, while the *Spirit of South Hadley* travels serene reaches of the river some 20 miles south. The sleepy old roads along both sides of the river are also becoming increasingly popular with bicyclists.

One of the state's most traveled bike paths follows an old railbed linking Northampton and Amherst, two towns that together represent one of the state's largest and most interesting concentrations of shops and restaurants. Lodging ranges from tents within sight of the eagles at Barton Cove to convention hotels in Springfield and includes both long-standing inns and a burgeoning number of B&Bs.

SPRINGFIELD AREA

One of the oldest cities in the country—it was founded in 1636 on the east bank of the Connecticut River between two waterfalls—Springfield has known booms and busts over three centuries. Unlike many other old New England industrial communities, it has tried hard to adapt creatively to change, although with mixed success. Today a city that once based its prosperity on manufacturing firearms is an increasingly popular tourist destination thanks to its central location, the worldwide craze for basketball, and the endearing characters created by local boy Theodor Geisel, better known as Dr. Seuss.

With a population of 152,000, Springfield is the third largest city in Massachusetts, and the metropolis of the Pioneer Valley. Although 33 square miles in area, most of its attractions—shops, restaurants, stately Courthouse Square (a monument to the city's glory days), the Museum Quadrangle, the Dr. Seuss memorial sculpture park, and the Civic Center (a sports arena and convention center)—are within a few blocks of each other in the compact downtown area known as Springfield Center. The Basketball Hall of Fame, the city's most popular attraction, is just a few minutes' drive away, as is the Springfield Armory National Historic Site.

Both Springfield Center and the Basketball Hall of Fame are well marked from Interstates 91 and 391. Within greater Springfield all you have to do to find downtown is follow signs with the impish image of Dr. Seuss's "Cat in the Hat," about as engaging a guide as you could ask for.

The Springfield you see today is largely the result of the young federal government's decision in 1794 to establish a national armory to manufacture muskets for the U.S. Army in the then small riverside village. The armory attracted skilled workers and developed machinery and manufacturing techniques that made Springfield one of the engines of the industrial revolution in America. Machine shops and factories utilizing tools and methods developed at the armory were established up and down the Connecticut Valley, which in time became known as "Precision Valley."

With the War of 1812 Springfield became an overnight boomtown, but it was the Civil War that really transformed the city, which doubled in population as it became the chief arsenal of the Union army. The armory produced more than half the rifled muskets used by northern troops, while nearby Smith and Wesson

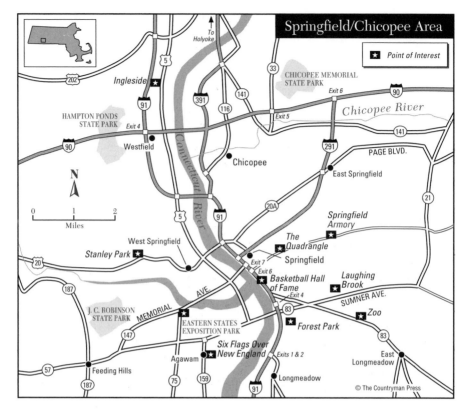

turned out 110,000 revolvers and the Ames Sword Company in neighboring Chicopee made 150,000 cavalry sabers.

After the Civil War, Springfield evolved into a prosperous diversified manufacturing city known for an impressive variety of inventions including the first gas-powered car and the first motorcycle, along with pioneering versions of airplanes and vacuum cleaners. The city was also the home to manufacturers of household-word products such as Breck Shampoo and Milton Bradley board games.

Most workers were well-paid craftsmen who could afford to buy their own houses, rather than live in rented tenement flats as in most New England cities, and Springfield boasted that it was "the City of Homes." Wealthy industrialists built themselves grand mansions, of course, but also supported the arts, endowing the Museum Quadrangle—an extraordinary civic amenity—and creating grand public spaces like Forest Park with its delightful zoo.

Theodor Geisel, born in Springfield in 1904, spent his childhood following his father, the city's superintendent of parks, around Forest Park. The zoo provided the inspiration for Dr. Seuss's whimsical creatures, his father was the model for the kindly zookeeper, and the park was the setting for many of his stories. A visit to Forest Park is particularly rewarding after seeing the sculptures in the Dr. Seuss Memorial in the Quadrangle and viewing the exhibit on Geisel's life in Springfield at the nearby Connecticut Valley Historical Museum.

Well-to-do local businessmen were also major supporters of self-improvement organizations such as the Young Men's Christian Association. It was at a YMCA training school for physical education instructors in Springfield in 1891 that Dr. James Naismith took a soccer ball and two peach baskets and created the game of "basket ball." His students, and other graduates of the school, took the game around the world.

The closure of the Springfield Armory in 1968 marked the end of an era for the already economically troubled city, which saw its industrial base continue to shrink and the population decline. Many formerly pleasant neighborhoods deteriorated into near slums, and once busy downtown department stores, hotels, theaters, and restaurants were forced to close their doors

Impressive but rather sterile urban renewal projects such as the Civic Center (currently being enlarged into a full-blown convention center) and the Town Square complex (a 29-story office tower and hotel with a shopping arcade and large parking garage) have brought life back to downtown, particularly after dark. However, many handsome 19th- and early-20th-century buildings that gave the city its distinctive character were bulldozed away to create them. Efforts are now being made to preserve landmark buildings and also to restore historic older neighborhoods.

Recent revitalization projects, such as Riverfront Park between I-91 and the Connecticut River, have a more human dimension than their predecessors. The park includes a 3.5-mile-long bicycle path and is also home to the new Naismith Basketball Hall of Fame.

Built at a cost of $45 million, the Hall of Fame is an architecturally striking building shaped like a basketball and with a 15-story spire topped by one 14 feet in circumference. At night, when it's illuminated in changing colors, the Hall of Fame looks like something from outer space and definitely brightens the Springfield skyline.

One local institution that has endured through Springfield's vicissitudes is the Eastern States Exposition—always referred to locally as "the Big E"—founded in 1917 and still going strong. Held mid-September through the first weekend in October in its vast fairgrounds in West Springfield, the Big E is the only annual event of its kind encompassing all six New England states. A huge and still basically agricultural fair, it also includes big-name entertainment and the Avenue of States, with replicas of the various New England state capitol buildings, each housing exhibits.

Also a survivor is the large amusement park just across the river in Agawam. Now called Six Flags New England and operated by the giant Six Flags national theme park corporation, it was originally Riverside Park and founded at the turn of the 20th century to provide inexpensive entertainment for Springfield factory workers and their families. The park was famous for its roller coaster and other scary rides back then—and still is.

AREA CODE 413.

GUIDANCE **Greater Springfield Convention and Visitors Bureau** (413-787-1548 or 1-800-723-1548; www.valleyvisitor.com), 1441 Main Street, Springfield

01103. The well-stocked and -staffed visitors center is open 9–5 weekdays.

William C. Sullivan Visitor Information Center (413-750-2980), 1200 West Columbus Avenue, Springfield 01103. Open March through October, daily 8–6. An attractive walk-in, staffed visitors center in the riverfront development area near the Basketball Hall of Fame, it offers information about the Pioneer Valley as well as Springfield.

GETTING THERE *By air:* **Bradley International Airport** (860-627-3594; www.bradleyairport.com). Eighteen miles south of Springfield in Windsor Locks, Connecticut, served by most national and regional carriers and major car rentals. See *Getting Around* for taxis.

By train: **AMTRAK** (1-800-USA-RAIL), 66 Lyman Street, connects Springfield with Hartford, New Haven, New York City, Philadelphia, Baltimore, Washington, D.C., and Chicago. There is frequent service from New York (change in New Haven). The bus depot is right around the corner from the train station.

By bus: **Peter Pan** (413-781-2900 or 1-800-237-8747), based in Springfield (with its own terminal at 1776 Main Street), connects with the airport, Boston, Hartford, Cape Cod, Albany, and New York City. **Vermont Transit** (1-800-552-8737) stops en route from New York and Albany to Vermont, New Hampshire, and Montreal.

By car: The route is trickier than you might think. From points north take I-91 to exit 7, and from points south to exit 6. From Boston, take the Mass Pike to exit 6 to I-291 to I-91 north to exit 2B (Dwight Street), which parallels Main; take it to State Street and turn left for the Quadrangle Museums; from Holyoke, I-391 is another connector.

GETTING AROUND **Pioneer Valley Transit Authority** (413-781-7882) serves the Springfield-Holyoke area.

By taxi: **City Cab** (413-734-8294), and **Yellow Cab** (413-739-9999).

PARKING The Quadrangle Museums, Springfield Armory National Historic Site, and Basketball Hall of Fame all offer parking (see map), and downtown parking lots are reasonably priced.

MEDICAL EMERGENCY Dial **911.**

Baystate Medical Center (413-794-0000), Chestnut at Spring Street.

✳ To See

MUSEUMS **Naismith Memorial Basketball Hall of Fame** (413-781-6500; www.hoophall.com), 1000 West Columbus Avenue, Springfield. (Just off I-91 and well marked: Look for the 15-story-high spire with the basketball on top.) Open Sunday through Thursday 9–6, Friday-Saturday 9–8, mid-June through September; opens at 10 AM the rest of the year. Admission $15 adults, $12.50 seniors, $10 youths (5–18). Dr. James Naismith invented basketball at a YMCA college in

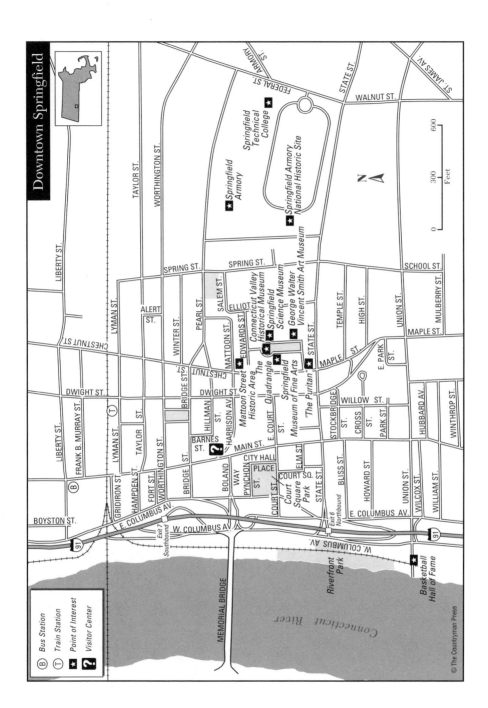

Downtown Springfield

- Ⓑ Bus Station
- Ⓣ Train Station
- ★ Point of Interest
- ? Visitor Center

Springfield Technical College

Springfield Armory

Springfield Armory National Historic Site

WALNUT ST.

STATE ST.

ST. JAMES AV.

FEDERAL ST.

ARMORY ST.

TAYLOR ST.

WORTHINGTON ST.

LIBERTY ST.

SPRING ST.

SPRING ST.

SCHOOL ST.

ALERT ST.

PEARL ST.

SALEM ST.

ELLIOT ST.

Connecticut Valley Historical Museum

Springfield Science Museum

George Walter Vincent Smith Art Museum

TEMPLE ST.

HIGH ST.

UNION ST.

MAPLE ST.

MULBERRY ST.

CHESTNUT ST.

WINTER ST.

MATTOON ST.

EDWARDS ST.

CHESTNUT ST.

The Quadrangle

Mattoon Street Historic Area

Springfield Museum of Fine Arts

"The Puritan"

STATE ST.

MAPLE ST.

E. PARK ST.

DWIGHT ST.

DWIGHT ST.

HILLMAN ST.

HARRISON AV.

E. COURT ST.

WILLOW ST.

STOCKBRIDGE

CROSS ST.

PARK ST.

HUBBARD AV.

WINTHROP ST.

BARNES ST. ?

MAIN ST.

CITY HALL

BOLAND WAY

PYNCHON ST.

COURT ST.

PLACE

COURT SQ.

Court Square Park

STATE ST.

ELM ST.

BLISS ST.

HOWARD ST.

UNION ST.

WILCOX ST.

WILLIAM ST.

LIBERTY ST.

FRANK B. MURRAY ST.

Ⓣ

Ⓑ

LYMAN ST.

GRIDIRON ST.

HAMPDEN ST.

TAYLOR ST.

FORT ST.

WORTHINGTON ST.

BRIDGE ST.

BOYSTON ST.

E. COLUMBUS AV.

W. COLUMBUS AV.

Exit 7 Southbound

MEMORIAL BRIDGE

Exit 6 Northbound

E. COLUMBUS AV.

W. COLUMBUS AV.

91

91

Riverfront Park

Connecticut River

Basketball Hall of Fame

N

0   300   600

Feet

© The Countryman Press

🐾 **The Quadrangle** (413-263-6800, www.quadrangle.org), 220 State Street. (The main entrance to the complex is on the Edwards Street side.) At this unique cultural common, four museums—a science and a history museum and two art museums—and the city's main library are all assembled around a grassy green. The Quadrangle green is now the site of a sculpture garden memorializing the work of children's book author and illustrator Dr. Seuss, nom de plume of native son Theodor Geisel. The museums are open Wednesday through Friday noon–4, Saturday and Sunday 11–4. Admission is $7 adults, $3 children 6–18, under 6 free; a bargain because it includes entry to all four museums. Inquire about frequent special events. The **Quadrangle Welcome Center** adjacent to the Science Museum contains the ticket office, a large gift shop, and a café.

✏️ **Dr. Seuss National Memorial** (413-263-6800; www.catinthehat.org), the Quadrangle. Open dawn to dusk daily. Free. This imaginative sculpture garden is the kind of humorous, fantastical tribute Theodor Geisel would have appreciated. The 22 bronze figures range in size from a tiny Lorax (a gnome with a walrus moustache) to a 14-foot-high trunk-waving Horton the Elephant, depicted stepping out of a giant book with Thidwick the Big Hearted Moose, Sam I Am, and other beloved Dr. Seuss characters. All the sculptures are the work of Lark Grey Diamond-Cates, Geisel's stepdaughter. The man himself is depicted sitting at his drawing board—and standing beside him, grinning mischievously, is Dr. Seuss's muse: "The Cat in the Hat." As you might imagine, this sculpture garden is kid-friendly: Sculptures can be climbed on, and there is even a bronze "storyteller chair" where parents can sit and read a favorite Dr. Seuss story to their child.

The Museum of Fine Arts (413-263-6800; www.quadrangle.org), the Quadrangle. A 1930s art deco building with a central court, the museum houses a surprisingly superb collection. You might expect the 18th- and 19th-century portraits and Hudson River landscapes (be sure to locate *New England Scenery* by Frederic Church), some memorable Winslow Homers and Frederick Remingtons, but what you don't expect is the wealth of early-20th-century paintings by

SAM-I-AM, ONE OF THE CHARACTERS IN HORTON COURT, AT THE DR. SEUSS NATIONAL MEMORIAL

HISTORICAL MONUMENT OF THE AMERICAN REPUBLIC (1876), BY ERASTUS SALISBURY FIELD, CAN BE VIEWED AT SPRINGFIELD'S MUSEUM OF FINE ARTS

Georgia O'Keeffe, Charles Sheeler, Charles Demuth, Reginald Marsh, and others. Paul Sample's *Church Supper* alone is worth a trip to see. The modern art collection is also far more than token. The museum's 20th-century as well as earlier paintings and sculpture are complemented in an interesting way by period furnishings and decorative art. Another surprise: Erastus Field's *Historical Monument of the American Republic,* a huge, absorbing fantasy depicting 300 scenes on 10 elaborate towers, a visual saga culminating with the triumph over slavery (note Abraham Lincoln rising to heaven in a fiery chariot near the top of the central tower). *The Newsboy,* a moment in 1889 captured by George Newhall, Springfield's leading late-19th-century artist, is also worth noting. Changing exhibits.

George Walter Vincent Smith Art Museum (413-263-6800; www.quadrangle.org), the Quadrangle. The first museum on the Quadrangle (1896), this is a one-man collection housed in a magnificent palazzo. G. W. V. Smith (always called by his full name locally) amassed a fortune in New York and married Springfield's Belle Townsley, retiring here at age 35. The couple devoted the next five decades to collecting ancient Japanese swords, armor, and art; Islamic rugs; the largest Western collection of cloisonné; and 19th-century landscape paintings. A recent addition to the museum is the Art Discovery Center, an interactive, colorfully decorated gallery designed to introduce children and families to the museum's collection. Like Boston's Isabella Stewart Gardner, the

Springfield Library & Museums Association

ANIMAL EXHIBITS IN THE R. E. PHELON AFRICAN HALL AT THE SPRINGFIELD SCIENCE MUSEUM

Smiths stipulated that the collection not be altered after their deaths, and their ashes are interred in the museum. The couple's portraits are just off the entry hall, surrounded by those of stern past captains of valley industry.

✐ **Connecticut Valley Historical Museum** (413-263-6800; www.quadrangle.org), the Quadrangle. A Colonial Revival mansion built in 1927 (note the replicated Connecticut Valley front door) houses an excellent genealogical library and interesting exhibits on Springfield inventions, personalities, and institutions. An imaginative permanent exhibit on Theodor Geisel called *Seuss on the Loose in Springfield* matches the sites of the author and artist's boyhood in Springfield with the landscape of his books (a turreted old National Guard armory became a castle, for example). There is plenty here for children to relate to and with, and the special exhibits are usually outstanding.

✐ **Science Museum** (413-263-6800; www.quadrangle.org), the Quadrangle. Dinosaur buffs will find a 20-foot-high model of *Tyrannosaurus rex* and the tracks of much smaller dinosaurs. Exhibits also include a vintage-1937 Gee Bee monoplane made in Springfield, a hands-on Exploration Center, an impressive African Hall full of animals, some great old-fashioned dioramas, Native American artifacts, and a new Eco-Center featuring live animals in realistic habitats—lifelike vegetation, fish that walk on land, turtles that look like leaves, and an Amazon rain forest. Planetarium shows daily. $3 adults, $2 children.

Springfield in 1891, and the Hall of Fame has been at various locations around the city since 1968. The present $45 million museum is Springfield's pride, its most visible landmark (it's shaped like a giant basketball and illuminated in different colors at night), and its biggest tourist attraction. A combination history museum, shrine, computer game arcade, and gymnasium—there's nothing else quite like it.

Basketball is anything but static and neither is the Hall of Fame, which has 41 interactive computer stations where visitors can, among other things, get answers to basketball trivia questions and play virtual reality basketball games. Some 70 TV screens are going all the time, showing interviews with players and coaches and highlights of championship games. There are also plenty of opportunities to toss basketballs around. The Hall of Fame gallery, the game's Valhalla, displays photos and mementos of basketball's greatest players, coaches, managers, and teams. Among the museum artifacts on display are Milwaukee Bucks' Bob Lanier's size 22 sneakers, a pair of gym bloomers worn by a member of the first women's basketball team (Smith College), and Naismith's not-very-well-typed 13 original rules of the game. The heart of the building is a regulation basketball court—pickup games are encouraged—directly under the 90-foot-high basketball-shaped dome.

Springfield Armory National Historic Site (413-734-8551; www.nps.gov/spar). Open Tuesday through Sunday 10–5:30. Armory Square (1 mile east on State Street from the Quadrangle; enter from Federal Street near the corner of State). Free. It was the presence of this federal armory, established in 1794 to manufacture muskets for the U.S. Army, that transformed Springfield from a sleepy village into a vibrant industrial city. The museum in the Main Arsenal Building, which dates from 1847, contains one of the world's largest and most comprehensive collections of firearms.

Exhibits include an array of weapons, from flintlock muskets to M-16 rifles, used in every American war since the Revolution. There are also film presentations, displays of innovative machinery invented at the armory, special exhibits on firearms development, and weapons firing demonstrations. Only about 20 percent of the armory's vast firearms collection is on view in the public galleries, but hour-long guided tours of the second-floor storage area, where the bulk of the collection is kept, are given one day each week. (Tours are limited to a maximum of 10 people. Call ahead to confirm dates and times. There is a $12 charge.) The imposing brick armory complex, which occupies more than 15 acres along a bluff above the city, was deactivated by the Defense Department in 1968, and most of the buildings are now used by Springfield Technical Community College.

Springfield Indian Motorcycle Museum and Hall of Fame (413-737-2624), 33 Hendee Street, Springfield. Open daily, March through November 10–5, and December through February 1–5. From downtown Springfield, take I-291 east to exit 4, then turn right onto Page Boulevard until you see the HISTORIC SPRINGFIELD sign. The museum is a brick, garagelike building in an industrial complex. The collection includes a wide variety of vehicles, from old Columbia bikes to motorized toboggans. You learn that Indian was the first commercially marketed, gasoline-powered motorcycle manufacturing company in the United States; production ceased in 1953. Admission $3.

***Titanic* Historical Society Museum** (413-543-4770; www.Titanic.org), rear of Henry's Jewelry Store, 208 Main Street, Indian Orchard. Open weekdays 10–4, Saturday 10–3. A large collection of thousands of objects recovered from the RMS *Titanic,* the world's most famous shipwreck (April 15, 1912, with a loss of 1,600 lives). The society's founder and president, Edward Kamuda, was inspired to begin the collection after seeing the 1953 film *A Night to Remember.*

Storrowton Village Museum (413-787-0136), 1305 Memorial Avenue, West Springfield, at the Eastern States Exposition grounds (Route 147). Open mid-June through late August, Monday through Saturday 11–3:30. $5 adults, $4 children. The gift shop is open year-round (closed Sunday). Donated to the exposition in 1929 by Mrs. James Storrow of Boston (the same family for whom Storrow Drive is named), this grouping of restored 18th- and early-19th-century buildings makes up one of the first museum villages in the country. The buildings, all of which were moved here from their original locations, include a vintage-1834 meetinghouse, an 1810 brick school, a smith, a huge and handsome vintage-1776 mansion, and a genuine 1789 tavern that would now be deep in Quabbin Reservoir if it hadn't been rescued.

HISTORIC HOMES AND SITES Court Square, bounded by Court and Elm Streets, Springfield. Springfield's "Municipal Group" recalls the city's golden era. Completed in 1913, the monumental, many-columned, Greek Revival City Hall and Symphony Hall buildings are separated by a soaring, 300-foot Italianate campanile. The **City Hall** interior is graced by 27 kinds of marble and fine wood paneling and includes a Municipal Auditorium seating 3,000. **Symphony Hall** is equally elegant and known for its acoustics. In the columned **Old First Church** (413-737-1411), check out the art gallery (open Monday through Friday 9:30–2:30 or by appointment), topped with a rooster shipped from England in 1749. The park here, created in 1812 to complement the first Hampden County Courthouse, is the scene of frequent events. Note the Victorian-era courthouse designed by Henry Hobson Richardson.

Historic Springfield neighborhoods. In the late 19th century Springfield became known as the City of Homes, reflecting the quality of the thousands of wooden homes—single- and two-family houses instead of the usual tenements and triple-deckers for the working class, and truly splendid houses for the middle and upper classes. Unfortunately, with the flight of families to the suburbs, several once-proud neighborhoods are now shabby, but still well worth driving through. **Forest Park,** developed almost entirely between the 1890s and 1920, is filled with turreted, Victorian, shingled homes, many built by the McKnight brothers (for whom the **McKnight District,** boasting some 900 of these homes, is named). Some of the city's stateliest homes, a number on the National Register of Historic Places, are found in the **Maple Hill District.** Right downtown the **Mattoon Street Historic District** is a street of 19th-century brick row houses, leading to the 1870s Grace Baptist Church designed by Henry Hobson Richardson.

FOR FAMILIES *⚓* **Six Flags New England** (413-786-9300 or 1-877-4-SIXFLAGS), 1623 Main Street (Route 159), Agawam. Open weekends mid-April through May, daily June through Labor Day, weekends in September; call for hours. Largest theme and water park in New England with over 160 rides (including eight roller coasters) and an 8-acre water park; also midway, arcades, food, and live entertainment. $39.99 adults, $24.99 kids; cheaper after 4 PM; $10 parking.

✿ **The Zoo in Forest Park** (413-733-2251). Off Summer Avenue/Route 83 (I-91 north, exit 2; I-91 south, exit 4). Open April 15 through November 15, weekends through December and February through April 15. Admission $4.50 adults, $3.50 seniors and children 5–12, $2 under 5. A small wild-animal zoo (deer, bears, woodland and exotic animals) and a petting zoo.

✿ **Eastern States Exposition.** See *Special Events.*

✳ Green Space

✿ **Forest Park** (413-787-6434). Three miles south of the center of Springfield (see directions to the zoo under *For Families*). Open year-round. Free for walk-ins, nominal charge for cars. The 735 acres include two small zoos. The park also offers paddleboats, 21 miles of nature trails, tennis courts, picnic groves, swimming pools, and summer concerts at the **Barney Amphitheater.** A magnificent, columned mausoleum built by ice-skate tycoon Everett H. Barney (his mansion was destroyed to make way for I-91) commands a great view of the Connecticut.

Riverfront Park, foot of State Street, Springfield. This 6-acre riverfront park offers a 3.5-mile-long bicycle path and a view of the Connecticut River, which is otherwise walled from the city by railroad tracks and interstate highway.

Stanley Park (413-568-9312), Westfield, open mid-May to mid-October, 8–dusk. Endowed by the founder of Stanley Home Products, the 300-acre park is known for its extensive rose garden (more than 50 varieties), mini New England village, 96-foot-high carillon tower, Japanese garden with teahouse, arboretum, and large fountain. Sunday-evening concerts range from singing groups to the Springfield Symphony Pops.

✿ **Laughing Brook Education Center & Wildlife Sanctuary** (413-566-8034), 789 Main Street, Hampden. From I-91 in Springfield, take exit 4 (Route 83) to Sumner Avenue, then go 3.6 miles. Nature center open Tuesday through Friday 10–noon, Saturday 2–4, Sunday 10–4, Monday and holidays 12:30–4. $3 adult, $2 child. Off any main route to anywhere, this is a popular destination for families drawn by the onetime home

FOREST PARK OFFERS TWO SMALL ZOOS FOR CHILDREN, IN ADDITION TO PADDLE BOATS, SWIMMING POOLS, AND NATURE TRAILS

Kim Grant

of storyteller Thornton Burgess. The house is now part of a 356-acre preserve owned by the Massachusetts Audubon Society; it includes hiking trails, fields, streams, a pond, caged animals, a picnic pavilion, and a "touch-and-see" trail.

✳ Lodging

The downtown convention hotels include the 265-room high-rise **Springfield-Marriott Hotel** (413-781-7111) and the 325-room **Sheraton Springfield Monarch Place** (413-781-1010), both right at the downtown I-91 exit, both with indoor heated pools and full health clubs. Marriott rates are $129–179 per couple, and Sheraton's are $99–159. A 12-story, 245-room **Holiday Inn** (413-781-0900), 711 Dwight Street (I-291, exit 2A), has an indoor pool and rooftop restaurant. $79–159 double, but inquire about specials. The **Hilton Garden Inn** (413-886-8000 or 1-800-234-3744; www.springfieldgareninn.com) is an attractive 143-room hotel adjacent to the Basketball Hall of Fame (they share a parking lot) with a large indoor pool. $89–159.

Berkshire Folkstone Bed & Breakfast Homes (413-731-8785), 101 Mulberry Street. This reservation service offers bed & breakfast in homes in Springfield and around Western Massachusetts. We were delighted with the one we stayed at; our host, a lifelong Springfield resident and enthusiast, insisted on giving us a tour of Forest Park. $75–350.

✳ Where to Eat

DINING OUT Student Prince & Fort Restaurant (413-788-6628), 8 Fort Street (off Main), Springfield. Open 11–11, Sunday noon–10. Sandwiches served all day. The Springfield business community's favorite spot since 1935: a grand old downtown beer hall with stained-glass windows, hung with beer steins. Serves imported wine and draft beers and offers a large menu of hearty German specialties—sauerbraten, Jaeger schnitzel and Wiener schnitzel, hunter's pie, and Hungarian goulash. Seasonal specialties include a February wild-game menu (where else can you try young bear or buffalo in wine sauce?). Lunch runs $5–12.95, dinner $10–22.

Caffeine's Downtown (413-788-6646; www.caffeinesdowntown.com), 254 Worthington Street, Springfield. Open for lunch and dinner. Handy to the Quadrangle Museums and Symphony Hall, a vaguely Mediterranean decor and menu, a good bet either for lunch or dinner. Interesting menu choices include lobster Tropicana soup, lamb salad (watercress with candied pecans, soft poached egg, and grape tomatoes all drizzled with truffle oil), and black cherry and ginger lacquered duck. Entrées $15–30.

Zaffino's (413-781-0900), Holiday Inn, 711 Dwight Street. At the top of a high-rise hotel, Zaffino's glass-walled dining room has a great panoramic view over the city and the valley. The food—mainstream American with some Italian dishes—is pretty good, too. Entrées $11.50–23.95.

Café Manhattan (413-737-7913), 301 Bridge Street, Springfield. Open 11 AM–2 AM. This attractive storefront meeting and eating spot, featuring a lounge and a piano (jazz starts about 8:30 PM), also includes the adjoining storefront (wonderfully deep, softly lit wooden booths). If a lunch sampling of blackened scallops served over mixed greens and "quiche of the day" (zucchini, caramelized onion, tomato, and Asiago cheese) is any test, the food is terrific. Dinner entrées $10–18.

Cara Mia Ristorante (413-739-0101), 1011 East Columbus Avenue, Springfield. Open Tuesday through Saturday 4–10. An upstairs place in "Little Italy" with red velvet decor, but delightfully nonstuffy. Jackets not mandatory, but the food is elegant and the wine list extensive. The veal and lamb dishes are particularly good. Live Italian popular and classical music Friday and Saturday nights. Entrées run $12.95–23.95.

Hofbrauhaus (413-737-4905), 1105 Main Street, West Springfield. The dining room features murals of German landscapes, and the atmosphere is quite formal but fun. Try deep-fried sauerkraut balls or goulash soup, a selection of good veal dishes, and a sparkling German wine. Be sure to leave room for a torte. Dinner entrées are $14–26.

L'Uva (413-734-1010) 1676 Main Street. Open for lunch and dinner. Specializes in eclectic dishes such as grilled marinated rack of lamb placed on a grape relish with Cabernet-flavored lamb demiglaze. There are some 500 different vintages on the wine list, more than 50 of which are available by the glass. Dinner entrées $15–30.

EATING OUT Gus & Paul's (413-781-2253), Tower Square, 1500 Main Street. A popular breakfast and lunch spot in downtown Springfield. Freshly baked bagels and deli sandwiches are the specialty; also egg dishes like egg and pastrami scramble, knishes, gefilte fish, blintzes, and chopped liver, not to mention knockwurst on a bagel with mustard and kraut. There is also always a choice of freshly made soups, sandwiches, and salads; beverages include Dr. Brown's Soda, including celery flavor (our favorite and seldom seen).

Tilly's (413-732-3613), 1390 Main Street, Springfield. Open 11:30–9 Monday through Wednesday; open later through Saturday; Sunday noon–8. Great homemade soups, deli sandwiches, quiches, breads and desserts, daily specials, full dinners. Try the Black Forest pie. A popular meeting place for lunch and after work.

Blue Eagle (413-737-6135), 930 Worthington Street, Springfield. Open from 11:30 daily, until 9 Sunday through Thursday, until 10 on weekends. Diner fans should drive (though not far from Main Street, this isn't a walking neighborhood) up Worthington Street to this popular place with 1940s touches like round windows in the door and glass-block windows.

GUS & PAUL'S DELI

Christina Tree

The menu is large and better than basic, ranging from a BLT to surf and turf, including lamb shish kebab and fried seafood dinners.

Mom & Rico's Market (413-732-8941), 899 Main Street, Springfield. Open Monday through Friday 8–5:30. A great Italian deli and grocery with a self-service buffet that usually includes lasagna, sausage and peppers, and eggplant parmigiana (better than your mother's). Pay by the pound or order from the large choice of grinders. This is headquarters for local bocci fans. For cappuccino and a cannoli, step next door to the Café La Fiorentina (883 Main Street; see *Snacks*).

Frigo's (413-731-7797), 1244 Main Street, Springfield. Open Monday through Friday 8–5, until 6 in summer. The blackboard menu features take-out specialties like pizza rustica, veal parmigiana, large and interesting sandwich combinations; a favorite with the downtown lunch crowd. If you have time, step around to **Frigo's Market** at 90 Williams Street, a cheese lover's mecca, also Italian cold cuts and take-out.

Lido (413-736-9433), 555 Worthington, Springfield. Open Monday through Saturday 11–11. Drive (don't walk) to this Italian favorite, good for the basics like lasagna and eggplant parmigiana and hot or sweet sausage. Best garlic bread in town.

Sitar (413-732-8011), 1688 Main Street, Springfield. Open Monday through Saturday for lunch and dinner, Sunday for dinner 5–10. Sampler platters and luncheon specials help the uninitiated choose from a large menu of Indian and Pakistani dishes.

Uno's Chicago Bar & Grill (413-733-1300), 820 West Columbus Avenue. Open daily for lunch and dinner. A large, moderately priced family restaurant next to the Basketball Hall of Fame. Deep-dish pizza is the specialty, but there is a full menu. Live music nightly in the garden courtyard.

SNACKS La Fiorentina Pastry Shop (413-732-3151), 883 Main Street, Springfield. Open Monday through Saturday 8–6, Sunday 8–2. The real thing. Mauro and Clara Daniele first opened La Fiorentina in 1947, using recipes for which Mauro's father Giuseppe had won awards for baking in Florence. Try the tiramisu (espresso, liqueur, mascarpone cheese, and cocoa powder layered between ladyfingers). Gelati, coffees, biscotti, many pastries, and known for rum cake soaked with rum and layered with custard and chocolate.

✳ Entertainment

City Stage (413-788-7033), 1 Columbus Center, Springfield. Professional theater, September through May.

Civic Center (413-787-6600; www.civic-center.com), Main at East Court Street. Contains a 7,500-seat arena and hosts concerts, conventions, trade shows, and sporting events, including home games of the Springfield Falcons hockey team.

Symphony Hall (413-787-6600 or 413-788-7033). The classic, columned music hall on Court Square is the home of the Springfield Symphony Orchestra. It also stages top-name performers, Broadway shows, and children's theater.

The Hippodrome (413-787-0600), 1700 Main Street, Springfield. A former 1920s movie palace, now the largest nightclub in Western Massachusetts, featuring live (frequently Latin) entertainment.

Showcase Cinemas (413-733-5131), 864 Riverdale Road, West Springfield; a multiplex showing first-run films.

✳ Selective Shopping

Tower Square (413-733-2171; www.visittowersquare.com), 1500 Main Street, Springfield. This indoor mall has some 30 shops and restaurants selling clothing, books, antiques, and more.

Quadrangle Gift Shop (413-263-6800; www.quadrangle.org), 220 State Street, Springfield. Located in the welcome center of the four-museum complex (adjacent to the Science Museum) beside the usual museum store items, this attractive shop has all the Dr. Seuss books and a wide assortment of Dr. Seuss–themed toys, stuffed animals, lunch boxes, and other gifts.

Holyoke Mall (413-536-1440; www.holyokemall.com) in the Ingleside section of Holyoke (I-91, exit 15, and Mass Pike exit 4). Open Monday through Saturday 10–9:30, Sunday 11–6. The biggest mall in Western Massachusetts and one of the largest in New England. There are nearly 200 stores, with Filene's, Lord & Taylor, JCPenney, and Sears among the anchors. Also a dozen food outlets.

✳ Farms

Bluebird Acres (413-525-6012), 747 Parker Street, East Longmeadow. Open April through December, daily 9–6. Some 80 different varieties of apples are grown and sold at this farm complex, which includes a grocery store and bakery.

Fini's Plant Farm (1-800-342-2205; www.finiplants.com), 217 James Street, Feeding Hills. Open May through October, Monday through Friday 8–6, weekends 9–5. A large selection of perennials, annuals, and herbs. There are wagon rides, corn and hay mazes, and a perennial garden.

Bird Haven Blueberry Farm (413-527-4671; www.birdhavenblueberry.com), 55 Gunn Road, Southampton. Open year-round, Tuesday through Friday 9–6, weekends 9–5. Homemade pies, jams, and jellies sold at the farm store. Pick-your-own flowers, blueberries, and raspberries in-season.

Calabrese Farms (413-569-6417), 257 Feeding Hills Road (Route 57), Southwick. Open April through September, daily 8:30–7. Has bedding plants, hangers, geraniums, and perennials in spring, its own corn, tomatoes, melons, and other produce in summer.

Coward Farms (413-569-6724), College Highway (Route 202), Southwick. Open from the day after Thanksgiving through the Christmas season. Cut-your-own Christmas trees (four kinds of fir trees and blue spruce), and also has wreaths, swags, and kissing balls.

Ray's Family Farm (413-569-3366), 723 College Highway (Route 202 and Route 10), Southwick. Open mid-April through December, daily 8–8. Annual bedding plants and farm-grown produce.

Kosinski Farms/North Country Harvest (413-562-4643; www.KosinskiFarms.com), 420 Russellville Road, Westfield. Open January through March, Tuesday through Sunday 8–5;

April through December, daily 6–8. Plants, flowers, apples, berries, also sweet corn, pumpkins, and other produce. The farm store also sells bread, muffins, mulled cider, and fresh fruit sundaes. There is a corn maze. Special events include blueberry, apple, and pumpkin fests as well as Santa visits the month before Christmas. There are daily hayrides September through November, with "haunted hayrides" on weekends around Halloween.

Pomeroy Farm (413-568-0049 or 413-568-3484), Russelville Road, Westfield. Sugarhouse open mid-February through first week in April; farm stand open seasonally selling fresh produce. Maple syrup, candy, and gift baskets are available year-round. B&B accommodation is available (413-568-3783).

❋ Special Events

Note: For event information, call 413-787-1548 or visit www.valleyvisitor.com.

May: **World's Largest Pancake Breakfast,** Main Street, downtown Springfield (413-733-3800).

June: **Taste of Springfield,** Court Square—more than 30 restaurants participate (413-733-3800).

July: **Star-Spangled Springfield**— Fourth of July celebration with live music, food, an arts festival, and fireworks in Court Square (413-733-3800).

July–August: Sunday performances by **Springfield Pops** in Stanley Park, Westfield. Theatrical and musical performances in Forest Park, Sunday evenings.

July–September: Free concerts in **Stearns Square** Thursday evenings.

September: **Harambee Festival of Black Culture,** Winchester Square, Springfield. **Eastern States Exposition** ("the Big E"), West Springfield, the biggest annual fair in the East— livestock shows, horse shows, giant midway, entertainment, Avenue of States; always runs 17 days, including the third week in September (413-787-0271). **Quadrangle Weekend,** Springfield—outdoor festivities, films, lectures, crafts demonstrations (413-737-1750). **Mattoon Arts Festival**— an outdoor fair on a downtown Springfield street lined with brownstones, gaslights.

October: **Columbus Day Parade** down Main Street, Springfield, to the Christopher Columbus statue in the South End.

November: **Parade of the Big Balloons,** downtown Springfield (day after Thanksgiving; 413-733-3800).

Late November–mid-January: **Bright Nights at Forest Park**—New England's largest Christmas light display, with themes like Seuss Land, Victorian Village, North Pole Village. Evenings from six o'clock (413-733-3800).

December 31: **First Night**—New Year's Eve celebration centered in the Quadrangle.

UPPER PIONEER VALLEY

FIVE-COLLEGE AREA

DEERFIELD/GREENFIELD AREA

T he Holyoke Range, running east–west across the valley, has been called the "Tofu Curtain" separating the Upper Valley from the more urban Springfield area. This northern two-thirds of the valley divides, in turn, into two distinct parts: (1) the northern, narrow, and rural stretch for which the big sight to see is the village of Old Deerfield and the commercial center is Greenfield; (2) the Five-College Area, with some 30,000 students on five very different campuses within an 11-mile radius.

Old Deerfield's mile-long march of 18th- and early-19th-century brick and wood buildings, set starkly against a thousand acres of cornfields, evokes the valley's first prosperous era so effectively that it's one of those rare places in which you can genuinely step back—through Historic Deerfield's period houses and Memorial Hall's wonderfully eclectic exhibits—a century or more. With the industrial revolution and advent of the railroad Greenfield replaced Deerfield as the area's commercial center, and it too now conjures another era—the 1950s.

Greenfield's century-old department store and vintage movie theater, its eateries, family-owned shops, and newspaper, and its fine community college all serve a lively community that extends west up into the surrounding hills, north up to the quietest reaches of the valley, and east to Turners Falls, smallest of the valley's mill villages with its most dramatic waterfalls.

The feel is totally different 20 miles downriver in Amherst and Northampton, dual but different hubs of the Five-College Area. They are sited on opposite sides of the Connecticut and connected by relentless road rash along Route 9 but also by the Norwottuck Rail Trail, a 10-mile bike path through the farmland.

The "five colleges" actually include the University of Massachusetts, as well as four small, prestigious private colleges. In cities, such academic concentrations are less noticeable. Here, against a backdrop of cornfields, apple orchards, and small towns, the visible and cultural impact of academia has been dramatic. The art collections in the college museums are exceptional and free, and the galleries, shops, and restaurants spawned by the academic community are numerous and appealing. Still, the Five-College Area is one of the state's better-kept secrets.

Interestingly enough, this entire stretch of the Connecticut River was recognized as one of the earliest tourist destinations in New England. A mineral spa in Northampton and hotel atop Mount Holyoke were must-stops in regional tours outlined in pre–Civil War travel guidebooks. The area's distinctive landscape—the abrupt mountains thrusting up from the valley floor—was seen as picturesque, and Mount Tom in Holyoke, Mount Sugarloaf in Deerfield, and Mount Toby in Sunderland were also capped with hotels. The paved roads and hiking trails up these mountains survive, reminders of the Upper Valley's first era as a tourist destination.

Admittedly, the White Mountains this isn't—and wasn't. The scenery that drew visitors to this valley was—and continues to be—as much human-made as it was—and is—natural. The farmland, while less pervasive than it was, still spreads along both sides of the wide, sinuous river. In summer this landscape, especially viewed from Mount Sugarloaf, is checkered white with the netting that shades tobacco plants and red with the many long, wooden tobacco barns in which it's cured. The entire Upper Valley continues to be, as it has been for many thousands of years, intensely cultivated. Nowhere in New England are farm stands more plentiful and varied.

This stretch of the Connecticut River itself is one of the most accessible as well as most beautiful along its entire 410-mile length. It includes the famous "Oxbow" and the beautiful backwater of Barton Cove. Fifty-two miles have, moreover, been preserved as the Connecticut River Greenway State Park, and many reaches are readily accessible by kayak, canoe, and excursion boat.

TOBACCO BARNS WITH VIEW OF MOUNT SUGARLOAF IN THE BACKGROUND, SUNDERLAND   Kim Grant

FIVE-COLLEGE AREA

The "five colleges" include the University of Massachusetts, as well as four small, prestigious private colleges. It's actually "UMass" that's affected this area most in recent years, beginning in the 1960s when its enrollment tripled and five 22-story dormitories plus one of the world's tallest libraries were built, towering above surrounding fields. Innovative Hampshire College opened in an Amherst apple orchard in 1970, and the Five College Consortium evolved from concept into reality.

During the academic year, buses now circulate among the five campuses (residents and visitors welcome). Thousands of students annually take courses at the other institutions, and all share a lively "Five College" calendar of plays, concerts, and lectures. Increasingly, too, graduates have opted to stay on in the valley, establishing the crafts and art galleries, restaurants, shops, and coffeehouses for which the area is now known.

Northampton, the valley's focal point both for students and visitors, is known not only for the quantity of its attractions (some 75 restaurants, roughly 100 shops, and a dozen major galleries) but also for the quality of the art and crafted work on display. It is increasingly a magnet in its own right for artists, including musicians and filmmakers, from throughout the country. Northampton is, besides, an architecturally interesting old county seat, with an outstanding art museum at Smith College and the country's oldest and most ornate municipal theater, the Academy of Music.

Amherst retains an appealing but small-town look and feel. The handsome common, framed by the Amherst College campus and 19th-century shopfronts, remains its centerpiece, connected to the UMass campus (curiously invisible, despite the high-rises, unless you go looking for it) by one long street of shops and restaurants that offers plenty of good eating, shopping, and book browsing but remains low-key.

Mount Holyoke in South Hadley is the country's oldest women's college and arguably has the most beautiful of the five campuses, an 800-acre spread designed by the firm of Frederick Law Olmsted with two lakes and majestic trees.

The fact that each of the five "colleges" is so different contributes to the beauty of their mix—a phenomenon best experienced during the academic year. Summer is, however, increasingly interesting in the valley. Entertainment options include concerts at Mount Holyoke College, at the Summit House atop Mount Holyoke, and in the garden at Forty Acres in Hadley, as well as both music and theater at UMass. Hiking trails run east–west across the valley, along the ridge of the Holyoke Range and through many miles of conservation land.

We include the small brick-mill city of Holyoke in the Five-College Area, designed from scratch by Boston developers in the 1840s, a contrast to the nearby ivy-covered communities. Industrial-architecture buffs will be intrigued by canal-side mill buildings, and families will appreciate the attractions conveniently grouped around the Holyoke Heritage State Park—the Children's Museum and a working antique merry-go-round. Mount Tom offers great views.

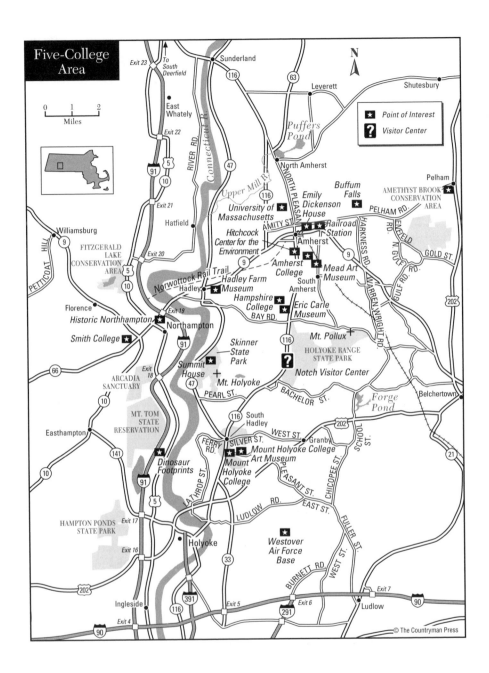

Five-College Area

Exit 23
To South Deerfield
Sunderland
116
63
Leverett
Shutesbury

0 1 2
Miles

91 5
10

East Whately

Exit 22

RIVER RD.

Connecticut R.

47

Upper Mill R.

North Amherst

Puffers Pond

★ Point of Interest
? Visitor Center

Exit 21

116

Pelham

Williamsburg
9

FITZGERALD LAKE CONSERVATION AREA

Exit 20

Hatfield

University of Massachusetts ★

Emily Dickenson House ★

Buffum Falls ★

AMETHYST BROOK CONSERVATION AREA ★

PELHAM RD.

HARKNESS RD.

ENFIELD RD.

N. GULF RD.

GOLF RD.

GULF RD.

AMITY ST.

Hitchcock Center for the Environment ★

★ ★ Railroad Station
Amherst ★

9

Exit 20

5
10

Norwottock Rail Trail

Hadley

Hadley Farm Museum ★

★ Amherst College

South Amherst

★ Mead Art Museum

WARREN WRIGHT RD.

PETTICOAT HILL

Florence

Historic Northhampton ★

Northampton

Smith College ★

Exit 19

91

Hampshire College ★
BAY RD.

Eric Carle Museum ★

Mt. Pollux +

202

66

ARCADIA SANCTUARY

Exit 18

47

Summit House +

Skinner State Park

Mt. Holyoke

116

?
HOLYOKE RANGE STATE PARK

Notch Visitor Center

Forge Pond

Belchertown

10

MT. TOM STATE RESERVATION

Easthampton

141

PEARL ST.

116

South Hadley

BACHELOR ST.

202

SCHOOL ST.

21

10

91

5

Dinosaur Footprints ★

LATHROP ST.

FERRY RD.

SILVER ST.

WEST ST.

Granby

Mount Holyoke College Art Museum ★ ★

Mount Holyoke College

PLEASANT ST.

CHICOPEE ST.

EAST ST.

FULLER ST.

LUDLOW RD.

HAMPTON PONDS STATE PARK
Exit 17

Exit 16

Holyoke

33

Westover Air Force Base ★

WEST ST.

BURNETT RD.

202

Ingleside

391

116

Exit 5

Exit 6

291

Exit 7

Ludlow

90

Exit 4

90

© The Countryman Press

Thanks to Amtrak from New York City and frequent buses from Boston and among the campuses, the Five-College Area is almost accessible without a car.

AREA CODE 413.

GUIDANCE Amherst Area Chamber of Commerce (413-253-0700; fax, 413-256-0771; www.amherstarea.com), 409 Main Street, Amherst 01002-2311. Sited off the main drag, down by the Amtrak station, open weekdays 8–4:30. An information booth on the common is open May through mid-October.

Greater Northampton Chamber of Commerce (413-584-1900; www.northamptonuncommon.com), 99 Pleasant Street (Route 5 south), Northampton 01060. Open Monday through Friday 9–5, also weekends June through October, 10–2.

For area museums, visit www.fivecolleges.edu/museums.

GETTING THERE

By air: **Bradley International Airport;** see "Springfield."

By bus: **Peter Pan–Trailways** (1-800-343-9999; www.peterpanbus.com) connects Greenfield, Amherst, South Hadley, and Holyoke with Boston, Springfield, Bradley International Airport, and points beyond. The local departure points are in Amherst, 79 South Pleasant Street (413-256-0431); in Northampton, 1 Round House Plaza (413-586-1030). From New York City, **Greyhound** (1-800-231-2222; www.greyhound.com) and **Vermont Transit** (1-800-552-8737; www.vttransit.com) serve Greenfield on north–south routes.

By train: **Amtrak** (1-800-872-7245; www.Amtrak.com), Amherst.

By car: The Mass Pike and Route 2 offer east–west access, and I-91 runs north–south. From Route 2, the quickest and most scenic way to the Amherst area is via Route 202 (exit 16), the Daniel Shays Highway, running down along the Quabbin Reservoir; turn west at the Pelham Town Hall.

GETTING AROUND The Pioneer Valley Transit Authority, or PVTA (413-586-5806), connecting Northampton, Amherst, and South Hadley, is free and frequent. It circles among the five campuses from 6:45 AM until 11:35 PM weekdays during the academic year, less frequently on weekends and in summer.

PARKING *In Northampton:* There is a 2-hour limit on the streets and in the lots, and even in the parking garage (Hampton Avenue behind Thornes Market) you have to prepay. The heavily patrolled lots are scattered throughout town with major areas just south of Main Street, accessible from Pleasant Street and from Hampton Avenue.

In Amherst: In addition to metered street parking, there are four downtown lots. The Boltwood lot (access from Main Street) is the handiest, with access to North Pleasant Street shops. Behind the CVS on North Pleasant Street is another lot, and there are also small lots on Spring Street (adjacent to the common) and Amity Street (across from the Jones Library). All are closely monitored.

In Holyoke: The downtown parking garage is on Dwight Street, one block from the Heritage State Park.

MEDICAL EMERGENCY Dial **911.**

Cooley Dickinson Hospital (413-582-2000), 30 Locust Street (Route 9), Northampton.

Providence Hospital (413-536-5111), 1233 Main Street, Holyoke.

✳ Villages, Towns, and Cities

Amherst. With significantly more students than Northampton (the town's population of some 35,000 includes a percentage of the 24,000 undergraduates and 5,500 graduate students at UMass, 1,600 at Amherst, and 1,200 at Hampshire College), Amherst is a lively college town. It's also walkable, with intriguing shops and restaurants lining two sides of its common as well as North Pleasant Street. More restaurants cluster around Boltwood Walk, squirreled away between North Pleasant and Main. As noted in the introduction to the "Upper Pioneer Valley," the vast and high-rise UMass campus, north of downtown Amherst, is curiously invisible. The far smaller Amherst College campus, just off the common, also eludes visitors but is well worth finding, both for its **Mead Art Museum** and **Pratt Museum of Natural History** and for its view down the valley to the dramatic Holyoke Range. Emily Dickinson buffs should visit not only her home but also the exhibits devoted to the poet's life in the **Jones Library,** just off the common. The Special Collections here form the literary heart of town, with exhibits and material devoted to Emily Dickinson but also an 11,000-item collection relating to poet Robert Frost. Portraits depict Frost not as the shaggy poet laureate we usually see but as the strikingly handsome young man who lived in Amherst from 1931 to 1938 and returned in the 1940s to teach at Amherst College. As noted in the Upper Valley introduction, Amherst has direct train service to Manhattan and a direct bus from Boston, as well as excellent local public transport and a bike trail to Northampton. It also offers a surprising amount of very accessible natural beauty, if you know where to look.

DOWNTOWN NORTHAMPTON

Kim Grant

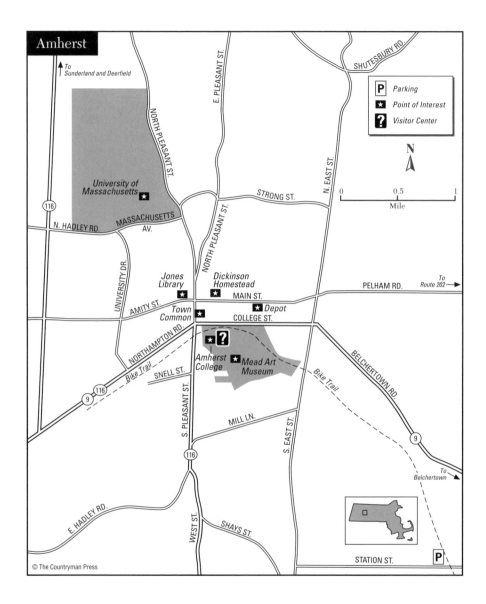

Amherst

P	Parking
★	Point of Interest
?	Visitor Center

To Sunderland and Deerfield

University of Massachusetts ★

Jones Library ★

Dickinson Homestead ★

Town Common ★

Amherst College ★ ?

★ Mead Art Museum

★ Depot

N

0   0.5   1
Mile

© The Countryman Press

Northampton. Despite a population of less than 30,000, this is a city, one with more art and music, film and drama, shopping and dining than most urban centers a dozen times its size. Thanks to Round Hill, an 1840s–1860 mineral water spa, Northampton loomed large on New England's pre–Civil War tourist map. In 1852 Jenny Lind, the Swedish Nightingale, spent a 3-month honeymoon at Round Hill and called Northampton "Paradise City," a name that's stuck (current local listings include Paradise City Travel, Paradise Copies, etc.). The brick hotel itself survives as part of the **Clarke School for the Deaf** (established 1867) on

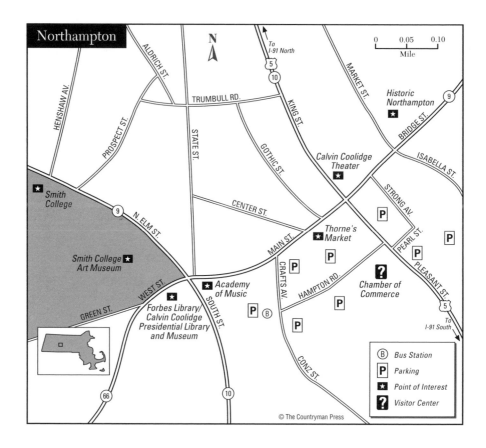

Round Hill Road, off Elm Street. Northampton is home to **Smith College** as well as to historic figures as different as the fiery 18th-century preacher Jonathan Edwards, the 19th-century food faddist Sylvester Graham (as in graham cracker), and the 1920s Northampton mayor and U.S. president Calvin Coolidge. The city's unusual history is nicely depicted in the **Historic Northampton** museum.

Northampton has reinvented itself several times over the centuries; the present Main Street lineup of restaurants, art galleries, and boutiques is relatively recent. Now known as Noho, Northampton continues to evolve, having a long tradition of tolerating people with dissenting religious and political views and non-traditional lifestyles. The town was a center of the peace movement during the Vietnam War and has a vibrant gay and lesbian community, the latter especially active in local cultural life. Civic pride runs as high as it did during the years the city's former mayor was sitting in the Oval Office (1923–29), a brief era in which the Hotel Northampton (which opened with a mini museum village attached, to serve as an auto touring destination) and several handsome art deco buildings appeared. These include a jewel box of a building featuring a stained-glass skylight that now appropriately houses Silverscape Designs; another splendid former bank is the setting for sculpture and prints (R. Michaelson Galleries), and the fabulously restored Calvin Theatre is regularly filled for stellar live performances.

Northampton these days illustrates synergy like no other place we know. It's not unusual to find the city's internationally famed Young at Heart Chorus of senior citizens sharing a stage with the Northampton Gay Men's Chorus, or for visitors to view a Matisse or Picasso in the Smith College Museum of Art and then stroll down the street to see a concert or a locally produced film at the municipally owned (since 1890) Academy of Music. Annual events include a Lyric Theater as well as arts and film festivals, and live music is a nightly given in several venues. Restaurants are so plentiful that patrons know they can always find a table within a block or two.

Don't overlook the village of Florence, still in Northampton, west on Route 9. Once known for silk mills, today its landmarks are the Miss Florence Diner and Look Park.

Hadley. The filler between Northampton and Amherst, Hadley is easy to miss because it's still predominantly tobacco, onion, and asparagus fields—beyond the Route 9 shops, greenhouses (the Hadley rose, the Talisman rose, and the Hadley gardenia were all developed here), and the many malls. Settled in 1659, it is the mother town of Amherst, South Hadley, Sunderland, Granby, and Hatfield, and was originally known as Norwottuck, a name resurrected for the bike path that threads its fields. In 1675 a white-bearded recluse, reputedly William Goffe (a Charles I regicide), saved the town from an Indian attack and has ever since been known as the Angel of Hadley. Turn off Route 9 at Middle Street to see the pillared town hall (1841), the **Hadley Farm Museum,** and the First Congregational Church (1808). The **Porter-Phelps-Huntington House** (1742) hidden away on the river (Route 47, north from Route 9) is a jewel.

Holyoke (www.holyoke.org). In 1847 Boston investors formed the Hadley Falls Company, buying 1,000 acres with the idea of utilizing the waterpower from the magnificent falls here. The company—and its dam—went bust but was soon replaced by the Holyoke Water Power Company, until recently the city's major political and economic force. Holyoke is a classic planned mill city. Its 4.5 miles of canals rise in tiers past dozens of mills; the commercial area is set in a neat grid above the mills. Housing changes with the altitude—from 1840s brick workers' housing on "The Flats" near the river, through hundreds of hastily built late-19th- and early-20th-century tenements, to the mill owners' mansions above, and above that the parkland on **Mount Tom.** In the visitors center at **Holyoke Heritage State Park** (413-534-1723; 221 Appleton Street; open Tuesday through Sunday noon–4:30; follow the signs for downtown), a short film conveys a sense of the city's late-19th-century vitality, of the era in which immigrants turned neighborhoods into "Little" Ireland, Poland, France, and half a dozen more bastions. If the film were remade today, it would note the last two decades' influx of Puerto Ricans, a group first drawn in the 1960s to work in the nearby tobacco fields. Specialty papers, from college bluebooks to hospital johnnies, remain

MOUNT HOLYOKE COLLEGE'S IVY-COVERED BUILDINGS, SOUTH HADLEY

Kim Grant

Holyoke's most notable product. Inquire about guided and leaflet walking tours and frequent special events. Mill-architecture buffs will appreciate the beauty of the canal-side Graham Mill (Second Level Canal near the Route 116 bridge). Inquire about the status of the **Holyoke Heritage Park Railroad,** dormant but not dead at this writing.

✳ To See

HISTORIC HOUSES AND MUSEUMS **The Amherst History Museum at the Strong House** (413-256-0678; www.amhersthistory.org), 67 Amity Street, Amherst. Open April through November, Wednesday through Saturday 12:30–3:30, or by appointment. $4 adult, $3 seniors and students. This circa-1750 gambrel-roofed house largely reflects several periods, including one in which it was a home and a "Young Ladies School." In addition to period rooms there are pictures and products (like palm-leaf hats) of Amherst past, also changing exhibits. The garden is 18th century. In 1899 it was the Amherst Historical Society's colorful founder, Mabel Loomis Todd, who secured this property. A room dedicated to her includes her paintings and souvenirs from world travels. Todd was Austin Dickinson's mistress and was responsible for editing and publishing early volumes of Emily Dickinson's poetry (see *Voice of the Valley*). Inquire about special events.

Porter-Phelps-Huntington Historic House Museum (413-584-4699), 130 River Drive (Route 47, 2 miles north of the junction of Route 9 and Route 47), Hadley. Open May 15 through October 15 for hour-long guided tours, Saturday through Wednesday 1–4:30. $4 per adult, $1 per child. **Wednesday Folk Traditions** (ethnic folk music) at 7 PM in June and July are staged in the garden, weather permitting ($8, $7 seniors, $2 children; picnickers welcome before concerts). **A Perfect Spot of Tea,** Saturdays in July and August (pastries and music at 2:30 and 3:30, $8). Also known as Forty Acres, this aristocratic old farm was built near the banks of the Connecticut River in 1752, and there have been no structural changes since 1799. The furnishings have accumulated over six generations of one extended family.

The Hadley Farm Museum (413-584-3120), Route 9 and Route 47, Hadley. Open May through October 12, Tuesday through Saturday 10–4:30, Sunday 1:30–4:30, closed Monday. Free. The 1782 barn from Forty Acres (see above) was moved in 1930 to its present site near the First Congregational Church and white-pillared town hall. It houses old broom-making machines (broom corn was once the town's chief crop), hay tedders and other old farm implements, pottery, an old stagecoach from Hardwick, and other assorted mementos of life in the valley.

In Holyoke
∞ **Wistariahurst Museum** (413-534-2216), 238 Cabot Street. Open Wednesday, Saturday, and Sunday, noon–5 April through October and noon–4 November through March; closed the last 2 weeks in August. Admission by donation. An opulent 19th-century, 26-room mansion with leather wall coverings, elaborate woodwork, and etched glass, built for the Skinner family, owners of the world's largest silk mill. It evokes the expansive spirit of Belle Skinner, the socialite who added a marble lobby, grand staircase, and great hall. Inquire about changing exhibits, concerts, and other events; also available for weddings, etc. The 3 acres of landscaped grounds include dinosaur footprints and fossil marks.

Also see **Holyoke Heritage State Park** under *Villages, Towns, and Cities* and the **Volleyball Hall of Fame** under *For Families.*

In Northampton
Historic Northampton (413-584-6011; www.historic-northampton.org), 46 Bridge Street (Route 9 between I-91 and downtown). Open year-round, Tuesday through Friday 10–4; Saturday and Sunday noon–4, when house tours are offered. The Museum and Education Center features *A Place Called Paradise*, a permanent exhibit dramatizing the city's history. Displays range from extensive Indian artifacts to Jonathan Edwards, industrial products to Coolidge years. There are also changing special exhibits. Three historic houses—the **Parsons House** (1719), the **Damon House** (1813, home of architect Isaac Damon), and the **Shepherd House** (1796)

PORTER-PHELPS-HUNTINGTON HISTORIC HOUSE MUSEUM IN HADLEY

Christina Tree

MORNING PICTURE (1890), BY EDWIN ROMANZO ELMER, IS SET IN ASHFIELD; THE PAINT-
ING CAN BE FOUND IN THE SMITH COLLEGE MUSEUM OF ART

ART MUSEUMS Smith College Museum of Art (413-585-2760; www.smith.
edu/artmuseum), Elm Street (Route 9, just beyond College Hall), Northampton.
Open Tuesday through Saturday 9–5, Sunday noon–5, until 9 Wednesday.
Free. This world-class art collection is second in Western Massachusetts
only to the Clark Art Institute in Williamstown. A recent 40-month, $35 million
remake added a third-floor, naturally lit gallery hung with works by Picasso,
Degas, Winslow Homer, Rockwell Kent, Marsden Hartley, Seurat, and
Whistler, and sculpture by Rodin and Leonard Baskin, also American primi-
tives and impressionists such as the starkly realistic oils by Edwin Romanzo
Elmer evoking 19th-century scenes from the nearby Hilltowns. From its 1870s
beginnings, the college's art collecting focused on "contemporary American
art" and by the 1920s included European "Modern Art." Curator Jere Abbott,
who had served on the founding staff of New York's Museum of Modern Art,
was instrumental in acquiring works like Picasso's cubist piece *La Table*. The
museum's second floor houses its European collection and a remarkable print
room; the first floor is devoted to special exhibits and includes a gift store
and what are undoubtedly the most artistic restrooms in any museum.

Mead Art Museum (413-542-2335; www.amherst.edu/mead), on the campus of Amherst College, Amherst. Open Tuesday through Sunday 10–4:30,
until 9 Thursday. The building, designed by McKim, Mead & White, has been
totally revamped within the past few years. The well-rounded permanent collection includes paintings by Thomas Eakins, Winslow Homer, Marsden Hart-

ley, and Childe Hassam. The stunning *Salome* by Robert Henri and *Morning on the Seine* by Claude Monet are usually on display; special exhibits are frequently contemporary and provocative. Totally unexpected is the Rotherwas Room, an ornately paneled, vintage-1611 English hall, a setting for furniture, portraits, and silver.

Mount Holyoke College Art Museum (413-538-2245 or 413-538-2245), Lower Lake Road, South Hadley. Open Tuesday through Friday 11–5, weekends 1–5. One

MAN WALKING, BY VINCENT VAN GOGH, ON DISPLAY AT THE SMITH COLLEGE MUSEUM OF ART

Smith College Museum of Art

of the oldest collegiate art collections in the country, but housed in a modern building, also recently redone with gallery space expanded. Permanent holdings range from ancient Asian and Egyptian works and Pompeiian frescoes, through Roman and medieval statuary, to some outstanding 19th-century landscapes by Albert Bierstadt and George Innes; also works by William Glackens, Robert Henri, and Milton Avery. Special exhibits are also frequently worth noting.

Mead Art Museum at Amherst College

SALOME (1909), BY ROBERT HENRI, CAN BE SEEN AT THE MEAD ART MUSEUM ON THE CAMPUS OF AMHERST COLLEGE

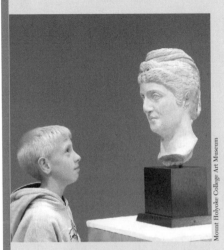

Mount Holyoke College Art Museum

A CHILD ADMIRES *FAUSTINA*, SCULPTURE OF EMPRESS FAUSTINA THE ELDER, ON DISPLAY AT THE MOUNT HOLYOKE COLLEGE ART MUSEUM

✎ **The Eric Carle Museum of Picture Book Art** (413-658-1100; www.picturebookart.org), 125 West Bay Road (off Route 116), Amherst. Open Tuesday through Saturday 10–4, Sunday noon–4. Admission: $4 adults, $3 seniors, $2 children and students, family $10. Opened in 2003 adjacent to the Hampshire College campus, this independently funded museum showcases the work of world-acclaimed illustrators and is aimed at "children of all ages." Local artist Eric Carle, author of *The Very Hungry Caterpillar* among many other books, contributed a founding gift and is frequently but not necessarily represented in the frequently changing exhibits—which are hung at child's-eye level. Facilities include a library of children's books, a hands-on painting room, a family-friendly café, and a big museum store.

Note: Art lovers should also visit Northampton's major art galleries (see *Selective Shopping*), which represent current artists whose work hangs in many of the world's major museums.

©1997 Eric Carle

A CAT AND A GIRL FROM ERIC CARLE'S FAMOUS *HEAD TO TOE*, AT THE ERIC CARLE MUSEUM OF PICTURE BOOK ART

reflecting lifestyles over three generations—are on their original sites, set in landscaped grounds. Inquire about special programs and events.

Calvin Coolidge Presidential Library and Museum at the Forbes Library (413-587-1014 or 413-587-1012; www.forbeslibrary.org), 20 West Street. Open Tuesday through Thursday 1–5 and by appointment or chance. The only presidential library in a public library, this recently renovated area contains all of Calvin Coolidge's papers from his years as governor, vice president, and president. The Amherst College graduate (1895) studied law and first hung out his shingle in Northampton. He became city solicitor, met his wife (Grace Goodhue was teaching at the Clarke School for the Deaf in Northampton when she met fellow Vermonter Cal), was elected a state representative, then mayor of Northampton (two terms). He became state senator, then governor, then vice president, and, when Harding died suddenly (August 3, 1923), president (for six years). The Coolidges had remained Northampton residents, and they returned to their Northampton house from Washington; Calvin died here in 1933. Personal belongings on display range from a replica of Coolidge's Northampton office, fitted with all its original furnishings, to an elaborate headdress presented by the Sioux nation, to an electric horse.

In South Hadley

Skinner Museum (413-538-2085), Route 116. Open mid-May through October, Wednesday and Sunday 2–5. Housed in the 1821 First Congregational Church that once stood in the town of Prescott (flooded by Quabbin Reservoir), this is a classic "cabinet of curiosities," some 4,000 items collected by Joseph Allen Skinner (1862–1946). The Skinner family owned major silk mills in Holyoke (see **Wistariahurst Museum,** above) and built The Orchards, a summer "cottage" across Route 116. Skinner's wealth permitted him to indulge his passion for collecting, which he did in his own world travels as well as those of his friends. To preserve it he acquired the once famous resort atop Mount Holyoke in 1916, and in 1930 he rescued this church and its surrounding buildings (a school and carriage house) with the idea of creating his own small museum village. Exhibits in the basement re-create a colonial hearth and early crafts, but the real wonder of this place is the eclectic mix of the collection, much of it displayed in high, old-fashioned glass cabinets—with and without labels: shells and fossils, scrimshaw, glass and china, here a huge old key to the Northampton jail, there two medieval sets of armor (one real and one fake—see if you can guess which is which).

MORE MUSEUMS **National Yiddish Book Center** (413-256-4900; www.yiddishbookcenter.org), 1021 West Street, adjacent to the Hampshire College campus, off Route 116. Visitors center open Sunday through Friday 10–3:30; closed Shabbat and Jewish and legal holidays. A cultural center, this handsome wooden complex of work, exhibition, and performance spaces is designed to resemble an Eastern European shtetl. Credit for the very idea of rescuing Yiddish literature (roughly a century's worth of works in the Yiddish language, beginning in the 1860s) goes to the center's director, Hampshire College graduate Aaron Lansky. This is a clearinghouse for books of a genre presumed almost dead when the

VOICE OF THE VALLEY: EMILY DICKINSON

Emily Dickinson (1830–86) was born in the staid, 1813 Dickinson Homestead not far from Amherst College. After attending Mount Holyoke Female Seminary for one year, she returned to her father's house, leaving rarely between 1855 and 1886, consumed with writing her honest puzzlings on the grand themes of love and nature, God and death, ragged-edged lines like:

"Hope" is the thing with feathers,
That perches in the soul,
And sings the tune without the words
And never stops—at all.

One of the most phenomenal aspects of Dickinson's story is that only 10 of these poems were published during her lifetime. The poet's work did not achieve widespread fame until well after her death.

The quality of the tour at the Emily Dickinson Museum is excellent. Dickinson's own room in the Homestead looks much as she knew it. The house itself was sold out of the family in 1916, but by 1965, when Dickinson's work was known worldwide, the house was purchased by Amherst College and opened to the public.

Though changes were made to the house, luckily the small world in which Emily Dickinson moved so intensely has been uncannily well preserved. The garden she tended remains a pleasant place to sit, and a path still leads next door to **The Evergreens,** an Italianate villa built in 1856 on the occasion of her brother Austin's marriage.

Emily and Austin's wife, Susan, were close friends, and Emily was a frequent visitor and present at social events with intimate friends and family. She was very much a part of this family, attached to their children, first a son and daughter and then, ten years later,

DAGUERREOTYPE PORTRAIT OF EMILY DICKINSON

Amherst College Archives and Special Collections

another little boy. When "Gib," the much-loved third child, died from typhoid fever, Emily grieved so deeply that she is said to have never fully recovered (dying two years later). Austin began an affair that is still the talk of the town, and many of his meetings with Mabel Loomis Todd, the lively wife of an Amherst College professor (she also founded the Amherst History Museum), were at the Dickinson Homestead, where his two sisters Emily and Lavinia still lived.

After Emily's death Lavinia first approached her sister-in-law Susan to edit Emily's poetry, but Lavinia later turned to Mabel Todd. Austin Dickinson died in 1895, and subsequent bitterness between the Todd and Dickinson families clouded publication of Dickinson's poetry for many decades after her death as competing versions of her verses appeared.

After Susan Dickinson died in 1913, her daughter, Martha Dickinson Bianchi, dedicated herself to publishing the Emily Dickinson poems she had inherited from her mother, and to writing about her memories of her aunt Emily. After the Homestead was sold out of the family in 1916, Bianchi began to establish The Evergreens as a destination for admirers of the poet's work, and she set up a room with her aunt's belongings that people could visit. Although some of these artifacts were subsequently transferred to the Houghton Library at Harvard University, The Evergreens retains its own original furnishings and interiors as well the feel of the house that Emily Dickinson knew so well. The quality of this experience is due in large part to Bianchi's heirs and to the work of the Martha Dickinson Bianchi Trust, established in 1988 to ensure the preservation of the house.

The Homestead and The Evergreens recently joined forces as the Emily Dickinson Museum. Both houses are now owned by Amherst College. The Dickinson Homestead—with its formal displays about Emily Dickinson and second-floor bedroom—and the magic of The Evergreens next door complement each other nicely.

For more about Emily Dickinson, visit the Special Collections rooms upstairs in the nearby Jones Library. Here panels depict the poet's life in Amherst. Several of her handwritten poems are among the collection of 8,000 items related to the history of Amherst.

Dickinson buffs might want to continue on to **West Cemetery** on Triangle Street. It's not difficult to find the Dickinson family plot, which is bounded by an ornate black iron fence. Here Emily lies surrounded by her grandparents, parents, and sister Lavinia. Note that on the Saturday nearest May 15 (the anniversary of her death), visitors are invited to meet at the Emily Dickinson Museum and walk to the cemetery. The museum offers other special events throughout the year. Also note the profile sculptures of Dickinson and Robert Frost in the

Christina Tree

THE EVERGREENS

small neighboring park, across from the puzzlingly grandiose Amherst Police Station (site of an apartment in which Frost wrote "Fire and Ice").

The Emily Dickinson Museum: The Homestead and The Evergreens (413-542-8161; www.emilydickinsonmuseum.org), 280 Main Street, Amherst. Guided tours June through August, Wednesday through Satruday 10–5, Sunday 1–5; September and October, April and May, Wednesday through Saturday 1–5; March, November, and early December, Wednesday *and* Saturday 1–5; closed mid-December through February. Call for specific times and to reserve a place. Tour of one house: $5 adults, $4 seniors and students, $3 children 6–18. Tours of both houses: $9 adult, $7 seniors and students, $5 age 6–18.

The Jones Library (413-256-4090), 43 Amity Street, Amherst. Open Monday through Saturday 9–8:30, Tuesday and Thursday until 9:30. The Special Collections rooms are open Monday 1–5, Tuesday through Friday 10–5, Saturday 2–5, but call to check.

center was founded in 1980; at the opening of the current facility in 1997 it had collected 1.3 million volumes, with an average 1,000 arriving weekly. Volumes are distributed to shops and libraries throughout the world. Exhibits change, but the quality of the artwork on display alone would have been worth our trip; also inquire about frequent lectures and performances.

✒ **Pratt Museum of Natural History** (413-542-2165; www.amherst.edu/~pratt/). Unfortunately this fabulous museum is closed as it moves to a new, renovated site. It reopens in 2006.

THE COLLEGES For an overview and current programs, see www.fivecolleges.edu.

Amherst College (413-542-2000; www.amherst.edu), Amherst. Founded in 1821 to educate "promising but needy youths who wished to enter the ministry," Amherst is today one of the country's most selective colleges. The campus is handsome and nicely sited, its oldest buildings grouped around a common overlooking the valley to the south and the Holyoke Range beyond. The **Mead Art Museum** (see *Art Museums*) is well worth a look.

Hampshire College (413-549-4600; www.hampshirecollege.edu), 893 West Street (Route 116), Amherst. Opened in 1970, this liberal arts college is predicated on cooperative programming with the other four colleges. Its 1,200 students design their own programs of study. Inquire about current exhibits at the College Art Gallery in the Johnson Library Center and events at the Performing Arts Center. Hampshire College president Greg Prince has encouraged a "cultural village" to evolve in the former apple orchard adjacent to the campus. To date it includes the **National Yiddish Book Center** (see *More Museums*) and the **Eric Carle Museum** (see *Art Museums*).

Mount Holyoke College (413-538-2000; www.mtholyoke.edu), Route 116, South Hadley. Founded in 1837, Mount Holyoke is the country's oldest women's college. The 800-acre campus, with its Upper and Lower Ponds and ivied buildings in a number of Revival styles, is home to some 2,000 women drawn from all 50 states and throughout the world. The adjacent Village Commons, a complex of restaurants, shops, and a theater, was designed by Graham Gund. Spend some time in the **Talcott Arboretum** (413-538-2116), open weekdays 8–4, weekends 1–4. This exquisite little Victorian-style greenhouse is filled with a jungle of exotic flora, featuring special late-winter and spring flower shows. *Note:* Prospective students, parents, and others with an MHC affiliation are welcome to stay at the attractive, on-campus Willits-Hallowell Center (413-538-2217). Be sure to see the **Mount Holyoke College Art Museum** (see *Art Museums*), marked from the South Hadley common.

Smith College (413-584-2700), Northampton. Founded in 1875 for "the education of the intelligent gentlewoman," the 125-acre campus now includes 97 buildings, an eclectic mix of ages and styles. Don't miss **Paradise Pond.** The newly renovated **Lyman Plant House** (413-585-2740), open daily 8:30–4, is known for its spring and fall flower shows; adjacent are an arboretum and gardens. Definitely don't miss the **Smith College Museum of Art** (see *Art Museums*).

University of Massachusetts (413-545-0111; www.umass.edu), Amherst 01003. Founded in the mid–19th century as the state's agricultural college, "UMass" now includes 10 undergraduate schools and colleges, also graduate schools, in more than 150 buildings on a 1,200-acre campus. Some 5,500 courses are offered by 1,000 faculty to 24,000 undergraduates and 5,500 graduate students. Sights to see at UMass: **Fine Arts Center and Gallery** (413-545-3670), changing exhibits. **William Smith Clark Memorial,** a half-acre memorial at the eastern entrance to the campus (off North Pleasant Street) dedicated to the first president of the university and his work in Japan, where he founded Sapporo Agricultural College, now the University of Hokkaido. The unusual memorial encompasses two circles linked by a spiral walk and twin steel walls depicting Clark's Amherst home and the Agricultural Hall at Hokkaido. Clark is widely revered in Japan, and many youth clubs are still dedicated to his memory. The memorial garden is sited on a hill with views extending across the campus to the river and hills. **Durfee Gardens and Durfee Conservatory** (413-545-5234), open weekdays 8:30–4:30. The conservatory dates from 1867 and houses tropical plants such as banana, coffee, and papaya divided by a 40-foot pool with an ornamental bridge and fountain. Five interlocking garden spaces offer benches, paths, and trellised wisteria and morning glories.

FOR FAMILIES ✐ **Dinosaurs.** The Pioneer Valley is a rich trove of dinosaur prints, said to range in age from 200,000 to 65,000 years old. The valley's dramatic topographical and climatic history is told in the **Springfield Science Museum** (see *Museums* in "Springfield") and at Nash Dinosaur Land (413-467-9566), better known as **"Dino Land,"** just off Route 116 north of the village of South Hadley. The sign on Dino Land's door reads PLEASE SOUND HORN. That fetches Kornell Nash from his house to this shop, which has been in the Nash family going on almost 60 years. Billed as the "world's largest dinosaur footprint quarry," Dino Land is the source of more than 3,000 dinosaur tracks sold ($50–500 apiece) over the years, clearly embedded in shale. Admission is $2 per adult, $1 per child. **Dinosaur Footprints** is in Smith's Ferry on Route 5, near Mount Tom, Holyoke. Look for a well-marked turnout on the river side of the road. A path leads down to a smooth rocks in which you can look for three-toed tracks, each 15 inches long and belonging to a 20-foot-long dinosaur *(Eubrontes giganteus)* that lumbered by 200 million years ago. Smaller tracks and other fossils have also been preserved. Also note the dinosaur footprints in the garden at **Wistariahurst Museum** in Holyoke (see *Historic Houses and Museums*).

✐ **Merry-Go-Round** (413-538-9838), next to the Holyoke Heritage State Park Visitors Center. September through June, weekends noon–4; July through Labor Day, Tuesday through Sunday 10:30–4. This vintage-1929 carousel with 48 hand-carved steeds, two chariots, and 800 lights was built for Mountain Park, an old-fashioned amusement park that closed in 1987. It was restored and moved to this handsome pavilion at a total cost of $2 million. Rides are $1; there's popcorn and a snack bar. Also available for private parties.

✐ **Children's Museum** (413-536-KIDS), 444 Dwight Street (across from the Heritage State Park Visitors Center), Holyoke. Open Tuesday through Saturday

9:30–4:30, Sunday noon–5. $5 per person. Children under 18 months, free. A
stimulating space with a Main Street that simulates downtown Holyoke's shops
and enterprises (the favorite is a working TV station), also a kids' TV studio and
"body of water" exhibit.

🖋 **Robert Barrett Fishway** (413-536-9428), Holyoke Dam, Holyoke, just off
Route 116 at the South Hadley Falls Bridge. Open in mid-June, Wednesday
through Sunday 9–5. Viewing windows and an observation platform overlook
American shad and Atlantic salmon as elevators help them bypass the falls on
their trip upriver to spawn.

🖋 **Volleyball Hall of Fame** (413-536-0926; www.volleyhall.org), 444 Dwight
Street, Holyoke. Housed in the Children's Museum complex (see above). Open
weekends noon–4:30, also Fridays in July and August. Invented in Holyoke in
1895, volleyball is commemorated here in a series of interpretive panels, an
interactive video presentation, and a model half court.

🖋 **McCray Farm** (413-533-3714), 55 Alvord Street, South Hadley. Open daily
year-round, with a dairy bar open spring through fall. A petting zoo, wagon and
sleigh rides depending on the season, maple breakfasts in March, and pick-your-
own pumpkins.

🖋 **Flayvors of Cook Farm** (413-584-2224), 129 South Maple Street, Hadley.
Open weekdays 8–7, 10–8 on weekends. Great ice cream (see *Snacks*) made
from the cows in residence.

🖋 **Look Memorial Park** (413-584-5457; www.lookpark.org), 300 North Main
Street (Route 9), Florence. Open Memorial Day through Labor Day. The many

MERRY-GO-ROUND NEXT TO HOLYOKE HERITAGE STATE PARK VISITORS CENTER

Christina Tree

Christina Tree

ENJOY DELICIOUS ICE CREAM AND THANK THE COWS IT CAME FROM AT FLAYVORS OF COOK FARM IN HADLEY

attractions of this 150-acre park include swimming and wading pools; pedal boating and canoeing on **Willow Lake;** bumper boats around "the lagoon"; a playground; the small **Christenson Zoo,** with native deer, peacocks, pheasants, and raccoons; the **Pines Outdoor Theater** (summer concerts and children's entertainment); and a miniature replica of an 1863 train that circles the zoo, as well as fishing in the **Mill River** (perch and small trout), an 18-hole miniature golf course, six all-weather tennis courts, a Picnic Store at which you can rent horseshoes, volleyballs, and other sports equipment, and plenty of places to picnic. Admission is free on foot or bike, but cars are $3 on weekends, $2 midweek, and there are charges for rides and rentals—but not for the zoo.

♦ **Western Massachusetts Family Golf Center Practice Range and Miniature Golf** (413-586-2311), Route 9 in Hadley. Open daily in season 8 AM–10:30 PM.

Also see *Entertainment.*

SCENIC DRIVES Rattlesnake Gutter Road and the Peace Pagoda. Assuming that you are coming from Amherst, the easiest way into this web of wooded roads is north from the lights in North Amherst, forking almost immediately right onto the road that becomes Route 63—but just before it does (there's a sign), turn right onto Depot Road, then left onto Montague. Rattlesnake Gutter Road is the next right, a dirt road that plunges down into a thickly wooded ravine—flanked by far deeper ravines. Continue to Moores Corner, turn left onto the North Leverett Road, and in a couple of miles turn left again onto Cave Hill Road; go left again in 0.9 mile at a small sign for the Peace Pagoda. Follow the dirt road to a small parking lot, from which you can climb up to the unlikely, white-domed Buddhist shrine and a hilltop view. Cave Hill Road runs back into Montague Road, which you follow back to Depot Road to retrace your route.

Route 47, South Hadley to Hadley. This beautiful road runs along the Connecticut River and through its floodplain, below Mount Holyoke. Be sure to turn in and follow the road through Skinner State Park to the summit.

Route 47, Hadley to Sunderland. The 9 miles from Route 9 in Hadley to the village of Sunderland shadow the river, passing through cultivated fields spotted with distinctive long tobacco sheds and some of the best farm stands in the valley.

Bay Road. For a quick sense of the beautiful farm country still surviving in Hadley at the heart of the valley, cut across Bay Road from Route 47 to Route 116. It runs along the southern foot of the Holyoke Range.

Note: Also see *Views*.

✳ To Do

BALLOONING Pioneer Valley Balloons (413-584-7980; www.northamptonairport.com). Hot-air balloon flights, daily, year-round weather permitting. Inquire about special events and flight instruction. $225 for a 2-hour ride.

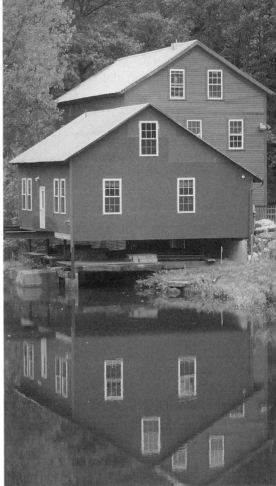

MILL NEAR EASTHAMPTON   Kim Grant

BICYCLING Given the number of young and young-in-spirit residents of this valley, combined with relatively level, quiet, unusually scenic rural roads, it's not surprising that bicycle touring is big here. At this writing it's possible to arrive on the Amtrak Vermonter in Amherst, unload your bike, and take off along the **Norwottuck Rail Trail,** a 10-mile bike path linking Northampton, Hadley, and Amherst along the former Boston & Maine Railroad right-of-way. You could also find a room within walking distance of the station and rent a bike (including a limited number of hand-cycles for handicapped cyclists) from **Valley Bicycles** (413-256-0880), 319 Main Street, Amherst, or from its annex right on the trail at 8 Railroad Street, Hadley (413-584-4466). Also **Laughing Dog Bicycles** (413-253-7722), 63 South Pleasant Street, Amherst.

Other access points to the rail-trail are at Mountain Farms Mall on Route 9 in Hadley and at **Elwell Recreation Area** on Damon Road (just north of the Route 9 bridge) in Northampton. The trail crosses the Connecticut on an old rail bridge and passes through open farmland, with views to the Holyoke Range to the south and to Mount Toby and Mount Sugarloaf to the north. Unfortunately a congested mile-plus gap presently exists between the western terminus of the Norwottuck Trail at Elwell Recreation Area and the eastern end of the **Northampton Bikeway,** which runs from State Street west 2.6 miles to Look Park. *Note:* The bikeway begins in a residential neighborhood without parking. Your best access option is the bike path entrance behind Stop & Shop on King Street. It's a great ride to do with kids; bring a picnic and explore Look Park (see *For Families*).

Bicycling the Pioneer Valley . . . and Beyond by Marion Gorham (New England Cartographics, 1998) is a valuable resource for touring this area by bike.

All the scenic drives outlined in this book lend themselves to bike touring, but there are many more loops. Inquire at local bike shops. For mountain biking trails, see **Northfield Mountain** in "Deerfield/Greenfield Area."

BIRDING **Arcadia Wildlife Sanctuary** in Easthampton (see *Hiking and Walking*) is the area's most obvious birding center, but there are others. The valley represents a major migratory flyway and is known especially for its many soaring hawks in fall. Prime watching spots include Goat Peak on Mount Tom and Prospect House on Mount Holyoke. **The Hitchcock Center for the Environment** (see *Hiking and Walking*) offers some birding workshops and is base for the Hampshire Bird Club. An excellent guide, *Birding Western Massachusetts: The Central Connecticut River Valley,* edited by Peter Westover for the Kestrel Trust and Hampshire Bird Club, is available in local bookstores. *Birding in Massachusetts* by Robert Tougias (New England Cartographics) describes 26 prime birding sites.

BOATING ♿ **Elwell Recreation Area,** just north of Route 9 at the Northampton end of the Coolidge Bridge, is a handicapped-accessible state-of-the-art boat dock.

River information. The **Connecticut River Watershed Council** (413-529-9500), 1 Ferry Street, Easthampton, publishes a canoe guide to the entire river and offers periodic guided canoe trips. **The Great Falls Discovery Center** (413-863-3221), Avenue A, Turners Falls, is also a source of river information. At **Barton Cove** (413-863-9300 or 1-800-859-2960), Northeast Utilities maintains tent sites, rents canoes and rowboats, and offers shuttle service to put-in places in Northfield. Also see *Connecticut River* in "Greenfield/Deerfield Area."

BOAT RENTALS **Sportsman's Marina** (413-586-2426), Route 9 at the Coolidge Bridge, Hadley, rents boats April through October (weather permitting): canoes, aluminum outboards, and pontoon boats. Bring a picnic and head for an island. **Brunelle's Marina** (413-536-3132) in South Hadley has a restaurant and launch area. There is also a state access ramp almost 1.5 miles north of Hatfield center, and another is off Route 5 at the Oxbow in Easthampton. The 16-mile stretch of the Connecticut River above the Holyoke Dam is heavily used on summer weekends by water-skiers, fishermen, and powerboat owners as well as canoeists. **Taylor Rental** (413-773-8643) in Greenfield rents aluminum canoes. **Oxbow**

Marina (413-584-2775), Island Road off Route 5 south of I-91, Northampton. The largest marina in the area offers a boat launch, rentals, instruction, a picnic area, and a beach.

BOAT EXCURSIONS *Spirit of South Hadley* (413-315-6342), an excursion boat based at Brunelle's Landing in South Hadley, offers seasonal 75-minute narrated tours up and down the Connecticut River, daily (weather permitting) at noon, 2, and 4; inquire about special evening cruises.

CANOEING AND KAYAKING Arcadia Nature Center and Wildlife Sanctuary (see *Hiking and Walking*), marked from Route 5, Easthampton, but on the Northampton–Easthampton line in Northampton, is a great place for novice canoeists to explore quiet waters. Inquire about guided canoe trips.

The 52-mile Connecticut River Greenway State Park (see "Greenfield/Deerfield Area") includes a 12-mile Connecticut River Water Trail that runs from the Turners Falls Dam in Montague to the Hatfield state boat ramp. The water along this trail is too shallow for powerboating, so the area is limited to small boats and canoes and to low-impact recreation. A detailed brochure guide to the trail is available from the Department of Conservation and Recreation (DCR; 413-586-8706, ext. 12), 136 Damon Road, Northampton 01060.

Fitzgerald Lake off North Farms Road (in Florence, turn off Route 9 onto Maple), Northampton. Roughly a mile long and a quarter mile wide, an oasis of quiet; look for a wooden dock about 100 yards off North Farms Road.

Puffers Pond, North Amherst (see *Swimming*). No powerboats allowed.

SPIRIT OF SOUTH HADLEY

Kim Grant

Adventure Outfitters (413-586-2323), Route 9, Hadley, rents canoes and kayaks.

GOLF Hickory Ridge Country Club (413-256-6638), West Pomeroy Lane, Amherst, is an 18-hole championship course with a clubhouse and snack bar.

Orchards Golf Course (413-534-3806), Silverwood Terrace, South Hadley. 18 holes.

Beaver Brook Golf Club (413-568-1636), Williamsburg. Nine holes.

Pine Grove Golf Course (413-584-4570), Highland Avenue, Northampton. 18 holes.

Ledges Golf Course (413-532-2307), 18 Mulligan Drive, South Hadley. 18 holes.

FISHING For licensing, see "What's Where."

The Connecticut River

The Pioneer Sporting Center (413-584-9944) in Northampton is a source of advice as well as equipment. To see migrating shad and salmon in mid-June, check out the **Robert E. Barrett Fishway** (413-536-9428) in Holyoke; viewing windows and an observation platform overlook the two elevators that hoist more than a million migrating fish over the falls.

Quabbin Reservoir

Quabbin Reservoir is open for fishing mid-April through mid-October, 6 AM to 1 hour before sunset. To rent a boat you must be 16 years or older and have a Massachusetts fishing license; licenses and bait are available from such local shops as Bill and Cathy Martel's **Bait Shop** (413-323-7117) at Gate 8 in Pelham. Much of the reservoir is off-limits, but Gate 8 (Route 202 in Pelham) accesses cold salmon- and trout-filled water. For detailed information, contact the **Quabbin Visitors Center** (413-323-7221). The **Charles L. McGloughlin Trout Hatchery** (413-323-7671) in Belchertown adjoins the **Swift River Wildlife Management Area,** which offers good fishing in the Swift River, as well as fields and woodlands webbed with trails.

HIKING AND WALKING

In Amherst and Pelham

The Amherst Conservation Commission (town hall, 413-256-4045) maintains some 1,450 acres scattered in 45 distinct holdings, with 60 miles of trails for walking, birding, and ski touring. It's worth stopping by the town hall or local bookstores to pick up printed maps or guides.

&. The most popular (and most heavily used) areas include **Upper Mill River** and **Puffer's Pond,** State Street off Pine, good for swimming and picnicking. Trails—including one designed for handicapped access and blind walkers—lead upstream from the pond along the Cushman Brook's cascades.

Hitchcock Center for the Environment (413-256-6006) at the Larch Hill Conservation Area, 1 mile south of Amherst center on Route 116. The 25 acres include hiking trails, formal gardens, and ponds. The center offers a variety of lectures and workshops; it also exhibits local artwork.

Mount Pollux, Amherst, is a favorite spot from which to watch the sunset, a gentle slope to climb through old apple orchards to a summit with a 365-degree view. The entrance is just off South East Street in South Amherst (turn left heading south). It's a very small sign and then a short way to the parking area, plus a brief walk to the top of a hill with the memorable view.

Amethyst Brook Conservation Area, Pelham Road, Pelham, is a great spot to walk or ski through woods and fields.

Buffum Falls, Amherst Road, Pelham. Heading east, turn left onto North Valley Road (almost a mile west of Amethyst Brook); look for a parking area on the left. Not particularly well marked but well used, an unusually beautiful spot. A 1-hour hike.

Between Amherst and South Hadley

Holyoke Range State Park (413-253-2883), Route 116 between Amherst and South Hadley. Trail maps are available at The Notch Visitors Center (staffed and with restrooms), which is open daily 9–4 except Tuesday and Wednesday in winter. Inquire about guided hikes. This dramatic east–west range rises abruptly from the valley floor. It is the most striking feature of the area, visible everywhere from Belchertown to Northampton. Mount Holyoke at its western tip (see Skinner State Park under *Views*) is the only summit accessible by road, but a trail traverses the entire 9-mile-long ridgeline. From the visitors center, a trail leads east to Mount Norwottuck (connecting with trails to Mount Toby in Sunderland and Mount Monadnock in New Hampshire). Ask about the Horse Caves below Mount Norwottuck in which Daniel Shays and his men supposedly sheltered after raiding the Springfield Armory (the caves are actually so shallow that two Boy Scouts and a pony would have trouble fitting in).

MOUNT POLLUX

Kim Grant

In Northampton

Fitzgerald Lake, in the Broad Brook Conservation Area, North Farms Road. A 550-acre town-owned preserve with 5 miles of well-marked trails, including a self-guided nature trail geared to kids. Much of the trail is right along the lake, under tall pines. Allow 2 hours. Maps are at the trailhead. No restrooms. From Route 9 in Florence, take Maple Street, which turns into North Farms.

In Easthampton

Arcadia Wildlife Sanctuary (413-584-3009; www.massaudubon.org), 127 Combs Road, on the Northampton–Easthampton line. Visitors center open Monday through Saturday 1–3, closed holidays. Trails are open daily dawn to dusk. Admission $4 adults, $3 children and seniors. Five miles of trail meander through meadows, marsh, and wetlands. Inquire about the canoe program.

Also see *Green Space*.

SWIMMING In Amherst the swimming hole is **Puffer's Pond** (413-256-4045), off Pine Street in North Amherst. Open June through September, dawn to dusk. It's a beauty, with a small beach and woods area, no lifeguards.

Carroll A. Holmes Recreation Area (413-367-0317) in Shutesbury, better known as Lake Wyola, is a sandy public beach with changing rooms on a wooded lake, maintained by the Department of Recreation and Conservation ($5 parking fee).

Musante Beach (413-587-1040), off Reservation Road, Leeds, Northampton. Open June 30 until Labor Day, 10–7. Nominal admission. Lifeguards and bathrooms.

ICE SKATING **Mullins Center** (413-545-0505), UMass campus, Amherst. Olympic-sized skating rink open to the public. Rentals; call for hours.

✳ Green Space

VIEWS What sets off this Massachusetts stretch from the rest of the Connecticut River valley is the number of abrupt mountains thrusting from its floor and the fact that so many old carriage roads, built to serve long-vanished 19th-century hotels, access their summits. Only by taking advantage of these amazing vantage points can you appreciate the valley's unusual mix of farmland and villages, cities and woods—a mix that has not altered essentially since Thomas Cole painted the Oxbow from the top of Mount Holyoke in 1836.

Mount Tom State Reservation (413-527-4805), access from Route 5 in Holyoke or from Route 141, Easthampton. This 1,800-acre mountaintop woodland contains 30 miles of trails, picnic tables, a lookout tower, and the Robert Cole Museum (theoretically open May 30 through Labor Day) with nature exhibits. Midweek, even in midsummer, the road out to **Goat Peak** is eerily empty; chances are you will be alone with the spectacular view north to Easthampton and off across the valley. In winter the road isn't plowed, but you can ski or snowshoe in. Lake Bray near the Route 5 entrance offers fishing in summer.

Skinner State Park (413-586-0350), Route 47, Hadley. Summit Road is open mid-April through mid-November; the Summit House, mid-May through mid-October. "The Paradise of America" is the way Swedish singer Jenny Lind described the view from the top of Mount Holyoke in 1850—the same view of the Connecticut River Oxbow, surrounding towns, and distant hills that Thomas Cole popularized in his 1836 painting. One of the first mountaintop inns to be built in New England (the first inn opened in 1821) and the only one preserved in any shape today, the surviving part of the Summit House (also known as Prospect House) is accessible by an auto road and hiking trails. In 1938 Joseph Skinner donated the Summit House and the surrounding 390 acres to the state. It's the setting for sunset concerts in summer.

Also see *Hiking and Walking*.

✷ Lodging

Note: "High" and "low" season rates tend to be pinned to the academic season. There are crunch periods in late May and early June during graduation, for instance; midweek in summer is relatively low season, while fall is high.

HOTELS AND INNS ⚭ ♿ **Lord Jeffery Inn** (413-253-2576 or 1-800-742-0358; www.lordjefferyinn.com), 30 Boltwood Avenue, Amherst 01002. Built in 1926 by the same architect who designed the matching Colonial Revival Jones Library across the common. College owned and obviously college geared, this is more a small hotel than an inn. The 48 rooms include 8 suites, all with private bath, phone, and cable TV; a number also have a balcony overlooking the garden. All rooms are periodically refurbished but look much as we remember them more than 25 years ago when we lodged our wedding guests here. Dining options include informal Elijah Boltwood's Tavern and The Windowed Hearth room (see *Where to Eat* for both). You can picture Robert Frost rocking on the porch. From $89 (for an economy double, low season) to $209 for the King Suite in high season. Sunday through Thursday from June through August is, incidentally, "medium" season, and most rooms are $109–159. Handicapped access.

✎ ♿ **Hotel Northampton** (413-584-3100 or 1-800-547-3529; www.hotelnorthampton.com), 36 King Street, Northampton 01060. Built in 1927, this is a proud, redbrick, five-story, 99-room downtown hotel, handy to all the town's shops and restaurants. The lobby has a hearth, wing chairs, and a soaring ceiling. The glass-fronted Coolidge Park Café serves breakfast, lunch, and dinner, and Wiggins Tavern Restaurant (see *Dining Out*) is a valley landmark. The one suite (No. 500) we've seen is a beauty, complete with Jacuzzi and a view of Mount Holyoke, but most of the standard rooms, though furnished nicely with reproduction antiques, wicker, and duvets, are small. Rates include continental breakfast, parking, and use of the exercise room. $135–245 per couple; "deluxe" rooms and suites are $127–495. Packages available. Amenities include valet and full room service. Four handicapped-accessible suites; children free under age 18.

Yankee Pedlar Inn (413-532-9494), at the junction of Routes 202 and 5,

Holyoke. This is an old standby: 28 inn-style rooms divided among the main inn and three neighboring clapboard buildings. $80–340.

BED & BREAKFASTS

In Amherst/Hadley

Allen House Victorian Inn and **Amherst Inn** (413-253-5000; www.allenhouse.com), 599 Main and 257 Main Street, respectively, Amherst 01002. Both houses have been lovingly restored by Ann and Alan Zieminski. Alan first became intrigued with the way Allen House still evoked the 19th century while lodging there as a student. Peacock feathers in chinoiserie vases, ornate Victorian-era wallpaper on ceilings as well as walls, and antimacassars on intricately carved Eastlake chairs don't usually turn us on, but this 1880s, stick-style Queen Anne home is a genuine period piece that's never really been on the market. The rush matting is as original to the house as the Eastlake fireplace mantels. Each of the seven bedrooms (all with private bath) is papered in hand-silk-screened copies of William Morris, Walter Crane, and Charles Eastlake, and all are furnished with appropriate antique beds and dressers bought locally. Rooms range in size from the back "scullery" to a large front room with three beds. All the comforts are here, including central air-conditioning.

Ann and Alan have since restored another, far less well-preserved big Victorian on Main Street, this one almost directly across from the Emily Dickinson Homestead. This is the Amherst Inn, now a handsome "painted lady" offering seven comfortable rooms (private bath, phone with modem, central air-conditioning). Ann

has lavished her considerable decorating skill on these rooms. We especially like the second-floor Ivy Room (a queen and double bed). Breakfast at either house might be Swedish pancakes, stuffed French toast, homemade fruit sauces, quiche, and fruit compotes. There's a sense of caring here: hot water and munchies on the sideboards, genuine attention to guests' needs. Fellow guests grouped around our breakfast table at the Amherst Inn hailed from London, Colorado, upstate New York, and Moscow. Well-behaved children over age 8 are welcome. From $75 in low season to $195 on graduation weekends. Rates include teas as well as breakfast.

✿ **Clark Tavern Inn Bed and Breakfast** (413-586-1900; www.clarktaverninn.com), 98 Bay Road, Hadley 01035. A 1740 tavern that stood on the other side of the Connecticut River until 1961, when it was slated for demolition to make way for I-91. Luckily, it was moved and restored. The house retains its "king's lumber" panels, wide pine floors, and much original detailing. The best news here is, however, the hospitality. Ruth Callahan is a nurse and her husband, Michael, is a physician's assistant, both obviously adept at ministering to the public. "It's so good to be able to make people feel great, not just better," Michael comments. The three rooms are each meticulously but not fussily furnished; the Fireplace Room has both a canopy bed and working fireplace; all have private bath and plenty of reading and relaxing space. Breakfast is served either on the large screened porch overlooking the extensive garden (with swimming pool), or in the Keeping Room, also overlooking the garden. The sound of birds, audible inside as well as from the porch, is so constant that we thought at first it must be a tape, but it isn't. A guest fridge is well stocked, and the Callahans are themselves a fund of local knowledge, happy to lend advice on dining, walking, biking, entertainment, whatever. $85–110 for the smaller room, $115–135 for rooms with working fireplaces. Rates include a very full breakfast and taxes.

☙ **Black Walnut Inn** (413-549-5649; www.walnutinn.com), 1184 North Pleasant Street, North Amherst 01002. The most imposing house in North Amherst, right in the middle of the village (at the traffic light), this Federal brick house meanders back through an 18th-century wing to a Victorian carriage house. Much of the house has been rebuilt from the floors up, but the integrity of the rooms survives. Furnishings are handsome, quilts are handmade, and the baths are private. Breakfast includes hot apple pie as well as other hot dishes like crêpes Suzette, three-cheese quiche, and Belgian waffles. Rooms geared to families are in the back wing; the Carriage House holds a meeting space good for 30 people. $115–150.

In Northampton
The Knoll (413-584-8164), 230 North Main Street, Florence 01060. An English Tudor–style home set well back from Route 9 on 17 acres 3 miles west of downtown Northampton, handy to the Northampton Bikeway and adjacent to Look Memorial Park. This has been Lee and Ed Lesko's home since 1963, when their former home by the Connecticut River was destroyed to make way for I-91. The house itself is quite grand,

but decor is homey and the three guest rooms (two with double and one with twin beds) are furnished simply and comfortably, sharing two baths. Breakfast is included in $70. No smokers, and no children under 12.

Lupine House Bed & Breakfast (413-586-9766 or 1-800-890-9766; www.westmass.com/lupinehouse), 185 North Main Street, Florence 01062-1221. On Route 9 west near Look Park, west of downtown Northampton. Evelyn and Gil Billings are the hospitable hosts of this pleasant 1870s house with its three guest rooms (our favorite is the Captain's Room) and private baths. The living room has a gas fireplace, and there's a guest fridge in a common area off the dining room where a full breakfast is served. For many years the couple also operated a summer B&B in York Beach, Maine (hence the lupine theme). Children over age 10 welcome. $65–85; $15 more for Saturday night only.

Sugar Maple Trailside B&B (413-585-8559; www.sugar-maple-inn.com), 62 Chestnut Street, Florence 01062. Kathy and Craig Della Penna's 1860s bicyclist-geared house is sited beside the Northampton Bikeway, no coincidence since Craig is a rail-trail activist who has written three books on rail-trails. The two guest rooms both have new bathrooms. Rooms are $60–80 weekdays, $70–90 weekends (with a 2-day minimum on weekends); $400–420 per week.

In Hadley
∞ 🐾 ♿ **Ivory Creek Bed & Breakfast Inn** (413-587-3115 or 1-866-331-3115; www.ivorycreek.com), 31 Chmura Road, Hadley 01035. Judy Loebel grew up in Hadley and

graduated from Mount Holyoke College ('65) then went on to live many places before returning with husband, Tod, to build this gracious retreat on 18 acres beside Skinner State Park. At first glance you assume the house is vintage 1890s, but the comforts include central air-conditioning, luxurious baths, and gas fireplaces in all the unusually spacious guest rooms. An attractive, totally handicapped-accessible first-floor room features a private deck. Each room is different, but furnishings throughout are tasteful and there's comfortable common space, a guest pantry, and an aviary with finches, parakeets, and parrots. Judy and Tod have nine (grown) children and 18 grandchildren, and children—dogs, too—are welcome in a garden-level room. $110–225 includes a full breakfast with yogurt, granola, and perhaps lemon soufflé pancakes or Tod's "Red Pepper Surprise."

Elsewhere

The Mucky Duck (413-323-9657; www.muckyduckinn.com), 38 Park Street, Belchertown 01007. "It's a smiling name," Annie Steiner replies when asked: "Why Mucky Duck?" Sited on the quiet side of the Belchertown common, this Greek Revival Gothic house is a smiling place to stay, as attractive inside as it is out. The exterior features a sharply peaked roof, a second-floor balcony, and an arched porch; inside is tastefully, deftly decorated, filled with interesting art, antiques, and sun. The two windows flanking the hearth are highlighted with stained glass Steiner has fashioned, and a carved oak armoire complements the hutch and sideboard in the dining room; both have been in her family for two centuries. Oriental rugs, comfortable

seating, and plenty of reading material make it all very inviting. All guest rooms have full bath, TV, and (in summer) air-conditioning. The Aylesbury Room (named for a white duck), decorated all in white and delft blue, features a king-sized four-poster bed and a balcony overlooking the common. In the Eider Suite the king-sized bed can also be twins; there's also a sunny dormer with a sitting area and a big, full bath with a free-standing glass-sided shower ("Superman's changing booth"). The Wood Duck Room, also upstairs, has wide pine floorboards and another king that can be twins. The ground-floor Mallard Room has a full-sized antique bed, hunter-green walls, and a full bath. Common space includes a comfortable parlor with a wood-burning stove and a small "business center" room with a phone and laptop hookup. There are also flowery rear gardens. Annie Steiner is Belgian, and breakfast may include Belgian waffles, Belgian pudding, or quiche, as well as a cheese tray and fruit. $85–115.

Ferry Hill Farm B&B (413-467-7751), 63 Ferry Hill Road, Granby 01033. Mona and Ed Parker's 1790s farmhouse isn't the easiest place to find, but it's been in Ed Parker's family for three generations. There's a homey living room and a breakfast room with a view and gas fireplace. The two guest rooms, one with twins, share a bath. $85 includes a full breakfast with Ed's maple syrup.

Mount Tom River Bed & Breakfast (413-584-4884), 4 Symansky Avenue, Mount Tom 01207. Open May until early November, weekends only during spring and fall. Sited 2 miles south of Northampton, just off Route 5, this big Victorian house was built as a lodging place in 1902. Beverly Wodick, the fourth generation of her family to live here, is a graphic-design professor, and rooms are tasteful, minimally decorated (nice prints, no fluff). The Yellow Room, a two-room suite with a sleep sofa, and the Rose Room (with a double sleigh bed) share a bath. The small, sunny White Room has its own. A full breakfast is served in the big, old-fashioned dining room. Common space includes a wraparound porch with a view of the Connecticut River as well as an an attractive, antiques-furnished living room. $75–90.

Note: A Five College Area Bed & Breakfast Guide (www.fivecollegebb. com) details more places to stay in this area. Also check out **Berkshire/ Folkstone Bed & Breakfast Homes** (413-268-7244 or 1-800-762-2751; www.berkshirebnbhomes.com).

MOTELS AND MOTOR INNS Autumn Inn (413-584-7660), 259 Elm Street, Northampton 01060. This is a splendidly built and maintained two-story, 31-unit motel, geared to the parents of Smith students. The 29 rooms are large with double and single beds, TV, phone, and private bath; a couple of one-bedroom suites have cooking facilities, and a third has a microwave. Breakfast and lunch are served in the coffee shop with a hearth, and there's a landscaped pool. $99–109 weekdays, $109–159 double, $20 more for efficiencies or suites and more than two guests.

Note: We don't pretend to have checked the following chain motels, but to omit them would be wrong, too. Rates vary with the day at the following:

Country Inn and Suites by Carlson (413-533-2100), 1 Country Club Road (Route 3 at Smith's Ferry), Holyoke 01040. Sited between I-91 and the Connecticut River, this new 61-room "inn" features luxurious rooms and suites with gas fireplace, two phones, and data port. Facilities include a pool and exercise room. $99–159. The Delaney House Restaurant (see *Dining Out*) is next door.

∂ **Clarion Hotel & Conference Center** (413-586-1211), junction of Route 5 and I-91, Northampton 01060. A good bet if you have children along: 124 rooms, an indoor and an outdoor pool, sauna, game room, and lighted tennis court; also a restaurant and lounge.

∂ **Holiday Inn** (413-534-3311 or 1-800-465-4329), Holidrome and Conference Center, junction of I-91 and the Mass Pike at Ingleside, Holyoke 01040. A 219-room, four-story complex featuring a tropical recreational area with 18-foot-high palm trees, a pool, a full spa, and, of course, a volleyball court. $79–135 per couple.

∂ **Holiday Inn Express Hotel & Suites** (413-582-0002; www.HIExpress.com/Amherst-Hadley), Route 9, Hadley 01035, offers 78 rooms, 22 suites, and an indoor pool.

∂ **Econo Lodge** (413-582-7707; www.hampshirehospitality.com), 329 Russell Street (Route 9), Hadley 01035, offers 63 rooms and an indoor pool.

∂ 🐾 **Howard Johnson** (413-586-0014; www.thhg.com), 401 Russell Street (Route 9), Hadley 01035. 100 rooms, outdoor pool.

∂ 🐾 **Quality Inn** (413-584-9816; qualityinnhadley@charter.net), 237 Russell Street (Route 9), Hadley 01035. 70 rooms, indoor pool.

⚓ **Best Western** (413-586-1500), 117 Conz Street, Northampton 01060. 65 rooms, outdoor pool.

✳ Where to Eat

DINING OUT This is recognized as one of the liveliest dining areas in New England. Because the largely academic clientele is unusually sophisticated but not particularly flush, many of the top restaurants are not that expensive.

In Amherst

& **Judie's** (413-253-3491), 51 North Pleasant Street. Open Sunday through Thursday 11:30–10, until 11 weekends. This cheerful, glass-fronted restaurant seems to be everyone's favorite: casual, friendly, and specializing in oversized, overstuffed popovers; we recommend the gumbo and basil chicken. Reasonably priced dinner entrées include a salad and popover or bread. Full bar. Entrées $13.75–15.50.

La Cucina di Pinocchio (413-256-4110), 30 Boltwood Walk. Open for dinner nightly. Mauro and Claire Aniello specialize in the cuisine of northern Italy and Tuscany and take pride in the elegant dining room with its white cloths and glass walls, its wines, antipasti like calamari insalata and carpaccio, and dishes like *risotto pescatore* ($18.95) and *filetto Tartufato* (marinated fillet of beef wrapped in prosciutto with a black truffle port wine sauce; $21.95).

The Windowed Hearth (413-253-2576), Lord Jeffery Inn, 30 Boltwood Avenue. Dinner served Wednesday through Sunday 5–9. Reservations suggested. This is the former library in this college inn, named for the distinctive window in its colonial-style hearth. It is now an intimate dining room with a varied menu. You might begin with lobster ravioli ($9) or poached mussels ($7), then dine on tenderloin tips sautéed with leeks and sun-dried tomatoes in a Gorgonzola cream sauce over fettuccine, or fire-roasted salmon topped with braised spinach and lemon-dill butter. Entrées $18–24.

Bistro 63 at The Monkey Bar (413-259-1600; www.mymonkeybar.com), 63 North Pleasant Street. Open daily 11:30–11:30. This sleek bistro offers a menu as hip as its decor. Lunch on coconut-breaded shrimp, blackened scallops, or a salade Niçoise. Dine on the bistro bouillabaisse or a pan-roasted pork chop. Outdoor seating in-season. Dinner entrées $11.95–18.95.

In Northampton

& **Del Raye Bar & Grill** (413-586-2664), 1 Bridge Street. Open nightly for dinner; the lounge closes at 11 PM, 1 AM Friday and Saturday. You can reserve—a plus on busy nights in Northampton, where most of the popular places are first come, first served—and the food is outstanding. The à la carte menu may include grilled smoked bluefish with tomato gazpacho, lobster risotto cake, and julienned vegetable ($25); truffled risotto with grilled shiitake and porcini mushrooms, oven-dried tomatoes, and asparagus ($22); or spice-rubbed lamb chops with an olive and anchovy demiglaze ($28). Entrées $16–23. Free parking in the rear of the building.

Green Street Café (413-586-5650), 62 Green Street. Open for lunch weekdays, dinner nightly from 5:30. Owner-chef John Sielski is a valley native who operated a restaurant in Brooklyn before opening this elegant storefront bistro. The plum-colored rooms are hung with original art; in winter the fireplace glows; and the menu is handwritten. You might start with mussels stewed in white wine, or homemade green ravioli with butter sauce. Entrées might include salmon baked *en papillote* with potato soufflé; chicken with apples and hazelnuts; or fireplace-roasted duck breast with figs. The restaurant grows its own vegetables and herbs. Inquire whether liquor is served. If the seasonal license isn't in effect, it's BYOB. Entrées $15–20.

India House (413-586-6344), 45 State Street. Open nightly for dinner. Decorated with Indian prints and featuring background sitar music, tandoori cooking, many vegetarian dishes; the valley's original Indian restaurant, the real stuff. Try the lobster masala in a sauce of curried tomatoes and ginger with onions ($15.95), or coconut scallops and shrimp ($16.95).

🍴 **Mulino's Northampton** (413-586-8900), 41 Strong Avenue. Open nightly for dinner. Anthony Bishop's popular trattoria remains as popular as ever. Antipasti are large, as is the choice of freshly made pasta dishes like ziti zuccala (julienne chicken, sautéed with prosciutto, zucchini, onions, garlic, and tomatoes, tossed with ziti and ricotta cheese). Pastas $14.95–18.95; entrées $17.95–23.95. *Warning:* Portions are large. Several fish and meat dishes are also standouts. Try the veal balsamico (scaloppine sautéed with olive oil in a balsamic vinegar, butter, and wine sauce). There's music nightly in the third-floor **Bishop's Lounge.**

Spoleto (413-586-6313), 50 Main Street. Open for dinner nightly. Featuring Spoleto Festival posters and creative "fine Italian" dishes like eggplant terrine (layers of eggplant, roasted red peppers, spinach, ricotta, mozzarella, and mascarpone cheese), or veal sautéed with mixed wild mushrooms in a peppercorn and cognac cream sauce with a touch of mustard. Entrées run $14.95–19.95. A local favorite; there can be a wait on weekends.

♿ **Eastside Grill** (413-586-3347), 19 Strong Avenue. Open for dinner weekdays from 5, weekends from 4. A popular place with a pleasant, multilevel dining room (try for a booth), as well as a big, reasonably priced menu with something for everyone. No reservations, so come early if you don't want to wait at dinner. A raw

DEL RAYE BAR & GRILL IN NORTHAMPTON

Kim Grant

bar features shrimp and oysters. Start with spicy beer-battered shrimp or gumbo, then maybe try barbecued salmon or seafood pasta jambalaya. Dinner entrées run $13.95–19.95.

Circa (413-586-2622), 57 Center Street. We're hearing mixed reviews for this ambitious restaurant with a menu that includes duck confit with fig sauce, sautéed spinach, and lentil jasmine rice pilaf ($18.75), or Tunisian rack of lamb with Harissa coulis, sausage, vegetable tagine, and almond couscous ($21).

Osaka (413-587-9548), 7 Old South Street. Open for lunch and dinner (until 11 most nights, and midnight Friday and Saturday). The word is that this is the best of several local Japanese restaurants. The menu is large with sushi bar entrées (a sushi and sashimi combination for two is $29.95) and chef's specials such as tuna steak or grilled beef with steamed vegetables, miso soup, and salad. Dinner entrées $16.95–20.95. Lunch specials $7.50–8.50.

Wiggins Tavern Restaurant (413-584-3100), 36 King Street. Open except Monday for dinner and Sunday brunch. When the Hotel Northampton opened in 1927, its owner, Lewis Wiggins, had this Wiggins Tavern moved here from Hopkinton, New Hampshire (where it had been built in 1786 by an ancestor), and attached to his hotel as the centerpiece of a mini museum village, which also included a country store, loom room, buttery, and more. The complex enhanced the hotel's appeal as a "motoring objective" in an era when "auto touring" was largely restricted to the wealthy. Unfortunately the tavern now occupies a dark, airless corner of the hotel, and we have heard

complaints of slow and sloppy service. The menu is traditional New England fare. Entrées range $17.95–22.95.

Elsewhere

Apollo Grill (413-517-0031), Eastworks Building, 116 Pleasant Street, Easthampton. Open weekdays from 9 for breakfast, lunch 11:30–3, dinner Tuesday through Saturday 5–10. Chef-owner Casey Douglas has created a winner, the hip dining spot in the valley. The decor is zany, the locale offbeat (ground floor of a vast mill, with tenants ranging from the registry of motor vehicles to several galleries). The reasonable menu is varied and the food, fabulous. Lunch on a hummus plate with eggplant, caviar, sundried tomato puree, grilled onion, and red pepper in a fried tortilla ($5), or apricot-glazed roast pork loin ($8); dine on wild mushroom risotto with garlicky spinach, or pistachio-crusted salmon with mango hollandaise, napa cabbage slaw, and purple sticky rice. Dinner entrées $13–21.

Yankee Pedlar Inn (413-532-9494; www.yankeepedlar.com), 1866 Northampton Street (Route 5 near I-91, exit 16), Holyoke. A landmark with a number of function rooms and a small, richly paneled dining room. The chef specialties are honest and local—chicken potpie, Yankee pot roast, New England baked scrod, and turkey dinner—but it's a vast and varied menu, and you can dine on Pedlar crab and lobster cakes or grilled filet mignon. Entrées $8.95–22.95.

Delaney House (413-532-1800), Route 5 at Smith's Ferry, Holyoke. Open nightly for dinner and functions. Now a franchise but still the same chef who has made this a local special-occasion place for many years. American cusine specializing in fresh fish and game. An à la carte menu, with entrées $13.95–25.

EATING OUT

In Amherst
Antonio's (413-253-0808), 31 North Pleasant Street. Ask any student around. This is simply the best pizza.

Amherst Brewing Company, 36 North Pleasant Street. Open daily for lunch and dinner; live entertainment Thursday through Saturday 10 PM–1 AM. The town's first microbrewery, with a reasonably priced menu that includes traditional pub food like Irish stew, shepherd's pie, and cock-a-leekie pie. Tell us what you think of the brew.

Amherst Chinese (413-253-7835), 62 Main Street. Open daily for lunch and dinner. A mural in the dining room depicts the restaurant's nearby farm, source of the vegetables in its dishes. Known fondly as AmChin, this

is a local favorite. Note the daily specials; no MSG.

Atkins Farms Fruit Bowl (413-253-9528), corner of Route 116 and Bay Road, South Amherst. Open daily; hours vary. Probably the fanciest farm stand in New England, this handsome redwood building sits amid thousands of fruit trees on the 190 acres that have been farmed for generations. There is a first-rate deli, but for some reason it's on the opposite side of the building from the bakery, where there's seating.

Daisy's (413-549-4085), 1185 North Pleasant Street, North Amherst. Open daily for breakfast and lunch, 6–3. Breakfast all day with daily baked muffins, vegetarian specialties.

Il Pirata Restaurant (413-256-1040), 27 South Pleasant Street. Pleasant decor and a reasonably priced, traditionally Italian menu. Good food.

PREPARED TO ORDER AT THE APOLLO GRILL IN EASTHAMPTON

Kim Grant

La Veracruzana (413-253-6900), 63 South Pleasant Street. Reasonably priced Mexican specialties.

Maplewood Brewery & Restaurant (413-256-3276; www.maplewoodfarm.net), 138 Belchertown Road (Route 9). Dinner nightly, except closed Monday. An unusual combination that works: farm-fresh ingredients, microbrew, and live acoustic music Saturday nights. The menu includes sandwiches and soups to go, vegetarian entrées, pastas to steak, and up to 15 varieties of Maplewood's beers on tap.

Elijah Boltwood's Tavern (413-253-2576), at the Lord Jeffery Inn, 30 Boltwood Avenue. Open for lunch and dinner. The inn's large pub is best known for its 8-ounce char-grilled Black Angus beef burgers, repeatedly voted best in the valley; veggie burgers and salmon burgers are also available, with an all-day menu ranging from salads to seasoned steak with mock chow ($19.95).

Pasta e Basta (413-256-3550), 26 Main Street. Open 11–11, until midnight Thursday through Sunday. An unusually attractive little trattoria with a wide selection of homemade pastas. Specialties include penne chicken, and broccoli cream and spinach linguine. The reasonably priced menu also includes grilled and skewered seafood and chicken.

The Pub (413-549-1200), 15 East Pleasant Street. Open daily at 11:30 through dinner, Sunday brunch. The name says it all: a classic college-town pub with a 10-page menu featuring everything from burgers to broiled scrod; a wide choice of beer. Children's menu, outside patio. Over 40 bottled microbrews plus half a dozen on tap.

Panda East Restaurant (413-256-8923), 103 North Pleasant Street. Open 11:30–10 daily, until 11 Friday and Saturday. This is part of an excellent local chain specializing in traditional Hunan-style Chinese food, also Japanese staples (sushi, tempura, and teriyaki). Full bar.

Nancy Jane's (413-253-3343), 36 Main Street. Open 6:30–2, Sunday 7–3, and for dinner Wednesday through Friday 5–8. This is a traditional downtown coffee shop serving dependably good, predictable food and recently expanding to comfort-food dinners.

Black Sheep Deli and Bakery (413-253-3442), 79 Main Street. A genuine coffeehouse-deli with exceptional pastries, deli sandwiches, and a deli with pasta and salads; good picnic makings. Folk music, weekends; periodic poetry readings.

In Northampton

♦ ✐ ♿ **Sylvester's Restaurant, Cafe & Bakery** (413-586-5343), 111 Pleasant Street. Open for breakfast and lunch. Named for and housed in the onetime home of pioneer vegetarian and whole-wheat advocate Dr. Sylvester Graham (as in graham cracker). The long, well-lit dining room and adjoining café are cheery, perfect for breakfast (try the Lox-Ness omelet); there's also a large choice of soups, salads, sandwiches, wraps, burgers, and hot entrées at lunch, from a Mango Tango Salada, to a "West of Woostah" (sliced avocado and veggies on homemade toast), to shrimp sautéed with spinach, garlic butter, white wine, artichoke hearts, and mushrooms, served over grilled polenta. Tea isn't from a bag, and coffees are from the café. The food is so good here, in fact, that we lament the fact dinner is no longer served. Come early for lunch. There's a special menu and trivia cards for kids. Beer and wine served.

❦ **Amanouz Café** (413-585-9128), 44 Main Street. Open for lunch and dinner. A narrow but deep storefront with great falafel, salads, kebabs, a selection of couscous dishes (including chicken or lamb), and both vegetarian and meat sandwiches, like *shawerma* (marinated lamb and beef, vegetables, and tahini).

❦ ♪ ♿ **Paul & Elizabeth's** (413-584-4832), entrances from Thorne's Market (150 Main Street) and from Old South Street. Open Sunday through Thursday 11:30–9:15, 11:30–9:45 Friday and Saturday. The town's oldest natural foods restaurant, a great space with big old second-story plate-glass windows overhung with fanciful stained glass and a high tin ceiling, plenty of plants and wood. The extensive menu specializes in but is not limited to vegetarian dishes, soups and salads, tempura and noodle dishes; also seafood, home-baked breads and pastries. Sides of baked brown rice, deep-fried tofu, sea vegetables, and more. Daily specials. Dinner entrées average $10.25–14.50. Beer and wine.

Cha Cha Cha (413-586-7311), 134 Main Street. Open daily for lunch and dinner, except closed Monday. This bright, busy spot in the middle of Main Street is a good bet for burritos and salads. Try the Cajun catfish tacos (flour tortillas filled with spicy fish, served with red onions, sour cream, and salsa).

Fitzwilly's (413-584-8666), 23 Main Street. Open daily 11:30 AM–midnight. One of New England's first fern bars: brick walls, plenty of copper,

antiques, hanging plants. It all works, including the immense menu with blue plate luncheon specials like chicken potpie and sandwiches; burgers are a specialty, along with "lotsa pasta."

La Cazuela (413-586-0400), 271 Main Street. Open daily, closed Monday off-season. One of the most popular places in town, specializing in spicy Mexican and southwestern fare, including plenty of vegetarian dishes. Try the spinach enchiladas or *pollo verde.* Full bar.

Northampton Brewery (413-584-9903), 11 Brewer Court. Open Monday through Saturday 11:30–11, Sunday 1–11. Housed in a 19th-century livery stable, this is a pleasant, multilevel space serving sandwiches, pizza, burgers, steaks, seafood, and stir-fries. Beer changes daily; live music Wednesday and Sunday evenings.

Café Casablanca (413-582-0755), 16 Main Street. Open Sunday through Thursday 8 AM–10 PM, weekends until 11. Same ownership as Amanouz but a slicker, café atmosphere. On a rainy spring day a yellow pot of orange pekoe tea and an omelet crêpe Provençal (spinach, tomatoes, mushrooms, and cheese) hit the spot. There's an espresso bar, fresh-squeezed juices, and a choice of shakes and smoothies.

♪ **Pizzeria Paradiso** (413-586-1468), 12 Crafts Street. Open nightly. This is all about wood-fired, brick-oven, very-thin-crust pizza, both white and red, unusual favorites like Chèvre Delight with goat cheese, sun-dried tomatoes, and roasted garlic cloves with mozzarella and Parmesan. Beer is served, along with kids-only pizza, finger food, and salads.

FRESH PASTA CO. ON MAIN
STREET IN NORTHAMPTON

Kim Grant

Spoleto Express (413-586-8646), 225 King Street. Open daily from 11 AM, until 9:30 Sunday through Wednesday and until 10:30 Thursday through Saturday. This offshoot of the popular Main Street dining spot (see *Dining Out*) is good for wraps in a tomato-basil tortilla or on grilled rosemary focaccia; also soups, pizzas, salads, and pastas. Eat in or take out.

Vermont Country Deli (413-586-7114), 48 Main Street. Open daily at 7 AM with freshly baked bagels and muffins, pastas, and plenty of deli choices all day. Seasonal outside seating.

Bela Vegetarian Restaurant (413-586-8011), 68 Masonic Street. Open

Tuesday through Saturday noon–8:45. A small, bright eatery with a full vegetarian menu: soups, pasta and tofu entrées, polenta. Try the butternut bisque and tempeh with zucchini in red wine rosemary butter, served with salad and brown rice.

Fresh Pasta Co. (413-586-5875), 249 Main Street. A cheerful corner storefront with white brick walls, a varied menu including focaccia, pizza, pasta, and chicken specialties (avoid the chicken potpie); try the grilled eggplant with fresh basil and goat cheese; wine and beer served.

Elsewhere

🍴 **Woodbridge's** (413-536-7341), 3 Hadley Street, South Hadley. Open daily for all three meals. Early-bird specials 4–6. This big, friendly old tavern (booths on the bar side, tables on the other) on the common is known up and down the valley for its clam chowder, but the menu is large and reasonably priced, including veal piccata and London broil as well as veggie melt, salads, and butcher-style deli sandwiches. Daily specials.

Dockside at Brunelle's (413-536-2342), 1 Alvord Street, South Hadley. Open daily for lunch and dinner (until 9); the lounge is open until midnight. A local favorite with a large, reasonably priced menu, nightly specials, live jazz nights, down on a scenic stretch of the river. This is departure point for the *Spirit of South Hadley*.

Zoe's Fish & Chop House (413-527-0313), 238 Northampton Street (Route 10), Easthampton. Open for lunch weekdays, dinner nightly. A big, bright standby with booths and function rooms, basic American restaurant featuring shellfish and fried fish. Vegetarians can opt for beer-battered artichoke with a sour cream dill dip. Not a place for calorie counters. It's a big menu, and there are plenty of meat dishes, including "pork mignon." Dinner entrées $12.95–22.95.

Gramps Restaurant (413-534-1996), 216 Lyman Street, Holyoke. Open for breakfast, lunch, and dinner. Closes Sunday at 3 PM. An attractive, easy-to-find Polish restaurant that's as genuine as they come, operated by Danuta and Krzysztof Wojick, long-time owners of the neighboring Polish deli. Pierogis and blintzes are made fresh each day. It's definitely the place for *golabki* (stuffed cabbage).

Aura (413-532-1664), Route 141 across from the Mount Tom Reservation entrance on the Easthampton–Holyoke line. Open Monday through Friday 4–9, Saturday and Sunday 1–9. Formerly the Harvest Valley, still with the same great valley view, now less formal with T-shirted staff and an Asian/American menu. Entrées $12–20.

Fernandez Family Restaurant (413-532-1139), 161 High Street, Holyoke. Open Monday through Wednesday 10–4:30, Thursday through Saturday 10–5, closed Sunday. A Puerto Rican eatery with some 20 dishes on display so that you can point rather than having to pronouce *surullitos* (sweet cornmeal with cheese), *boquito* (crabmeat fritter), or *mofongo* (plantains, garlic, and bacon).

Smokin Lil's BBQ (413-527-5566), 82 Cottage Street, Easthampton. Minimal western decor and a choice of chicken and pork barbecue dishes as well as many vegetarian options make this a local favorite.

DINERING OUT Miss Florence Diner (413-584-3179), 99 Main Street, Florence (Northampton). Open for early breakfast through late dinner, 3 miles west of downtown Northampton. Known locally as Miss Flo's, this is the most famous diner in Western Massachusetts, in the same family since the 1940s. Forget the banquet addition and stick to the stools or booths. Unexpected specialties like clam and oyster stew and baked stuffed lobster casserole, a soup and salad bar, and full liquor license. Good beef barley soup and coconut and macaroon cream pudding.

Bluebonnet Diner (413-584-3333), 324 King Street, Northampton. Open

MISS FLORENCE DINER

Kim Grant

Monday through Friday 5:30 AM–midnight, Saturday 6 AM–midnight. A classic diner with "home cooking." Full bar, smoking section. Dinners average $6.95.

Look Restaurant (413-584-9850), 410 North Main Street, Leeds (Northampton). A landmark with a 1950s look and menu, "homestyle cooking," breakfast available all day. Fresh-made breads, muffins, and pies.

SNACKS AND BREWS **Bart's** in Amherst (103 North Pleasant Street) and Northampton (249 Main Street). Open Sunday through Thursday until 11, Friday and Saturday until midnight. Since 1976, milk from local cows is used for great ice cream in 100 flavors like mud pie, blueberry cheesecake, and orange Dutch chocolate.

La Fiorentina Pastry Shop (413-586-7693), 25 Armory Street, Northampton. Facing the parking lot, a hidden jewel of a coffee shop with delectable desserts like sfogliatelle and tiramisu as well as coffees, Italian soft drinks and juices, gelati, and memorable biscotti. For the story of the original Fiorentina, see "Springfield."

✐ **Flayvors of Cook Farm** (413-584-2224; www.cookfarm.com), 129 South Maple Street, Hadley. Open year-round, daily, seasonal hours. Milk from the resident cows is used to make outstanding ice cream (try the ginger!). Also available: turkey pie, chili, soups, and salads. The setting is one of the most beautiful in the valley, surrounded by fields at the foot of the Holyoke Range. Plenty of outside tables and plenty of cows, both behind the fence and in the neighboring meadow. Sunday music 2–5, the kind to please both kids and cows.

✐ **McCray Farm** (413-533-3714), 55 Alvord Street, South Hadley. The dairy bar, open spring through fall, features homemade ice cream. This working dairy farm is near the river, with a small petting zoo; maple breakfasts during sugaring season.

Rao's Coffee Roasting Company (413-253-9441), 17 Kellogg Avenue, Amherst. Sequestered behind North Pleasant Street, this is an attractive café beneath a leafy canopy in summer; also inside seating. The aroma of coffee from dozens of stacked bags of beans and from the roaster hits you the moment you walk in.

Normand Bakery and Konditorei (413-584-0717), 192 Main Street, Northampton. Open Tuesday through Saturday 7:30–5:30. Tempting German tortes and other pastries, also breads plus cookies for the stroll.

"A Perfect Spot of Tea" at the Porter-Phelps-Huntington House (see *Historic Houses*). Saturdays in July and August at 2:30 and 3:30, served on the back veranda with pastries and live music ($8).

The Moan and Dove (413-256-1710; www.themoananddove.com), 460 West Street (Route 116 south), Amherst. A serious new pub with 20 beers on tap, several casks, and some 125 bottled brands to choose from.

Paper City Brewery (413-535-1588; www.papercity.com), 108 Cabot Street, Holyoke, offers Friday-evening "tastings" 6–8. A microbewery: amber ale, Cabot Street wheat, and Irish stout.

✳ Entertainment

For the academic year consult the *Five College Calendar of Events,* published monthly and available at all campuses as well as at http://calendar.fivecolleges.edu. A typical month lists more than 27 films, 30 lectures, 19 concerts, and 32 theatrical performances. Visitors welcome.

The Valley Advocate, with weekly arts listings, is published Thursday. It's free and everywhere in Northampton/Amherst, also online: www.valleyadvocate.com.

Academy of Music (413-584-9032; www.academyofmusictheatre.com), 274 Main Street, Northampton. This Renaissance-style, century-old, municipally owned, 300-seat theater features a balcony and a baby grand in the women's lounge. It schedules live entertainment as well as films.

The Calvin Theatre (413-584-1444), 19 King Street. First opened in 1924 as a 1,300-seat vaudeville house, splendidly restored, the venue for stellar live performances 3 to 6 nights a week during the academic season, less frequently in summer. Check out **Bar 19** after the show.

Mullins Center (413-545-0505), UMass campus, Amherst. A 10,500-seat sports and entertainment arena with a year-round schedule of theater and concerts as well as sports.

Fine Arts Center (413-545-2511; www.fineartscenter.com), UMass campus, Amherst. Performing arts series of theater, music, dance.

The Commonwealth Opera (413-586-5026; www.commonwealthopera.org), with offices at 140 Pine Street, Florence, stages a fall opera, a December *Messiah,* a March Broadway musical, and other performances at local venues.

Center for the Arts (413-584-7327; www.nohoarts.org), 17 New South Street, Northampton. Theater, dance, art exhibits.

MUSIC Northampton Box Office (413-586-8686 or 1-800-THE-TICK) serves the Calvin Theater, the Iron Horse, and Pearl Street.

The Iron Horse (413-584-0610), 20 Center Street, Northampton. This is only open when there's a performance, but that tends to be nightly. Live folk, jazz, and comedy, plus 50 brands of imported beer; dinner served. According to *Billboard* magazine, the Iron Horse "boasts one of the richest musical traditions in the country."

Pearl Street (413-584-7771), 10 Pearl Street, Northampton. Dancing on Friday and Saturday, live music several nights a week. DJ.

Musicorda (413-532-0607; www.musicorda.org), Chapin Auditorium, Mount Holyoke College, South Hadley. Six Friday-evening (8 PM) chamber music concerts feature strings and piano music by artists from around the world.

Jazz in July at UMass (413-545-3530) in Amherst, a series of summer concerts and workshops celebrating jazz music.

The Mount Holyoke Summit House (413-586-8686) is the scene of a sunset concert series (folk, jazz, barbershop), 7:30 Thursdays; **Look Memorial Park Sunday Concerts** are held Sundays at 4 PM, late June through mid-August, in Look Park, Route 9, Northampton.

Pioneer Arts Center of Easthampton (P.A.C.E.; 413-527-3700; www.PioneerArts.org), 41 Union Street, downtown Easthampton. A coffeehouse with a lively calendar of music, stand-up comedy, and more.

THEATER *Note:* For on-campus performances during the academic year, check www.fivecolleges.edu/theater.

🍃 **Pioneer Valley Summer Theatre** (413-529-3434; www.summertheatre. net) at Williston Northampton School (P.O. Box 53), Easthampton 01027. The theater is in Scott Hall on Payson Avenue. Performances late June through mid-August. Inquire about **Theater for Young Audiences,** Wednesday through Saturday at 10 AM during the company's season.

New Century Theatre (413-585-3220; www.smith.edu/theatre/nct). Over the past decade this regional company has developed a reputation for quality performances, staged late June through mid-August at the air-conditioned Hallie Flanagan Studio Theatre within the Mendenhall Cen-

RICHARD MICHELSON, OWNER OF
R. MICHELSON GALLERIES

Christina Tree

ter for Performing Arts at Smith College on Green Street, Northampton. **New WORLD Theater** (413-545-1972; www.newworldtheater.org), based at UMass, stages productions featuring ethnic and minority themes during the academic year and on weekends in June and July.

FILM **Academy of Music** (413-584-8435), 274 Main Street, Northampton. Art films and general releases alternate with live performances (see above).

Cinemark at Hampshire Mall (for movie times, 413-587-4237), Café Square, Hampshire Mall, Route 9, has 12 theaters.

Pleasant Street Theatre (413-586-0935), 27 Pleasant Street, Northampton. First-run and art films, one theater upstairs and the well-named Little Theater in the basement.

Tower Theaters (413-533-2663), 19 College Street, South Hadley. First-run and art films; seats may be reserved.

Note: Progress with the ambitious Amherst Cinema Center project can be checked at: www.amherstcinema-center.org.

✴ Selective Shopping

ANTIQUES Northampton antiques shops are just east of its big higher-rent shops. Check out the **Antique Center of Northampton** (413-584-3600), 91/2 Market Street. Open 5 days 10–5; closed Wednesday; Sunday noon–5. A multidealer shop on three levels. **American Decorative Arts** (413-584-6804), 3 Olive Street, has become something of a mecca for collectors of early-20th-century furniture. **Collector Galleries** (413-584-6734),

11 Bridge Street. Open daily 11–5, Sunday noon–5. This is one of the oldest and biggest shops around, a good bet for furniture.

ART GALLERIES *Note:* In recent years Northampton has become an arts center in its own right as aspiring artists gather to study with established names. Many restaurants and coffeehouses also mount constantly changing work (for sale) by local artists. There's even a distinctive Northampton school of realism. Amherst, too, has its share of galleries; an **Amherst Gallery Walk** is held the first Thursday of each month.

R. Michelson Galleries (413-586-3964; www.rmichelson.com), 132 Main Street, Northampton, and 25 South Pleasant Street, Amherst. Open Monday through Wednesday 10–6, Thursday through Saturday 10–9, Sunday noon–5. Since 1976 Richard Michelson has maintained galleries at various locations, in 1995 moving into the huge and handsome two-story-high space designed in 1913 for the Northampton Savings Bank. The gallery showcases work by 50 local artists, including Leonard Baskin, one of America's most respected sculptors, painters, and printmakers, with work selling here from $100 to $100,000. Other well-known artists whose work is usually on view include Barry Moser, Gregory Gillespie, Linda Post, and Lewis Bryden. Note the special gallery devoted to original children's book illustrations featuring work at nationally known local illustrators.

The Hart Gallery (413-586-6343), second floor, 102 Main Street. Open daily, until 8 Thursday through Saturday, noon–5 on Sunday. At street level this appears to be simply an art shop, but the upstairs gallery showcases work by top area artists.

Wm Baczek Fine Arts (413-587-9880), 36 Main Street, Northampton.

The Canal Gallery (413-532-4141; www.TheCanalGallery.com), 380 Dwight Street, Holyoke. Open Thursday 1–5, Saturday noon–4, and by appointment. A 19th-century mill building houses this major gallery specializing in modern art, sculpture installations, and performance art.

CRAFTS Some 1,500 craftspeople work in the valley and nearby Hilltowns, and Northampton is their major showcase, known particularly for handcrafted jewelry, pottery, and furniture. One Cottage Street in Easthampton, the Cutlery Building in Northampton, and the Pro-Brush Building in Florence all house

THE CANAL GALLERY

Kim Grant

THE CANAL GALLERY

artisans. For periodic tours and open houses, check with the Northampton Chamber of Commerce (see *Guidance*).

The valley is also the venue for several major crafts and fine arts happenings: **The Paradise City Art Festivals** (413-527-8994; www.paradisecityarts. com)—held in late May or early June (depending on th college graduation calendar) and on the Columbus Day weekends at Northampton's Tri-Coun- try Fairgrounds—are rated as the state's premier showcases for fine, con- temporary juried crafts and art. In Easthampton dozens of crafts studios hold open house twice a year, once in early June and again the first weekend in December (www.ArtsEasthamp- ton.com).

In Northampton

P!nch (413-586-4509; www.epinch. com), 179 Main Street. A variety of artistic, functional pottery and decora- tive accessories.

Skera (413-586-4563; www.skera.com), 221 Main Street. Open daily, Sunday from noon, Thursday until 9. Long- time owners Harriet and Steve Rogers specialize more and more in stunning handcrafted clothing, "wearable art."

Silverscape Designs (413-586-3324; www.silverscapedesigns.com), 1 King Street, Northampton; also 264 North Pleasant Street, Amherst (413-253- 3324). The Northampton store (open weekdays 10–6, Saturday until 9, Sun- day noon–5) is a beauty, the Tiffany's of the valley—a former bank building with art deco detailing and a glorious stained-glass skylight. The old tellers' windows are still in place; there's also a cascading fountain. A wide variety of jewelry and accessories, also Tiffany-style lamps.

Don Muller Gallery (413-586- 1119), 40 Main Street. An outstanding store displaying a wide variety of crafted items, specializing in art glass, always exhibiting the deeply colored signature orbs handblown by locally based Josh Simpson.

Artisan Gallery (413-586-1942; www.theartisangallery.com), Thornes Market, 150 Main Street. A quality selection of jewelry, pottery, wood- work, and glass; kaleidoscopes are a specialty.

Claytopia (413-584-9323), 157 Main Street. Open daily (except Sunday and Monday) 11–6, Thursday until 9, Friday and Saturday until 7. Billed as an "art studio for you to paint beauti- ful, unique pottery"; you buy a piece of dishwater-, microwave-, and oven- safe pottery and are equipped with the paints and stencils with which to decorate it. If you aren't in town long enough to pick up the final product (it takes 3 days to fire and process), they ship.

Bill Brough Jewelry Designs (413- 586-8985), 104 Main Street. Original jewelry designs in gold, diamonds, pearls, and special stones.

Ten Thousand Villages (413-582- 9338), 82 Main Street. Open Monday through Wednesday 10–6, Thursday through Saturday until 8. Fairly trad- ed handicrafts from around the world.

In Amherst

Fiber Art Center (413-256-1818; www.fiberartcenter.com), 79 South Pleasant Street. Open Tuesday through Saturday 10–6. Changing exhibits in the gallery plus a retail shop specializing in woven, quilted, and other quality fiber arts, both local and worldwide.

ARTISANS AT WORK AT THE MILL AT ONE COTTAGE STREET

Kim Grant

Gallery A₃ (413-253-4171), 28 Amity Street at the Amherst Cinema Center. Open Wednesday through Sunday noon–6. The Amherst Art Alliance mounts changing exhibits, frequently first rate.

Alfredo's Photographic Gallery (413-253-1707), 39 South Pleasant Street. A serious gallery with changing exhibits as well as work by photographer Alfredo DiLascia.

Also see **R. Michelson Galleries** and **Silverscape Designs** in Northampton.

In Easthampton
One Cottage Street. This five-story, mid-19th-century mill building has been a hive of artists' studios for 20 years, ever since it was acquired by Riverside Industries, Inc., the service organization that trains disabled people for jobs. Most studios are accessible only during the biannual (first weekend in June and December) open houses sponsored by Arts Easthampton (www.ArtsEasthampton. com).

Kaleidoscope Pottery (413-527-6390; www.Kscopepottery.com). Evelyn Snyder's "Leafware" is made by hand without a potter's wheel by impressing the leaves into stoneware clay. Each piece goes through 16 stages to create a fossil-like image. The resulting platters, baking dishes, trays, and bowls are stunning, safe for oven, microwave, and dishwasher use.

Latimer Glass Studio (413-527-5567). Lynn Latimer makes striking African-influenced glassware, beautiful tableware, and functional art.

Eastworks, 116 Pleasant Street. Another vast factory building. Formerly Stanley Home Products, this is now a small business and arts incubator, also housing the Apollo Restaurant (see *Dining Out*) and the registry of motor vehicles.

Nashawannuck Gallery (413-529-9393), 40 Cottage Street. Fine arts, crafts, jewelry.

BOOKSTORES Book browsing is a major pastime in this area.

In South Hadley

Odyssey Bookstore (413-534-7307 or 1-800-540-7307; www.odyssey-bks.com), Village Commons, 9 College Street. Open Monday through Saturday 10–8, Sunday noon–5. An independent bookstore. Large children's books and poetry sections, author readings and other special events, across from the Mount Holyoke College campus.

In Northampton

Beyond Words Bookshop (413-586-6304 or 1-800-442-6304), 189 Main Street. A large bookstore featuring books for inner development; also music, stationery, gifts.

Broadside Bookshop (413-586-4235), 247 Main Street. A general trade bookstore with a strong emphasis on fiction and literature as well as personal advice.

Booklink (413-585-9955), 150 Main Street. Specialties include travel and local books.

Bookends (413-585-8667), 80 Maple Street, Florence. Nine rooms of quality used books.

Raven Used Books (413-584-9868), 4 Old South Street, specializes in scholarly titles, women's studies, and philosophy.

In Amherst

Jeffery Amherst Bookstore (413-253-3381), 55 South Pleasant Street. A full-service bookstore with a strong children's book section, specializing in Emily Dickinson.

Amherst Books (413-256-1547), 8 Main Street, has a wide selection of new books, specializing in poetry, literature, and philosophy. Frequent author readings.

Book Marks (413-549-6136), 1 East Pleasant Street (Carriage Shops). A wide selection of used books specializing in art, poetry, photography, and Emily Dickinson.

Food for Thought Books (413-253-5432), 106 North Pleasant Street, featuring gay and lesbian, progressive political, and African American titles.

Laos Religious Book Center (413-548-3909), 867 North Pleasant Street, an ecumenical bookstore with both Christian and Jewish titles.

CLOTHING

In Amherst

Rural chic is the look at **Zanna** (413-253-2563), 187 North Pleasant Street, and **Clay's** (413-256-4200), 32 Main Street.

In Northampton

Zanna (413-584-8866; www.zanna.com) is at 126 Main Street, and **Wild Rags** (413-587-9560), 229 Main Street, is worth checking, along with **Taylor Women** (413-585-0785) and **Taylor Men** (413-585-0785). **Talbots** (413-858-5985) is at 34 Bridge Street; **Cathy Cross** (413-596-9398), 151 Main Street; **Country Comfort, Ltd.** (413-584-0042), 153 Main Street; and **Eileen Fisher Store**, 24 Pleasant Street.

OTHER SPECIAL STORES AND ENTERPRISES

Northampton Wools (413-586-4331), 11 Pleasant Street, Northampton. Linda Daniels's small shop just off Main Street is crammed with bright wools and knitting gear; workshops offered.

Faces (413-584-4081), 175 Main Street, Northampton. Open daily. A hip, student-geared department store with toys, clothing, furniture and furnishings, cards, and much more.

The Mountain Goat (413-586-0803), 177 Main Street, Northampton. The area's premier outdoor "funfitters"; mostly clothing, some hiking and camping equipment, a great selection of shoes.

Table & Vine (413-584-7775 or 1-800-474-2449; www.tableandvine.com), 122 North King Street, Northampton. Open Monday through Saturday 9–9. Featuring more than 5,000 wines, 400 beers, over 100 cheeses, dozens of kind of olives, pastas, and thousands of other delicacies plus glassware, books, and kitchen accessories. Inquire about wine tastings.

SHOPPING CENTERS **Thornes Marketplace,** 150 Main Street, Northampton. An incubator for many Northampton stores: a five-story, 30-shop complex with high ceilings, wood floors.

The Village Commons in South Hadley. A whimsical, white-clapboard complex of shops designed by Boston architect Graham Gund to house shops, restaurants, and a movie theater (two screens).

Holyoke Mall (413-536-1440) at Ingleside (I-91 exit 15, and Mass Pike exit 4), open Monday through Saturday 10–9:30 and Sunday 11–6. The single biggest mall in Western Massachusetts, second largest in all of New England, with Filene's and JCPenney anchors.

FARM STANDS

In Amherst
Atkins Farms Country Market (413-253-9528), 1150 West Street (Route 116 south). Open daily 8–6 except holidays, later in summer. The valley's largest and fanciest farm

stand, a vast redwood market with a huge selection of quality produce, much it from the family's 290 acres and 25,000 fruit trees; the complex includes a popular deli café (see *Eating Out*) and is surrounded by apple orchards (see *Pick-Your-Own*).

Delta Organic Farm (413-253-1893; www.deltaorganicfarm.com), 352 East Hadley Street, sells herbs, syrup, and organic produce; also soup and salads to go.

J&J Farms (413-549-1877), 324 Meadow Street, North Amherst. Open June to November, daily 9–7. Fourth-generation farm open for seasonal produce specializing in sweet corn, tomatoes, peppers, squash, strawberries, and six varieties of potatoes.

In Granby
Red Fire Farm (413-467-SOIL), 7 Carver Street. Open May to November daily. Over 30 types of certified organic

Kim Grant

vegetables grown and over 50 varieties of tomatoes test-tasted at the August Tomato Festival. Fruit and berries from other local farms also sold.

In Hadley

Hibbard Farm (413-549-5684), 311 River Drive. Open May to December, 9–5; asparagus in May and June, then carrots, asparagus, beets, peppers, pickles, turnips . . .

Mapleline Farm (413-549-6174; www.maplelinefarm.com), 78 Comins Road. Farm-bottled milk and other products.

Dion Pumpkin Farms (413-584-6170), 28 Middle Street. Pumpkins, Indian corn, Chinese lanterns, gourds, apples, farm tours, horse-drawn hayrides, and a game farm.

In Hatfield

Teddy C. Smiarowski Farm (413-247-5181), 487 Main Street. June 7 through July 8. Fresh-picked asparagus and strawberries.

Szwawlowski Potato Farm (413-247-9240), 103 Main Street. Open except Sunday May through November 7–5, weekdays off-season. Potatoes—all varieties!

FLOWERS **Andrew's Greenhouse** (413-253-2937), 1178 South East Street, Amherst. Open daily April through June, and except for Tuesdays in July and August. A favorite source of perennials, herbs, bedding plants, and cut-your-own flowers.

Hadley Garden Center (413-584-1423), 285 Russell Street (Route 9), Hadley. Open daily, year-round. Herbs, orchids, bulbs, bird food, indoor plants, firewood, and gardening workshops.

Wanczyk Evergreen Nursery (413-584-3709), 166 Russell Street (Route 9), Hadley. Open daily April 10 to November. A great source of perennials and nursery plants.

PICK-YOUR-OWN **Atkins Farms** (413-253-9528), 1150 West Street (Route 116 south), Amherst. Pick-your-own apples in fall. (Also see *Farm Stands* and *Eating Out*.)

Lakeside U-Pick Strawberries (413-549-0805), 281 River Drive, Hadley. Open daily in season, 7:30–7.

Sapowsky Farms (413-467-7952), 436 East Street, Granby. Pick-your-own strawberries. They also sell milk, cheese, eggs, syrups, honey, jams, and firewood.

Teddy C. Smiarowski Farm (413-247-5181), 487 Main Street, Hatfield. Asparagus. (Also see *Farm Stands*.)

SUGARHOUSES **North Hadley Sugar Shack** (413-585-8820; www.northhadleysugarshack.com), 181 River Drive. Open mid-Feburary until Christmas week. Maple syrup, maple candy, and maple ice cream; sugaring breakfasts February into April. Then strawberries, asparagus, pumpkins, squash, Harvest Moon Pumpkin Festival in late October.

✳ Special Events

Spring–fall: Farmer's markets are held on Saturdays in Northampton (on Gothic Street) and Amherst (on the common); in Holyoke on Thursday afternoons (2:30–5:30, Hampden Park off Dwight Street); in Greenfield, Saturdays 8–1.

March: **Annual Bulb Show,** Smith College (first 2 weeks). **St. Patrick's Day Parade,** Holyoke (Sunday after St. Patrick's Day).

May: **Emily Dickinson's World Weekend. Western Massachusetts Appaloosa Horse Show,** Three-County Fairgrounds, Northampton.

May or June: **Paradise City Arts Festival** (www.paradisecityarts.com).

June: **Taste of Amherst, Community Fair**—sampling of local restaurants (413-253-0700).

July: **Fireworks** (July 4), Amherst. **Amherst Crafts Fair** (weekend after Indpendence Day). **Morgan Horse Show,** Northampton.

August: **Amherst Teddy Bear Rally** (first weekend). **Taste of Northampton**—more than 40 restaurants participate (second weekend).

Three-County Fair at the Three-County Fairgrounds, Northampton.

Weekend before Labor Day: **Celebrate Holyoke** at Heritage State Park—a 4-day, multicultural music festival, food, dancing.

October, every other year: **Book and Plow Festival,** Amherst—3 days honoring local writers and farmers.

November: **Northampton Film Festival.**

December: **Open crafts studios** at Eastworks in Easthampton (first weekend; 413-527-1000; www.Arts-Easthampton.com). **First Night,** Northampton (New Year's Eve).

DEERFIELD/GREENFIELD AREA

Old Deerfield isn't just one of America's best-preserved early villages. It's also one of the country's first tourist attractions.

Even before the Civil War, the village's mile-long street of 18th- and early-19th-century houses was drawing history buffs. An 1848 crusade to save the so-called Indian House (still bearing the marks of a tomahawk embedded in it during a 1704 raid) is now cited as the first effort in this country to save a historic house. The door, at least, survived and is displayed, along with this country's first "period room," in Memorial Hall, a village historical museum that opened in 1880. Over the next few years the 18th-century Barnard Tavern and Frary House were restored as a center and showcase for an arts and crafts movement dedicated to reviving traditional handicrafts—not unlike those for which the area is currently known. Several local hotels were established to accommodate visitors, including one that opened in 1864 atop nearby Mount Sugarloaf in the village of South Deerfield.

The road up Mount Sugarloaf (now state owned) survives, and the view from its summit is a must-see: The wide, shimmering ribbon of the Connecticut River stretches south as far as the eye can see, flanked by a baffle of trees and broad patchwork of yellow and green fields, spotted with century-old wooden tobacco sheds and walled on the south by the magnificent east–west march of the Holyoke range.

The commercial strip along Routes 5/10 in Deerfield has become a destination in its own right. Yankee Candle, with its Bavarian Village, counts more than 1.5 million customers a year, and word is spreading about Magic Wings, a nearby year-round butterfly conservatory and gardens.

Bicycle or drive up or down River Road through farmland along the Connecticut in Deerfield and Whately, Sunderland, Montague, and Northfield. Patronize the many farm stands selling fresh-picked produce and flowers: asparagus in May, lavender and strawberries in June, blueberries in July, apples and peaches in September, and pumpkins in October. And get out on the Connecticut. Above Turners Falls the river itself is accessible by excursion boat as well as by rental kayaks and canoes.

Greenfield is the Franklin County seat and the commercial center of the Upper Pioneer Valley. It remains a classic New England town—one with some architecturally interesting buildings, a rare sense of community, and a salting of galleries, shops, and cafés. It's the hub of a remarkably varied rural area that extends upriver to Bernardston and Northfield, east to Montague and Wendell, as well as south to the long-settled river towns of Sunderland, Whately, and Deerfield.

AREA CODE 413.

GUIDANCE Franklin County Chamber of Commerce (413-773-5463, daily, 24 hours; fax, 413-773-7008; www.franklincc.org), P.O. Box 898, 395 Main Street, Greenfield 01302. This Regional Tourism Council covers a broad area, including many of the Berkshire Hilltowns as well as the northern half of the

TOBACCO BARN

Kim Grant

Upper Valley. Request a map and guide. It operates the **Upper Pioneer Valley Visitor Information Center** (413-773-9393) just off I-91 (exit 26) at the Route 2 rotary behind Appleby's on Route 2A east, open daily 9–5 (until 8 on Friday), with restrooms and local products as well as information. Also check www.MassCountryRoads.com.

GETTING THERE *By bus:* **Peter Pan–Trailways** (1-800-343-9999; www.peterpanbus.com) connects Greenfield, Amherst, South Hadley, and Holyoke with Boston, Springfield, Bradley International Airport, and points beyond. The local departure point is town hall, Court Square, Greenfield.

By car: Route 2 is the quickest as well as most scenic access from east or west, and I-91 is the way north and south.

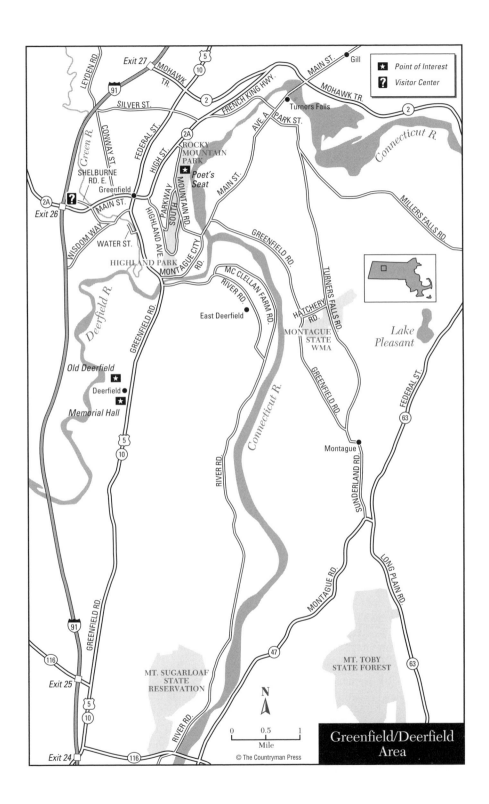

Greenfield/Deerfield
Area

© The Countryman Press

PARKING *In Greenfield:* Metered parallel and angled parking on Main Street and in the lot across from the chamber of commerce.

MEDICAL EMERGENCY Dial **911.**

Franklin Medical Center (413-773-0211), 164 High Street, Greenfield.

✳ Towns and Villages

Deerfield (population: 4,750). Founded on a lush plain between the Deerfield and Connecticut Rivers in 1669, Deerfield is best known for the mile-long street of 18th- and early-19th-century homes in **Old Deerfield.** The current town center with its shops and restaurants is 6 miles south in South Deerfield, also the site of **Mount Sugarloaf** and (on North Main Street) of the obelisk marking the site on which most of the town's first male settlers were killed in 1675. This region was the homeland of the Pocumtuck tribe, which had farmed the land for many centuries. Deerfield's natural as well as human-made beauty is unusually accessible: Follow River Road north along the Connecticut from Route 116 to its terminus in East Deerfield, also great for bicycling. Or hike the **Pocumtuck Ridge Trail,** the **Channing Blake Meadow Walk,** and the **Mahican-Mohawk Trail. Yankee Candle** is found along Routes 5/10.

Greenfield. This proud old town (population: 18,170) is sited at the confluence of the Green and Connecticut Rivers, and also at the junction of Route 2 and I-91. Main Street is distinguished by a number of interesting buildings in a wide variety of styles, several by native son Asher Benjamin, the unsung hero responsible for the architectural look of much of rural New England. In the 1790s, a period when much of Western Massachusetts and northern New England was quickly settled, Benjamin was keenly aware of the need for a "do-it-yourself" guide to the new architectural styles being introduced in Boston by Charles Bulfinch. In 1796 Benjamin wrote *The Country Builder's Assistant,* followed by six more books that resulted in the construction of thousands of homes and hundreds of churches—the distinctive three-story houses and high-steepled churches that remain the pride of New England villages. The **Greenfield Public Library** (413-772-1544), 402 Main Street, said to be the first building designed by Asher Benjamin, has an exceptional children's room and an interesting historical collection. Greenfield's entire Main Street is, moreover, remarkable because it has all the downtown essentials that most towns used to have but have lost since the 1950s. They're all here: the coffee shops, the movie theater and family-owned department store, the banks and bakeries, sporting goods shops and grocery store, plus people who all seem to know each other. The interesting new community of **Energy Park** off Main Street (50 Miles Street), created by Northeast Sustainable Energy Association (NESEA), features sculptures, climbing structures, and exhibits demonstrating solar energy, transport alternatives, and more. The **Poet's Seat Tower** up in the Highlands above town is also well worth finding, as is the quiet farmland along the Green and Deerfield Rivers. The **Greenfield Historical Society** (413-774-3663), 3 Church Street (open summer Sunday afternoons and by appointment), offers eight rooms filled with furnishings, portraits, early Greenfield artifacts, and photos. You learn that

Greenfield's J. Russell Company, "America's first cutlery factory," was once known for its Green River buffalo skinning knife.

Northfield (population: c. 3,000). Bisected by the Connecticut River and bounded on the north by both Vermont and New Hampshire, Northfield has an unusually wide and long Main Street lined with many houses built during the heyday of river traffic and sheep farming. It's best known today for the two college-sized campuses of Northfield Mount Hermon, founded as two distinct prep schools by the evangelist minister Dwight Moody in the late 19th century. The trails at **Northfield Mountain** and rides aboard the excursion boat *Quinnetukut II* also attract visitors, and both golf and bicycle options are outstanding. Stop by the **Northfield Historical Society** (413-498-2901) to learn more about Dwight Moody and the Stearns brothers.

Montague. Few towns with a population of just 8,500 encompass as many contrasting villages. By far the biggest of these is **Turners Falls,** sited at the "Great Falls" (visible from Route 2), one of the first waterfalls in the country to be circumvented by a transportation canal (begun in 1794, completed in 1800, operating until 1856). The town is named for Captain William Turner, whose company massacred virtually all the local Indians (the Pocumtucks) near the falls in 1617. This brick mill town was, however, designed and built in the 1860s by Colonel Alvah Crocker. Its sophisticated power canal system functioned from 1860 to 1940, attracting cotton, silk, and cutlery factories as well as three paper mills, collectively employing between 1,200 and 1,500 in their heyday. The town's seven churches served German, French Canadian, Italian, Lithuanian, Bohemian, Irish, and Polish immigrants. Note, in particular, **Our Lady of Czestichowa Catholic Church** (413-863-4748), 84 K Street (turn off Avenue A onto 7th and then left up K); open Saturdays 7–4 and otherwise 3–6:30. The painting of the Black Madonna, the famous Polish icon, is an object of special veneration, a 1920s copy of the original embellished with the jewelry of parishioners. While the most elegant of the town's four hotels have

MONTAGUE MILL, MONTAGUE

Kim Grant

vanished, many handsome buildings survive, and the original 1860s building of Montague Paper (once a 15-building complex covering 5 acres) now houses the federally funded **Discovery Center,** a combination visitors center and museum of natural history focusing on the Connecticut River and its watershed. **The Shea Theater** (see *Entertainment*) is a community theater staging frequent music and drama. Turners Falls sits at a bend in the Connecticut River, which surrounds it on three sides—wide and placid as it enters town at Barton Cove (which offers camping, paddling, and nesting eagles), then magnificently wild as it plunges over the dam beneath the bridge linking the town with Route 2, then dividing into two narrow strips, one a power canal, the other the river. The new **Canalside Rail Trail** follows the canal south from the Discovery Center to riverside roads, ideal for biking. The brick commercial buildings and blocks of mill housing flanking the town's wide, grandly conceived Avenue A (down which trolleys once ran to Amherst and Northampton) are quietly beginning to fill with studios and galleries. Unity Park overlooking Barton Cove is a great picnic site.

Montague Center, south of Turners Falls (best accessed from Route 2 via Route 63 south) has a classic New England green, the site of Montague Old Home Days and the town's Independence Day activities. Nearby Montague Mill (see *Selective Shopping*) is an early-19th-century gristmill on the Sawmill River, now housing crafts studios, a large antiquarian bookshop, and a café. The town's other hidden gem is **Lake Pleasant,** off Route 63 north of Montague Center, a pristine lake (the town's drinking supply) rimmed by 19th-century gingerbread cottages built as a spiritualist camp in the late 19th century. It's still the site of frequent "psychic fairs" on the first Saturday of every month (call 413-774-4705). East of Lake Pleasant lies one of the state's most extensive pine barrens. The town also includes **Millers Falls,** another small mill town just off Route 2, bisected by the Millers Falls River.

Sunderland (population: 3,777). Settled as "swampland" at the turn of the 18th century, this riverside town represents some of the richest and best-protected farmland in the state, much of it still planted in shade-grown tobacco. Early industries included covered buttons, and the big sight-to-see in town is the **Buttonwood Tree,** said to be the largest of its kind (a variety of sycamore) east of the Mississippi and dating from the 18th century. It's on Main Street (Route 47), which is lined with handsome old homes. The brick town hall here, built in 1867 to double as the school, is the new home to the Blue Heron, one of the area's most popular restaurants. Routes 47 and 116 meet in the middle of town and then diverge again, both heading south through farmland. Follow Route 47 north and fork onto Falls Road for a scenic route along the river to Greenfield or follow it northeast, turning down Reservation Road to find the access to trails up **Mount Toby** (1,269 feet), which offers an observation tower and fine view across the valley. Also look for access to trout-stocked **Cranberry Pond.** The Division of Fisheries and Wildlife maintains a trout hatchery on Route 116 south, and the **Cronin National Salmon Station** (413-548-9010) is also open to the public, theoretically 8–4.

Whately (population: 1,771). Motorists from Canada to Florida know Whately's "Fillin' Station," a 24-hour diner just off Route 1-91, but the town itself is blessedly little touristed, from the farm stands salted along River Road by the Con-ing from the tiny village of West Whately. Whately Center is just off Route 5, a classic old town center with two general stores, an old town hall, library, post office, church, and inn.

To See

Old Deerfield. Old Deerfield's serene good looks belie its ups and downs during the 19th and 20th, as well as the 17th and 18th, centuries. Founded in 1669, the first settlement here was deserted in 1675 after King Philip's Native Americans burned the town and killed most of its young men in an ambush that's remembered as the Bloody Brook Massacre. Seven years later, however, the settlers were back, harvesting crops and listening to Sunday sermons in the square, tower-topped meetinghouse (reconstructed on a smaller scale as the present village post office). In all there were 30 attacks in the community's first 50 years, the most famous one on a blustery February night in 1704, when more than 100 villagers were carried off to Montreal. Today visitors are amazed by the richness and sophistication of life as it was lived here during and after the Revolution—as judged from the quality of the architectural detailing, furniture, silver, and furnishings on view. Ironically, after all those early struggles, Old Deerfield survives today as a unique sampling of life in the late 18th and early 19th centuries.

By the 1820s, however, Deerfield had been upstaged by Greenfield as the local commercial center. Already it had become a place to come to school (Deerfield Academy was founded in 1797) and to visit "historic" sites. In 1830 an elaborate granite obelisk replaced the vintage-1720s wooden marker at the site of the Bloody Brook Massacre in South Deerfield; it's believed to be the first historic monument in what became the United States. In 1848 a campaign was mounted to save the Indian House, which still bore the mark of the hatchet implanted in its door during the 1704 raid. Though the campaign failed, it is now cited as the first effort in this country to save a historic house; the door was acquired by a Boston antiquarian, which so outraged local residents that he had to return it. For some time it was displayed in the Pocumtuck House, a hotel that stood on the village common.

Deerfield's zeal for self-preservation was fanned in the 19th century by George Sheldon, a self-appointed town historian given to raiding his neighbors' attics. Sheldon organized the **Pocumtuck Valley Memorial Association** in 1870 and a decade later acquired a striking, three-story brick building designed by Asher Benjamin (it had been the original Deerfield Academy building). The society filled this Memorial Hall with local relics ranging from the Indian House door to colonial-era cooking utensils, displayed in what is now recognized as the first "period room" to be seen in any American museum.

Sheldon also enticed his cousin C. Alice Baker back to town. Born in Deerfield, Baker had become a teacher and noted preservationist in the Boston area (she was involved in the campaign to preserve the Old South Meeting House) and was familiar with the then-current attempts to restore colonial buildings in and around the village of York, Maine. Back in Deerfield, Alice Baker acquired the

Frary House and restored it. At this time two societies were also founded to revive colonial-era crafts such as weaving, hearth cookery, pottery, and basketry. Visitors came. They came by rail and later by rural trolley, stayed in local farms and several now-vanished hotels (including Jewitt House atop Mount Sugarloaf), and shopped for arts and crafts in local homes and studios.

By the 1930s Deerfield was again forgotten. The 1937 *WPA Guide to Massachusetts* described it as "the ghost of a town, its dimness almost transparent, its quiet almost a cessation, but it is essential to add that it is probably quite the most beautiful ghost of its kind, and with the deepest poetic and historic significance to be found in America."

Following World War II Deerfield Academy headmaster Frank Boyden came to the rescue of the old houses, persuading Deerfield Academy alumnus and parent Henry Flynt and his wife, Helen, to buy a number of decaying Old Deerfield buildings. The Flynts subsequently restored many of these buildings, incorporating them as the nonprofit Heritage Foundation (now Historic Deerfield) in 1952. The entire town of Deerfield has been remarkably lucky in preserving some 5,900 acres of cultivated land. Although tract housing sprouted in several fields in the late 1980s, a Deerfield Land Trust was subsequently established and is now dedicated to preserving local farmland.

The largest property holder in Old Deerfield is **Deerfield Academy,** and there are two more private schools—Eaglebrook up on a hill and Bement School—in the village. Also in Old Deerfield: The Brick Church, built in 1824, has arched doorways and a closed wooden cupola. It's the scene of frequent special events as well as regular services. The Old Burying Ground (walk along Albany Road) has many 18th-century stones and the mass grave of the English colonists killed in 1704.

FOR FAMILIES ❧ **Yankee Candle Company** (413-665-2929; www.yankeecandle.com). Routes 5/10, a quarter mile north of I-91, exit 24, South Deerfield. Open daily 9:30–6, except Thanksgiving and Christmas. In 1969 Michael Kittredge used his mother's kitchen to make his first candles. Now billed as "the world's largest candle store," Yankee Candle is a huge complex that includes a Bavarian Village complete with year-round falling snow, a make-your-own-country-candles kitchen, and (new in 2003) Santa's Enchanted Toy Shop, complete with animatronic elves and a countdown-to-Christmas clock. Attractions also include a castle courtyard and waterfall, nutcracker castle, a Candle Making Museum, Yankee Candle Home with home furnishings for the bath, kitchen, and garden, and Chandler's Restaurant (see *Dining Out*).

❧ **Magic Wings** (413-665-2805; www.MagicWings.net), 281 Greenfield Road (Routes 5/10), South Deerfield. Open spring and summer 9–6, fall and winter 9–5, closed Christmas and Thanksgiving. $7 adults, $5 seniors, $4.50 age 3–22. Dozens of varieties of butterflies flit though this vast glass conservatory filled with bright flowers and lush vegetation. A glassed display also reveals the evolution of butterflies. There's a bright café and, of course, an extensive gift shop.

❧ **Old Greenfield Village** (413-774-7138; www.crocker.com/Greenfield/ogv.html), Route 2 west from Greenfield. Open mid-May to mid-October, Saturday and holidays 10–4, Sunday noon–4; weekdays by appointment. $5 adult, $4 seniors, $3 students (6–16), free under age 6. This is a genuine, Yankee kind of phenomenon that has disappeared almost as completely as the thousands of artifacts it displays. What's here are the basics found in stores, in dental offices, churches, barbershops, and tool shops around the turn of the 20th century, all collected over 30 years by retired schoolteacher Waine Morse—not a man with a lot of money, but just a sense of where to find what, when. Morse also constructed the buildings himself. Raising the church steeple alone, he admits, was a bit tricky.

✈ **Great Falls Discovery Center** (413-863-3221), Avenue A, Turners Falls. (Open Friday and Saturday 10–4 at this writing.) A publicly funded, family-geared showcase for the entire Connecticut River watershed, focusing on natural history, with displays as well as live animals, fish, and reptiles native to the area. The landscaped grounds include an amphitheater, and nearby **Unity Park** offers picnicking facilities and a playground.

✈ **Northfield Mountain Recreational and Environmental Center** (413-659-3714 or 1-800-859-2960; www.nu.com/Northfield/), Route 63 in Northfield. Open Wednesday through Sunday 9–5. A film about the construction and operation of the plant can be viewed in the visitors center. The project utilizes water from the Connecticut, draws it up into an artificially created lake on top of the mountain, and uses the stored water to generate power during high-use periods. The powerhouse itself is hidden in a cavern as high as a 10-story building, as wide as a four-lane highway, and longer than a football field. The center also houses superb displays dramatizing the story of the river's 18th- and early-19th-century flat-bottomed sailing barges for which canals were constructed in the 1790s. The story of steamboating and the advent of the railroad is also told, along with subsequent industrialization, logging, and the present hydro uses of the river's "white gold." See *To Do* for late-June through mid-October cruises on the Connecticut aboard the *Quinnetukut II*.

SCENIC DRIVES

River Roads
Along the western shore of the Connecticut all the way from Hatfield north to the confluence with the Deerfield, **River Road** is lined with farms, tobacco sheds, and fields. It's flat except for the monadnock, Mount Sugarloaf, which thrusts up all alone; be sure to drive to the top (see *Views*). See *Selective Shopping* for farms along this road, and note the old headstones in **Pine Nook Cemetery** some 4 miles north of Route 116.

Along the eastern side of the Connecticut, follow **Falls Road** (also known as the North Sunderland Road) forking left off Route 47 beyond the Buttonwood Tree, keeping along the river as far as you can. You pass falls as well as farms.

River Road in Northfield runs south from the landing (off Route 63) at Northfield Mountain to Route 2. It's also beautiful.

Route 2 to Montague Center to either Greenfield or Deerfield. Turn off Route 2 at Route 63 south to Swamp Road (a right). Stop at the Montague Mill, with its crafts, bookstore, art studio, and the Blue Heron Restaurant. You might also want to detour less than a mile south to Montague Center, a classic village

HISTORIC DEERFIELD

HISTORIC DEERFIELD (413-774-5581; www.historic-deerfield.org).
In Old Deerfield, marked from Route 5; 6 miles north of exit 24 off I-91, or 3.5 miles south of Greenfield (off I-91 and Route 2). Open all year 9:30–4:30, daily except Thanksgiving, Christmas Eve, and Christmas Day. Admission is $12 adults, $5 children 6–21; May through October the fee includes admission to Memorial Hall. Tickets (good for 2 consecutive days) are sold in the Hall Tavern (be sure to see the upstairs ballroom). Guided and self-guided tours through this museum of New England history and art are presently offered of 12 buildings displaying a total of some 30,000 objects made or used in America between 1650 and 1850. The **Flynt Center of Early New England Life** houses objects not on display and a "visible storage gallery" featuring some 2,500 historic household furnishings, also special exhibitions. Detailed descriptions of items are available on computers. Inquire about antiques forums, frequently on the decorative arts. The historic houses include:

The **Wells-Thorn House** (sections built in 1717 and 1751) shows the dramatic changes in the lifestyles in Deerfield through two centuries. The **Ashley House** (1733), with its elegantly carved cupboards and furnishings, depicts the lifestyle of the village's Tory minister (note his 1730s Yale diploma). The **Asa Stebbins House** (1799/1810) is the first brick home in town, grandly furnished with French wallpaper, Chinese porcelain, and Federal-era pieces. The Wright House (1824), another brick mansion, is a mini museum of high-style furniture and ceramics. The **Sheldon-Hawks House** (1743) is furnished with pieces from the Connecticut River valley and Boston and is still filled with the spirit of George Sheldon, the town's colorful first historian. The **Frary**

House/Barnard Tavern (1740/1795) has a classic tavern look, ballroom, and 1890s restoration by C. Alice Baker. The **Ebenezer Williams House** (1750s, rebuilt 1816–20), furnished from an 1838 inventory, is surprisingly airy and modern, with touches like the light-toned rag stair rug, "glass curtains," venetian blinds, and exceptionally beautiful patterned wallpapers and floorcloths. A **Children's History Center** is slated to open in 2005.

    Memorial Hall (413-774-7476; www.old-deerfield.org), Memorial Street, Old Deerfield. Open May through October, 9:30–4:30 daily including weekends. $6 adults, $3 youth and children (6–21); a combination ticket with Historic Deerfield is $12; $5 for youth and children. In addition to the "Indian House door" and country's first period room (see above), this beautiful old building houses the Pocumtuck Valley Memorial Association's wonderfully eclectic collection. You learn about the Pocomtuck tribe, caught between the English who had settled in the lower valley and the Mohawks to the west. In 1675, you learn, these people seized the lands they had been tilling for centuries, replanting their cornfields until they were again dislodged by settlers, from whom they again attempted to wrest their ancestral homeland in 1704. Among "The Many Stories of 1704" you hear the Reverend John Williams describe the massacre in which his wife and children were murdered and a son and daughter kidnapped, how the son was ransomed but daughter refused to return, visiting 40 years later but remaining in a Mohawk community near Montreal until her death at age 81. Deerfield's 1890s–1920s era as an artistic center is illustrated with paintings by the Fuller family, among others, and by an extensive collection of work by the Deerfield Society of Blue and White Needlework. **The Old Indian House** (open daily July 4 through Labor Day, then weekends through Columbus Day, 11–4:30), a 1929 reproduction of the Sheldon House (demolished in 1848), houses activities geared to young visitors. Also see *Special Events.*

MOCCASINS, CIRCA 1880, ON DISPLAY AT MEMORIAL HALL IN OLD DEERFIELD

ENGLISH BARBER'S BOWL, CIRCA 1700–1720, ONE OF MANY COLONIAL ARTIFACTS AT HISTORIC DEERFIELD

Pocumtuck Valley Memorial Association

Penny Leveritt

with a Congregational church designed by Asher Benjamin and a brick town hall on its common. Otherwise continue west (Swamp changes at the mill to Ferry Road) and turn north (right) onto Greenfield Road; take a left onto Montague City Road and cross the river. To reach the Poet's Seat, turn right onto Mountain Road. For Old Deerfield, continue to Routes 5/10 and turn left; Old Deerfield is a mile or so south, on your right.

Route 2 to Turners Falls to Old Deerfield. This is a shortcut rather than a scenic drive, but it's handy to know since it lops off several tedious highway miles. Leave Route 2 at Turners Falls and cross the high bridge onto Avenue A, the main drag of this classic, late-19th-century mill town. You might stop for a meal or at least pie at the Shady Glen Restaurant; also stop by the Great Falls Discovery Center across the way. Continue south on Avenue A, which turns into the Montague City Road, and cross the iron bridge, bear left to Routes 5/10, and watch for an OLD DEERFIELD sign.

Mohawk Trail. The stretch of Route 2 designated in 1914 as the Mohawk Trail, New England's first official tourist trail, begins in Greenfield and heads west, abruptly uphill. Shelburne Falls, the hub of the Mohawk Trail, is just 8 miles west of downtown Greenfield. (See "Along the Mohawk Trail.")

Deerfield to Greenfield, the scenic route. From "The Street" in Old Deerfield, head south, continuing as the village ends and it becomes Mill Village Road, flanked by farmland. Turn right onto Stillwater Road and follow it along the Deerfield River. Turn right on the bridge across the river (this section of the Deerfield is popular with tubers) and follow the West Deerfield Upper Road through more beautiful farmland. Note Clarkdale Fruit Farms (303 Upper Road), a fourth-generation family farm offering pick-your-own apples, peaches, pears, and pumpkins; great plums and cider, too.

Route 116 west from South Deerfield climbs steeply and quickly out of the valley and up into Conway. (See "Hidden Hills.")

Route 47 north from Sunderland runs through farmlands, past the turnoff (Recreation Road) for Mount Toby, farm stands, and sugarhouses.

✳ To Do

BICYCLING The river roads described under *Scenic Drives* are all suited to bicycle touring. The 4-mile **Canalside Rail Trail,** due for completion in 2004, runs from the **Discovery Center** in Turners Falls south along the river.

Mountain biking is also popular in summer on the 40 miles of trails at Northfield Mountain. Rentals as well as advice are available from **Northfield Bicycle Barn** (413-498-2996), Main Street, Northfield (look for Al's Convenience Store; the Barn is behind the neighboring house).

Basically Bicycles (413-863-3556), 83 3rd Street, Turners Falls, offers rentals as well as sales and service. Closed Sunday.

BOATING EXCURSIONS The *Quinnetukut II* (413-659-3714 or 1-800-859-2960) cruises the Connecticut from the Riverview picnic area at the **Northfield Mountain Recreation and Environmental Center,** Route 63 in Northfield.

The 6-mile cruise is through French King Gorge downstream to the Turners Falls Dam. Departures are three times per day from late June through mid-October. Call for reservations. $9 adults, $8 age 55 and over, $5 children 14 and under. Inquire about special children's cruises and sunset cruises with live jazz.

CANOEING AND KAYAKING **Northfield Mountain's Barton Cove** facility (413-863-9300 or 1-800-859-2960) on Route 2 just east of the bridge to Turners Falls, offers rental kayaks and canoes and shuttle service as far north along the Connecticut as Vernon Dam (20 miles). This is also a source for information about canoeing sites that Northeast Utilities maintains for public access: **Munn's Ferry Campground** (with Adirondack shelters and tent sites, accessible only by boat), and **River View,** a float dock, picnic tables, and sanitary facilities on the river across from the entrance to Northfield Mountain.

FISHING **The Connecticut River** offers outstanding fishing for bass, shad, yellow perch, all kinds of sunfish, carp, walleye, and trout (check out the mouths of feeder streams). Cranberry Pond in Sunderland is known locally for trout. The most user-friendly put-in place for visitors is Barton's Cove; see *Boating* for further rentals.

Pipione's Sport Shop (413-863-4246), 101 Avenue A (the main drag), open daily from 7 AM, is a source of advice, as well as equipment and licenses.

Note: The nearby **Quabbin Reservoir** is the state's premier fishing hole, and the **Deerfield, West,** and **Millers Rivers** are nationally famed among anglers for fly-fishing.

GOLF **Crumpin-Fox Golf Club** (413-648-9101), Route 10, Bernardston. 18 holes. The front nine were designed by Robert Trent Jones himself, and the back nine by his firm.

Northfield Golf Club (413-498-2432), 31 Holton Street, Northfield. A nine-hole, par 36 course.

Oak Ridge Golf Club (413-863-9693), 231 West Gill Road, Gill. Nine holes, par 36.

Thomas Memorial Golf Club & Country Club (413-863-8003), 29 Country Club Lane, Turners Falls. Nine holes, par 70.

CROSS-COUNTRY SKIING **Northfield Mountain Ski Touring Center** (413-583-9073), Route 63, Northfield, open December through March, Wednesday through Sunday, offers cross-country and snowshoe rentals for use on its 40 km of doubletracked trail.

✳ Green Space

THE CONNECTICUT RIVER As noted in the introduction to "The Pioneer Valley," the Connecticut River flows through the heart of this area, and while no longer its transportation spine, the river itself is a vantage point from which to enjoy the greenery on either shore. You can ride an excursion boat or paddle down the middle of the river, pedal a bike across it on a former railroad bridge, and watch salmon surmount its dams via the fish ladder in Turners Falls. You can also spend a day walking, driving, or fishing along its banks. Not much, however, is obvious. You have to know what's there.

The **Connecticut River Greenway State Park** (413-586-8706) encompasses 4,000 acres in numerous locations along the 138 miles of the river's shoreline in Massachusetts, and collectively these properties form a state park.

Great Falls Discovery Center (413-863-3221), Avenue A, Turners Falls. Phone for hours. Just over the bridge from Route 2, a major publicly funded interpretive center focuses on the entire Connecticut River watershed, from the sound all the way up to the Canadian border. Exhibits are on natural and human history, from Native Americans to the present day. This is also a visitors center, dispensing information about eco- and heritage tourism.

The visitors center at **Northfield Mountain Recreational and Environmental Center** (see *For Families*) has exhibits on the river.

VIEWS **Mount Sugarloaf State Reservation,** off Route 116, South Deerfield. A road winds up this red sandstone mountain (said to resemble the old loaves into which sugar was shaped) to a modern observation tower on the summit, supposedly the site from which King Philip surveyed his prey before the mid-17th-century Bloody Brook Massacre. There are picnic tables, restrooms, and great views down the valley.

Poet's Seat Tower and Rocky Mountain Trails, off High Street in Greenfield (or see *Scenic Drives* from Turners Falls). This medieval-looking sandstone tower on Rocky Mountain honors local 19th-century poet Frederick Goddard Tuckerman, who liked to sit near this spot. You can understand why. A Ridge Trail (blue blazes) loops along the top of the hill.

Mount Toby, at 1,269 feet the tallest mountain in the valley, offers great views plus caves and waterfalls. As is the case with Mount Holyoke and Mount Sugarloaf, a hotel once capped its summit, but now there is just a fire tower. Access is off Route 47, 4 miles south of Sunderland center. It's a 3-hour round-trip hike, but you can go just as far as the cascades. From Route 47 in North Sunderland, turn right onto Reservation Road; the parking area is in half a mile.

HIKING AND WALKING **Barton Cove Nature and Camping Area** (1-800-859-2960), Route 2, just east of Turners Falls in Gill. The office and information center is on Route 2 in the former Rainbow Bend Restaurant. An interpretive nature trail meanders along a rocky ridge overlooking the Connecticut River, and there's a picnic area in addition to tent sites. During nesting season, eagles are usually in residence. Canoe and boat rentals available.

Along Route 2, Millers Falls and Gill
French King Bridge (Route 2 west of Millers Falls) spans a dramatically steep, banked, narrow stretch of the Connecticut, 140 feet above the water. Park at the rest area and walk back onto the bridge (there's a pedestrian walk) for the view. Note the mouth of the Millers River just downstream. The bridge is named for

PICNICKING AT THE TOP OF MOUNT SUGARLOAF

Christina Tree

French King Rock below. The king was Louis XV, and the rock was reportedly named by one of his subjects in the mid-1700s. It's funny how some names stick.

In Deerfield

Channing Blake Meadow Walk in Old Deerfield. A half-mile path through the village's north meadows and a working 700-acre farm begins at the northern end of Deerfield Street; inquire at Historic Deerfield about special family tours and nature activities.

Pocumtuck Ridge Trail, South Deerfield. Take North Main Street to Hillside Drive (across from Hardigg Industries) to Stage Road. Turn left at the top of the hill onto Ridge Road for the trailhead for paths through Deerfield Land Trust's 120-acre preserve.

Mahican-Mohawk Trail. The first 1.5 miles of this 7.5-mile trail, said to be the actual 10,000-year-old route along the lower Deerfield, is accessible from Deerfield. Request a map at the Hall Tavern in Historic Deerfield. Drive south on Deerfield Street and instead of turning back onto Route 5, jog right and then south along Mill Village Road and turn right at the small stone building at the corner of Stillwater Road; at 0.9 mile take Hoosac Road, and you will see the trailhead at 0.2 mile. The trail follows an abandoned railbed to the South River. For a description of the rest of the trail, see "Along the Mohawk Trail."

In Northfield

Northfield Mountain, Route 63, Northfield (see *For Families*).

Bennett Meadow Wildlife Management Area, also maintained by Northeast Utilities, maintains space to park by the west side of the river in Northfield.

In New Salem

Bear's Den Reservation. Off Elm Street, less than a mile from Route 202. This Trustees of Reservations site is a grotto on the Middle Branch of the Swift River with a sparkling waterfall. Local legend says that in 1675 King Philip met here with this chieftains to plan the attack on Deerfield.

✳ Lodging

INNS ᵰ **Deerfield Inn** (413-774-5587; outside Massachusetts, 1-800-926-3865; www.deerfieldinn.com), 81 Old Main Street, Deerfield 01342. Open year-round. A newcomer by Old Deerfield standards (it opened in 1884), the antiques-filled inn is dignified but not stiff. It is the place to stay when visiting Historic Deerfield, enabling you to steep and sleep in the full atmosphere of the village after other visitors have gone. There are 23 rooms, all with private bath, 12 in an annex added since the 1979 fire (from which townspeople and Deerfield Academy students heroically rescued most of the antiques). Rooms feature wallpaper and fabric from the Historic Deerfield collection, and furnishings are either antiques or reproduction antiques; some canopy beds. Attention to details, phones. Some annex rooms are quite spacious. $181–248 includes breakfast. Rates vary with the season, not the room, which strikes us as strange since rooms vary in size and feel, and come with and without ghosts.

BED & BREAKFASTS ✎ ☙ **The Brandt House** (413-774-3329 or 1-800-235-3329; www.brandthouse.com), 29 Highland Avenue, Greenfield 01301. This expansive, 16-room Georgian Revival house is set on more than 3 acres and offers seven guest rooms, all with private bath. Common rooms include a tastefully comfortable, plant-filled living room, the dining room with large sash windows overlooking the garden, a game room with a full-sized pool table, a wicker-furnished porch and patio, and an upstairs sunroom stocked with local menus, a microwave, and TV; there's also a clay tennis court. Guest rooms are all relatively small but tastefully furnished, two with working fireplace, and the top floor harbors a two-room suite. $100–225 includes a full breakfast. There's also a lower "corporate rate" weekdays (single occupancy). Children and well-behaved dogs are accepted ($25 extra for a dog).

∞ **West Winds** (413-773-3837; www.westwindsinn.com), 151 Smead Hill Road, Greenfield 01301. Sandy Richardson designed this contemporary dream house with cathedral ceilings and great spaces, and her husband, Tim, built it. There are now nine guest rooms, all with private bath. Several feature patios and balconies overlooking a sweep of valley and hills beyond, and some are fitted with Jacuzzi. Breakfast is served in the light-filled dining area with a field-stone fireplace off the open kitchen. Rates include a full breakfast. $125–225 in high season, $160–165 off-season. Continental breakfast weekdays, full on weekends.

∞ **The Ashley Graves House** (413-665-6656; www.ashleygraveshouse.com), 121 North Main Street, Sunderland 01375. One of the finest houses around, proudly built in 1830 and lovingly preserved but centrally air-conditioned by Carole and Mike Skibiski.

Guests enter through The Barn Room, a large comfortably furnished common space with guest fridge and adjoining dining and breakfast rooms. The King Philip Suite is a beauty with skylights in a post-and-beam ceiling and a "Vermont crazy window" in the wall. It's huge, with a king-sized bed, private entrance, and private bath with whirlpool tub ($175). There is also a room with twins, another with a lovely antique double bed and a balcony, and a second-floor suite with a queen bed and a pull-out sofa in the adjoining sitting room. All rooms have private bath and are tastefully furnished with antiques, as is a front parlor with a brick fireplace. From $150, including a full breakfast.

Hillside House (413-665-5515; www.hillsidehousebb.com), P.O. Box 183, 60 Masterson Road, Whately 01093. Julia and Ed Berman searched the country before picking this hillside home as their B&B. A modern home wasn't what they had in mind, but when you step into its airy, glass-walled spaces and out onto the deck, you understand why anyone would like to spend much of their life here. Furnishings are comfortable and tasteful with some exceptional pieces, art and mementos from their far-flung travels. The "pink guest room" is what you want here, spacious and bright with the valley view—but the "yellow guest room" also has its charm, and both have private bath. There is also a "spa room," and a swimming pool is set below the house in landscaped gardens. The Bermans dine out around the valley and share with guests their critiques of local restaurants. Children over age 12 are welcome. $95–145 includes a generous breakfast.

✎ **Hitchcock House** (413-774-7452; www.thehitchcockhouse.com), 15 Congress Street, Greenfield 01301. Jennifer and Jeffrey Capers's Victorian-style house sits on a quiet residential street within walking distance of downtown Greenfield. The three second-floor guest rooms are furnished with antiques and quilts, equipped with private or shared baths. The third-floor rooms can be linked as a suite, good for a family of four. Both Jen and Jeff are graduates of the Culinary Institute of America, and breakfast features fresh pastries, fresh fruit, and the specialty of the day, included in $90–110 per couple. Children welcome.

∞ **Old Tavern Farm Bed & Breakfast** (413-772-0474; www.old-tavernfarm.com), 817 Colrain Road, Greenfield 01301. A quiet byway today in the lush Green River part of town, this was a main road between Boston and Albany when the tavern was first licensed in 1746. Present hosts Gary and Joanne Sanderson are devoted to preserving the feel of this very special place, which retains its classic old ballroom (still a great place for a dance). Common space includes the sunny, low-ceilinged dining room, warmed by a soapstone woodstove, and an attractive former "ladies' parlor," as well as the old taproom with fireplaces and attractive but authentic antiques, some rather rare and special. The master bedroom is warmed by a Rumford fireplace and features a vintage-1814 Sheridan bird's-eye maple four-poster. There is also a smaller upstairs bedroom and a downstairs suite with a genuine feather bed. Bathrooms are shared, and breakfast is full. Gary is a local sportscaster and also a licensed fishing and hunting guide. $135–205 for a suite. The house and ballroom can be rented for small weddings.

🐾 **Sunnyside Farm** (413-665-3113), River Road, Whately 01093. Mary Lou and Dick Green welcome visitors to their big yellow turn-of-the-20th-century farmhouse, 5 miles south of Deerfield. It's been in their family since it was built and stands on 50 acres of farmland that grew tobacco and is now leased in part to the neighboring berry farm. All three guest rooms overlook fields. Two spacious front rooms with small TVs face River Road. There's a small but appealing corner double, and a back room has a king-sized bed; baths are shared. Guests have full access to the downstairs rooms, which include a comfortable living room and a dining room in which everyone gathers around a long table for breakfast. Don't miss the porch swing. $65–100.

🐾 **Centennial House** (413-498-5921 or 1-877-977-5950; www.thecentennialhouse.com), 94 Main Street, Northfield 01360. Built in 1811 and formerly the headmaster's house for the Mount Hermon School, this handsome old home was designed and built by the town's premier builder, Calvin Stearns. There are four guest rooms, including a third-floor (air-conditioned) suite with skylights, a kitchen, dining and sitting areas, and both an antique sleigh bed and a twin. All guest rooms are furnished in antiques; three have fireplace. Common space includes a pine-paneled living room with a hearth, a gracious parlor, and best of all, a glassed sunporch overlooking the 2-acre "back meadow" with its sunset views. The house sits on Northfield's long, wide Main Street,

which invites strolling. $95–160 includes breakfast.

🐾 **Prior House** (413-498-5957; thepriorhouse@aol.com), 55 Main Street, Northfield 01360. A federal home built by the Stearns brothers for Isaac Prior in 1820. There are pleasant shared spaces with good original art. A private-entrance suite (where pets and children are accepted) features a kitchen and a sitting area with TV as well as twin beds and a sleep sofa and bath ($95–110). Upstairs are two more cheerful, antiques-furnished guest rooms with a shared bath (from $65). Rates include breakfast with self-serve cereals, fruit, cheese, yogurt, hard-boiled eggs, and breads; also hot eggs, sausage, and potatoes if desired.

∞ 🐾 **Bullard Farm** (978-544-6959), 89 Elm Street, North New Salem 01355. This 1792 farmhouse, on 400 acres just a mile from Quabbin, has been in Janet Kraft's family for many generations. The farm has its own walking and cross-country ski trails and adjoins the Bear Den Reservation. Deer and flocks of wild turkeys from the reservation wander onto the property. If you must have a private bath, Laura Ashley wallpaper, and mints on your turndown, this isn't the place for you. But if you appreciate the authentic feel of a country bedroom with a comfortable bed and windows overlooking fields, this is a good place to know about, especially if you like to bicycle quiet roads down to forgotten places like New Salem Village. The house offers four guest rooms with period furniture (sharing two baths), and there is ample common space in addition to a meeting and function room in the barn. Breakfasts are full, and if you come during blueberry season, you will likely have berries-to-go. Janet delights in turning guests on to this remote and least touristed part of the valley. Rates are $75 single, $95 double, including breakfast.

🐾 **Yellow Gabled House** (413-665-4922; www.yellowgabledhouse.com), 111 North Main Street, South Deerfield 01373. Overlooking Bloody Brook (now tamed to a small stream) and the obelisk-shaped memorial to the 1675 massacre on the site, this Gothic Revival house is both snug and elegant. There are three carefully furnished upstairs guest rooms, all with fan and air-conditioning. Two rooms (one with queen-sized beds and matching tailored Greef fabric spreads and window treatments; the other has a canopy bed) share a bath, and a suite has a tall posted bed, adjoining sitting room with TV, and private bath. Host Julia Stahelek is a cartographer and local historian who feels so strongly that her guests should visit Historic Deerfield that she offers complimentary tickets. $80–145 includes a full gourmet breakfast.

House on the Hill B&B (413-774-2070; www.thehouseonthehillbnb.com), 330 Leyden Road, Greenfield 01301. High on a quiet green shoulder of the valley. Donna and Alain Mollard's big old white-clapboard house offers a wraparound porch and three second-floor air-conditioned guest rooms (two queens, one king), all with private bath and TV. Shared space includes a living-dining area with a large fireplace. Another ground-level guest room with private bath is available on request.

MOTELS 🐾 ☀ 🐾 **Fox Inn** (413-648-9101 or 1-800-436-9466; www.sandri.

com), Route 10, Bernardston 01337. An unusually attractive motel just off I-91, exit 28, but with an out-in-the-country feel. Rooms all overlook greenery; request one with peaked ceilings. $55–76 double. Handy to golf.

☀ **French King Motor Lodge** (413-423-3328), Route 2, Millers Falls. A good bet for families, 18 units with a swimming pool and restaurant near the French King Bridge. $65–95.

OTHER Barton Cove Nature and Camping Area (for reservations prior to the season, phone 413-659-3714; otherwise, 413-863-9300), Route 2, Gill. This is an unusual facility maintained by Northeast Utilities on a peninsula that juts into the Connecticut River. Wooded tent sites are available.

✳ **Where to Eat**

DINING OUT Blue Heron Restaurant (413-367-0200; www.blueheron-dining.com). Owners Deborah Snow and Barbara White have won rave reviews for their American regional cooking—which, until 2003, was served up at the Montague Mill. Their new home is the Sunderland Town Hall, and while they are in transition at this writing we trust that they will be back in business by the time this book appears, serving entrées that might range from a Moroccan vegetable tagine (chickpea stew with tomatoes, kale, leeks, preserved lemon, raisins, and cracked green olives served over couscous), to grilled Black Angus rib-eye steak "Tuscan style," with truffle oil, garlic mashed potatoes, and sautéed greens. Entrées $18–25.50.

Deerfield Inn (413-774-2359), The Street, Old Deerfield. Open daily for lunch, dinner nightly. Reservations advised. This is a formal dining room with white tablecloths, Chippendale chairs, and a moderately expensive lunch menu. At dinner you might begin with escargots in puff pastry with Brie and garlic butter ($7.25), then dine on roasted half duck with poached pear in cider ($27), or fresh salmon steamed in orange juice, ginger broth, and vegetable pot-au-feu ($23). Wine is available by the glass, and the wine list itself is extensive. Inquire about late-afternoon carriage rides as part of the dinner package.

Sienna (413-665-0215), 6 Elm Street, South Deerfield. Dinner from 5:30 Wednesday through Sunday; reservations a must. An unpretentious storefront is the setting for this restaurant that's always ranked among the best in the valley. Richard Labonte's menu changes frequently and always features local produce. You might begin with a baby artichoke tart, then feast on pan-seared Atlantic cod with crabmeat mashed potato and crispy hearts of palm with lobster demiglaze; other options might range from forest mushroom potpie to grilled beef tenderloin. Leave room for desserts like a strawberry napoleon, or a Chardonnay-poached pear with mascarpone-pistachio filling and ginger-champagne sabayon. The one complaint we hear is that the wine list is overpriced. Entrées $21–26.

Chandler's Restaurant at Yankee Candle (413-665-5089; www.yankeecandle.com). Open for lunch and dinner, with Mystery Dinner Theater Wednesdays at 6:30 ($30 includes a specially selected menu). The decor is both rustic and romantic, with dinner lighting by candlelight (some 200 candles). Lunch on sun-dried tomato, basil, mushroom, and onion quiche or a Caesar salad, and dine on carrot ginger soup followed by veal roulade or crispy roast duck. Entrées $18–24. Inquire about brew and wine tastings.

Bella Notte (413-648-9107), Huckle Hill Road, Bernardston. Open nightly for dinner, closing Monday and Tuesday November through early April. Reservations please. A glass-faced, hilltop building with the best views of any restaurant in the valley. The huge menu features northern Italian dishes: many appetizers, pastas, veal, chicken, and seafood dishes. Entrées $10.95–24.95.

Whately Inn (413-665-3044 or 1-800-WHATELY; www.whatelyinn.com), 193 Chestnut Plain Road, Whately Center. Open daily 5–10, Sunday 1–9. Reservations suggested. Chef-owner Steve Kloc packs them in with a big menu, good food, and lots of it. Dinner entrées are $16.95–24.95, but that includes everything from soup to nuts: appetizers like chopped liver pâté and soup du jour, followed by entrées such as rack of lamb Dijonnaise, fettuccine with wild mushrooms, frog legs Provençal, veal Oscar, or roast prime rib, complete with garden salad, dessert, and coffee.

Stearns Tavern (413-498-0098), 61 Main Street, Northfield. Open Wednesday and Thursday 4–9, Friday, Saturday, and Sunday 4–10. Housed in a post-and-beam barn, fine dining with an emphasis on steaks, filet mignon, and prime rib.

Also see **Green Emporium** in nearby Colrain under "West County."

In and around Greenfield

The People's Pint (413-773-0333), 24 Federal Street, Greenfield. From 4 PM. A first-rate brew pub that's also a great people place; good food, too. Specialties include soups, breads, and "the ploughman classic" (crusty sourdough topped with sharp cheddar, a pickle, and mustard) and reasonably priced entrées like New Orleans red beans and rice, and grilled chicken salad. Chess, board games, and darts weekday evenings, live music Saturday night, Celtic music Sunday.

China Gourmet (413-774-2299), 78 Mohawk Trail (Route 2A), Greenfield. Open for lunch and dinner, until 10 most nights and to 11 Friday and Saturday. A local favorite, light on the MSG, a reasonably priced menu and new sushi bar. Szechuan and Hunan specialties include hot-and-sour seafood soup, General Tso's chicken, and "Hot Lovers Triple Treat."

✿ Bill's Restaurant (413-773-8331), 30 Federal Street, Greenfield. Open daily at 4, Sundays 11–8. This friendly, traditional restaurant remains a local favorite; liquor served. Plenty of pasta and fried dishes. Lobster pie is a specialty, and there are "Lite Dinners" for kids and seniors.

Brad's Place (413-773-9567), 353 Main Street, Greenfield. Open 6–3, Saturday 6–2. "Serving downtown for 30 years," this is the kind of place in which everyone knows everybody—but visitors are also served quickly and well. Daily specials, burgers, soups and sandwiches, a long counter and booths.

Green Fields Market (413-773-9567), 144 Main Street, Greenfield. This natural foods cooperative occupies a former JCPenney and includes a tempting deli and "from scratch" bakery with attractive seating space near the windows.

Café Koko (413-774-2772), 204 Main Street, Greenfield. Open Sunday through Wednesday 7 AM–9 PM, until 11 Friday, Saturday, and Sunday. An invitingly casual café serving a light menu, coffees and teas, beer and wine. Live entertainment on weekends and frequently during the week, ranging from storytelling to folk music and open mike.

Elsewhere

Wolfie's (413-665-7068), 52 South Main Street, South Deerfield. Open 11–10 Monday through Saturday. This

CAFÉ KOKO IN GREENFIELD

Kim Grant

is our kind of place: wooden booths, fast friendly service, an appealing family restaurant. The menu features a blackened Wolfieburger (Cajun charbroiled 5-ounce ground round with melted cheddar, etc.), a "big bad wolfburger" (8 ounces of ground round with melted cheese, etc.), many sandwiches, grinders, and salads as well as dinner specials starting at $8.95, draft beer, mixed drinks and wine.

Blue Skies Café (413-863-9684), 104 4th Street, Turners Falls. Open Tuesday through Friday 9–3, Saturday 11–9. Bright colors, fresh flowers, murals, occasional live music, and dependably fresh homemade breads and pastries make this a place worth finding, just off the main drag. Lunch on soup and salad or sandwiches. We recommend the veggie wrap with avocado, hummus, baby spinach, olives, feta, and more.

Bub's Bar BQ (413-548-9630; www.bubsbbq.com), Route 116, Sunderland. Open at 4 weekdays, noon Saturday and Sunday. Rated "best barbecue joint in New England" by *Yankee,* this place offers great variety: kielbasa and blackened fish, "spicy dirty rice" and "orange-glazed sweet potatoes," as well as pulled-pork back ribs.

Smiarowski Farmstand and Creamery (413-665-3415), 320 River Road, Sunderland. Polish specialties like *golabki,* "lazy cabbage pierogi," and kielbasa; also Snow's ice cream, farm-fresh salads, and desserts. Self-serve.

ROAD FOOD

Off Route 2

🍴 ♿ **Shady Glen Restaurant** (413-863-9636), 7 Avenue A, Turners Falls. Open Monday through Saturday 5 AM–9 PM, closed Sunday. No credit cards. A real step back to the 1950s, this diner with its L-shaped counter and eight cozy booths is just off Route 2—over the bridge across the Great Falls. For some years John and Linda Carey have devoted their lives to this gem, unquestionably the center of Turners Falls.

Countree Living Restaurant (413-423-3624), 63 French King Highway (Route 2), Erving. Open Wednesday through Sunday for dinner (4:30–8), Saturday for breakfast, too (11–2). Basic American fare with dinner specials, entrées $10–18. Full liquor license.

French King Restaurant (413-659-3328), handy to Route 2, Millers Falls. A family restaurant, open (except Monday) for lunch and dinner.

Off I-91

Tom's Hot Dog, Routes 5/10 south of I-91 exit 23 in North Hatfield. Legendary steamed hot dogs.

Fillin' Station (413-665-3696), Routes 5/10 just off I-91, exit 24. The best we can say is that this classic chrome diner is open 24 hours, adjacent to a gas station–truck stop. The flashy decor is great, but on a recent visit the service was slow, food below par.

The Four Leaf Clover Restaurant (413-648-9514), Route 5, Bernardston. Open daily for lunch and dinner, until 9 Friday and Saturday. Just off Route I-91 exit 28, a family restaurant that's a local favorite, good for chicken potpie, baked haddock, and liver and onions as well as homemade soups and bread pudding.

7 South Bakery (413-648-0070), 7 South Street (Route 5), Bernardston. Open 6:30 AM–5 PM, closed Sunday. A pleasant coffee stop, great breads, pastries.

✳ Entertainment

Arena Civic Theatre (413-773-9891) presents musicals and comedies, mid-June through August, in various Franklin County locations.

Shea Community Theater (413-863-2281), 71 Avenue A, Turners Falls. Call Tuesday through Friday noon–3 to inquire about performances by the resident community theater and visiting professional theater companies.

Music in Deerfield (413-625-9511 or 1-888-MTC-MUSE; www.musicin-deerfield.org). A fall-through-spring series of performances by nationally known musicians, presented by Mohawk Trail Concerts at the Brick Church Meeting House in Old Deerfield.

1794 New Salem Meetinghouse (978-544-5200), off Route 202, New Salem. A beautiful setting for music—choral, folk, and jazz—also an assortment of live performances May through July.

Full Moon Coffee House (978-544-2086), Wendell. Monthly concerts held in town hall on the Saturday night closest to the full moon.

Pioneer Valley Symphony and Chorus (413-773-3664) based in Greenfield. One of the oldest symphony orchestras in the country.

FILM Northfield Drive-In (603-239-4054), Route 63 north of Northfield. Half in New Hampshire and half in Massachusetts, an old-fashioned drive-in showing new releases, open seasonally.

Greenfield Garden Cinemas (413-774-4881), 361 Main Street, Greenfield. No longer the movie palace it once was but still a place to see first-run films.

✳ Selective Shopping

ANTIQUES AND AUCTIONS This is a particularly rich antiquing area. Auction houses include:

Douglas (413-665-2877), Route 5, Deerfield (Friday nights); and **Ken Miller** (413-498-2749), Northfield, auctions on Monday nights (6:30) in summer and fall, Saturdays (10–5) in the off-season, also flea markets Sundays, mid-April through October, 7–3.

Yesterdays Antique Center (413-665-7226), Routes 5/10 in Deerfield. Open Tuesday through Sunday 10–4; some two dozen dealers, displaying everything from books to major furniture pieces.

ART AND CRAFTS GALLERIES
Battelle Harding Gallery (413-834-2359; www.battelleharding-gallery.com), 267 Main Street, Greenfield. Open Sunday through Thursday 11–6, Friday and Saturday 11–8. Closed Wednesday. A serious gallery, well worth checking out, with changing exhibits featuring painting, sculpture, photography, and works on paper.

Room with a Loom (413-367-2062), at the Montague Mill, doubles as a studio for Karen Chapman and as an exceptional gallery displaying work by local craftspeople and artists.

Millworks Gallery at the Montague Mill features Louise Minks's outstanding acrylic screen prints, mostly landscapes with many local subjects. Her cards alone are worth a trip.

Artspace Gallery (413-772-6811),

Mill Street, Greenfield. Changing crafts shows represent area artists and artisans.

Green Trees Gallery (413-498-0283), 105 Main Street, Northfield. A very attractive consignment gallery featuring handmade pottery, weaving, paintings, and sculpture. Art classes are also offered, and when we stopped by there was talk of opening a restaurant.

DeGraff Studio Pottery (413-774-7763), 83 Newton Street, Greenfield, displays Leslie DeGraff's striking pottery.

Pure Light Gallery (413-863-9652; www.purelightgallery.com), 37 3rd Street, Turners Falls. Open Thursday and Friday 10–2, Saturday 10–3, or by appointment. Probably a sign of things to come, a serious photography gallery. Turners Falls is also home to the **Hallmark Institute of Photog-raphy** (www.hallmark-institute.com).

Tim de Christopher (413-586-7496; www.ohmysoul.org), Williams Garage (147 2nd Street), Turners Falls. The sculptor has converted a classic 1940s garage into a studio for his garden and other creations.

Tom White Pottery (413-498-2175), 205 Winchester Road, Northfield. Sited at the corner of Pierson and Winchester Roads, this studio is a source of wheel-thrown, porcelain production work that's obviously been influenced by traditional Chinese forms and glazes. Call ahead.

Opus (413-773-7701), 186 Main Street, features crafts along with furnishings and gifts.

BOOKSTORES Meetinghouse Books (413-665-0500; www.meetinghouse-books.com), 70 North Main Street, South Deerfield. Open Wednesday

PURE LIGHT GALLERY

Christina Tree

through Friday 10–6, weekends noon–6. A destination for browsers for more than 20 years: Judith Tingley and Ken Haverly have filled an old wooden church with their eclectic selection of thousands of used and out-of print books, literature, history, the arts, and much more, "priced to every budget."

World Eye Bookshop (413-772-2186; www.worldeyebookshop.com), 156 Main Street, Greenfield. Open daily. This well-stocked book- and gift store serves a wide upcountry area.

Book Mill (413-367-9206; www.montaguebookmill.com) in the Montague Mill, Greenfield, and on Depot Road, Montague. Open daily 10–6. Used books in a picturesque old mill by a rushing stream. From Route 63, turn off to Montague Center. At this writing the picturesque complex also includes the Lady Killigrew Café, the Room with a Loom, and Millworks Gallery.

Whately Antiquarian Book Center (413-247-3272), Route 5, Whately. Open 10–5:30, Sunday noon–5. A group shop with 45 dealers and 20,000 good used and rare books.

CLOTHING **Zemi** (413-774-7079), 176 Main Street, Greenfield. Larger than it looks from the street with a wide variety of women's clothing and bargains in the back.

SPECIAL STORES **Wilson's Department Store** (413-774-4326), 258 Main Street, Greenfield. Open Monday through Saturday from 9:30, most nights until 6 PM; to 8 Thursday and 9 Friday. In business since 1882, one of New England's few surviving independently owned downtown department stores: four floors with

MEETINGHOUSE BOOKS IN SOUTH DEERFIELD

Christina Tree

everything from appliances and bedspreads, through cosmetics, to toys, cars, and clothing.

Longview Tower (413-772-6976), 497 Mohawk Trail. The first vintage tourist stop heading west from Greenfield along Route 2. It comes up so quickly you tend to miss it, but don't: There's a petting zoo as well as souvenirs, fudge, and the "three-state view."

Magical Child (413-773-5721), 134 Main Street, Greenfield. A first-rate toy and children's clothing store.

Pekarski's Sausage (413-665-4537), Route 116, South Deerfield. Homemade Polish kielbasa, breakfast sausage, smoked ham, and bacon.

Millstone's (413-665-0543). 24 South

Main Street (Route 47), Sunderland. The store's name and design, both featuring genuine millstones, date from 1929. Known for its meat, this is an exceptionally friendly store featuring local produce.

Richardson's Candy Kitchen (413-772-0443 or 1-800-817-9338; www.richardsoncandy.com), Routes 5/10, Deerfield. Open daily 10–5:30. Handmade chocolates and specialty candies with a wide and enthusiastic following.

Also see **Yankee Candle** under *For Families*.

The Textile Co., Inc. (413-773-7516), Power Square, Greenfield. Open Monday through Saturday 9–5:20, Friday until 8:20. Closed Monday in June, July, August. Customers come from far and wide to this old-fashioned, quality fabric store good for cottons, silks, polysters, vinyls, linen, acetate, calicos, notions, and patterns.

FARMS AND FARM STANDS Clarkdale Fruit Farms (413-772-6797), 303 Upper Road, Deerfield, a fourth-generation farm, operates a major farm stand specializing in their own fruit, also offers PYO.

Smiarowski Farm Stand and Creamy (413-665-3880), 320 River Road (Route 47), Sunderland. Open May through November, 8–6. The thing to order here is Karen Smiarowski's "Polish Power Plate": a *golabki*, a "lazy cabbage pierogi," and a chunk of kielbasa, plus homemade potato salad, baked beans, and rye bread. Desserts change with what's in season, beginning in June with rhubarb pie, then strawberry shortcake, then crisps—blueberry, peach, and finally apple in September and

October. Fruit toppings for the Snow's ice cream are also homemade. The self-serve snack bar (picnic tables) is attached to the family's post-and-beam farm stand.

Hamilton Orchards (978-544-6867), 22 West Street (just off Route 202), New Salem. Open July and August, daily 9–5; September and October, weekends 9–5. Bill and Barb Hamilton have been welcoming visitors to their 100-acre hilltop farm since 1943. In fall, with four kinds of apples to pick and tables piled with apple pies and dumplings, the place is hopping and the snack bar is open. In summer there are PYO raspberries and blueberries. Picnic tables overlook the hills.

Greenwood Farm (413-498-5995), 265 Millers Falls Road (Route 63), Northfield. Open June through October, 10–6. Antique and heritage apples, unpasteurized cider, maple syrup, homemade ice cream.

Upinngil (413-863-2297), 411 Main Road, Gill. Open June through October. Organically grown asparagus, melons, sweet corn, potatoes (many varieties), pumpkins, winter squash, honey, hay, maple products. Strawberries picked and U-pick.

Riverland Farm (413-665-2041), 197 River Road (Route 47), Sunderland. Open early June to late October, daily. A large selection of farm-grown organic vegetables, plus other local milk, cheese, eggs, goat cheese, fruit, and maple syrup.

Warner Farm (413-665-8331), 159 Old Amherst Road, Sunderland. Open May through October, 10–6. Farm-grown produce: asparagus, strawberries, peas, beans, peppers, sweet corn, pumpkins, and squash. Pick-your-own strawberries in June.

APPLE FARM ON RIVER ROAD IN SUNDERLAND

Kim Grant

September through October: "Mike's Amazing Maze" (www.mikesmaze. com), the area's first and only corn maze, 9–5 at 23 South Main Street (Route 47).

Golonka Farm (413-247-3256), 6 State Road, Whately. Open June 15 though October, daily 9–6. Specializing in sweet corn, but a variety of other home-grown vegetables.

Long Plain Farm (413-665-1210), 149 Christian Lane, Whately. Open May through December, 9–5. Onions, potatoes, cabbage, eggplant, summer and winter squash, pickle and salad cucumbers, sweet corn, Halloween and sugar pumpkins.

Chee Chee Mamook Farm (413-498-2160), 341 Caldwell Road, Northfield. Open year-round. Hours by appointment. This is a visitor-geared alpaca farm with a store selling homespun alpaca-fleece yarn and clothing.

FLOWERS Baystate Perennial Farm (413-665-3525), 36 State Road (Routes 5/10), Whately. Open mid-April through September, daily 9–6. New and unusual as well as proven classic perennials, shrubs, and vines. Free gardening workshops and informal garden walks/talks.

Blue Meadow Farm (413-367-2394), 184 Meadow Road, Montague Center. Open April 15 through July. An acre of display gardens noted for unusual annuals and perennials makes this a popular destination. Request the catalog, featuring perennials, ornamental grasses, woody plants, annuals, and herbs. The prettiest way to come is from Sunderland, forking onto Falls Road off Route 47 north of the "Buttonball Tree," then onto Meadow Road. Coming from Millers Falls, it's not far south of the Montague Mill.

Mill River Farm (413-665-3034), corner of Routes 5 and 116, South Deerfield, across from the fire station. Open April through late June, September through October, and Thanksgiving weekend through Christmas.

Annuals, herbs, hanging baskets, mums, asters, pumpkins, Christmas trees, perennials.

PICK-YOUR-OWN **Clarkdale Fruit Farms** (413-772-6797), 303 Upper Road, Deerfield, has PYO apples, pumpkins, peaches, pears, and great cider.

Nourse Farm (413-665-2650; www.noursefarms.com), 41 River Road, South Deerfield. This 400-acre riverside farm ships some 15 million "virus-free plants" throughout the world. While most business is through its catalog and web site, it also welcomes PYO customers June through October daily (8–4) for whatever is in-season: strawberries (24 varieties) and several kinds and colors of raspberries.

Ripka's Farm (413-665-4687), Routes 5/10, Deerfield. Farm stand open daily for pick-your-own straw-berries.

Quonquont Farm (413-575-4680), 9 North Street, Whately. Open mid-July through early November, 10–6. Closed Monday and holidays. Pick-your-own blueberries, peaches, and apples. Farm stand with fruit, cider, and preserves. A blueberry maze.

SUGARHOUSES Maple producers who welcome visitors include **Williams Farm Sugar House** (413-773-5186; www.williamsfarm.com), Routes 5/10 in Deerfield, open mid-February to mid-April, 8:30–5, with pancake breakfasts served daily and sugarhouse tours; products available year-round; **Brookledge Sugarhouse** (413-665-3837), 159 Haydenville Road (2 miles fom Whately Center), Whately; **River Maple Farm** (413-648-9767), Route 5, Bernardston; **Ripley's Sugarhouse**

(413-367-2031), 195 Chestnut Hill Road, Montague; and **Old Homestead Farm** (413-367-2802) on Route 63, Montague.

✱ Special Events

February: **Greenfield Winter Carnival,** at Highland Pond, Beacon Field, and all around town—ice sculpture contest, ice skating, cross-country skiing, sledding (first weekend; 413-772-1553). **Chocolate Festival** (Saturday before Valentine's Day; 413-339-5756).

March: **Sugaring**—local sugarhouses invite the public; check the listings above or visit www.massmaple.org.

April: **River Rat Race**—over 300 canoeists congregate on the Millers River in Athol.

May: **A Classic Day in Greenfield**—downtown street fair (413-774-2791).

Mid-May through June: The **Fish Ladder** behind town hall in Turners Falls, operated by Northeast Utilities, offers views through a window behind the falls of shad and occasional Atlantic salmon finding their way up the Connecticut River.

Spring–fall: Farmer's markets are held in Greenfield, Saturday 8–1.

June: **Old Deerfield Summer Crafts Fair** at Memorial Hall—more than 200 exhibitors (last weekend; 413-774-7476; www.deerfield-craft.org). **Lavender Day Festival and Tours**—a self-guided tour of farms and gardens with workshops, lavender products, entertainment (413-625-9708). **Old Deerfield Sunday Afternoon Concert Series**—chamber music (413-774-3768).

July: **Old-Fashioned Independence Day** in Old Deerfield (413-774-3768).

Greenfield Garden Club Tours (usually the weekend after July 4; 413-773-5819). **Green River Festival**—a mid-July spectacle, sponsored by the Franklin County Chamber of Commerce at Greenfield Community College, with nationally known musicians, a crafts fair, and hot-air balloon launches (413-773-5463). **Sundays in the Park**—six Sunday evenings of music in Greenfield Energy Park including jazz and world music. Inquire about the **Annual John Putnam Fiddler's Contest,** also in Energy Park (413-774-5051).

Late August: **Montague Old Home Days**—games, an auction, food, music, and a footrace in Montague Village and Montague Center (413-367-9467).

September: **Franklin County Fair,** held at the fairgrounds in Greenfield—livestock, crafts, music, a midway, and food (first weekend after Labor Day). **Old Deerfield Fall Craft Fair**—more than 200 juried exhibitors from throughout the country, featuring traditional crafts (413-774-3768).

October: **Greenfield Fall Festival,** Main Street—craftspeople, music, children's entertainment, sidewalk sales (Columbus Day weekend). **Antique Dealers of America Historic Deerfield Antiques Show** (early October; www.adadealers.com).

INDEX